1995

W9-AEE-682

We Are Your Sons

We Are Your Sons

The Legacy of Ethel and Julius Rosenberg

written by their children
Robert and Michael Meeropol

Second Edition
with a Foreword by Eric Foner

University of Illinois Press   Urbana and Chicago

This book is printed on acid-free paper.

A portion of this book has appeared in *Rolling Stone.*
The authors gratefully acknowledge permission to reprint from *Invitation to an Inquest* by Walter and Miriam Schneir (copyright © 1965, 1968, 1973, 1983 by Walter Schneir and Miriam Schneir) and from "Were the Rosenbergs Framed?" a transcript of a public debate held 20 October 1983 at the Town Hall, New York City (copyright © 1983 by Walter and Miriam Schneir).

LIBRARY OF CONGRESS CATALOGING-IN-PUBLICATION DATA

Meeropol, Robert.
  We are your sons.

  Bibliography: p.
  Includes index.
    1. Rosenberg, Julius, 1918–1953. 2. Rosenberg,
Ethel, 1916–1953. 3. United States—Social conditions—
1945– . I. Meeropol, Michael. II Title.
HX84.R6M43 1986   364.1'31'0922[B]   85-30892
ISBN 0-252-01263-1 (alk. paper)

Contents

Foreword

THE PUBLICATION OF this expanded edition of *We Are Your Sons* comes at a time when the trial and execution of Julius and Ethel Rosenberg command renewed public attention. Thousands of documents recently released from the files of the FBI and other agencies have shed new light on the weaknesses of the government's case in the "crime of the century"—the alleged theft and transmission to the Soviet Union of the "secret" of the atom bomb—as well as revealing new evidence of serious misconduct by the prosecution and Judge Irving R. Kaufman. And the debate inspired by *The Rosenberg File,* the most sophisticated brief for the prosecution yet to appear, has directed attention to the still unresolved questions surrounding one of the most famous political trials in American history.

When it appeared a decade ago, *We Are Your Sons* was immediately recognized as a contribution to the literature on both the Rosenberg case itself and the Cold War's impact upon American society. In lengthy excerpts from the condemned pair's letters, the book revealed the Rosenbergs as warm, passionate individuals, deeply concerned over the fate of their children, convinced of their own innocence, and seeking every means of overturning the verdict against them (a far cry from the portrait of soulless automotons and intentional martyrs invented by the prosecution and echoed by Ronald Radosh and Joyce Milton, authors of *The Rosenberg File*). But *We Are Your Sons* is also a testament of growing up in the 1950s and of sixties political activism. Although Michael and Robert Meeropol's situation was, of course, unique, their experience in many ways paralleled that of thousands of other "red diaper babies" who played so important a part in the history of the New

Left. In this sense, the book joins works like Jonah Raskin's *Out of the Whale* as chronicles of the process by which the legacy of the Old Left was both embodied and transformed by the New.

Containing three new chapters, this expanded edition continues the narratives of Michael and Robert Meeropol, examines the implications of the documents released under the Freedom of Information Act, and subjects *The Rosenberg File* to a searching and devastating critique. For these reasons alone, it constitutes a significant addition to an ongoing debate that shows no sign of ending.

Beyond the question of guilt and innocence, moreover, lie other historical issues suggested by the book and deserving further work by historians. What was the nature of the Communist party, and what effect did the case have upon the Left as a whole? Too often, writings on the Rosenberg case accept uncritically a portrait of American Communism now undergoing substantial revision by a generation of historians, such as Maurice Isserman and Mark Naison, who have moved beyond polemics to investigate the actual social and political history of this poorly understood organization. Rather than the nest of Soviet spies portrayed by the FBI, or creatures of Moscow incapable of independent thought, the party emerges in new work as a complex and diverse organization that, one might say, became Americanized almost in spite of itself. Yet once demonology is laid aside, further questions about the case present themselves for historical analysis: why was the Rosenbergs' defense so poorly handled; why did so much of the Left remain silent during their trial; why did the party, in this as in so many other cases, seek to avoid the issue of Communism rather than forthrightly confronting it? And in addition to the case itself, historians need to look further at the enduring legacy of McCarthyism in affecting the subsequent development of institutions like trade unions, churches, and universities purged of a Left presence during the 1950s. The execution of the Rosenbergs was only the most extreme example of a broader pattern of shattered careers and suppressed civil liberties. This determined effort to root out dissent from American society had profound consequences, many scarcely anticipated by the liberals who played a part in the anti-Communist crusade, only to see its logic turned against themselves.

One thing is even more clear today than when *We Are Your Sons* first appeared—by any reasonable standard of justice, the case against the

Rosenbergs was weak, and the death penalty an abomination. Even those who defend the prosecution and FBI now acknowledge that virtually no evidence existed against Ethel Rosenberg and that crucial portions of the testimony of Harry Gold and David Greenglass, the main witnesses for the government, were fabricated shortly before the trial. And although in the aftermath of Vietnam and Watergate we have become accustomed to governmental misconduct, the relentless pursuit of the death penalty by FBI director J. Edgar Hoover and Judge Kaufman stands out as singularly reprehensible.

Truly, as they themselves write, Michael and Robert Meeropol are "Orphans of the Cold War." Julius and Ethel Rosenberg were indeed guilty—if not of espionage, then of being Communists, a "crime" almost as heinous in 1950. The two children deprived of their parents were in a sense the most innocent victims of the entire affair; their experience, a devastating indictment of American jurisprudence, bears witness to one of our nation's most lamentable epochs. If the original publication of *We Are Your Sons* played a part in the campaign to force the release of government documents concerning the Rosenberg case, this new edition stands as a reminder that enough unanswered questions remain to justify a full-scale national inquiry, with access to all documents still withheld from public scrutiny. Like the trial of Sacco and Vanzetti, the Rosenberg case should serve as a constant reminder of the fragility of justice, and the ways the rule of law can be perverted to serve the ends of power.

ERIC FONER

Preface to the Second Edition

A DECADE HAS PASSED since we put together the first edition of *We Are Your Sons*. While the first edition was primarily our family's personal story, what is new in this second edition is a detailed argument in support of our view that our parents were innocent. Here, we will sketch out what we've been up to since 1974.

Between 1974 and 1979, our primary commitment was to the "re-opening effort." The primary vehicle of that effort was our lawsuit under the Freedom of Information Act (FOIA) that ultimately led to the release of over 200,000 pages of previously secret government documents concerning our parents' case. That FOIA case is still pending; an appeal was argued in September of 1985. The lawsuit against Louis Nizer for copyright violation was settled out of court without coming to trial. One of the terms of the settlement was that we were not permitted to divulge the content of that overall agreement.

In support of our FOIA lawsuit, we worked first with the National Committee to Reopen the Rosenberg Case (NCRRC) and later with the Fund for Open Information and Accountability (FOIA). Both organizations still exist and are based in New York City. Our work centered on organizing support, publicity, and fund raising to continue the lawsuit and keep the case before the public. Many people made significant contributions of time, energy, and money to our campaign. They are too many to mention individually here. Some coordinated or participated in local committee chapters. Others organized and took part in demonstrations. Many people from local committees attended monthly meetings of the steering committee of the NCRRC as well as less frequent national committee meetings. Individuals not associated with local organizing efforts also worked with either the NCRRC or

FOIA, some as paid staff, others as voluntary participants. Some people arranged speaking engagements for us, and others concentrated on publicity. Some planned fund-raising parties and events while others, through slide shows, talks, and movies, carried out educational efforts. Some provided us with transportation, and some welcomed us into their homes. Lay volunteers and legal professionals worked more directly on the lawsuit while other professionals helped organize mass mailings and large public meetings. Cultural workers, both amateur and professional, in music, art, drama, poetry, prose, and signing have volunteered their time and expertise at events large and small, some repeatedly. Many, many others, whatever their other involvements, made generous financial contributions to the lawsuit, to the NCRRC, or to FOIA.

We thank you one and all. Although the courts have not yet overturned the verdict and are unlikely to do so in the foreseeable future, particularly given the current ideological makeup of the Supreme Court, your work was essential in securing the release of government material that overwhelmingly demonstrates the monstrous crime that was perpetrated against our family and the American public when the government framed and executed two innocent people. In a time when it is often hard for people of good will to see the positive effect of years of struggle, the production of this proof has undoubtedly altered the course of history, even in a small way, to the benefit of all people. You should all be honored for your work.

The years 1978 and 1979 marked a turning point for us. For five years our lives had focused on our parents' case. We wished to lead our lives in our own right. Michael wished to devote more time to teaching and economics, while Robby wanted to figure out what he was going to do. Five years of travel and publicity had been difficult for our families. Our parents had been taken away from us by the government, and we did not wish in turn to absent ourselves from our children's lives. We supported others who continued the struggle, but we no longer considered it the central focus of our existence.

Robby and his family, now increased by the birth of Rachel Anne in 1975, moved to Berkeley, California, for two years. He became the managing editor of *Socialist Review*. Michael intensified his teaching efforts. In 1980 he and Ann returned to Cambridge, England, with Ivy and Greg for his sabbatical. We remained politically active. Robby and his family returned to Springfield in late 1981; he entered Western New England College's School of Law in the fall of 1982 and graduated in May 1985. Michael continues to teach and was promoted to full professor in 1985. The events of the last decade have not altered our views of our parents' innocence, our belief that the basic nature of American society must change before our government and economic system will cease to be a menace to the world's ecology and peace, and our profound sense that political involvement in an effort to make the world a better place for all people provides the best avenue for leading a constructive, meaningful life.

Some reviewers of our first edition faulted our failure to make a case for our parents' innocence. The book was our family's personal story and as such was not designed to provide more proof. Instead, we directed readers to the excellent work of Walter and Miriam Schneir, John Wexley, and William Reuben for evidence that our parents were framed. We felt and still feel that this was the proper focus for the book. At that stage in our knowledge, we had only one or two items to add to the work of the Schneirs and others, and we did include some of that on pages 190–92 below. Our personal story was the most significant new material we wanted to add, and we candidly stated that in the first edition.

This new edition alters this course. The personal story remains, but now we provide systematic arguments that our parents were innocent. We do this with three new chapters. In the first, Robby gives the reader a summary of the facts, evidence and testimony from the trial, and outlines the proof we had available to us in the mid-1970s. This is done by using a typical speech either Michael or Robby could have given on the college lecture circuit then. It was reconstructed through the use of notes and outlines from those speeches and is an accurate representation of them. Robby then supplements this material with information from the FBI files that makes our case even stronger.

The second chapter shows some of the results of the FOIA lawsuit. In it, Michael uses FBI documents to demonstrate the unethical, and at times possibly illegal, behavior of our parents' trial judge, Irving R. Kaufman. In the third chapter, Michael uses the files to demonstrate that *The Rosenberg File*, written by Joyce Milton and Ronald Radosh, presents a thoroughly distorted picture of what is in those files. In this process he demonstrates how the files reinforce our claims that the government's case was built on perjuries. Though that does not directly "prove" our parents were innocent, once the original "proof" of guilt is shown to be fraudulent, the presumption of innocence until guilt is proven should return to govern our judgments. In the last part of that chapter, we provide an overview of how the files should be approached and speculate as to the meaning of the widespread media acclaim for Radosh and Milton's book.

We feel our shift in course is warranted. We have now engaged in many years of speech, debate, and research on our parents' case. We have analyzed many of the files as they have been released. We know much more than we did when the first edition was written. But we are primarily compelled by the disservice the Radosh/Milton book does to our parents, the files, and the truth. We and many others devoted a great deal of effort to securing the release of these files. It is infuriating to see Radosh and Milton misrepresent what is in them to the public and to have the media blandly accept what Radosh and Milton say as gospel without making an independent effort to ascertain that is actually in the files. How ironic! Prior to our FOIA lawsuit, the public didn't have access to files that would show much of what actually happened. Now such access exists, but instead of explaining the files, Radosh and Milton and much of the media have misused them and misinformed the public. What is new in this edition seeks to correct this travesty. With this edition we seek to set the record straight so all can see what is really in the files. An open-minded reading of them inexorably leads to the conclusion that our parents were framed.

In saying this we want to make clear to the readers that we are not angry at Radosh and Milton because they have used the files to make a case for our parents' guilt. We are angry because they have **misused** the files and misused interviews in an effort to make the evidence fit the case they desired to make. Our anger, despite our personal interest, is the anger of experts in any area of inquiry when someone achieves acclaim for work that violates all the canons of serious discourse. To the average reader who might doubt that we can maintain our honesty when looking at the material, we ask that you read carefully and ask yourselves, if we have accurately quoted the files, why do Radosh and Milton ignore/distort what is in them in their book? To the student of history, we ask only that you check our footnotes. The intellectual fraud perpetrated by *The Rosenberg File* will last as long as readers do not think critically about what is in that book. We have confidence that the reading public will not be intellectually lazy. Once the Radosh and Milton smokescreen is cleared away, we believe that all readers of this book will agree with us that a full-scale governmental inquiry into the case while the still-living participants can be forced to testify under oath is essential. We hope you will join us in petitioning the House Judiciary Committee to undertake such an inquiry.

Acknowledgments
for the Second Edition

THE TWO CHAPTERS I WROTE for this edition would never have been possible without the partial success of our Freedom of Information Act lawsuit. The efforts of our lawyers, Marshall Perlin, Max Millman, Bonnie Brower, and the late Samuel Gruber and David Rein, were coupled with energetic support, both political and professional, from scores of members and supporters of the National Committee to Reopen the Rosenberg Case and the Fund for Open Information and Accountability. Because the lawsuit has continued to this day, the files released so far have been located in New York. Thus, I have had fewer opportunities to research them than others. Therefore, it is with deep appreciation that I acknowledge the research efforts of Walter and Miriam Schneir, Jerry Markowitz, Marshall Perlin, Ann Mari Butraigo, and others who have discovered many of the files referred to in these chapters. I have had, however, the opportunity to go over much of the material covered in these chapters and have personally seen all of the files quoted. Therefore, I want to make it clear that I take full responsibility for the accuracy of my quotations from FBI files utilized in these chapters.

John Anzalotti, Noam Chomsky, Jack Gold, Stephen B. Oates, Marshall Perlin, and Walter and Miriam Schneir all read the last chapter. The manuscript was significantly improved as a result of some of their comments. Robby and Jerry Markowitz must be singled out for special thanks since they helped in the many rewrites the manuscript went through from September 1983 to the present. Jerry's collaboration with me on an article in *Science and Society* on the scientific evidence in the case only scratches the surface of my debt to him as a researcher and dear friend. His own review article of Radosh and Milton's *The Rosenberg File* should demonstrate how much I am in his debt. Marshall Perlin, Stephen B. Oates, Jerry and Robby also read my chapter on Judge Kaufman. Again, I must repeat that I alone am responsible for any errors of omission or commission that remain even after receiving the expert and loving advice it has been my good fortune to obtain.

Finally, I thank my family, Ann, Ivy, and Greg, for putting up with the intensity of my commitment to this struggle over the last twelve years. Our children are young adults, ready for college and new challenges. I know they forgive me for times when my mind (or sometimes body) was elsewhere. Ann has held down a full-time job, gone back to school for graduate degrees, and begun the joyful but painfully difficult process of becoming a professional writer. I know my activities for the last twelve years have at times been very trying. She has stayed with it, with strength and good humor, and I am forever grateful.

M. M.

I'D LIKE TO THANK Phil Harris, Bruce Miller and Fred Sokol, who read and commented on the manuscript of the chapter I wrote for this edition. I take full responsibility for its contents and any errors are mine. My brother, Michael, deserves special thanks, not only for assisting with this chapter but for being the driving force behind this new edition.

I am also indebted to my wife, Ellen, and my daughters, Jenny and Rachel, for providing me with the space and encouragement I needed. It is difficult enough to put up with a full-time law student; I deeply appreciate their positive support for this "extracurricular activity."

R. M.

WE WISH TO ALSO THANK Richard Wentworth and Cynthia Mitchell of the University of Illinois Press for their encouragement, advice and professional assistance in seeing this second edition through to publication.

M. M. R. M.

We Are Your Sons

To the memory of Anne Meeropol,
who was a creative, courageous person and
a strong, dynamic and loving parent.

To Abel Meeropol, who continues
to struggle with energy and foresight;
his gentleness and humor gave and
still give us laughter.

Preface

FOR MANY YEARS we planned to eventually republish our parents' prison correspondence. While much of the material in these letters does not fulfill the legal requirements of evidence, we felt they represented one of the strongest proofs in our parents' behalf. Since their side of the story has never received a complete airing in the mass media and previous publications of their letters had been extremely fragmentary, or of limited circulation or were distorted, getting the letters out to the largest possible audience seemed of primary importance. It was with this end in mind that we approached Houghton Mifflin Company in the fall of 1973. In preparing their letters for publication, we noted our parents' recognition of the fact that the courts were not impartial arbiters of justice but would rule on their appeals in response to political pressures. Our parents came to feel that getting their story before the public was their only hope. We found ourselves in a similar situation vis-à-vis the public. Before deciding to issue these letters, we had filed a law suit against Louis Nizer in the Federal District Court in New York, *Meeropol* v. *Nizer et al.,* #73 Civ. 2720, charging him with copyright infringement, misusing and distorting some of our parents' letters in his book, *The Implosion Conspiracy*; that with malice he created false, fictitious and distorted writing about our parents, us, and our relations with them, thus defaming us and invading our privacy; and damaged our common law copyrights in our parents' unpublished letters. Since the institution of this action, which is still pending in the District Court, our claims based upon defamation and invasion of privacy were dismissed. If and when a final adverse judgment is entered in the case, we will appeal; in the interim we have filed a supplementary complaint restating our charges of defamation and invasion of privacy. Sharing our parents' skepticism about the courts, we resolved not to rely solely on their impartiality to force Nizer publicly to retract the lies with which we charged him. Instead, we have combined the letters with our own stories to, in part, set the record straight.

Portions of 192 letters were published in *Death House Letters of Ethel and Julius Rosenberg*. An expanded edition was later published with 26 more letters. Fragments of twenty-four previously unpublished letters were included in a chapter of *Invitation to an Inquest* (Penguin, 1973), a fine investigation of the case by Walter and Miriam Schneir.* We now have in our possession 523 letters. We would appreciate any person holding original letters from our parents or knowing of their location letting us know through our publishers. Many letters selected for this volume have not been previously published. We chose them in an attempt to present as clear and honest a portrait of our parents as space would allow. We excerpted rather than edited, save for the corrections of obvious misspellings. Whenever possible we printed letters in their entirety.

Our parents came to realize that their correspondence could be utilized as aids in the campaign to save them. They authorized their lawyer and dear friend, Emanuel Bloch, to publish the letters and before their execution the first volume, *Death House Letters of Ethel and Julius Rosenberg*, was released by a corporation he organized.

Section I contains the story of all four Rosenbergs in the years 1950 through 1954. In addition to personal recollections, Michael drew on the memories of those he interviewed, and on published works about the case to present a few of the reasons we believe our parents were framed. This book is not an attempt to prove that frame-up. We hope readers will be drawn to more thorough investigative accounts of the trial which are referred to in our book.

Section II covers the next twenty years, 1954–1974. After the execution life continued. Robert describes how we survived and the sustaining effect of the memory of our mother and father. He

---

*The most recent revised edition of the Schneirs' *Invitation to an Inquest* was published by Pantheon in 1983.

focuses on the events surrounding our political education. Little attempt is made to lay out the theoretical underpinnings of our political beliefs or activities or to prove the correctness of these beliefs. Though our political philosophies have changed, we feel there is a great deal of consistency in the ultimate goals and sentiments shared by Ethel and Julius, Anne and Abel and ourselves. We leave it to the reader to decide if we acted reasonably.

Our parents' last message to us was, "Always remember that we were innocent and could not wrong our conscience." We have taken that admonition to heart and love and revere their memory. We are firmly committed to exposing the fraud of their conviction and revealing the truth of their innocence. We hope this book contributes to bringing all the facts to light — facts which the government still refuses to release from the files of the FBI — and which we are convinced will only make our case stronger.

Acknowledgments

IN PUTTING TOGETHER the narrative for 1950 to 1954, I have interviewed several individuals to supplement my own memories. I am grateful to Elizabeth Phillips, my former social worker; Rabbi Irving Koslowe, the Jewish chaplain at Sing Sing; Frances Minor, Michael Minor, my aunt Ethel, Leon Summit, Cedric Belfrage, Marshall Perlin, Michelle Alman Harrison; another former social worker and my mother's psychiatrist (both of whose privacy I've chosen to respect). In addition, Gloria Agrin Josephson not only consented to an interview but permitted me access to Emanuel Bloch's files where I found a recording of his September 1953 speech mentioned in the book. Long before this interview I had learned much from my long conversations about the case with Gloria. Similarly, Emily and David Alman have provided a wealth of information during our long friendship. Emily gave me access to her files and discussed with me many of the issues raised in the case. Similar discussions with Walter and Miriam Schneir have been helpful and greatly appreciated. I also want to acknowledge the importance to me of John Wexley's excellent book, *The Judgment of Julius and Ethel Rosenberg*. Alice Citron and Dr. Frederic Wertham kindly responded to important questions through letters. In writing and revising, I have benefited from the comments of Cedric and Mary Belfrage, Allen Young, Ann V. Meeropol, Abel Meeropol, Adrienne and Gerald Markowitz, all of whom read an early draft. Sonia Bach, Leon Summit and Marshall Perlin checked certain portions of the manuscript for accuracy. Conversations with Victoria Ortiz, Mary and Cedric Belfrage and Emily Alman were very beneficial. Needless to say, none of these people should be held accountable for any weaknesses in these sections. Neither should Robert though he provided me with written material of his memories of our early years. Though we have read each other's sections, we are both stubborn enough to resist even a brother's urging at times! Finally, I want to acknowledge the love, joy and sustenance I derive every day from Ann, Ivy and Gregory Meeropol.

M.M.

The second section came almost entirely from inside my head. Michael helped correct my faulty chronology and supplied me with many of his significant memories of these years. While writing this section I visited old friends whom I thank for pleasant times, putting up with a tape recorder, sharing their recollections and providing insights which made my work easier. Abel Meeropol gave me material, encouragement and sound advice. Ellen Meeropol read the manuscript a number of times and offered useful suggestions and corrections. Beth Schneider, Fred Miller, Rayna Reiter, Randy Reiter and Hernán Drobny read and criticized this section. Without their help I would not be as certain of the accuracy of events described since 1965. I am responsible for any errors that appear. I thank Ellen Meeropol and Margery Rosenthal for giving me the needed space to work. Thank you, Jenny, for making me smile.

R.M.

This book was made possible by all the people who helped us survive as individuals who loved our parents. To these loving, courageous adults and contemporaries who fought when it was simpler to hide, we owe our happy lives and our sanity. Some deserve special notice, but there are many, too many, to list here. They know who they are and so do we. We are most deeply grateful to those who worked with the Committee to Secure Justice in the Rosenberg Case as well as those who struggled to insure our living with the Meeropols. We thank the National Committee to Reopen the Rosenberg Case for its continued support.

We are indebted to Hank Perlin and Marshall Perlin for helping assemble the letters and for reading the manuscript. We also thank Lawrence Libow for aid in the duplication of the letters. Rachel Wilcox deserves special credit for meeting our often unreasonable typing deadlines. We thank Ellen Joseph, our tireless editor on this project. Her professional expertise and enthusiastic support are as responsible as any other factors in enabling us to complete this book. We feel warmly toward her personally as well.

Chronology of Important Events

1950

Feb. 3   Klaus Fuchs, German-born British scientist, confesses in England to having given atomic information to the Soviet Union.

February   David Greenglass, brother of Ethel Rosenberg and formerly a machinist employed at the Los Alamos Atomic Project while in the army during World War II, visited by the FBI and questioned about persons he might have known while stationed at Los Alamos and about some uranium missing from the project.

May 23   Harry Gold, a Philadelphia chemist, states that he had been the American courier for Fuchs in 1944–45.

June 15   David Greenglass signs confession that he was an accomplice of Gold's in 1945.

June 16   Julius Rosenberg, brother-in-law and former business partner of David Greenglass, questioned by the FBI, but not arrested. Retains Emanuel Bloch as counsel.

June 25   Korean war begins.

July 17   Julius Rosenberg arrested on charges of having recruited David Greenglass into a Soviet spy ring in late 1944.

Aug. 11   Ethel Rosenberg arrested on the charge of conspiracy to commit espionage with her husband, Greenglass and Gold.

Aug. 12   Michael and Robert (aged 7 and 3), the children of Julius and Ethel Rosenberg, move in with Ethel and David's mother, Tessie Greenglass.

Aug. 16–18   Morton Sobell, former classmate of Julius Rosenberg, kidnaped from his Mexico City apartment, allegedly deported to the United States, and arrested by the FBI on charges of having been part of the same ring as the Rosenbergs.

November   Michael and Robert are transferred to the Hebrew Children's Home, a shelter in the Bronx.

Dec. 9   Harry Gold sentenced to thirty years in prison.

1951

March 6–29 Julius had been imprisoned for eight months, Ethel and Morton for seven, when their trial began before Judge Irving Kaufman. The jury listened to two weeks of testimony and then returned a guilty verdict.

April 5   Morton Sobell sentenced to thirty years in prison. Julius and Ethel sentenced to death, executions set for May 21, 1951 (automatically stayed pending appeal).

April 6   David Greenglass sentenced to fifteen years in prison.

April 11   Ethel Rosenberg transferred to Sing Sing prison in Ossining, N.Y., and housed as the only woman prisoner in the Condemned Cells, thus separating her from contact with Julius and family.

May 16   Julius Rosenberg transferred to Sing Sing's Death House.

June   Having partially recovered from an illness, Julius' mother, Sophie Rosenberg, takes Michael and Robert into her home.

Aug. 1   After a year of separation, Michael and Robert begin visiting their parents in Sing Sing.

August–   The *National Guardian,* a small left-wing news weekly,
September   publishes a series of articles concluding that the Rosenbergs are innocent and demanding a new trial.

November   The National Committee to Secure Justice in the Rosenberg Case is formed.

1952

Feb. 25   Convictions of the Rosenbergs upheld by United States Circuit Court of Appeals, Judge Jerome Frank writing the unanimous opinion. Sobell conviction affirmed, Judge Frank dissenting.

July   Michael and Robert move in with Ben and Sonia Bach, friends of Julius and Ethel, in Toms River, New Jersey.

Oct. 13 The Supreme Court denies *certiorari*, refuses to review the case or pass on the merits of the appeal. Justice Hugo Black dissents.

Nov. 17 Supreme Court refuses to reconsider its original ruling, Justice Black again dissenting.

Nov. 21 Judge Irving Kaufman sets the second execution date for the week of January 12, 1953.

Dec. 10 Motion for hearing based on evidence of perjury and prejudicial publicity heard by Judge Sylvester Ryan. Motion denied; stay of execution denied.

Dec. 30 Judge Kaufman hears motion to reduce sentence.

Dec. 31 The Court of Appeals upholds Ryan's denial of a hearing.

1953

Jan. 2 Judge Kaufman refuses to reduce sentence.

Jan. 5 Court of Appeals denies stay of execution.

Jan. 10 Petition for executive clemency submitted to the President; executions stayed until five days after determination is made.

Jan. 21 Tessie Greenglass visits her daughter at Sing Sing in an effort to induce her to confess and back brother David's story.

Feb. 11 President Eisenhower refuses clemency.

Feb. 16 New execution date set for week of March 9.

Feb. 17 Court of Appeals stays executions so the Supreme Court can consider a new petition for a review.

May 25 Supreme Court again refuses *certiorari*, Justices Hugo Black and William Douglas dissenting.

May 29 Judge Kaufman sets new execution date for week of June 15.

June 2 John V. Bennett, Director of the Bureau of Prisons, visits Sing Sing and personally offers Julius and Ethel their lives if they will "fully cooperate."

June 8 Judge Kaufman hears arguments for new hearing charging that newly discovered evidence proves perjury and subornation of perjury. Kaufman immediately denies motion, refuses to stay the executions.

June 9 Appeals Court orders Rosenbergs' lawyers to argue their appeal from Judge Kaufman's ruling on the spot.

June 11   Appeals Court affirms Judge Kaufman's decision; denies stay.

June 14   Michael and Robert travel to Washington where Michael hands a letter addressed to President Eisenhower pleading for clemency to a White House guard.

June 15   Supreme Court refuses stay of execution so a new petition for *certiorari* might be filed to appeal Kaufman's June 8 decision. Vote is 5 to 4, Justices Black, Douglas, Frankfurter and Jackson dissenting. Application for stay made to Justice William Douglas.

June 16   Another application for a stay made to Justice Douglas via a "next friend" brief based on the view that the Atomic Energy Act of 1946 should have applied to the case.

Michael and Robert together with Emanuel Bloch visit Ethel and Julius in Sing Sing. New clemency petitions signed.

Clemency petitions filed with the Pardon Attorney at the Justice Department.

June 17   Justice Douglas grants stay of execution until the lower courts can decide the new issue raised in the "next friend" brief.

Acting on the request of Attorney General Brownell, Chief Justice Fred Vinson recalls the court into special session to consider the point on which Douglas granted the stay.

June 18   Oral arguments before the Supreme Court.

June 19   Supreme Court vacates Douglas' stay, Justices Hugo Black, William Douglas and Felix Frankfurter dissenting. That afternoon, defense lawyers argue for a stay of execution with the Court of Appeals in New Haven, Connecticut.

Eisenhower again refuses clemency.

Ethel and Julius Rosenberg are executed. Their wills name Emanuel Bloch guardian of Michael, 10, and Robert, 6.

Fall   The Superintendent of Schools in Toms River, New Jersey, decides that since Michael and Robert are not state residents, they cannot be permitted to attend public school in New Jersey.

December   Michael and Robert move back to New York City and are provisionally placed with Abel and Anne Meeropol by Emanuel Bloch.

1954

Jan. 30   Emanuel Bloch dies suddenly at the age of 51.

Feb. 18   Judge Jacob Panken of the Children's Court Division of New York County has Michael and Robert secretly "remanded" to a children's shelter in Pleasantville, New York, pending consideration of a petition alleging neglect filed by the Society of the Prevention of Cruelty to Children.

Feb. 20   State Supreme Court Justice McNally paroles Michael and Robert in the custody of Sophie Rosenberg.

April   Surrogate Collins of New York County appoints Sophie Rosenberg and Kenneth D. Johnson (Dean of the New School of Social Work) as co-guardians of Michael and Robert.

September   Michael and Robert move in permanently with Anne and Abel Meeropol.

1957

February   With the approval of Dean Johnson and Sophie Rosenberg, Michael and Robert are legally adopted by Anne and Abel Meeropol.

Part I
The Long Nightmare
by Michael Meeropol

Sweetheart Darling,

Here it is still two more days before a young man's fancy turns to love and already I am "pleur de amor" for you my sweet Ethel (as always my dove). Everything seems to be in tune. The season of the year is approaching with the bright sunny days that quicken the pulse, freshen the spirit and a glorious feeling of youthfulness encourages newer accomplishments. For in essence, advancement, always displays the vigor of youth. The world has come to recognize the true nature of our case and the people, the most effective force on earth are behind us and are demonstrating a thorough awareness that they know how to fight for peace and freedom. Politically not only has this miscarriage of justice inspired but it has exposed our Government by the barbaric sentence of death against two innocent people for their progressive views. Then, too, the level of the campaign at home has entered the phase where the public is beginning to understand the full meaning of our case. Therefore, my morale is at a very high point and my profound love is in harmony with it but cries out for proper expression. There is no doubt that we've received great satisfaction from our firm maintenance of high moral and ethical standards and from working for a good cause but still the flesh and blood will not be assuaged until we are together again with our children at home.

I've been thinking darling it is almost three years since we've lived with our children. How we treasured every moment with them and how wonderful it was to share each and every accomplishment of theirs. A new painting, a nice block building, a particularly meaningful action of our boys, signs of growth, indications of abilities for music, art and the general problems of joy, worry and pain that goes with the beauty of family life. And so Robbie will be six and Mike is ten and they and we have been denied our birthrights by beasts. If we write with conviction and we're strong it's because the truth is indelibly made part of us by the deep marks of pain. When I see the spark of understanding in Michael's deep blue eyes and the warm smile of feeling in Robbie's face, then I know the reason we can stand this great suffering. Inside of me I guess I'm a softie for when I think of our sons and you I get such tender feelings and although I don't show it my heart is crying.

You know I've been reading a great deal lately, books on nature, the physical laws, economic problems, political and scientific works and because I know man can work with nature and better the world I realize how important it is to work to make this a reality. This is the only way to truly love my children. Dearest when I sit across from you separated by the power of tyranny, my eyes, my voice and my demeanor conveys to you my wholehearted devotion and admiration for you and assures you that I will forever be true. So for the coming day, a breath of spring, the perspective that will make all year the seasons of youth, for the full bloom of life, I love you and I'm confident.

Your young man — JULIE

1

The Arrests and the Dissolution of the Family

ON JULY 17, 1950, while Robby was asleep and I listened to "The Lone Ranger," the FBI came to our apartment to arrest our father. The radio episode concerned bandits trying to frame the Lone Ranger by committing crimes with "silver-looking" bullets. Just as someone was exposing the fraud by scraping the bullets to show they were softer than silver and only silver-colored, an FBI man turned off the radio. I turned it on; he turned it off again. We kept this up until I finally gave in, attracted by my mother's sudden shout, "I want a lawyer!"

I have a memory flash of driving in a car with my mother and one or two FBI men. I asked her if Daddy were coming home and she said, "No, not tonight." Intending to be friendly, I told one of the agents that I listened to him on the radio show, "This Is the FBI."

The night of my father's arrest I stayed up to listen to Lyle Van's eleven o'clock news to hear about him. Very soon after the arrest, I became aware that he was charged with spying and that he faced the death penalty. I somehow made a nightmare prediction that stayed with me for the next three years: conviction, followed by the failure of appeals, followed by execution. This was more a fear than a prediction. At that time, I didn't know details about appeals, clemency, etc., but the possibility of death was first planted in my mind as early as those first few days following my father's arrest.

In describing his arrest, I talked as if I had seen it on TV or heard it on the radio. My father had been taken away by the FBI. My father was a bad man, the FBI was good. A few nights later, again on Lyle Van's newscast, I heard that my father had termed the charges against him ridiculous, "like my kids listen to on the radio." That statement quoted over the air, marked the beginning of the reassertion of rationality. Though I had doubts and needed to be reassured, I do not believe I was ever again as convinced of my father's "badness" or the FBI's "goodness."

Three days after his arrest, my father wrote to us:

July 20, 1950

Dearest Wife & Two Boys:

I am feeling well and getting along. My day (Eleanor)* starts at 6:30 A.M., make the bed, get dressed, washed, etc. Breakfast about 7:30. Stewed fruits, cereal, cake, coffee. I am assigned to 2nd floor detail and after each meal we sweep down the corridors and swab the floors. Then I sit down with a book and do some reading. 11:30 A.M. lunch — kidney stew, succotash, browned potatoes, cake, lemonade. Then we have two one-hour periods on the roof in the sunshine. Ping-Pong, handball and just chewing the fat with the men. I met some nice guys here and they've been keeping me in cigarettes, cookies and oranges. This Friday when the Commissary opens, I'll get my own. One of the gang lent me "The Wall" by John Hersey. I am up to page 45 at this writing. Good book. 5:00 P.M. supper — Jellied soup (n.g.) pork-beans, cornbread, salad, chocolate drink. It is now 5:30 P.M. after this letter I'll go up on the roof for an hour tonight, do some reading, possibly play some cards, shower and go to bed at 10:00 P.M. I am allowed to send you three letters a week. You'll be able to explain to the family that you will be the source of all information coming from me. I received a receipt for the $10.00 you sent in for me. Tomorrow I'll get a lock for my locker, toothbrush, comb, brush, razor, blades, shaving brushes, fruit, cookies, candies. We are allowed $2.50 a week for such items. This afternoon before supper I had a talk with the visiting Rabbi. He's a nice guy & if the front office will permit him he will call my Mom and tell her I'm alright. I hear your brother David was shipped off to the

* "My Day," a syndicated column by Mrs. Eleanor Roosevelt, was published for the entire decade of the 1950s.

"Tombs." * When you have a chance tell my lawyer to see me at his earliest possible convenience. I hope the business** will not cause you much trouble and I'd like to have a report on the billing and expenses each week you see me. If they can make it, ask my brother and sister to come. To Michael. I want you to remember all the games we play together, baseball, checkers, cards, cowboys and when you play them with your Mommie, remember I'm enjoying them too. Of course I miss you, but you must understand Daddy is occupied elsewhere and make the best of the situation. Play as much as possible with your brother and be nice to him. I particularly remember the times you've phoned me at my place and how nice it was to hear your voice. To Robert: "Is that my Robbie, this is your Daddy" just like on the phone call to the shop. Don't forget his lucky ride every night Mommie. Of Course don't forget a trip with the boys now and then. I hope I'm not going off the deep end and giving you a tough job with them. There are many times my mind wanders but with a couple of kids like I've got and a wonderful wife I feel much better. Send my love to your mother and family, my mother and my family and regards to all our friends. With all my love and constant thoughts of you I am looking forward to seeing you this Sunday. Hugs and kisses to my boys and all my affection to you.

JULIUS

July 24, 1950

Dearest Honey Wife, —

There was so much to tell you and talk about before I saw you but somehow when I saw you yesterday words came hard and all I could seem to talk about was the business. After you left and until I fell asleep, I thought of how you looked and what you said. Eth, believe me I did not want to convey the idea to you that I am hard and that you were weak to cry and feel so badly. It will take more than my inadequate words to

---

* David Greenglass, arrested one month earlier, was housed on the eleventh floor of the "Tombs" (the so-called "Singing Quarters") with Harry Gold. There they rehearsed their stories so that at the trial they meshed perfectly.
** My father was a struggling small businessman. He owned a machine shop and was trying to pay off the money he'd borrowed to set it up.

convey to you my profoundest feeling and love for you. It is so much more difficult because of the kind of relationship we have. You looked so pretty and your dress looked so well on you. I am sure you were able to get some of the good feeling I obtained from seeing and talking to you. Thinking of this I am suggesting that you become the secretary and active participant in my legal defense.* That is, you should be present at all important confidential conferences between my lawyer and myself. You realize that you will be an important witness in my case. The best results are obtained by a very complete preparation of my defense before I go on trial. You will take this up with Mr. Bloch. Concerning visiting. Come at the earliest possible hour and waste the time before visiting with the necessary red tape inspection so that we can have the full time alloted to me. Before I go further I want you to understand that you've acted better than was to be hoped for considering the adverse conditions you are presently facing. Give these instructions to Charlie. Bill Air-Duct Installation $291.50 less handling costs (not to exceed $10.00). Bill Centennial for 155 assemblies $4.00 ea. [He is being allowed no more than 25¢ for assembly.] We will handle Templet's bill as they owe us a considerable balance. Offer Coil Winders the test equipment with a 30% discount from the price a legitimate outfit such as Newark Sales or others that are located at Cortlinat Street would charge. Sell Aristocrat all the small heads we have at 30¢ ea. He can take all the stainless steel & aluminum for his job at a 10% discount off our cost. I want us to keep my personal tools such as, slide rule, drawing instrument micrometers, scales, etc. and the parts and tools for the jumping booster bars. Try to make some progress in selling the shop but don't be too hasty. Sweet Michael boy, I know how much you love me and it always makes me feel better to hear you keep on saying it and asking about me. I am very happy we were able to spend such nice times together, at such places as South Beach Amusement Park, Central Park and Prospect Park.** Sometimes I think of

* Ethel had typing and stenography training, so this would also be a way of saving expenses.
** South Beach was a great excursion. It used to include a trip on the Staten Island Ferry, then a train ride on the Staten Island Rapid Transit (surface subway trains) to the Lower

the nice baseball games we played in the East Pine Drive Park. I could just close my eyes and see you bang that ball way over my head for a home run. Don't you worry, we'll be playing games again as soon as I can straighten out this trouble I'm in. When it comes to my Robbie all I can say I miss him as much as I miss his big brother and Mommy. I can just imagine him sitting with his trucks, cars, blocks and toys in his room playing with them and then rushing in to yell, "Come see what I made." No I can not forget all these joys and they give me sustenance. All my love, hugs and kisses to you my wife and to you my boys. Regards to our families — love —

JULIUS

Meanwhile, our mother struggled to carry on with us and his business.

July 25, 1950

Dearest Honey,

This will, of necessity, have to be brief as it is now close to 1:00 A.M. and my eyes ache for lack of sleep.

Just got through hanging the clothes as Mike didn't get to sleep until 11:30 P.M. Have an awful lot scheduled till I get to see you again. Was supposed to discuss matters with Templet today but never got around to it — The accountant is coming in Thursday morning about taxes — Got a call from someone concerning Pitt's* future which did not sound phony to me — However, I made no commitments of any kind and will simply turn over the name and address to Mr. Bloch when I see him . . .

Billed Lo-Man today for 135 pcs. which comes to a sizable amount. Therefore, Sunday should give you some picture of things . . . Love you darling — miss you and can't wait till Sunday. Best from your two kiddies who never stop asking for you. Why haven't I heard from you yet? Hope everything's

---

Bay shore of Staten Island. The trips clearest in my mind are the ones to Prospect Park, the Bronx Zoo and South Beach.

* The name of the business was the Pitt Machine Products Co., Inc.

O.K. with you. It's all so strange without you, my dear one. I love you, sweetheart, goodnight.

ETHEL

Though my father wrote that he'd be back as soon as he could "straighten out this trouble," the tone of these letters indicates resignation to a long separation from the family. In prison awaiting trial he agreed with a fellow prisoner's assessment that he would be convicted. He understood that, given the temper of the times, he had very little chance with the jury. His attorney, Emanuel Bloch, concurred. Under those circumstances the defense strategy at the trial was restricted to creating a good impression in the hope of forestalling the death penalty, even if it meant not challenging all the prosecution's assertions.

In these first letters there is a theme that runs throughout their correspondence over the three years — concern for the family and a desire that the family act as a contact with the outside world as well as provide sustenance. This support, no matter how frightened and half-hearted, from the Rosenberg relatives was very welcome. My father had three sisters, one of whom was institutionalized, and a brother. Sophie, his mother, was still living. The family split with the Greenglasses was all the more wrenching for the importance such support would have had. My mother had two brothers in addition to David, and her mother, Tessie, was also still living.

From the time of my father's arrest until the nature of the "deal" between David and Ruth Greenglass and the prosecution was understood, Julius sent regards to Tessie Greenglass and other members of that family. Ethel, free, saw the hostility building up.

Returning from her first Grand Jury appearance on August 7, she entered her mother's house to collect Robby and me and the conversation between Tessie and Ruth stopped. When my mother admired Ruth's infant daughter, Ruth turned beet-red and wouldn't respond. In the course of the ensuing conversation, Tessie slammed her hand down on the table and said, "If you don't talk, you're gonna burn with your husband."

"But Mama, I've lived with him. I know he didn't do those things."

Neither Robby nor I have any significant memories of the period between our father's and our mother's arrests. On July 29, one of our father's first letters finally arrived and our mother immediately set about following his instructions regarding the business.

Dearest Julie,
Finally got your letter this morning. First to take up the practical matters: . . . What I did today was go over your letter bit by bit with Charlie and make notes of his replies alongside. So here goes. He is going to get that Carbide Milling Cutter. He's working on the valves and Danny is working on the Lo-Man job, . . . The MRM bushings were canceled Tuesday morning. So were the drills, so you don't have to worry about them being returned. Incidently, Dun and Bradstreet came in wanting information from Charlie which, of course, he was unable to give them. Letters have already been sent out to their subscribers cutting you off from any more credit. Charlie spoke to Du-Fast, who said he must be paid C.O.D. as he had parts ready, so Charlie called customer to whom parts were to go and the customer agreed to take parts. When we bill, we'll deduct handling charges. . . . As for the parts you mention having to do with Templet, when 4 parts were finished, Continental picked up same and made arrangements to work directly with Templet — a cancelation in effect . . . as for Coil Winders, what would you consider a satisfactory offer for the electrical test equipment? . . .
. . . Charlie . . . feels there should be some more definite understanding well in advance of the finish of the work. I assured him that if and when we decided to close the doors he'd receive enough notice not to be left jobless suddenly and unexpectedly. Personally, my feeling is it is imperative to sell the shop. It is ridiculous to temporize . . .
Gladdy has responded extremely well to the new treatment,

so much so that Bernie sounded really elated. It knocked the temp. from somewhere bet. 103 and 104 down to normal at once, and she is feeling a lot stronger. Oh how wonderful it would be if a real cure could be effected * . . . Poor Mike, he simply can't see why he shouldn't be permitted to see you or at least talk to you by 'phone. And he keeps repeating that I shouldn't neglect to tell you how much he misses you and loves you. Robby too, asks for you constantly and I have all I can do not to break down continuously. Please, darling, do take care of yourself and be assured of how much I am trying to justify your faith in me. I miss you terribly, though, how much I love you —

See you Sunday,
ETHEL

July 31, 1950

My Darling —

9:30 P.M. The Playing cards have been collected & we're locked up for the night and we are now listening to the Dodger ball game. I received your letter of the 25th of July, as soon as I got back from Foley Square, *note* the 6 day delay. Concerning your questions on the bills. They are due in 30 days but in this case we can go a little beyond this time. Look through the checkbook and note the previous checks to see which are due to the Telephone Co. and other firms. Before sending any checks make certain there is a reserve in the bank to cover at least one payroll in advance.

It was very refreshing to see you looking so well and so nicely dressed this morning. I can also thank you for your excellent taste in making my selections. At present I am thinking about your parting remark & it makes me feel good. Eth, I believe that we should use some moderation as to when it is necessary for you to be present as it may take too much out of you. Honey, let's leave it to you and Mr. Bloch's discretion. I am very sorry we did not have an opportunity at this hearing to talk about the kids as I am very much concerned about Michael's

---

* Gladys Greenglass, the mother of our cousin Sharon and the wife of Bernard Greenglass, was suffering from Hodgkin's Disease.

health. I would like you to have him send me a letter about his experiences with his uncle Bernie and cousin Sharon in the country. His cold must have deprived him of a chance to go swimming. I hope an opportunity presents itself for you to take the boys to the beach. Now that summer school is out the little one must be leading you a merry chase. I would like to make a repeat request for photos of you and my boys. That reminds me see if you can get the FBI to return the stuff they took from our house such as watches, picture books and the typewriter.* I want you to convey my thanks to Bernie for taking Michael for the weekend and send him and Glady my best wishes. Don't fail to send my regards to your mother and let me know how she's been feeling. Keep me posted on my mother's health. Send her my wishes for a speedy recovery and all my love. Tell her it isn't appropriate for a grandmother like her to behave in this manner, after all, everybody is counting on her. Call my sister and let her know what's what. I am trying to keep away from telling you how much I miss you but it's no use. Things are so different without you and the kids and only the passing of time and the looking ahead seems to make any sense. All my thoughts are constantly of you and the children & how we spent our time together. Love, more love and hope.

JULIUS

August 4, 1950

Dearest Honey Wife —

Friday — I just had some baked fish, baked potato, string beans and watermelon. A good lunch. My attorney visited me before lunch. It is always good to have a visit from him to discuss the case and get the latest news on things concerning you and the kids. I am so glad to hear that you are in good spirits and conducting yourself in a very noble manner. Remember darling that you are a big factor in my morale. I love you very much and miss you more than my written words can express. There are many moments during the day that I think of you and the kids, exactly what you're doing and how

* As of the end of 1974, those things were still in the custody of the government at Foley Square in New York City.

you're managing. Eth, try to write me in detail about you and the kids . . . Send my best wishes to all our family and friends especially to both our mothers. I am feeling fine and in the best of health and loving you more and more. A big hug and many kisses to my dear boys.

DADDY — JULIUS

Unaware that our mother was about to be arrested, our father wrote to his sister, Ethel,* appealing directly to his family for help.

August 11, 1950

Dear Ethel,

I find myself in a predicament, by force of circumstances, without being guilty of any crime. Ever since childhood I can remember the close family relationship and loving cooperation that has always existed among our relatives. In these days of stress more than ever your help is needed. At a time when Ethel is so taken up with our children and my defense, she may be forced to go to work. I know you're not millionaires but all practical help, moral support and love is needed by my wife and children. In the past, when necessity called, my wife and I were never found wanting, on the contrary, we contributed to the best of our ability. I want you to understand, I am not begging or am I demanding, however I am asking you to stand by me, my wife and children.

I am limited to three letters per week, therefore, I would appreciate it if you let Lena, Dave and my wife read this letter. Any news you can send me about you, your husband and children will be most welcome, as I hunger to hear from my family and letters help the time pass pleasantly. Send my best wishes to ————** Congratulations are in order for your daughter ————*** for her successful graduation. All my love and regards to ————, ————**** and of course you my beloved sister.

YOUR BROTHER JULIUS

*My father had a sister named Ethel as well as a brother named David. The resemblance between his brother and my mother's brother ended with their first names.
**Our uncle.
***Our Aunt Ethel's older daughter
****Our Aunt Ethel's two other children

P.S. To Mamma, Dave and Lena,

I am sending my letters to my wife, who will communicate them to all of you. I sent this letter to Ethel as she lives near you, my dear brother and very often she and her family drive down to visit with my sweet mommie and darling sister Lee. If my correspondence were not limited and I would send each of you my dearest personal letters but am sure you will all understand I am doing my best considering the restrictions I am under. Send my love to your respective husband, wife and my niece and nephew.

As for myself I'm in the best of health; and hope to hear the same from you. To a great extent my morale depends on my family. I want you to know it is very high and I'm positive I can count on each everyone of you to help continue to keep it that way.

All my love, JULIUS   Hugs and Kisses

On August 11, after her second session before the Grand Jury, my mother was arrested and held in $100,000 bail. A woman hired for the day looked after us; though my mother thought she might be arrested, she had not had time to make plans to have us taken care of. I can still hear her on the telephone telling me she was under arrest. I have been told that my reaction was a heart-rending scream which continued to give her nightmares the rest of her life. I have completely blocked this out.

August 12, 1950

Dearest Ethel,

I heard the news over the radio last night and after strenuous efforts to see you or contact you I've been given permission to write this letter. Let me know as soon as possible how you are feeling. How are the children? Has any provision been made for them? I am fine and all's well. I expect the lawyer to see me this morning and I'll instruct him to send you commissary money, newspapers and all the little things he can do to make it easier. Tell me your plans for the children and I'll try to have

the lawyer arrange a meeting for us to decide on the children.
Keep a stiff upper lip. all my love

YOUR JULIUS

August 12, 1950

My dearest darling Julie,

By now you must know what has happened to me. Darling, I
wish I could say that I am cool, calm and collected but the fact
is that although, contrary to newspaper reports, I have not been
hysterical at any time, I have shed many anxious tears on behalf
of the children and have been feeling badly that I won't be
seeing you on Sunday. My heart cries aloud for you and the
children. Now indeed it is harder to be inside than out because
each of us knows the other is not free to care for our dears.
How unfortunate it was that I never got around to discussing
arrangements for them with the proper people. I had been
planning to do that very thing this week so that the kids should
be subjected to as little strain as possible, in the event I was
detained — and I must confess my mind does leap ahead to the
frightening possibilities for them. However, I guess I will feel
lots better after I see Mr. Bloch and ask him to get in touch with
those people who can help us in the matter of the care of the
children. By all means, sweetheart, if you have any ideas about
this and/or any of our other problems, please communicate
with our lawyer and also write me about same . . .

Sweetheart, I talk with you every night before I fall asleep
and cry because you can't hear me. And then I tell myself that
you too must be choking with the same frustration and
wondering if I can hear you. Darling, we mustn't lose each
other or the children, mustn't lose our identities. I try to think
of the good, fine life we've led all these years and I am agonized
with my longing to go on leading it.

All my love and my most devoted thoughts to you, my
dearest loved one. Please write me as soon as you can.

I love you,

ETHEL

August 14, 1950

Dear Michael,

Hi son how are you getting along and how do you feel? As for me all's well and I'm doing nicely. I received both your letters and they were sweet. Keep up the good work. You, your brother Robert and your mother are always in my mind. I love all of you very much and I am glad to hear that you are managing so nicely.

You remember that Lone Ranger story about how his little nephew* even though all alone managed so well. He was able to do this because he cooperated with the one who was put in charge of him and even as he learned new things he enjoyed himself doing it. I am so glad you are able to play with your clay, blocks crayons and toys and get so much out of it. These things are just like the tools your Daddy used in the shop to do his work with only your tools are your play things.

I was so impressed with your Hop Along Cassidy story that I'll write you one

"Crime of the Bar-Q"

One day as two cowboys Michael and Robert were riding along the trail to the Bar-Q ranch to see the boss man Mr. Jones, they heard shots coming from the direction of the ranch house. "Let's Go," yelled Mike to Robert "Giddap" roared Robert as they dug their spurs into their pintos and they raced forward. Rounding a bend in the road they saw three men swiftly mounting their horses to make a getaway. Michael drew his six-shooter and fired from the hip "Bang Bang." One of the outlaws fell off his horse shot through the head. As their horses came up to the door of the ranch house they heard, "Help, Help. I'm wounded" They rushed into the house and found Mr. Jones lying on the floor badly wounded. "Quick Robert ride to Doc Thomas and bring him back at once. I'll stay here with rancher Jones," said Michael. "Who were these hombres and what did they want?" asked Michael. Jones replied, "The Adams gang robbed me of $100,000 cattle money." "Don't worry we'll get those owl hoots for you." After making sure

* Dan Reed who rode one of Silver's sons, Victor.

that Jones was out of danger and Doc Thomas was on hand, Mike and Robert carefully trailed the remaining two outlaws to their hideout. While the outlaws slept Mike and Robert surprised them and took them prisoners and so ended the "Crime of the Bar-Q."

Give your brother a big hug and kiss for me. Darling I want you boys to remember your Daddy is always thinking of you and wants to hear all about you. See if you can write again real soon. If I have the time I'll try to make up a story about a space ship and a trip to one of the planets. Now be good have a lot of fun and keep on playing. I hope to see you soon. With all my love Your Daddy Julius Love & Kisses & Hugs.

Our mother also wrote:

August 15, 1950

Dearest Michael boy,

I am so sorry you have had to wait so long to hear from me. I am also sorry that I didn't have more time to speak to you on the phone after I was arrested.

Believe me, sweetie, I think of you and Robby all the time and I know how you must be missing your Mommy and Daddy. I know also that it's harder for you to do the usual things when the person you're used to isn't around to help you do them. When you're having a hard time of it, try to remember that I am wishing like anything that I were there taking care of you and that I am also hoping you are cooperating as much as possible with the people who are there in my place. For instance, you can make things easier by telling them where your clothing is what you and Robby are used to eating and how you're used to having things done generally. In the meantime Mr. Bloch has already called Mrs. Phillips and when she comes to see me, we will work out the best kind of arrangements possible for you and Robby. So be as happy as you can and try not to mind too much, darling. Your Mommy and Daddy have not forgotten about you. All my love to my dearest boys.

The woman hired to take care of us stayed in our apartment that night but the next day she took us to Tessie Greenglass, who lived in a tenement on the Lower East Side.

Her neighborhood was filled with old walk-up buildings, with clapboard fences in the backyards. There were also plenty of empty lots with roosters strutting around in them — sometimes even goats. Junk and garbage were strewn in these lots. I often watched large trucks loaded with fish pull up to the curb of the seafood stores. Workers caught the fish in nets and dumped them in barrels which were carried into the store and the fish were poured into large tanks. When a customer selected a particular fish, the woman (it was usually a large-armed woman with an apron and a look of strength about her) laid it out on the table. With one whack of a rolling pin she killed the fish. Then, she cut off the head, slit it down the middle and removed the bones and organs.

When our maternal grandfather "Zade Barnett" * was alive he ran a sewing machine repair shop in front of the ground-floor apartment where he and Tessie lived. Her sister, Chutcha, lived upstairs. He died in 1948 so I barely remember him as a thin, bald-headed man with rosy cheeks and a cheery smile. However, I do have a clear memory of the junk-filled room which served as his shop. Tessie stored many seltzer bottles in that room. I never drank seltzer and thought it useful only to scare away cats, dozens of which hid in the junk in the room as well as in the backyard.

I spent a lot of time in the kitchen watching Grandma build a fire in the old wood stove or sitting at the kitchen table drawing railroad tracks on paper. I don't know why I was so fascinated by railroad tracks, but between the ages of six and thirteen I must have drawn miles of them. (Suddenly, at thirteen, I lost interest.) These tracks were not art work, I didn't try to reproduce a visual image. I simply drew two lines to represent the track. I liked to draw switches and the route a train would take switching from one track to another. I often drew an express train that passed a lot of stations. Once I dictated a story to my mother about "Big Fierce Track" in which one track constantly switched into others, and

* "Zade" is a Yiddish word for Grandfather.

trains running on that track had the right of way. I thought of every switch as some kind of victory for the track/train being switched.

During this period, my parents' major contact with us was Mrs. Elizabeth Phillips, the social worker at the Jewish Board of Guardians whom I had been seeing since early 1950. My mother had brought me to the J.B.G. because I was tense and becoming very difficult to control. There may have even been some school problems when I was in second grade. While at my grandmother's, I continued to see Mrs. Phillips regularly.

August 20, 1950

Dearest Sweetheart,

It's 7:15 and I'm in the Recreation Room. I've showered and washed my things and hung them to dry. At 7:30 I'll be heading for my "house" (that's what the girls call their cells), and at 8:00 they'll lock each of us in for the night. Lights out by 9:00 and up the next morning at 6:30 . . .

Darling I'm thinking of your second letter which came when I was in the sorest need of it. In the main, I would say that I'm taking the situation fairly well, but there are times when I'm terribly blue and depressed. Saturday was just such an unhappy day. Sunday was a little better because a good part of the morning was spent at Protestant and Christian Science services. Right after breakfast, these services are held and by the time we return it's close to 11:00 A.M. I like it because it constitutes a diversion which is also personally enjoyable because it gives me an opportunity to sing. Incidentally, it took them just a few days to realize that I could sing so almost every night now I receive various requests. One morning, at breakfast, I was pleasurably surprised to hear a number of girls in corridors other than my own, away across the hall, express their appreciation.

Last Friday I attended the Jewish Services which were all too short. Too bad there was no singing, but the Rabbi intoned the prayers so beautifully that I couldn't help but enjoy it.

During the week there is a lot more to take up one's time. There's visiting, commissary, an hour on the roof in the afternoon and yesterday just as I came down I was told to go to Social Service and there Mrs. Phillips sat awaiting me, bless her. She told me that a very good homemaker is now helping my mother and that Michael has been coming to see her (Mrs. Phillips) very willingly. Last week she took him home in a cab after getting him a sandwich he asked for. Hope I get to talk to you in Court today, darling.

Love you,
ETHEL

August 29, 1950

My dearest darling Julie,

I am hoping that by now you have received my second letter. By now I know that my first one finally reached you.

Oh darling, even though we were able to spend some time together the day we went to court, it seemed to me when I had returned here that there were so many other ways I might have expressed my feelings to you, so many other things I might have said. So let me say them now, my dear one. And yet, I couldn't ever say enough what pride and love and deep regard for you I feel. What you wrote me about ourselves as a family, and what that family means to you made my eyes fill. There came to me such an abiding sense of faith and joy, such a sure knowledge of the rich meaning our lives have held that I was suddenly seized with an overwhelming desire to see you and say it to you and kiss you with all my heart.

Sweetheart, we must go on pouring out all that we feel towards each other, in our letters as I know how this strengthens the deep bond between us, that bond you described as well in your last writing. How frustrating it is, though when we have been accustomed to day-to-day association to have only this means of communication. I treasure the time we spent together last Wednesday (which already seems so long ago) and can't wait for our next meeting . . .

Love you sweetheart,
YOUR ETHEL

My reaction to life with Grandmother was very poor. On one

occasion I blurted out to one of my father's sisters who lived in the neighborhood that I wanted to run into the street and get killed by a car. My social worker noticed that I was not eating and combined each weekly visit with a trip to a local luncheonette where I ravenously devoured a hamburger. I think that was the origin of my belief that the hamburger was the greatest food invented, a view I held until I was a teen-ager.

For Robby (then three years old), Grandma Tessie and Chutcha — he remembers her as "Cheh-cheh" — were cold and unfriendly. Our parents' lawyers were made to understand that we were unwanted, a message also conveyed to Robby and me. I remember Tessie's house as a place where I did nothing but read comics, draw tracks and walk around the neighborhood. Referring to my parents, Grandma would say things to me like, "You're lucky they're born here or they'd be deported." Considering their fate I guess we weren't so lucky.

Tessie's oldest son, Sam, shared her anger at my mother when it appeared she would not back up David's story. He wrote:

Dear Sis —

Today I visited Mom — I also saw Robert and Michael. I told Michael that I had spoken to you. His first words to me were "My mother is innocent" — "She would not do anything that was wrong" — Well, you certainly built up a lot of faith in this poor child. — How can you have the bitter thought on your conscience to let this child down in such a horrible way.

When a stranger walks into the house — his first question is "Is she from the child welfare or is she an investigator —. I don't want to go to a foster home — I want to stay here."

How can Mom keep those two children — They are wearing her away very quickly — I must say you have done and are still doing a very wonderful job — There is not much more disgrace you could bring to your family — but now your great problems seems to be — to get rid of them — one at a time — First Mom — Then Chuch — The children in a foster home — your brother in jail — what an excellent job — . . .

. . . In my lousy heart there is only contempt for you and your kind — but spurred on by the emotions and a Mother and an Aunt* who unselfishly give of their lives so that poor defenseless and innocent children can have a temporary shelter and comfort and protection —

For these I ask again — give up this wild ideology — come down to earth, give yourself a fighting chance (I may be able to help you) so that someday you may possibly be a mother to your two children — and not a number in some jail — rotting away your years. — I mention again that I may be able to help you but I must have your co-operation.

Your brother
SAM

Once when I complained about how horrible life was there, Grandma retorted, "Good, send your momma a telegram and tell her! Ask her to get you out of here." She thrust the phone into my hand. Tremulously, I dictated a telegram to my mother at the Women's House of Detention, careful not to upset her: "I am having a nice time. I miss you very much. Love, your son, Michael." Someone from the prison called back but Grandma never gave me the message. I don't know if my mother ever received that telegram.

Despite all this, my memories are not entirely negative. I did enjoy Chutcha taking me on subway and El rides. I had always enjoyed these rides with my father and at least continued to get that kind of pleasure from Chutcha. Standing in the first car, I watched the switching tracks.

Nevertheless, life with Tessie and Chutcha was very upsetting for the four of us. I slept in Chutcha's bed upstairs; Robby slept with Grandma. Robby would grind his teeth all night and keep her awake. I insisted on staying up late enough to hear Lyle Van's eleven o'clock news in the hope of hearing something more about my parents. Though I don't remember my parents teaching this at home, I would continually shock my religious grandmother by saying, "Grandma, how many times do I have to tell you there is no such thing as God." She would turn pale and warn, "God will punish you." After a number of these encounters, I relented to please her. "All right. Now I believe in God."

* Tessie and Chutcha.

An angry letter to my mother dated October 25, 1950, from Bernard Greenglass' sister-in-law describes the zoo at Tessie's house:

> . . . I'm there all day every day but Saturday and Sunday and all I ever see the woman* doing is cleaning the floors, the windows, or ironing. Your kids roam the streets and the only time I see anything done for them is when your Ma calls them in for feedings . . .
>
> Your Ma reviles and rants about you and the situation you & Julie brought on her family and how much trouble the kids are and how bad they are and how bad you are, and why don't you do what Ruthie did so you too could be with your kids and why I don't go and tell you that . . .
>
> . . . even if you think I'm deranged call the proper authorities and get your kids out anywhere but with them, please.

Some unpleasant memories have been blotted out of my mind.

> . . . when I see your kids pushed around screamed at, have to listen to your being spoken about badly and cursed and your Ma talking bad about your in-laws and poor Michael going into temper tantrums when your Ma curses you I want to hit her over the head.

I did not know at the time the family's self-protective position: Julius is responsible for getting David into trouble; Ethel is responsible for refusing to talk. The Greenglasses rallied to David and Ruth's side. Part of this is explainable by the Greenglass family's desire to associate themselves with people who cooperated with the government rather than with those whom the government and newspapers were vilifying. Part by the fact that my mother, as the only daughter, was very much overlooked by her family.

Tessie threatened to dump us at the nearest police station as soon as she could. She had to be forced to care for us and finally

---

* Someone hired by a family service agency to help with Robby and me.

succeeded in arranging for us to be transferred to the Hebrew Children's Home, a shelter in the Bronx. When we were told we had to leave, I was scared and didn't want to go. Tessie and Chutcha indicated that our leaving was for the best as we wouldn't be able to stay through the winter — the apartment got cold, even the water in the toilets froze. Seizing this reason I said to myself, "Oh, well, I guess we have to leave." I wouldn't have been so willing to accept that if I hadn't really *wanted* to leave. Robby has a clear memory. "I spent a few intense minutes gazing down the toilet trying to fathom why someone would say it was frozen when there wasn't any ice." Later, when Robby was five, he called canned pears, a dessert he hated, "the Cheh-Cheh thing" to emphasize its awfulness.

The Greenglasses' abandonment of the Rosenbergs in favor of the repentant "spies" David and Ruth was a bitter pill for our parents to swallow. Unfortunately, the support and sustenance our parents received from the Rosenberg family did not include us. Our father's two sisters and one brother did not offer to take us in and, in fact, only the sister living near Grandma ever visited us there.

At first my father's family was shocked and frightened by his arrest. Then, his mother, Sophie, a tough, courageous woman, visited him in prison. She asked him what this was all about and when he answered, "Mamma, I don't know anything about this stuff," she returned to her other children and said, "Go visit your brother in jail. He's innocent." She refused to be cowed by political hysteria and convinced her children of her position. But they remained scared of publicity, of what their other relatives and friends might think. In short, though the Rosenberg family believed in Julius and Ethel's innocence, activity in their behalf, especially taking care of their children, terrified them. My father's letter of July 31 shows that his mother, sixty-two, was ill at this time. Had she been well she would have provided a home for us, and after she got better she did.

Grandma Tessie and a social worker (not Mrs. Phillips) took us to the Hebrew Children's Home. Robby started to cry when he realized Grandma was abandoning us. The director of the shelter, Mr. Bernard Witover, whom I picture as a pleasant if distant man,

picked Robby up and carried him down some stairs into the building. I glumly trailed after, not yet crying. We had arrived at our third home in four months.

Robby is lucky that he has no time sense of being there. Though we remained at the shelter from November until June, his memory is of a few days at most. The place has been described to us as a poor institution with poor food, cold, drafty dormitory rooms, a setting worthy of a Charles Dickens novel with some (but not all) of the brutality omitted. I hated it. The initial shock of being placed there took a long time to wear off. I felt I must have done something wrong; being there was my punishment. My voice breaking, I pleaded with anyone — an older kid, a worker — who would listen: "I've been here a whole week, don't you think that's enough and that they'll let me go home now?" Such hopes were rekindled every weekend. If someone came to pick us up Saturday morning, we were free for the whole weekend. Every Saturday for the first few months, I kept hoping against hope that someone in our family (Tessie and Chutcha took us for weekends, alternating with the Rosenbergs who took us on Sundays) would allow us to stay with them.

Following an early visit, Tessie further pressured our mother by sending this telegram on November 9:

DEAR ETHEL WENT TO SEE CHILDREN LAST SUNDAY AND SAW THEM TWICE DURING THE WEEK BUT THEY DIDN'T SEE ME. THEY WERE CRYING STEADILY. WOULD COME TO SEE YOU BUT WOULD NOT BE ABLE TO TAKE IT. ALL BROKEN UP WITH HEARTACHE. LET ME HEAR FROM YOU LOVE —

MOTHER

At the "home" as Robby and I called it (and still refer to it) I had my first confrontation with authority. I had always been a finicky eater. Hot cereal and soft eggs, staples in institutions, were high on my list of dislikes, and I gagged on them. The women who worked there were not trained teachers or licensed practical nurses. They were underpaid, for the most part young, black women who were supervised by a white Jewish registered nurse and put upon by disturbed, unhappy, whiny (for the most part)

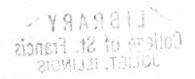

white Jewish kids. Our first breakfast at the home was hot cereal. When confronted by my refusal to eat, they responded as all authority figures probably had responded to them — they came down hard. "You eat everything or you eat nothing!" I prepared to starve but Robby was hungry. Picking up his spoon he shoved the poison into his mouth. "Robby," I shrieked. "Don't!" I put my arms around him. "I know you want to eat the bread but don't eat that stuff." A more kindly woman came over and asked, "You want bread?" I said, "Yes" and they let us have bread. That was the last concession they made. Though Manny Bloch remembers that I lived on grape jelly for months, I remember many meals in which I didn't eat anything. A new woman was hired and the others proudly informed her of how they "deal" with me. "He likes bread, see; and if he don't eat what's put before him, we don't give him no bread." Also, Robby and I were separated during meals. After we moved to New Jersey, I built the experiences at the home into a concentration camp story. As I told the story, I described myself so starved that I weighed less than Robby, though I hadn't the slightest idea how much I weighed or whether I had lost weight. Looking back, I did have some good times, but I still recall life there with horror.

Robby and I slept in separate dormitories, which were large with high ceilings and contained metal beds and drably painted walls. The rooms were sterile but dirty. We were permitted daily contact with each other, usually at bedtime, even though the younger group slept in a different dormitory. My "conversion" at Grandma Tessie's was reinforced at the home because we all said prayers ("bruchas") before meals. Every night I coaxed Robby to say his prayers. He knew how to get my goat. I recited, "Now I lay me down to sleep," etc., trying to persuade him to repeat it after me. He'd start, then insert "Goddammit" in a giggly voice. I implored him not to curse because it was a "bad sin." He'd finally say the entire prayer, and I'd go to bed worried and exhausted from the ordeal. Robby recalls, "I made a joke out of it. I'd say the prayer only after many warnings from Michael that I would go to hell if I didn't. He was very earnest about praying, but I never took him seriously. I was a nonbeliever even then. God never made any sense to me."

In the concrete playground behind the home I learned my first sport, "Knock out," which was dodge ball without boundaries. I also enjoyed afternoons and Saturdays with a young high school (or college) student, Gerald, whom we called Mr. Gerald. He was genuinely interested in us, and once protested to Mr. Witover that some of the women were mistreating us. He even got one of the harshest women fired.

Miss A—— was angrier and treated the kids with more contempt than most of the other women. One day, I think on a Saturday, I misbehaved. Miss A—— sent me to the dormitory to be punished. I cried bitterly, maybe even cursed, and threw my clothes all over the room, getting into bed naked. She came up after me, dragged me into the shower and repeatedly slapped me. After that incident I hated her with the consuming passion I have reserved for very few choice people. My plan of revenge, however, showed reverse psychology. I became an incredible "goody-goody" around her, going out of my way to say, "Hello, Miss A——" or "Goodbye, Miss A——," whichever was appropriate. If I was in the middle of a game or ready for bed, I called across the room to her. After a while, she noticed my fawning behavior and in my presence laughed to another woman about my always saying hello and goodbye to her. I was glad of my ability to make her think I had been "tamed"; every salutation was an obvious (to me) mockery of her authority.

I was able to indulge all my contempt and hatred for her while at the same time protecting myself from her physical and verbal abuse. Soon, I was free of Miss A——, in fact as well as spirit. Mrs. S——, the registered nurse, who often washed out kids' mouths with soap, had on numerous occasions expressed horrified disbelief at some of our stories about the extent of corporal punishment, not only from Miss A—— but from others. When Mr. Gerald complained about the same thing, we knew something would happen. One night as he was leaving, Miss A—— exploded in a tirade of angry expletives. He just kept walking. Shortly thereafter she was fired. We all knew he was to be thanked for getting rid of her, and we were tremendously relieved that she was gone.

I made a concentrated effort to get on Mr. Gerald's good side.

In school I drew him a birthday card and worked hard to win good conduct marks from him. I was a perfect little brown-nose. At the same time, I was not averse to being punished in order to gain his attention. I guess this was part of my perception that being at the home was a result of having done something wrong. Punishment seemed logical there. Though it never happened to me, kids often had their mouths washed out with soap. The angry young women responsible for us physically punished us often and roughly. Not the "therapeutic slap," as parents like to define their spankings — it was raw anger at their lives and at us who were part of their lives.

At one point I volunteered for punishment. A group of us had crowded into Mr. Witover's office. I hung back but may have entered his outer office. One kid actually got near his desk and started talking to him when Mr. Gerald came charging in and shooed us out. Why the hell Witover didn't say, "Let them stay; I'd love to visit awhile" is beyond me. Mr. Gerald demanded that everyone in Mr. Witover's office sit down. I remained standing though I wasn't really sure if I was guilty or not. Angry that so few people "owned up," he had us turn around, ordering all who were guilty to raise their hands. I was totally confused, and, not knowing why, I raised my hand. At least, I thought, he won't be mad at me now. My "volunteering" earned me more than I bargained for. On a gloriously beautiful day I had to sit on a bench indoors for the afternoon. I was furious. I didn't cry, though if I'd spoken to anyone I probably would have. I spent the entire time plotting revenge. I didn't scheme against Mr. Gerald or the staff at the home; instead, I plotted against various members of the Greenglass family. How many ways did I plan to dismember Ruth and David! Also, I have always been partial to the "Just You Wait" version of revenge. In the song from *My Fair Lady*, Eliza promises, "You'll be broke, and I'll have money. Will I help you? Don't be funny . . ." In my scenarios I would suddenly appear in the future, able to dispense gifts to those who had harmed me and now had fallen on bad times. They would beg for help and then I would reveal that I was the person they had wronged. Overcome with remorse they'd plead for forgiveness and help. I'd entertain one of two endings for this scenario:

magnanimous forgiveness or connivance in their total downfall. I'm not sure which ending I'd choose today.

To impress upon me the seriousness of my crime, Mr. Gerald stretched my punishment to two weeks. This became too much for me. Firmly convinced I had "volunteered" for punishment erroneously, I tearfully explained to the home's social worker, "I was raising my hand to ask a question." To this day I don't know which version was the truth and I'm not sure it matters. My social worker whittled my punishment to less than a week.

True to form, I remained friendly with Mr. Gerald. When he initiated a plan of checks (for good behavior) and crosses (for bad behavior), I tried very hard to earn checks. One week I won the most checks and was made the judge who meted out punishments to those who had earned X's that week. His system was no doubt considered too punitive after Mrs. S——'s son was convicted in my "court" and sentenced to missing television all week. In any event, the next time I tried to earn a check by straightening up the chairs in a room while he was watching (he never gave a check if you called attention to your own good behavior; being good was supposedly its own reward!), he sorrowfully offered me a lollipop. I think I understood immediately that his program had been scrapped. Though he was in many ways a disciplinarian, Mr. Gerald was my favorite adult at the home.

The women who didn't make a habit of beating us were nevertheless in angry or contemptuous moods most of the time. Ridiculing one child before the whole group was a usual pastime. One poor guy who was always making in his pants, for instance, was paraded in front of the dormitory as we were going to bed. He had no clothes on and the angry attendant — as I recall she was the white night worker we called Aunt B—— — demanded our attention: "Look! Look at this!" She flung the boy around and we saw liquid shit on the backs of his legs. Some kids gave a short, loud burst of embarrassed laughter and then grew silent as the boy, released, raced into the bathroom to clean himself off.

Invariably, the only times the women were friendly and respectful to us were on Sunday afternoons as the relatives we had visited dropped us off at the home. I wished they would stay in those "good moods" all week. I didn't understand how they could be so nice and kind on that day and so awful the other six days. Eventually I realized they wanted to make a good impression on our relatives.

Despite the fact that Grandma Tessie had thrown us out, I looked forward to the Greenglass family visits. Unlike the Rosenberg relatives, Tessie and Chutcha took us for the whole weekend. I would draw tracks all day Saturday. We might have stayed a weekend or two with a Rosenberg relative, but usually they came for us on Sunday afternoons. We'd walk in the neighborhood, talk a little, maybe play catch — the visit was short. The Rosenbergs remained torn. They were convinced of their brother's innocence but terribly afraid of being publicly associated with him. They continued to visit my parents and later became actively involved in the struggle to develop new evidence and force clemency either from the sentencing judge or President Eisenhower, but they still did not take Robby and me in. Until Grandma Sophie got well, we were stuck in the home.

A bright aspect of life there was that I had an excellent school year at P.S. 30. Having missed more than a month of the third grade by not going to school while living with Tessie and Chutcha, I was at first stuck into the second grade. I quickly proved my reading ability, so I was transferred to the third grade. During school hours I felt happy and content. This is a bit puzzling considering our predicament. Perhaps it was the familiarity of academic activity — reading, spelling, math which came easily and for which I was praised. In the unfamiliar setting of the institution, of Mommy and Daddy being away, of conflicts over eating, I was secure with my school work and good grades which I knew would please my parents. Probably school reminded me of simpler days in the past when a good report card was one of the happy things I shared with them. One of my more unfortunate trademarks developing at this time was an incredible stubbornness and arrogant self-confidence that would drive anyone with a different answer or point of view into a rage. Being a very good student and having received a tremendous amount of positive reinforcement increased my stubbornness and self-confidence. At this age I did not yet use scholarly excellence as a competitive edge to impress my fellow students. I enjoyed school and worked hard because I had been taught that to do so was important, not because I looked upon high marks as a gateway to superiority in the eyes of others. In school and at the home, I even made friends. To Robby the kids seemed tough, and he wasn't but somehow managed to stay out of trouble. I was not as introverted as Robby and liked the kids, becoming particularly attached to Adam Mericus. The first night he arrived at the home the other kids started teasing him, saying his name was Atom Bomb. We'd walk home from school together, and I'd start, "Adam Marias, Adam Marisse, Adam Mer-ee-cuss . . . (pause) Atom Bomb!" Then I'd playfully run away as if afraid he would chase me. He didn't seem to mind the kidding.

In April I received some news that I knew I should respond to with sadness. Moping, I walked outside and to everyone interested or within hearing distance, I repeated over and over, "We lost the trial." * I'm not sure I was immediately informed of the death sentence, but probably I was aware of it anyway. From listening to Lyle Van's news programs, I'd no doubt learned that my parents faced the death penalty. Thus my "nightmare prediction" was reinforced. I remained conscious all along of the "worst possible" outcome. In the three-year period between arrests and executions, my worst nightmares came true. I didn't *expect* them to, but I *feared* they would and anticipated the worst. But for some reason I couldn't get upset over the "loss" of the trial. The most personally upsetting thing, separation from our parents, had already occurred. I didn't comprehend that the fulfillment of my "nightmare prediction" was more likely now that they had been convicted. So I pretended to be upset though I didn't really know enough to *be* upset. My parents, however, knew enough to be overwrought and were.

April 10, 1951

Precious Woman,

Ethel, my darling, you are truly a great, dignified and sweet person. Tears fill my eyes as I try to put my sentiments on paper. I can only say that life has been worthwhile because you have been beside me. I firmly believe that we are better people

* See page 57 for the description my social worker gave my father of my reaction.

because we stood up with courage, character and confidence through a very grueling trial and a most brutal sentence, all because we are innocent. It's very difficult for people who are uninformed and who have no feelings to understand our stamina. Our upbringing, the full meaning of our lives, based on a true amalgamation of our American and Jewish Heritage, which to us means freedom, culture and character, has made us the people we are. All the filth, lies and slanders of this grotesque political frame-up, in a background of world hysteria; will not in any way deter us, but rather spur us on until we are completely vindicated. We didn't ask for this; we only wanted to be left alone, but the gauntlet was laid down to us and with every ounce of life in our bodies we will fight till we are free.

Honey, I think of you constantly, I hunger for you, I want to be with you. It is so painful that such a great hurt can only mean that I love you with every fiber of my being. I can only repeat over and over again that the thought of you more than compensates for this pain because of all the happiness you have brought me as my wife. Sweetheart, I can't let go of you; you are so dear to me. If you are able to get just part of the sustenance you engender in me I am sure you will have the strength to withstand the hardships that face us.

Now I'd like to talk about our greatest possession, our two dears. I got a wonderful letter from Michael and it moved me very deeply. I promptly wrote, reassuring him of our love and answering his two questions on a level he could comprehend. I told him we were found guilty and I also explained about the appeal to the higher courts and let him know everything will finally come out all right. That we want very much to see him and we are making every effort to get permission from the court for us to have a visit with the children. On the whole I think Michael will be able to understand. I did not tell him of our sentence. I said we will tell him all about our case when we see him. It is cruel to be separated from our children but it is good to know they are well and growing up. Something very big is missing. It all seems so unreal but yet the cold reality of the steel bars are all around me. I eat, sleep, read and walk four paces back and forth in my cell. I do a lot of thinking about you and the children and I intend to write at least once a week to each of you. My family is 100% behind us and it encourages me. I know as time goes on more and more people will come to our defense and help set us free of this nightmare. I caress you tenderly and send all my love.

Your own
JULIUS

To understand the hysteria of the times, one need only peruse the relevant portions of Judge Kaufman's sentencing speech:

> The issue of punishment in this case is presented in a unique framework of history. It is so difficult to make people realize that this country is engaged in a life and death struggle with a completely different system. This struggle is not only manifested externally between these two forces but this case indicates quite clearly that it also involves the employment by the enemy of secret as well as overt outspoken forces among our own people . . . I consider your crime worse than murder . . . I believe your conduct in putting into the hands of the Russians the A-bomb years before our best scientists predicted Russia would perfect the bomb has already caused, in my opinion, the Communist aggression in Korea, with the resultant casualties exceeding fifty thousand and who knows but that millions more of innocent people may pay the price of your treason . . .
>   . . . In the light of the circumstances, I feel that I must pass such sentence upon the principals in this diabolical conspiracy to destroy a God-fearing nation, which will demonstrate with finality that this nation's security must remain inviolate; that traffic in military secrets, whether promoted by slavish devotion to a foreign ideology or by a desire for monetary gains must cease.

The judge maliciously went out of his way to add a note of cruelty in his unfounded charge, that

> . . . the defendants Julius and Ethel Rosenberg placed their devotion to their cause above their own personal safety and were conscious that they were sacrificing their own children, should their misdeeds be detected — . . . Love for their cause dominated their lives — it was even greater than their love for their children.

The first step in the effort by the United States government to have my parents confess had been taken.

The trial had begun on March 6, 1951, and after listening to fourteen days of testimony, the jury retired to reach a verdict. A day later, on March 29, they judged my parents guilty of conspiracy to commit espionage. The jury's verdict upheld the prosecution's charge that my father had enlisted David Greenglass in his spy ring. David allegedly supplied him with atomic information from research conducted at Los Alamos, New Mexico. Working through another co-conspirator, Soviet Vice-Consul Anatoli Yakovlev, my father supposedly sent Harry Gold to Albuquerque to get the information from David and pay him for it. Later, in my parents' apartment, David claimed he sketched an implosion bomb and wrote a description of it which my mother typed.

By charging conspiracy rather than treason or actual espionage, the government was able to have otherwise inadmissible testimony introduced as evidence. David and Ruth Greenglass, alleged co-conspirators, were the only significant witnesses to attribute any espionage activity to my parents.* This oral testimony was all the prosecution needed to make its case, providing the jury believed its witnesses.

There were obvious lies in key prosecution testimony, and the jury was never informed of the truth in these events. David and Ruth stated that a console table in my parents' apartment was a present from the Russians and a hollowed portion underneath the table enabled them to microfilm secret material. Our parents said they had purchased the table at Macy's. The prosecution did not produce the table and never disputed our father's testimony that it was in the apartment at the time the FBI arrested him and conducted an extensive search. The defense believed the table had been sold when the apartment was abandoned. The prosecution submitted illustrations of console tables as an exhibit.

Another crucial prosecution exhibit was a replica of the sketch of the implosion bomb dropped on Nagasaki which David allegedly gave to our father in 1945. The prosecution claimed this

---

* The Court of Appeals said of the Greenglasses, "Doubtless if that testimony were disregarded the conviction would not stand."

drawing illustrated the secret of the atomic bomb. In 1966, in an affidavit for co-defendant Morton Sobell, Philip Morrison, co-holder of the patent on the Nagasaki bomb, stated that the Greenglass sketch was a worthless "caricature" with many errors. He asserted that the only secret of any importance was that such a bomb could be made — and that fact was demonstrated at Hiroshima. Responding to Morrison's testimony, the prosecution stated that the value of the sketch was now immaterial, only the intent mattered.

A third significant government exhibit was the photostat of the hotel registration card signed by Harry Gold. This card supposedly proved that Gold visited David and Ruth in Albuquerque on June 3, 1945, for their only meeting. When Walter and Miriam Schneir, authors of *Invitation to an Inquest*, examined this exhibit they discovered two conflicting dates on the card and the forged initials of a hotel clerk. This forgery was substantiated by a leading documents expert, Elizabeth McCarthy. (The original card was never introduced as evidence, so the government returned it to the hotel in August of 1951, and it was subsequently destroyed.) During his testimony, Gold stated that the cardinal lesson for a spy is never to use his own name. Gold's name is written on the forged registration card.

As additional evidence that our parents and the Greenglasses were engaged in spying, photographs of the Greenglass family were introduced. David and Ruth testified that these pictures were taken for passports after our father urged them to flee the country. (After Klaus Fuchs was arrested in England, our father supposedly advised David to leave the country as the chain of couriers led from Fuchs to Gold to David.) However, the owner of the photograph shop that had supplied the photos told the Schneirs that these were not standard poses or sizes customarily used on passports, which indicated to him that they were not passport photographs. The prosecution palmed off family portraits as passport photographs.

Harry Gold himself was a major weakness in the prosecution's case. Though the prosecution claimed that his credibility was unquestionable, he had revealed in an earlier trial before Judge Kaufman (and the same prosecutor) that he had constructed a fantasy life which for many years he presented to his friends and acquaintances as the truth. (The jury never knew of this admission.) Gold never testified that he had met our parents, yet the prosecution linked them to espionage through Gold's incriminating password, "I come from Julius." The Schneirs uncovered actual recordings made by Gold prior to our parents' trial in which this password is "Benny sent me . . ." or "Bob sent me . . ." On the recent public television documentary, *The Unquiet Death of Ethel and Julius Rosenberg*, an ex-FBI agent admitted that he supplied the name Julius to Gold "as a suggestion."

To increase the pressure, my mother was transferred to the Death House at Sing Sing prison in Ossining, New York. The government was undoubtedly aware of her having had psychotherapy since 1949. She discussed the possibility of continuing treatment with her lawyer, Emanuel Bloch,* as the following letter, written in October of 1950 (it is undated), indicates:

Dear Mr. Bloch:

. . . I am not at all satisfied that I understand just what you brought out to Dr. ——— concerning my feelings and I am also not at all satisfied that what you did bring out was what I expected you would bring out. By the same token, I am not satisfied as to what he then brought out to you about me and that it was what I wanted him to bring out. Certainly, I told you myself that I didn't expect to break down, certainly I told you myself that I had made "remarkable progress" under treatment, & certainly I told you also that my problems stemmed from way back in my childhood not from more recent date. To find these things out, I should have thought was not the sole purpose of your interview with him but rather to ascertain of what benefit or harm, for that matter, could further treatment possibly be to me and the case as a whole.

To have reached some understanding about this would have

---

* At the trial, Alexander Bloch, Emanuel's father, was officially my mother's lawyer, but the younger Bloch was the chief defense lawyer.

necessitated our giving him a fairly detailed picture of the case up to now, pointing out the nefarious role my brother D and other members of the family are playing, what kind of a person they are making me out to be and what possible capital you figured the opposition might make of my having undergone psychiatric treatment. It would also have necessitated his giving you a fairly detailed picture of what constituted my problems, in what direction I was moving in order to solve them, in what way and up to what point psychoanalysis had loosened certain blocks for me and why I am therefore finding it so difficult now to reconcile 1) My development up to the time I stopped going to him 2) the enforced clamp on that development since my incarceration and 3) the conflicts engendered thereof.

If, on the basis of this type of discussion between you and if, after further discussion concerning ways and means of actually effecting contact (and I have a few ideas myself on this score) between Dr. ——— and myself, it is still considered unadvisable, I will abide by the decision we have all had fair opportunity to make . . .

In an interview with me, my mother's psychiatrist explained that when she began treatment with him in 1949 she was anxious and needed someone to hold on to while she sought to discover the sources of her anxiety. In his opinion the root of the problem was her relationship with her immediate family. She felt she was "looked down upon" by her mother and brothers. Her mother had always dominated the family and treated her brothers as the consequential human beings. My mother never felt her own mother really loved her. Though she was burdened by the demands we placed on her, our mother's problem was not related to the presence of children. Further, the doctor remembered nothing to indicate that her marriage even slightly contributed to her unrest. She felt she had been shortchanged in the family relationships encountered since childhood.

In therapy she allowed her resentment of her family, the burdens of motherhood to surface and became certain that "life was possible." She desired to continue her close relationship with

Dr. —— in prison. When my father was arrested, she discontinued these sessions. Dr. —— connected the name in the newspapers with my mother and called her. She offered to let him off the hook, saying, "Oh, you don't have to see me anymore." He assured her he was not concerned about being "tainted," that he *wanted* to see her. Crying a little over the phone, she said she'd be in touch. Then she was arrested, and Dr. —— was not permitted to see her in the Women's House of Detention while she awaited trial.

The details of her problems and treatment were not of great interest to the authorities, but the *fact* of her need for therapy might have given the Justice Department officials who determined such things the idea of removing her to Sing Sing to center the pressure on her. They isolated her by keeping my father at the Federal House of Detention in New York City, in a special kind of confinement with almost no exercise and no contact with other prisoners, but, more significantly, away from my mother.

This enforced separation from family visitors, the prospect of not being able to confer with my father during attorneys' visits and the deprivation of all human contact save for one matron at a time began to tell on my mother:

April 17, 1951

My very own dearest husband,

I don't know when I've had such a time bringing myself to write you. My brain seems to have slowed to all but a complete halt under the weight of the myriad impressions that have been stamping themselves upon it minute upon minute, hour upon hour, since my removal here. I feel, on the one hand, a sharp need to share all that burdens my mind and heart and so bring to naught, make invalid the bitter physical reality of our separation, yet am stabbed by the implacable and desolate knowledge that the swift spinning of time presents a never-to-be-solved enigma.

Be that as it may, (and you know my perfectionist's passion for chronological sequence and detail) I shall seek to console myself by recounting for you all that it is humanly possible for me to do, at one writing or another, though the incident described, the thought circumvented, the emotion captured be not of that exact moment's making.

Darling, do I sound a bit cracked? Actually I am serious about it and find that I must at least express my deep-seated frustration so that you will comprehend all I must endure in order to "wrest from my locked spirit my soul's language" . . .

As you see, sweetheart, I have already embarked on the next lap of our history-making journey. Already there appear the signs of my growing maturity. The bars of my large, comfortable cell hold several books, the lovely, colorful cards (including your exquisite birthday greeting to me) that I accumulated at the House of Detention line the top ledge of my writing table to pleasure the eye and brighten the spirit, the children's snapshots are taped onto a "picture frame" made of cardboard, and smile sweetly upon me whenever I so desire, and within me there begins to develop the profoundest kind of belief that somehow, somewhere, I shall find that "courage, confidence and perspective" I shall need to see me through days and nights of bottomless horror, of tortured screams I may not utter, of frenzied longings I must deny! Julie dearest, how I wait upon the journey's end and our triumphant return to that precious life from which the foul monsters of our time have sought to drag us!

. . . Darling, I love you.

ETHEL

Immediately, Emanuel Bloch filed in court for a writ of *habeas corpus* to return my mother to New York. In her supporting affidavit, she asserted:

. . . my removal to and detention in the Sing Sing Death House was made with the object and purpose of demoralizing my spirit and overcoming my will to resist efforts of the Government to compel me to admit guilt of the crime for which I have been convicted although I am innocent of any such charge . . . I am sealed in the gray walls of this prison as if in a tomb. I am alone in an entire building except for the matron who guards me. I see no other human being from morning to night and from night to morning. I have no occupation other than to sit immured in the aching soundlessness of my narrow cell. I have no recreation other than to walk on a bare patch of ground, surrounded by walls so high that my only view is a bare patch of sky. Sometimes I can see an airplane passing by; sometimes, a few birds; sometimes, I hear the noise of a train in the distance. Otherwise, there is always dead silence. The power to transform a vital human being into a caged animal is a power to coerce that rivals the deliberate infliction of physical torture and pain.

However, she tried to put her best face on in letters to Julius, Manny Bloch and members of the family.

April 16, 1951

Dear Manny,

Even though you may get to see me before this letter reaches you, I feel compelled to discuss a number of things which were of necessity neglected on Saturday. Incidentally your visit was a shot in the arm and even though I was inclined to be a bit tearful after you had gone, I was also greatly encouraged. Perhaps in time I shall truly become one of those people whom you once characterized as having that "kind of spirit that can never be extinguished." I am certainly going to try hard enough!

1) I forgot to tell you that you are permitted to send me newspaper clippings via the mail. First of all, I am just conceited enough to want to see the latest pictures and publicity concerning my removal here. But seriously, I feel the adoption of such a regular procedure to help keep me in touch with things between your visits will serve an excellent morale purpose. Kindly implement said obviously agreeable purpose at once.

2) The more I think of it, the more I am inclined to believe that it would be extremely valuable for me to see Mrs. ———* before my contemplated visit with the children. I know there may be complications involved but it might be worthwhile to broach the question to her supervisor on the basis that I have not seen Mrs. ——— in months and since I am therefore very much behind on matters concerning the kids, I will be at a

* My social worker at the Hebrew Children's Home.

distinct disadvantage when I see them and may pull some unnecessary boners.

If for any reason, however, she can't make it, I feel it absolutely imperative for her to write me in detail what kind of questions they have been asking, what answers people have been giving them, on what level they have generally been discussing us & the case, & any other information concerning their development up to this point she thinks it might be helpful for me to know. In any case, there is no reason she cannot at least see Julie & give him such a picture as I have outlined. Personally, I would urge every effort on the agency's part to see me directly. There are so many questions bumbling about in my head regarding the kids and I feel so strongly about making their initial visits both to me & Julie as positive an experience for us all as I can, that I am most anxious to see her. . .

. . . for heaven's sake, read this letter to Julie and tell him to be patient just a little while longer and he will get a nice big, juicy book from his silly wife who perversely (it might seem to him) writes her lawyer before she gets around to writing him! I am still trying to kind of catch my breath and so far I think I've made progress, only it shouldn't happen to two dogs!

One more technical item. I have just been informed that unless a pass for a visitor is filled out here by me by Tuesday, said visitor will not be allowed in for a Sunday visit. In other words, it may be better for my in-laws to try to get here some time during the week (at least for this week) because I can't very well fill in such a form when I don't know who intends to come here Sunday, if anyone. After a while things will regularize and we'll all get into the swing of things; it is irksome and frustrating, however, in the meantime. I've written to you rather than Julie & his folks first to save time and to try to avoid unnecessary repetition and confusion.

Affectionately,
ETHEL

April 18, 1951

Dearest Ethel,

I received your wonderful letter this afternoon. Frankly, I've been impatiently awaiting news from you. Whenever Manny comes to see me he tells me all he knows about you. He described in great detail how you live (that is as much as he is aware of) and how Sing Sing affects one as sensitive as you . . .

Your letter is so terrific that I took time out to analyze it. The first impression I got is that the situation as it confronted you was overwhelming and to some degree you were a bit emotionally shocked. This is no doubt the effect one expects. However, in spite of this initial observation and most important, I notice a marked clarity and steadfastness in all this turbulence. It is certainly remarkable to see that at this early date your pendulum of emotions still hovers about a stable core and already you have begun to organize yourself. Your perfectionist passion for detail will do you stead. Now that you have made yourself as physically comfortable as possible, I advise you to regiment yourself to a very strict schedule of reading, writing and also to embark on a course of self-study whether it be music, psychiatry, or both. This, darling, is the only way to overcome these hardships and at the same time maintain one's own equilibrium. Of course, every effort will be made to see that the lawyers and members of my family visit you as often as is humanly possible. If our lawyers do not succeed in bringing you back to the Women's Detention House at 10th Street in New York, I will move heaven and earth to be sent to Sing Sing to be nearer you and in order to be able to see you whenever it is possible. I beg you not to try to sway me from this decision as this is what I must do. This single document is indelible proof that not only are you a tremendous person but you have the courage, confidence and enlightened perspective to come through this hell and then some with flying colors. My wife, I stand humble beside you, proud of you and inspired by such a woman.

Manny is truly a jewel. He is doing a lot of running around but contrary to the proverbial expression, "like a chicken without a head" such brains can only fit in two heads and the unfortunate thing is that he has only one body so he can't be in two places at once. All power to him as he is doing a magnificent job. Certain things I will not put in letters but leave for our attorneys to convey to you by word of mouth. You understand the American Gestapo is all "eyes and ears" in their drive to establish thought control over the people. The undemocratic "Loyalty" oaths, political frame-up trials through which they parade perjured stool pigeons and professional witnesses, all these are links in their witch hunt to shackle the minds or bodies of the great freedom-loving American nation. As surely as they will fail in this effort so, too, we will succeed in winning our freedom with the help of those same forward-looking people. It is impossible to keep the truth and facts of our case hidden from the public. Sooner or later, the true picture will become known to all. Many people have already expressed to our lawyers and my family their sentiments and desire to help us. Take heart and know that we are not alone. The monstrous sentence passed on us, which at first stunned the people, will, as time goes on, result in an avalanche of protest and this great movement, coupled to our legal fight, will set us free.

Sweetheart, I am not trying to minimize all the difficulties you face — believe me, I am fully aware of the nightmares, the pain and the hurt you feel. My heart cries out for you. I want so to shield and protect you, to be with you in this time of need and to hold you in my arms. Yet I feel so sure of you that I just know you will always be there and that is the assurance that we will some day find each other again and return as you say to our precious life and wonderful family.

Ethel, you are just my girl and nothing on earth can change that. In a couple of days, the Passover celebration of our people's search for freedom will be here. This cultural heritage has added meaning for us, who are imprisoned away from each other and our loved ones by the modern Pharaohs. It has such meaning to us and our children. Yes, we are missing a lot but this, too, shall pass and we will have cause for greater celebration. Since we are unable to do much but talk about our sons, do not worry as everything possible is being done for their welfare . . .

Always your very own,
JULIUS — Love.

April 19, 1951

Dearest Lee,*

I have just finished putting fresh linen on my nice comfortable bed, Groucho Marx is on the radio and I'm eating an apple for a change. Before that, I had spent two hours in my very own exclusive sunny yard, had splashed around in my substantial stall shower (I wear a pretty lilac-colored plastic cape and wrap into a warm terry robe when I'm through bathing), and then had stowed away a sardine and onion sandwich canned peaches and milk. I was so tired from all these exertions that I then proceeded to enjoy a two-hour nap . . .

By now I hope it has grown clear to you that I'm not in the worst place in the world; on the contrary everyone has been most pleasant and cooperative, thus far, and I don't see any reason this encouraging state of affairs shouldn't continue. Even in the short time I've been here, they must already have realized that I'm an intelligent well-balanced person who intends to put my energies to good use here. I'm already halfway through one excellent book and expect to really catch up on my reading, now that there is no longer a trial to concern myself with.

Manny Bloch was here Saturday and his Dad turned up today. Bless them both each is equally wonderful in his own way; how can we fail with two such precious, dignified human beings in our corner! I beg you to believe me Lee, that although I don't kid myself that I can really be happy under the circumstances, and although the picture is actually not the rosy one it might seem from all the cheerful things I have said — I still beg you to believe me that I am already recovering from the initial dismay of my removal and have begun to dig in and come to grips with the situation.

So take heart all my dear family; I wish there were some way to truly convey to you the tremendous confidence, the unwavering faith I have that decency and justice must triumph. How is my dear mother bearing up under all this inhumanity? (You don't mind sharing her with me, do you) Tell her to have

* My father's sister Lena.

a most enjoyable Passover for Julie and me . . . All my love
                                                    ETHEL

April 20, 1951

Dearest Julie,

My most heartfelt greetings to you, darling, on this, the evening of the first Passover Seder. How bitter it is to be spending it away from all my loved ones! I sit behind the indifferent gray bars and listen to the ticking of the indifferent clock, and know the full agony of the heart's deep yearning.

But enough of this. I have lots to tell you about myself and my doings here, that I know you are anxious to hear. By dint of patient but persistent prodding I have now become an established and respected (although female) member of the Sing Sing community, and have set up jailkeeping in earnest! On my sink there reposes a giant-size tube of Colgate's tooth paste inside an imposing red box, on top of which my long black comb lies stretched out ready, willing and able to obey my slightest command. A sturdy, red toothbrush stands stiffly in its holder in the middle of the basin and two cakes of soap, (the coarse white for laundering purposes and the gentle green for the gentlewoman), sit quietly at its side. The toilet plunger is gaily camouflaged by my bright salmon-colored wash cloth while the white toilet paper directly below it presents a sharp and unashamed contrast. My book case (prison style of necessity, and therefore fashioned of vertical round bars and horizontal flat metal strips across them), is a handy catch-all for stationery, newspapers, dust cloths and Sapolio, as well as a good supply of books. A paper carton for old letters and clippings stands beneath my writing table which displays among other things (for example, the children's snapshots, greeting cards & blue plastic glass) my latest and highly prized acquisition, a small desk calendar. And a smaller box for current mail, literary notes, commissary bills, money receipts and all the other paraphernalia that so eloquently bespeaks the rich and varied life that may be led within these walls if one works assiduously at it (and knocks one's brains out doing it) — this box completed the picture. Ah, yes, the bed — clean and comfortable, with the necessary supplies of sheets and blankets and face towels hanging on the white metal head post; the bed, cold and chaste and uncaring of its lone and lonely occupant!

Seven A.M. finds me reluctantly crawling out from under its covers and after a leisurely breakfast of toast and coffee, eaten in my terry robe, I don my prison finery and sally forth onto my own private little Riviera, where I bang a ball around the four towering brick walls and run like mad as I dribble it along the concrete floor. I am now the proud possessor of 1) a pair of comfortable, low-heeled, ugly black oxfords, 2) a pair of thick, seamless, brown cotton stockings 3) a pair of long heavy drawers which by tacit consent are known as my "ski pants" and which have a way of sliding down past my derrière and over my knees and coming perilously close to slipping off altogether as I dash about the yard, 4) two surprisingly pretty printed cotton dresses, not too ill-fitting, either 5) a really nice looking, soft, well-made, navy blue, wool cardigan 6) a pair of roomy brown leather bedroom slippers 7) a fairly good-looking double-breasted mannish sport coat in a rough-textured, grayish black flannel material with which the tailor proudly presented me. After looking like a scarecrow for a week in an oversized, heavy, itchy, clumsy one with tremendous pockets that reached to my knees, (I'd put it on like a cape and say I was George Washington about to cross the Delaware), one of the four matrons who look after my needs and I successfully grappled with a tape measure and I am now a thoroughly presentable inmate. 8) a number of other lesser items of clothing which the guards have delicately referred to as "unmentionables" and so I shan't offend against their good taste by giving details. (It is enough that I described my "ski pants," the likes of which have not been seen, I am certain, since Hector was a pup, and which I will happily discard just as soon as the weather permits.)

And now with the purchase of cold cream, deodorant, powder, lipstick and side combs to help me look neat at all times, an accomplished fact, I am "at home" and ready to receive all comers. Pop had openly complained at seeing my pale, wan map and unruly locks, and Manny's first remark, by way of greeting on the occasion of his second visit was "Where'd you get the lipstick?" 'S a funny thing, though, this ungracious ungratefulness on my part. It is like the kid who goes to camp for the first time in his life and writes his parents of all the wonders and glories of it and then concludes his letter by mournfully wailing, "I wanna go home!"

To speak now in more serious vein, your letter (with Michael's pathetic, touching one enclosed) finally arrived after landing first at the House of Detention. Sweetheart, how eloquently you expressed to me the quality of the love that is mine. How humble I am before you and yet how proud and happy that I should be the one capable of inspiring such noble thoughts in another human being. When shall I find answering words to match the fine integrity of your own? Dearly do I love you, my sweet and dearly do I desire you to understand what warm comfort your writing brought with it and what warm response it evoked in my own heart. I look forward with eager anticipation to our continued correspondence and grow ever more certain of our eventual release. Let the jackals bray while they still may, for the winds of time are fashioning a sound and a song that must finally and inexorably drown out their ugly voices!

Darling, I had meant to discuss also the subject of the children, every thought of whom brings such stabbing anguish and pain, as I cannot describe, but the mail is going out right away and I want this letter to go with it.

Until I write again, then, and it will be soon, I promise, I embrace you in all love and tenderness and reluctantly say good-bye.

As ever,
ETHEL

On April 24, my father decided to save the letters they were writing and asked Manny to keep them together in an album. From then on they copied letters and sent them to him.

April 24, 1951

Hello Honey Wife:

Tuesday night Bob Hope is on the loud speaker system and it's hard for me to concentrate but I'm a persistent fellow, so here goes. I've been hearing glowing reports about you. I read the two letters you sent Lena, and Manny related all the details of his last visit. It all adds up to this: You are your old self again, full of spirit, spunk, and in the groove.

Darling, I'm a little jealous. Everybody is being buoyed up by you. You're a fountain of encouragement to my family. The lawyers are confident you'll stand up and I'd like to be able to lean on your shoulders and get a little special comfort from you too. You know, the real stuff. Just a little warmth and love. How I miss it. But enough of that — as jailbirds, our lot is supposed to be a mechanical one, devoid of many physiological needs. Present-day penology is said to be rehabilitative and constructive. Sufficient for me to say I could write a book on its present evils and another on recommendations I would make to humanize and modernize it.

April 25, 1951

. . . Ethel, you're a lovely ninny, sweet and wonderful. Of course I'm quelling* from you. (Some Yiddish-English!) The glowing description you gave of Sing Sing is both encouraging and inviting, and since I expect to be there anyway soon I am looking forward to experiencing for myself the wonders of Ossining Manor. However, since I know you well, I am sure the physical set-up is the least important but the emotional security and mental stimuli are the paramount things. My witty one, your letter is conclusive. As the popular prison expression goes, "You've got it made." What you wrote was so refreshing that I took the liberty of sharing your wonderful gift with my chess opponent. He remarked, "A terrific letter. She's in better shape than you!"

Last Monday after the regular roof period they finally let me have a half-hour of fresh air. Even though I was alone except for a guard who accompanied me and another one who

* This Yiddish word translates as "deriving pleasure from."

watched us from a tower I enjoyed every minute of it very much. The cool breeze and sunshine were invigorating. I am trying to have this established as a regular exercise period as it is essential for continued good health and it serves as a break in the monotony and closeness of my cell . . .

It is easy for me to gather from your letters and my own personal experiences and feelings that we're both trying very hard and we'll do the best under the circumstances, and we miss each other very much. There is no substitute for our being together. I feel like screaming from the rooftops: "Hark, people! A tragedy has been perpetrated!" The gruesome reality is that our case is being used as a camouflage to establish a fear paralysis among the outspoken progressives and to stifle criticism or opposition to the mad drive to atomic war. The public must be made aware of this political trick especially for us since our personal fight is thereby linked to this general movement for peace. We see it and somewhere, somehow, as soon as possible, everyone must be made aware of it.

I read in the newspapers that two of the new crop (I believe I misspelled it) of government informers, the stool pigeons, David and Ruth Greenglass, have sold their story to a Sunday magazine (Collier's?) Note: à la Budenz and Bentley fashion. History records that David Greenglass stands without parallel and ahead of even Judas Iscariot in infamy.

Michael scribbled a couple of words in a letter Ethel sent me. He is a peach and so sweet. How I long for our boys. The kids are doing fine so don't be concerned. It is hard to leave but I must go to bed now. Gosh how sad without you. All my love,

Your own,
JULIUS

Responding to my father's admonition not to try and deter him from transferring to Sing Sing, my mother argued against any such action.

April 25, 1951

My dearest, sweetest, most precious idiot,

Whatever in the world am I going to do with you? And since

when does this wife obey this husband without question? At this late date, sweetheart, it is folly on your part to attempt to make a decision that concerns me so vitally without permitting me that kind of voice in the matter which I have rightly come to expect, after nearly twelve richly creative years with you. Beg me as you may, then, I can brook no such arbitrary abrogation of my wifely rights in the matter as you intend I should, and on the contrary, my dear lord and master, for all that I do truly adore you, I must insist that you hear me out, or it giffs murder!

Let's be really honest about this thing and examine the dynamics involved. Isn't it the fact that when the authorities decreed the harsh punishment of incarceration at Sing Sing for me, they also dealt your manhood a severe blow? Every last ounce of prideful masculinity in you (and mind you I bear you nothing but the deepest kind of respect for the tender protectiveness and strength said masculinity actually constitutes) stands outraged at a fate that perversely persists in forcing me to bear the full brunt of its fury . . .

Love you, dearest.

ETHEL

On the same day she wrote to Manny reiterating her determination not to take the easy way out by giving a false confession, and expressing her anxiety about us as well.

April 25, 1951

Dear Manny,

. . . I am making progress here at a fairly rapid pace, I should say. Already the outlines of my routine begin to take shape and I feel somewhat like a runner, breathing deeply with each slow, deliberate, relaxed intake of air, yet tensing in anticipation of the challenge. Indeed, there is even an eagerness for the race, a quiet, calm acceptance, and a genuine humility in the realization that it should have been given to two ordinary people like the Rosenbergs to stand up and be counted. Whatever may come to pass, it will never be said that we ever permitted ourselves to be counted as anything but *decent* people!

To come down from my exalted heights, for a minute, I confess I am worried sick about the children. I implore you to concentrate most of your efforts on the solution of this pressing problem, as I simply won't rest until they are in the family's hands. Please don't think me an ingrate, however. I am fully aware, believe me, that you are leaving no stone unturned in your concern for them and us. The truth of the matter is, Manny dear, (and the devil take the censor) that I love you! Can I be any plainer than that? Give my best as per usual to your Pop and my old sweetie pie!

Salud and No Pasaran! *

ETHEL

Because she understood the authorities were using her to put pressure on my father, she urged him not to give up his proximity to the defense efforts and his human contacts with fellow prisoners in New York.

April 29, 1951

Dearest sweetheart,

. . . does "moving heaven and earth to be with me" (bless you, dearest, I love you for it) really help me as much as refusing to permit yourself to fall into the very trap the authorities have so craftily laid for you and standing by your guns at West Street while I stand by mine at Sing Sing! For one thing, you have the incalculably valuable opportunity of associating with your fellows (and they are people who regard you with the utmost kind of liking and respect); for another, you are easily accessible to Manny and your folks and you can therefore actually participate in the development of the campaign for our release.

Of course, even though I don't deny that I could certainly do with some of the emotional gratification my being able to see you would promote, it won't constitute a major disaster if you remain in the city. Darling, I know how much like rejection this

---

* *No Pasarán* was the cry of the Spanish Republican armies defending Madrid against Franco's troops in 1936. My parents' support for the Spanish Republic was used against them at the trial to show their "Communism."

must sound to you and what hurt I may therefore be inflicting upon you. I know, too, however, how deep your understanding of our situation goes and in what a true light that understanding must help to frame my seemingly harsh words. In all humility I tell you it is your love for me and mine for you (even though the expression of it must, of necessity, now be dammed up) that is enabling me to strive ever more consciously to reach that height for which I seem somehow to have been singled out. In view of all that has transpired, I can come to but that one conclusion.

No, stay where you are, my dear love, if so you can do, and be my voice for me, since mine dissipates itself upon the Ossining air even while I raise it. So you to your job and I to mine and together we will make the victory! . . .

As ever,
ETHEL

After learning the nature of my father's special kind of solitary confinement, my mother wrote:

May 4, 1951

My dearest sweetheart,

. . . I had no way of knowing just what kind of an inexcusably harsh, severe, physically and mentally debilitating regimen had been foisted upon you; you may well imagine, then, how appalled I was to read of the shocking circumstances of your present mode of life.

Oh, my poor darling, how I ached for you and how ashamed I felt to have had to scold you for wanting to come here! Small wonder, I thought scornfully, that I was able to set such an example and send such encouraging letters to the folks.

Upon closer examination of your situation, however, and a more honest appraisal thereof, (laying aside, of course, my needlessly guilty feelings about the bright spots of my own existence) you actually have the edge over me in that you are still associating (even if to a much lessened degree) with the other inmates, and visiting presents no difficulties. Still, I am filled with indignation that you have had to convince them about such an elementary and easily supplied need like outdoor exercise! For heaven's sake, bunny, it is imperative for you to maintain a certain minimum standard of health and somehow I get the impression that you are inclined to take the matter of your physical comforts a little too lightly. I don't "appreciate" such a state of affairs one tiny bit and strongly suggest you begin to "perform" * accordingly, until you succeed in instituting some vitally important & long-overdue changes.

. . . Hold me close to you, always closer when you go to sleep; I miss you so terribly! Your own loving

[ETHEL]

* Jitterbug language by the courtesy of the late lamented but still fondly remembered House of Detention!

Despite the hardships she still tried to maintain her sense of humor..

May 5, 1951

Dearest darling,

Believe me, this dear lady* and I are a proper pair of lunatics; indeed, we are both thoroughly convinced that we simply didn't meet each other soon enough! The hilarious shrieks that issue forth from the Women's Wing (the No-Man's Land in which I am spending my summer vacation, *a zuch in weh***) would certainly incline any listener to believe he had landed at Luna Park, not the death house! Ooh, I just got a brilliant idea; tomorrow when she arrives at 6:30 A.M. I am going to panic her (by way of greeting) with a gay little ditty entitled, "Who's Afraid of the Big Electric Chair, they can shove it up their "spine" For all I Care" (Variation: "They Can Dump it in the Hudson For All I Care")!

Be sure of it, begorra, it is stir-crazy she'll be goin', long before me; and don't think, m'pretty one, it isn't worried she is abaht it; already she's admittin' to hearin' bells when they don't ring! (you ought to hear the magnificent Irish brogue I've developed; it tickles the Irish in *her* no end!)

* One of the matrons.
** A basically untranslatable Yiddish expression that may be approximately translated, "Woe is me."

But she isn't the only zany in these parts. There's still another one who rounds out this delightfully cozy little family circle, a willing vessel for my increasingly perverted sense of humor, whom I am fast converting from a "square" into a "hep-cat," House of Detention style. You just never appreciated just what kind of a little ray of sunshine you possessed! And why not? To be a Condemned-nik, I'm absolutely refusing — If you'll be so kindly, I'll already better taking "paskudnik"! My God, that book's got me coming and going!

However, she couldn't always resist her depressions.

May 6, 1951

Pussy-cat, I'm lonesome. Last night I went to sleep with streaming eyes and full heart. The reason? Manny's usual Saturday visit which evokes a tremendous intellectual and emotional response from me and which for that very reason, hurts all the worse when it's over and he's departed for that bright world I shan't be knowing for many months & possibly many years to come. Yet never fear, beloved — I stand steadfast though my eyes weep and my heart breaks.

Your always loving wife

May 8–9, 1951

My Dearest Wife,

Upon reading your message of May 4th I want you to calm your fears as to my physical surroundings and more important I am surprised to hear you admonished yourself because you had wrongly felt your situation was worse than mine. Truthfully, you are suffering a harder incarceration than I. Darling, neither of us is exactly living in comfort or enjoying a life of milk and honey. You are to be congratulated for your stamina and excellent adjustment to such a horrible and barbaric confinement. Your conduct is admirable and your bearing is praiseworthy. I am both proud and happy that you are doing so well. Keep up the good work honey.

There has been a slight improvement in my routine in so far as I am presently allowed one half hour on the roof almost

every day of the week. Since I am not permitted to have a belt
or shoe laces my handball performance is not exactly professional. Falling pants or a shoe slipping off my foot hinders my
speed and gives me a handy alibi for the fearful trouncings
administered to me . . .

Ethel I was terribly shocked to read that Willie McGee was
executed.* You know how I am affected by these things . . .
My heart is sad my eyes are filled with tears. I must yell Shame
America! Shame on those who perpetrated this heinous act!
Greater Shame on those who did not lift their voices and hands
to stop the Mississippi executioner. It seems to me that the
Federal Courts have adopted the abominable medieval practice
of the Southern Bourbons, legal lynching of Negroes and is now
attempting, as in our case, to apply this to political prisoners.
Mark my words, dearest, the harsh sentence passed on us is part
of the atomic hysteria designed to brutalize the minds of the
people in order to make it easier for them to accept as a
commonplace thing long prison terms and even death sentences
for political prisoners. It serves the added nefarious purpose of
establishing a fear paralysis among progressive Americans.
Before it is too late, our countrymen must be awakened to the
hideous plans of the war makers who are utilizing these fascistic
acts to pave the way for spilling rivers of human blood in
modern, efficient and scientific way. Now! Today! People
must stand firm on these issues as life itself depends on it. The
most important thing is that the camouflage has to be ripped
away, the loud braying of jackals of hate has to be answered
with reason and fact and only positive organization of free
people and their ensuing direct action can successfully save the
peace and assure freedom in our country. That is why I am
positive growing numbers of people will come to understand
our fight and join with us to win so just a cause. McGee's death
spurs me on with added determination. I am impatiently
awaiting news of the beginning of a great campaign to save us.
Right is on our side and we must be successful.

* Willie McGee, a black World War II veteran, was charged, convicted, and executed for
raping a white woman. He had in fact slept with her but the rape charge was bogus. See
Cedric Belfrage, *The American Inquisition* (Indianapolis: Bobbs Merrill, 1973), pp. 141f.
Manny Bloch had represented McGee on several of his appeals.

Mrs. ———* was over to see me yesterday and we had a lengthy discussion on the welfare of our two dears. By the time the jury pronounced us guilty, Michael had already heard a great deal of the comments on our trial from the radio, television and the Greenglasses all great purveyors of the "truth." When he saw the social worker he asked what was the sentence and in all truthfulness she answered she did not know. Whereupon, he replied my Mommy and Daddy could not get the death penalty as they didn't kill anybody and many people would have to be killed for them to deserve that. He was aware that the Greenglasses were witnesses against us and he wanted to know who lied and more about the case. He asked many questions and Mrs. ——— told him there is good and bad in all people even in herself and Mr. Witover. After exhausting his questions he laid his head on her lap, began whimpering and sucking his thumb. The boy told her he would not be able to get up. She comforted and soothed him and after fifteen minutes he was himself again. He knows we are in prison kept behind bars and we are not allowed to leave. Do you know that he said it's like the North Koreans and Americans. They both say they are right and maybe both are. Can you beat such a mature statement from our eight-year-old. He has progressed to the point where at times he tells her to come next week as he is too busy to interrupt his playing by talking to her. There is definite improvement emotionally and in his eating habits. He looks well and is healthy. As for Robert she can also report advances. He has learned to play with other children and is developing normally. The baby still tries to latch on to a grownup for support. With the proper guidance and supervision both boys will continue to grow mentally and physically well. They need us so and to say the least we need them too. She will try to see you to give you a personal briefing on your sweet boys . . .

Your very own
JULIUS

* My social worker at the Hebrew Children's Home.

May 7, 1951

Hello, honey dear,

Thank you so much for your most beautiful letter of May 2nd which arrived on Saturday . . .

Darling, your letter brought you right into a cell grown suddenly quiet as a tomb, much as though you, too, were visiting me, moving me profoundly and stirring me to the depths. . . . The unutterably sweet expressions of love and devotion contained in this last episode filled me with such a deep and abiding happiness and brought you so close, I could almost (but not quite) reach out and touch you.

Indeed, after a listless game of handball (played solo, of course), a shower, dinner and an evening of enchanting music, during which you made passionate love to me, I could no longer withstand the disquieting sense of dismay that had been steadily gnawing at my vitals, and finally succumbed to homesick tears. It is a luxury I rarely permit myself, however, and you will be happy, I know, to hear that I am your own good girl once more!

Oh, darling, how greedy I am for life and living. All at once I want to see and hear all there is to see and hear, know and be all there is to know and be! I've never been quite so conscious of all the glowing beauty that beats within me, feel quite such an aching desire to share it, nor been so aware of my own powers as an individual. My voice wells up now way down deep inside me somewhere, and my heart bursts with the burden of my song! And of what do I sing? Of noble Man & Woman, of noble freedom! Were there ever any more precious words? For of what value be the love and joy of Man and Woman, without the right also of its truest and most untrammeled expression?

Bunny, I'm beginning to sound like a real old graybeard am I not.

Oh, mail call —

Goodbye, my dearest love
ETHEL

But behind all the "continuous improvement" in my mother's situation, lay the stark reality that isolation had taken its toll. A well-known psychiatrist, Dr. Frederic Wertham, was approached by Manny for expert testimony about the effect of my mother's isolation. Dr. Wertham recalled the events in a letter many years later:

> . . . Emanuel Bloch . . . was very much concerned . . . that she [Ethel] might suffer a serious mental breakdown, being all alone and not being able to see and confer with her husband . . . I was given permission to testify in court under oath about Mrs. Rosenberg's mental condition, but permission to examine her first was refused . . . So I had to rely for my opinion on communication with Mrs. Rosenberg through an intermediary, Mr. Bloch. There was no doubt that she was in a bad way. She was evidently a courageous woman, but the strain of being isolated in the Death House was becoming too much for her. Except for a guard she was kept all alone in an entire building and could not see or speak to any other person from morning to night. She had difficulty eating and sleeping. She herself felt that her thought processes were "slowed" (a typical symptom of depression). The uncertainty and anxious dreams took a great toll. Sometimes she was near despair. Her greatest concern was what would be done with and to her children . . . Aggravating her emotional state was the mental torture she was exposed to. The electric chair was used as psychological pressure: it was a matter of talk or die; if you'd only "name names" their lives could be spared and she could save her husband's life . . . In my testimony . . . I stated that if the absolute separation of husband and wife were to continue so that Mrs. Rosenberg could not confer with her husband there was a definite and strong probability that she would break down and develop a prison psychosis . . . within a few days after my testimony Washington completely reversed itself. Mr. Rosenberg was transferred . . . to the Death House in Sing Sing. After visiting with her husband, Mrs. Rosenberg's depression lifted and her spirits revived.

2

Pulling Together

May 17, 1951

Hello My Love,

You are so close at hand and yet you being in a different corridor separated by so much steel, locked away from my sight and beyond my hearing range the frustration is terrific. Tonight I was able to hear your voice when a few of the high notes of one of your arias was faintly audible. To insure a daily contact I will try to write you a note each day and I hope you can manage to do the same. Yesterday even though it was wonderful was to some extent overwhelming due to the excitement of seeing you and Manny at the same time. While I was with you two lovely human beings it was great. I felt so good and confident talking over our defense and personal problems but when it was over there was a terrible letdown. Darling, I miss you so much and I am so concerned for your welfare and peace of mind. All during the lawyers' consultation I couldn't take my eyes off you nor could I get myself to express the tender and deep love I feel for you my precious. Something prevented me from telling you my innermost thoughts and I guess I'll get around to them after I am more relaxed. Only one who experiences this nightmare is capable of comprehending the tremendous emotional pressure of this type of incarceration. Ethel please keep on holding your chin up as it does so much for our confidence. The other men here are swell. They're helping me with commissary until I am able to buy my own. . . . Physically, I am fairly comfortable and already in the routine of things. The food is much better than West St. and so far I manage very nicely in the eating department. As for recreation besides the sunshine and exercise in the yard, and incidentally a keeper plays handball with me in the afternoon, I read about six newspapers a day. I play chess . . . by remote control with another inmate and I am reading "The Old Country" by Shalom Aleichem. Most important the other men here are nice and kid around quite a bit and the time passes pleasantly. . . . I'm sure we'll make it darling. With decency and justice we'll be delivered from this darkness to beautiful life and freedom.

Goodnight my wife

YOUR OWN JULIUS

Their first meeting since their sentencing more than a month earlier had to await Manny's presence for a legal conference.*

May 19, 1951

My own dear Sweetheart,

How loath was I to leave your fond embrace, how loath; and how reluctant my step as I approached my cell. It was there waiting for me, silent, inexorable, disdainful, seemingly unaware of its occupant's departure but smug in the knowledge of her eventual return.

It's only three days ago that my lips clung in desperate hunger to yours and my glance kindled to behold the long-loved, oddly familiar, oddly strange being, close to whom I had lain and sweetly slumbered through how many nights. It's only three days by the calendar, yet am I certain that eons have elapsed and that I dreamed our meeting, in any case. Darling, you state it for me, too, when you say you were overwhelmed. The staircase I had just climbed, the sight of you as I entered, Manny's voice that I heard only dimly, the room itself — all rushed upon my consciousness with such a mad pounding, I was unable to give response to the very tumult of my response. And then before I could fully savor the painful taste of our physical salutation, while yet keenly aware of an even greater

* Later, weekly visits without Manny were permitted. A cage was placed opposite my mother's cell in the women's wing and they conversed through the bars.

thirst as I drank, we were apart and the table stood immovable between us!

How my heart smote me for your pale, drawn face, for your eloquently pleading eyes, for your slender, boyish frame, your evident suffering. My dearest husband, what heaven and what hell to welcome you to monotonous days and joyless nights, to endless desire and endless denial. And yet here shall we plight our troth anew, here held fast by brick and concrete and steel, shall our love put forth gripping root and tender blossom, here shall we roar defiance and give battle; yes, and here shall we expose the predatory plan of our madmen to institute thought control and drag our people to slaughter!

Sweetheart, I know how impatiently we both sat watching the clock yesterday, longing for one of the Blochs to turn up and bring us together. Doubtless they were engaged elsewhere on some other sector of the fighting front, on our behalf, so we must swallow our disappointment, bitter though it surely is and bide our time. Pussy cat, of course you couldn't give free tongue to all the crowding thoughts and sensitive feelings, nor could I. Did you expect that it would be easy to open our hearts to each other under those cold, forbidding circumstances? And yet I confess I had myself anticipated a tremendous release, an end to anguish. And when such surcease was not forthcoming and there remained instead a vague sense of loss and anticlimax, I was, like you, quite overcome with frustration. Indeed, until your letter arrived (for which many kisses) I couldn't even begin to express it on paper. So glad for you, my dearest, that you are handling the situation with your usual élan. Ah, Monsieur, je t'aime, je t'adore.

Your lonely wife,
ETHEL

She copied the letter for Manny and when she sent it out, the warden enclosed this stern note:

May 21, 1951

Dear Sir:
From the enclosed letter which is being sent to you by Mrs. Ethel

Rosenberg, it is noted that she states that she was "longing for one of the Blochs to turn up and bring us together."

It is not desired to establish a practice for you to visit them here for the express purpose of bring them together. Your visits with your clients should be confined strictly to legal matters. Arrangements for personal visits between them will be arranged here.

In the event that it is found that your visits are made just for the purpose of their conducting a social visit together, it will become necessary for me to have you see your clients one at a time.

Very truly yours,
WARDEN

May 20, 1951

Dearest Julie,

Today I am at such loose ends I don't know where to turn for comfort. There has been a fine intermittent rain all afternoon and I have sat in my chair at the entrance of the yard, drinking in the fragrance of flowers growing somewhere unbeknownst to me, and watching the bedraggled sparrows picking dispassionately at the bread I had scattered earlier for them. Every once in so often, the rain lets up and then I stalk disconsolately about inspecting the few green things I possess miraculously pushing their way up through the apparently unyielding concrete; here growing between the brick wall and the stone walk are sprigs of crisply curling bright green parsley, and there along another wall, the shapely leaves of a wild violet plant luxuriously unfold while under them two buds cozily nestle, only vaguely aware as yet of the world outside. Now I kneel down and glumly scrutinize a crevice in the concrete, filled with earth painstakingly accumulated from the under part of moss, small velvety clumps of which cling to the damp, cool parts of the yard where the rays of the sun seldom penetrate. In this earth, an apple seed which I had carefully planted some few days before and which I had ever since been patiently watering, is bravely sprouting, but I sigh and turn away from the all but visible bit of green . . .

YOUR OWN ETHEL

May 21, 1951

My Sweetest Darling,

When I finished writing you Friday evening I was told mail is not picked up until Monday morning so I lapsed into a lazy existence of eating, sleeping, some reading and daydreaming about you. I spent quite a bit of time on my bed absorbing as much as possible of the full reality of my being here. What you wrote, Ethel, so eloquently expresses our profoundest frustrations, our understanding and deep love for each other. The hemmed-in solitude that surrounds us and the oppressive nature of this somber tomb must not succeed in removing our strong ties to the vibrating and pulsating outside world. We caged here can only protest our innocence and stand up firmly but it is the task of the American people to stay the executioner's hand and see that justice is done. I gaze at the walls of my cell and contemplate the great sufferings of my wife and children and I am helpless to aid them. My heart aches as I tell myself your job is to stay strong so that you can clear your name and in that way bring the greatest comfort to your loved ones. The most difficult thing for me to take is that you, my heart, are also in this Gehenna* and only your splendid steadfastness has made it possible for me to stand up. I ask myself over and over again why it is necessary for them to keep us apart and I find no satisfactory answer. . .

Do not be concerned about my looks as I feel healthy and can take care of myself. Sunday afternoon I heard you telling the guard that you wanted to have some of your Commissary Cream Cheese with your supper. I was thrilled to hear your voice. This occurred while I was resting on the yard steps and I believe the door to your corridor was slightly ajar. Honey, we have a license and we should be allowed to set up housekeeping here. In all earnestness only your complete freedom will satisfy me. Always impatient to see you and be near you. Until we meet I send my kisses

YOUR OWN JULIUS

* Yiddish for "Hell."

Both my parents continued to stay in contact with members of Julius' family via the mails as well as personal visits.

May 26, 1951

Dearest Ethel,

. . . Darling, thanks so much for quoting me Michael's letter to his father. What was his and Robby's reaction to the one I wrote them, thanking them for their Mother's Day Cards? Oh, Ethel, how indescribably bitter it is to be separated from one's children. Can the heartache ever really be measured? I am a vessel filled to overflowing with so much sorrow, so much pain, it seems as though I shall never be quite free of these feelings again. My desire to see my two pussy cats grows steadily with each passing hour, yet must I curb my longing, & bid myself to be patient yet a while more. The thought of my sweet husband ever comforts and sustains me; I simply must not be found wanting in his hour of need!

The most wonderful thing happened on Friday right after lunch. My sweetheart was allowed in the Women's Wing and under the double surveillance of a matron and a guard, of course, visited "his monkey in the cage," as I gaily characterized myself to him when he walked in. We spent a most enjoyable hour, as you may well imagine, exchanging notes as to our respective doings and expressing our love for each other thru the all too inadequate means permitted us. A thick screen separated us, through which he managed, nevertheless to pick out his son standing proud & tall among the other children in his class; I am referring to the picture Michael had seen fit to yank off the wall at the home and turn over to Mrs. Bloch as a gift for me, bless his sweet thoughtfulness! Give everybody my love.

As ever,
ETHEL

May 27, 1951

Dearest darling one,

Of course, you experienced the same pangs of unfulfilled

hunger at the termination of our visit as I did; and yet what sweet gratification there was for us in the simple fact of our being together. Do you know how madly in love with you I am? And how utterly shameless were my thoughts as I gazed at your glowing face through the double barrier of screen and bar. Bunny dear, I wanted you so much, and all I could do was to kiss my hand at you! . . .

There was once a wise man, I forget his name, who marveled about the "indestructibility of human character." Beloved, we shall prove him right upon my soul we shall prove him right: perhaps then will other human beings believe in their indestructibility, too and rally in ever increasing numbers to our defense and their own. For they who have the courage and the foresight and the decency to aid the Rosenbergs' fight for freedom ensure their own eventual release.

My sweet husband, your miserable wretch of a woman salutes you but why must you sleep in one bed and I in another? Tch, tch, the State is awfully wasteful shame on them!

YOUR OWN GIRL . . .

Following the first Jewish religious service they attended together, they exchanged these letters.

May 29, 1951

My dearest loved one,

. . . My darling, what dear solace to hear your voice during the Jewish Services. And the contribution you made to the general discussion following the sermon was certainly very much apropos. Did you agree with my comments, incidentally? I think the Rabbi is a very fine, intelligent, sincere and decent young man and what he has to present always gives me food for thought. What was the reaction among the other men? I sense a warmth and spirit of good-will toward him and toward me, for that matter, which is most gratifying. Today I felt this friendliness reaching out to encircle you too; in sooth, I have an idea, my one and only, that you have very definitely arrived, and are now a veritable pillar of "CC" society. Am I correct?

My thoughts turn not to those newspaper articles you

recounted for me, insinuating that we don't want our folks to visit us and are not interested in requesting visits for ourselves. What vile disgusting lice crawl forth their petty days upon this wondrous earth of ours, spewing forth their filth upon people who wouldn't lower themselves to spit at them! I have nothing but the most profound contempt and loathing for this kind of worm; lo, when the Judgment Day comes, they will be ground into the dust where they belong!

Dear one, it is torture to be without you! All my love and the intense longings of my body & soul don't stop you.

ETHEL

May 31, 1951

My Dearest Wife,

By now Manny has received copies of the two letters you sent me and they have been made part of my treasured archives . . .

As for our budding poet Michael. His birthday card to me had a picture of a sailboat on a lake and the printed verse said,

> On the tides of deep affection, Dad
> This thought sails on its way
> To hope you'll have more Birthday Joy
> Than words can ever say!

He added in his own precious hand these beautiful thoughts

> The Merry Wind is blowing
> My lovely words are flowing — Michael

This my dearest is our pride and joy eight-year-old.

The Jewish services were rather novel and impressive. Without doubt the Rabbi is a sincere, intelligent and learned man and the method he uses to integrate prayer with present circumstances and obtain uniform participation is very effective. Naturally, light of my life, your contribution hit the core of the topic under discussion by going to the principle of the argument. The men here have deep respect for you and keep you in high regard. You impress them as a "balla busta" * and

---

* Translated "a strong, independent woman."

one who knows how to handle herself. This is not me speaking. I just shep nachass.*

Lena sent me a letter and told me how they repaired your old ironing board, like new, washed my shirts and socks and put all our clothes in order. You see our loved ones are all prepared for our eventual homecoming.

Shut away from the world by layers of massive steel, concrete and numerous locks, reading blasphemous lies about ourselves in newspapers that are poison spread by pen prostitutes and, finding myself and my wife condemned to an early doom it takes every ounce of my strength and all my understanding to stand up to all this. However, seeing you, hearing your voice and receiving such letters gives me terrific stimuli and it seems easy to take all this in my stride. Your words are so expressive, and full of meaning and I adore you for every bit of the person you are. To me love is all inclusive, the culmination and the ultimate creative expression of life itself. If I am not expressing some of my innermost thoughts it's because I want to keep these private for the two of us and most important just knowing that you're always there is sufficient comfort for me. Through all of this you stand out in dignity and character as a woman. I am proud of you my lovely wife. I too miss you very much but this is our unfortunate lot . . .

YOUR OWN JULIUS

Every week the prison's Jewish chaplain, Rabbi Irving Koslowe, conducted services in the men's wing of the Condemned Cells. My mother, the only woman in the Condemned Cells, was allowed to attend services. She could not see the male prisoners, nor they her. These services provided human contact for the prisoners. Some regarded them as a break in the boredom of prison existence, others as a sincere religious experience. The rabbi could not determine the priority for my parents, "but if they came only for an opportunity to hear each other, it would be understandable."

The letters indicate a positive response to the services, which is puzzling in the light of family members' feeling that they were in

* Translated "experience great pride."

fact not religious in the traditional sense. I have no memory of being inculcated with belief in a Supreme Being. An aunt recalls that when my father first became involved in political issues — perhaps it was the Scottsboro case* in the 1930s — he attempted to enlist the aid of several rabbis. When they refused, he lost faith in the value of organized religion. Life on earth was more important to him than spiritual communion with God. My mother agreed, as the following fragment should indicate:

September 30, 1951

I am thinking now of the darkened streets of the Lower East Side; early tomorrow morning throngs of people will be hurrying to the synagogues to pray. I earnestly hope their prayers are answered, yet life has taught me that theory without practice can be a pretty empty, meaningless gesture, lip service simply does not bring about the peace and goodwill and security all decent humanity so bitterly craves; we must not use prayer to an Omnipotent Being as a pretext for evading our responsibility to our fellow-beings in the daily struggle for the establishment of social justice. Jew and Gentile, black and white, all must stand together in their might to win the right!

In prison I believe they coordinated the purely ritualistic aspect of the service with their political interpretation of their Jewish heritage. Certain themes in this history, particularly that of the struggling underdog, helped them retain their sanity, patience and courage.

October 2, 1951

. . . I was unutterably moved to hear the Shofar, sounding amid the grim stark grayness of our surroundings during Jewish

---

* A famous case in which a group of blacks were framed on a rape charge. The case aroused the concern and anger of the entire nation, and through the efforts of political organizations and volunteer lawyers who braved lynch mobs to intercede, convictions were overturned a number of times. One of the accusing women (they were both prostitutes) recanted her testimony. Landmark Supreme Court decisions were handed down regarding the right to counsel in State Courts and the illegality of the exclusion of blacks from Southern juries. Finally, four defendants were released and three others pardoned.

Services today; truly am I proud of the inheritance of an ancient people who have made an eternal contribution to the civilization of mankind and with whom I shall ever be privileged to be identified.

. . . Love you darling

YOUR OWN GIRL ETHEL

October 4, 1951

My Most Precious Darling:

. . . I too share your sentiments about the Rosh Hashanah holidays and to us it has a special significance because the great history and culture of the Jewish People is one based on justice freedom and peace among all peoples. I am proud of this heritage and the contribution to world culture, literature, science and social enlightment my fellow co-religionists have made. When it's possible for us as people to see the decent role we play then we can have the courage to face all this hardship. As the children of Israel were freed from bondage so too will progressive Americans help us win our freedom. Sweetheart, honey wife I take you in my arms and hold you close — All my love —

YOUR MAN JULIUS

My parents sought whoever or whatever was on hand to sustain them — services, individual talks with the rabbi, the visits from her psychiatrist, the family, Manny Bloch, and evidence from the newspapers they received of activity in their behalf. I asked Rabbi Koslowe if he thought my parents were religious, if they believed in God. He found it a very difficult question.

I found them responsive at all times and respectful. I read some material about the fact that they had a disdain for religion. I read this in the newspapers. From my contact with them that was not apparent at all. I never found your mother or father either disrespectful in any way towards any religious practice or ritual or service. They participated in each one. They responded to each one.

Though our parents knew they might die, for the most part, they remained optimistic. Dr. —— (Manny was finally able to arrange regular visits for him) recalls a sense of optimism. Though they began in early May, his visits did not reflect the extreme depression sensed by Dr. Wertham. To Dr. ——, she'd become a resolute person, her own person, as it were. Therefore, "she found me really unnecessary as a therapist, but saw me as a person who was interested in her and who she was interested in and wanted to talk to, and I was available." Dr. —— and the rabbi both observed their constant distress over Robby and me.

Another element of their prison existence, which is playfully and seriously reiterated in their letters, is sexual frustration. I asked the rabbi and doctor about this, and despite their admission of the reality of the problem, they feel it was not a high-priority concern. Rabbi Koslowe said, "You and your brother were high on the ledger."

Still the adjustment was not complete. Also, problems boiled over at their weekly meetings.

June 27, 1951

My own dearest, darlingest one,

. . . Darling, this last visit was particularly distressing due to the mutual agitation engendered by the painful subject we were forced to attempt to analyze. I am so terribly, so achingly regretful for the wounds you are suffering through my seeming inability to render the sting of a certain group of poisonous snakes of my sorry acquaintance powerless against me. Love of my heart, in all humility, I ask your forgiveness; I solemnly promise you that I shall take the necessary steps to break loose once and for all from the emotional trap that has held me a prisoner, far more than the bars behind which I have been living some eleven months now ever have! . . .

Love,
ETHEL

July 1, 1951

My Sweetest Wife,

Before I go any further I want one thing understood. You are not to admonish yourself or have any guilt feelings because you act and react emotionally as your person dictates. You should know by this time that it is most important that you don't negate your innermost feelings and this is especially so because you have just cause and it is a necessary process for you. I kept kicking myself and feeling bad that I did not take an objective approach to this problem and let my passions run away with me. Believe me you have done exceedingly well and I am more than satisfied at the pace you're going. I'll be patient, I promise, until you can honestly and sincerely arrive at the point that there is a complete unity between your conscience and your emotional makeup and then you will really be master of yourself. It is because I too have experienced similar contradictions that I can comprehend the true status of your entire psychological makeup. By this I mean not all its detailed ramifications but the scope of it, so that each part can be judged in its proper perspective. What do you think? I'm beginning to sound like an analyst tch! tch! . . .

Forever your own —

JULIUS

August 9, 1951

My own darling Julie,

. . . While rummaging around "among my souvenirs" today, I could not help looking once more at your exquisitely lovely Mother's Day card with its genuinely touching, unusually expressive tribute and remembering how simply floored I was to receive it. And even though you were not there to deliver it personally (along with the appropriate embraces, of course, — and lots of them) I can't think of anyone more eminently fitted to be your emissary than Manny Bloch was that day. This self-styled "cynic" simply glowed to see my tremulous response but it was when with peaceful flourish, he produced the piece de resistance, Michael's class picture, that the man's rich, deep-flowing humanity manifested itself in all its blazing splendor. What warm, sweet feeling was then shared between us as I gazed on the inspiring sight of the child. How merry and bright are the eyes in the softly rounded, tender face of him and his teeth are coming along nicely in so far as I could determine from the crooked smile of him. And he is standing at the end of the back row with such an air of belonging and mature cheeriness, that I am positively thrilled.

I also experience such a stab of mother longing that I could howl like a she animal who has had its young forcibly torn from her! How dared they, how dared they, the low, vile creatures lay unclean hands upon our sacred family? And tell me, oh, my sister Americans, how long shall any of your own husbands and children be safe if you permit by your silence, your inertia this foul deed to go unchallenged! Shall you sir, too, in a soundless horror, entombed, buried alive, ears forever strained for the voice of a friend, eyes forever filled with nightmare terror, upon your brain forever stamped a thousand shocking imprints, heart forever fraught with mute, abysmal anguish! Shall you? — —

Lovingly,
ETHEL

August 16, 1951

My very dearest Sweetheart,

I believe I attempted to describe somewhat, the last time I wrote, the latest frame of mind toward which I seem to be gradually progressing. Actually, it is a very difficult mood to capture on paper, since there are quite a few apparently unrelated facets that comprise its format, that yet are all one and the same thing. For example, I have the curious feeling of living in a world beyond whose walls no other exists; in jail terminology, I've "made it," I've "arrived," because the "street" no longer contributes the magnet, the painfully plaguing goal, it once did. The carefully restricted demarcations of the area in which I am permitted, have dissolved because there is no longer any other area. I am conscious of a need to remain immersed in my own being that amounts to an actual resistance to showing my thoughts and feelings. Oh, I make plans about the children, Manny, and Dr. ———, but it's all so mechanical, it's as though I don't really believe these events will actually transpire; they are dreams I have yet to dream. I am withdrawn into myself and a lethargic lassitude envelopes me, yet there is awareness of a stronger bond with you and all these others, if anything, just because I don't feel so driven to overtake you and them. In other words, this outside world which I have to all intents and purposes, renounced, is more sharply with me than ever, by dint of the fact that the situation of which I am presently a part holds so much less strangeness and terror for me than it did.

I know it's all very paradoxical and maybe my brain is so worn with poking and pulling that it cannot function keenly enough to properly expound the particular ideas that have been streaming back and forth across it, of late. So take them for what they are worth to you, and perhaps I'll try my luck another time, along these lines . . .

ETHEL

August 16, 1951

My Most Precious Darling Ethel,

Overwhelming longings have taken hold of me and I desire so to hold you in my arms. It is not enough to see you and talk to you. My love for you is overflowing and it cries out for more adequate expression. After all the highest emotional and mental feeling are culminated in the physical sense. Because of these thoughts of you I have driven myself to higher efforts. My eating habits are improving to the extent of lowering my food intake. Setting up exercises to keep me in better physical shape have been started and I hope to be able to continue this effort. To our two dears I sent a lovely letter. Honey, you may not think so but you are the determining influence in my stability. Of your beauty I can sing. Your loveliness is so satisfying to my eyes and your sweetness warms my heart. The time I am with you I am completely removed from this tomb of steel and concrete and filled with sufficient inspiration, emotional uplift and mental stimulation to make me strong to stand erect in facing the daily hardships. My words are not able to express completely how tremendous an effect you have on me. If only we could spend the time together the torture and hurt would not be so great. However reason and humane treatment is not the criteria here. It is so hard to take and conceive particularly because we are so completely innocent of this charge and are only victims of a hideous political frame-up. How the pattern

keeps on unfolding, more political arrests, arrogant disregard
for the rights of people or the Constitution of our land and a
greater hysteria spreads through the country. Now is the time
for the people to stand up and defend their rights. We see so
clearly the similarity with all of this of our own case and the
complete identity of our position with that of the American
people's fight for Democracy and peace. It is essential that the
truth and the facts be known to all. Lee sent me a letter and
among other news told me of Michael's sleeping problem. She
said she'll discuss the problem when she sees us this Saturday.
We know this problem and I am sure you will be able to
recommend the correct remedy. Just like his Mother and
Father he thinks all the time and finds it difficult to fall asleep.
This kind of stuff tears my heart out. So much strength is
needed to withstand such heartaches. Only our complete
freedom and an early reunion with our family can serve to heal
the harm done to us. No matter what I'll continue to fight for
our vindication.

All my love,
JULIUS

While our parents were "adjusting" to life in the Death House
and trying to settle in for the long haul of appeals leading to, they
hoped, ultimate vindication, Robby and I had achieved some
form of adjustment to the "home." So it came as almost an
anticlimax in June 1951 when our grandmother, Sophie Rosenberg, whom we called "Bubbie," was finally well enough to set up
an apartment and take us into her home. Unlike the rest of her
children she was not frightened by the situation — for her, blood
was more important than "community standing." At the same
time the obvious unfairness of the lenient treatment for David and
especially Ruth Greenglass as opposed to our parents' sentence
outraged her. She often bitterly commented that Ruth was
"walking around" free. My aunts and uncle did help with
expenses and visited us regularly. I was pleased to be leaving the
shelter, but since I had grown accustomed to it, I didn't have the
great sense of relief and release I would have had earlier. Also, I
was somewhat surprised that the Rosenberg side of the family was

taking us. Their visits had been short, and since our grandmother had been ill, we had seen very little of her.

Our parents were extremely pleased and gratified.

June 17, 1951

Dearest Bunny Girl,

Friday! It was glorious. Seeing my lovely woman and hanging on to every word of wisdom that uttered from her sweet lips. Sparkling, twinkling, meaningful eyes that seemed to devour all they could encompass and lend color to your youthful pretty face. Agile mind, always probing, deep in thought, precise in analysis and exacting in detail and no hasty decision and an outside observer who knows you can bank on your studied conclusions. Is it possible that such treasure can hide endless pain, profound emotional torture and deep agony? Through it all you convey to me a warm, glowing and tender love. How I hoped I could have been with you the moment my sister told you the splendid news about the children. I heard your joyful shout and it was sweet music to my ears. Honey we have passed another milestone and I'm positive this will ease that ache in your heart and soothe some of the pain of your motherhood. Over and over again my Mama wanted to see you and tell you all she will do to give our children all the love, comfort and understanding and she is constantly hoping and praying for us to come home soon and take our rightful places as the parents. When I see you I'll try to recall all the details as she told them to me. She sends you a warm embrace and best wishes for a speedy homecoming . . .

Yours —

JULIUS

Though I had seen more of Tessie Greenglass, even in the years prior to my parents' arrests, my grandmother, "Bubbie," was more willing to play with Robby and me, was not as sour as Tessie. Bubbie and I used to play a game in which as "Michael Engineering" I pretended to be an engineer on a train. She probably imagined an engineer like my father, a college graduate

(CCNY, class of 1939), a professional. In the game she called me whenever the naughty boys (pronounced by her "naughty boy-yes") were misbehaving. I rushed into the room and beat up the entire imaginary gang until she urged me to desist. But while we lived with her, and in fact for the rest of her life, she never seemed to be in the mood to play that game.

We lived with her in upper Manhattan on Laurel Hill Terrace. Her apartment next to the Washington Bridge overlooked the Harlem River.* Perhaps the thing I loved most about moving in with Bubbie was that she cooked food that I liked. Chicken, meat, fish, potatoes, corn, vegetables. No chow mein, no cut-up hot dogs in awful pea soup, no hot cereal — none of the foods that caused me to starve myself at certain meals in the home. I also appreciated the fact that she was not a source of discipline. Basically, I did whatever I wanted. A registered nurse, S——, helped her because Grandmother was still suffering from high blood pressure. S—— hoped to provide discipline for us.**

Robby and I remember perfectly the physical layout of the apartment. As we entered the apartment (on the second floor) there was a short foyer. On the right was a small kitchen. Straight ahead was the living room which was as wide as the foyer and kitchen combined. Both the living room and the kitchen had two windows each overlooking the backyard. The yard was full of scraggly plants, rocks, garbage, and junk, including the hulk of an old truck or car. The living room was furnished with a couch, a combination radio-record player, a low chest of drawers on which was later placed our first television set, and a small table*** from our previous apartment for the telephone directory. The phone number was LOrraine 8-0821. Robby and I shared a bedroom and there was one bathroom. Someone had given me a globe when we moved in, and I kept it in our bedroom. I spent hours spinning it and looking at the different countries. When friends or

---

* Not the George Washington Bridge, I was told, which goes to New Jersey. The Washington Bridge, which now connects 181st Street in Manhattan with the Cross Bronx Expressway as well as local Bronx streets, was then just one of the many Manhattan-to-Bronx bridges that connected local streets; like the ones on 135th Street, 145th Street, 155th Street, only this one had a name.

** See below, pp. 101–103 for the problems that developed later on.

*** Little did we know the important role this console table had played in the trial and would play in the future.

family came over, I pointed to various nations and asked which sides these countries fought on during the two World Wars.

Bubbie's room was the only room that looked out over Laurel Hill Terrace. On Saturdays Robby watched through her window the huge earth movers a mile away across the river. They were in the process of building the Major Deegan Expressway, the New York City link of the New York State Thruway, though of course he didn't know that at the time. It seemed to him that they were just practicing moving earth this way and that with no apparent purpose.

Robby also spent time staring out the kitchen window and watching the hordes of cats that roamed the backyard. Sometimes Grandma threw scraps to them. He was fascinated by animal behavior (and still is). An apple tree grew so close to the window that its branches poked through the fire escape and onto the sill. All summer he watched the blossoms and the apples grow. We ate some of the apples in the fall.

June 24, 1951

My Dearest Darling Boy Michael,

Welcome to your own home son. Your mother and I told you not to worry as we'd do all in our power to see that you were well, comfortable and happy. Now that all arrangements have been completed you and Robert will have a nice big room, your own beds all your old toys and of course your sweet Bubbie Sophie and a nice lady to help take care of you. We your parents still can't come home as our appeal to the higher courts has not as yet been heard. Be patient honey as everything will turn out alright and we'll come home too, when all this is over. I see your mommy regularly and we talk about you two fellows. We look at your pictures and hug and kiss you with all our hearts. You are very dear and precious to us and I send you all my love. We'd like to hear from you as to all the things you do, see and hear. You write so well and it gives us so much pleasure to hear from you. Oh by the way thank you for the lovely Father's Day and Anniversary cards you sent me. Imagine you are becoming a poet taking after your wonderful mother. Well there is the erector set and many things you can build. I remember the fun we had, with the cranes and boom derricks and how we used it with the tracks trains and blocks. It's fun to play and build so let's hear about it. How is my baseball champ getting on? Did you have a chance to go swimming? Summer is here and you'll have a chance to go places on trips and see many new things and I've been told you'll always have people near you who understand and love you and I'm positive you are going to make new friends and have many good times.

Hello Robbie boy I've already been told by my lawyer that both you fellows were very happy when you heard the good news. From your picture I can tell you're growing up to be a big fellow like your brother. Yes sweetheart play, enjoy yourself and have fun. Your mother and I are always looking out for you and we send all our love to you.

By the way Mike send our love and best wishes to your Grandma Sophie and the nice lady and tell them I'm sure that everything will work out all right because we are all working together, from the heart and we are doing a wonderful thing for all of us. We are well and glad to hear such good news about you. We will be home you can bet on that —

YOUR OWN DADDY JULIUS

Robby had no friends and didn't seem to miss them. He was withdrawn, slowly learning that the best way to get along in this world in which our parents had mysteriously disappeared was not to draw attention to himself. If Grandma sat outside he did, too; if she took walks, he accompanied her. He had Grandma and me — we were safe and enough. He refused to go to day camp that summer, even after S —— offered to stay with him. I guess he'd had his fill of groups of kids. However, as I'd been somewhat accepted by the kids at the home (I corresponded several times with a couple of them and once phoned Mr. Witover to say hello), I was not afraid. I enjoyed camp, my only unpleasant experience being having to bathe under the hard spray of shower water before swimming. I delighted in learning to swim and quickly progressed from non-swimmer to "B" swimmer (for "better"). In the final week I progressed through the two most advanced levels and was permitted to swim in the deepest (eight feet) part of the pool on the last day of camp. I wrote my parents about this achievement.

July 22, 1951

My dearest honey Boy,

When I saw your sweet Mommy this week she was smiling and oh so happy. Of course, it was a splendid letter from her wonderful son Michael. Naturally the first thing I did was read the news you wrote in nice round penmanship on ruled lines. Yes we were both justly proud of you as you had progressed to the high swimming group "B." This is only one example of the pleasure you can get from trying, learning new things and accomplishing something concrete. Such is life for all people to advance themselves and create new joys in living. At this point play is very important to you as you find out how to get along with others. You see your own worth that you too can achieve things and improve yourself. How I'd like to be with you and talk to you and together we can grow and desire so much fun. But I am forcefully kept from you and we have to be patient until the time I am free to once again live with my own family. However until that time all of us in our own jobs and ways will continue to work hard to improve ourselves in order for us to better be able to live a healthy happy life. From your letter and all that your Aunt Ethel told me this week I know you are more than holding your own. You like Day Camp and it is helping you find more relaxation and comfort. The care and love of Bubbie Sophie, the help and warm understanding of the other lady S—— and the fact that you have your own things and home makes it a lot easier to get along. Know that no matter what the situation your mother and I with the help of many devoted people, both family and friends, think of you, plan to do all we can to help you and we are moving heaven and earth to win our appeal and go home to our dear children. You boys are our greatest pleasure and joy in life and we love you more than anything else in the world. Do not worry conditions will change and all will be well again. Robbie fellow you too are beginning to learn that things are improving for you, and it's

wonderful to be home again. People who see us confirm that
you are much happier and adjusting nicely in your new home.
Let me take you in my arms my sons, hug you tightly, smother
you with kisses and be consumed with the happiness of my love
because we are together. Have a good time and be happy
boys. . . .

YOUR OWN DADDY — JULIUS

Unfortunately, I had not been taught the breathing that goes with
the front crawl and never became an accomplished swimmer.

Two occurrences that summer were of very great importance.
Robby and I actually visited our parents in prison, hugged them,
kissed them and talked with them after more than a year of
separation. Though Manny Bloch had become a well-loved figure
by that time, he only *represented* them to us. In addition, William
A. Reuben's series in the *National Guardian*, which began running
in August 1951, broke the press monopoly in the country of
newspapers approving of the guilty verdict. I started reading the
series in the second or third installment and was thrilled to learn
that people thought our parents were innocent. I understood the
demand for a new trial though of course I couldn't absorb all the
material, but the tone and unmistakable conclusions of these
articles encouraged me. It was during this period of my life that I
became engrossed in politics. This interest undoubtedly prompted
my questions about different countries on the globe. But, more
importantly, I began firing questions about our parents' case. I
asked anyone and everyone about the case — why our parents
were framed, who framed them, what we were going to do, how
long the appeals would take, etc. Upon being told at one point, I
suppose by S——, that the government had framed my parents, I
exploded in my deepest eight-year-old voice, "Damn the government!" Grandma looked at the walls and fearfully shushed me.
S—— lamely countered, "Well, it was only some people in the
government," and I very meekly (in a more normal high-pitched,
ingratiating voice) said to the walls, "It wasn't the government,
anybody who heard me."

I have a clear memory of being told that Manny had caught
Dave Greenglass in a lot of lies on the witness stand. My mind

immediately conjured a courtroom (at the time I avidly listened to courtroom radio shows like "Amicus Curiae" and one called something like "Friend of the Defenseless" about an idealistic woman attorney) in which Manny, transformed into a grinning happy elf, leaped about the room gleefully shaking his finger at Dave Greenglass and chirping, "Aha! That's a lie! That's a lie!" I didn't ask why these exposed lies hadn't convinced the jury that my parents were innocent but I should have. After all, I didn't understand the hysteria of the times. I was only vaguely aware of the Korean war and initially thought Russia, as in World War II, was our ally. In any event, I knew the verdict had been unjust and thus agreed with the *Guardian* and my parents and Manny that they were entitled to another trial.

Generally, the prison visits to our parents were wonderful experiences. I wish I could disentangle in my mind the many pictures from different visits, but for Robby and me they merge into a composite with only the first and last ones being distinguishable. We do not even have the slightest inkling how many visits there were, though they continued for almost two years, August 1951 to June 1953.

The prison had the usual turrets for machine guns and despite what it respresented, it was not a forbidding, scary place to me. It was where Mommy and Daddy lived. The guns were sort of exciting, reminding me of the many FBI and private detective radio shows I had listened to both at home and at Grandma's house. Somehow, I never got the impression that the prison, the guards, etc., were the enemy. To get to the Death House we first had to enter the main prison and check in. Then we waited on one of the long benches in the waiting room. I was intrigued by the bars and the large metal doors opened by oversized keys. The trip to and within the prison resembled one of my radio shows. I liked the fact that the guards in official-sounding voices always called Manny "Counselor." From the waiting room we walked through a big steel door and out into a yard where a van took us to the Death House (or in polite parlance, the Condemned Cells — CC for short). From there it was more doors and up a flight of stairs (we never saw either of our parents' cells; everyone advised it would be traumatic) to a room with a long table, a lot of chairs and one or two high windows, with bars on them, of course. We both anticipated this and every visit with excitement.

It was probably on the first visit that I asked if I could see the electric chair.* On the same visit we even insisted the guards frisk us. I don't know if they did.** Our parents, anxious about our reaction to seeing them in prison, were particularly fearful of our first reunion. My father wrote:

July 25, 1951

. . . Right now I'm looking forward to seeing my own sweet sons after more than a year of forced separation. Even though it's an entire week off the tension is mounting and I'm going to have to exercise a maximum of control to keep my anxiety down. I want so for this to be a real positive experience for the boys. I am glad you are going to break the ice with them because I am certain you will come through with flying colors and set the stage for my visit. You know I just got a wonderful idea. The children will get a kick out of it. I'll make pages of pictures of trains, boats and buses and I'm positive Michael and especially Robbie will like them. What do you think of this idea? . . .

YOUR JULIUS

Our mother was writing on the same day.

July 25, 1951

My darling Sweetheart,

. . . The most important thing to remember is that Rome wasn't built in a day; better to take the attitude that we won't be able to answer every question with all-inclusive finality and

---

* Louis Nizer in his malicious book, *The Implosion Conspiracy*, has put this request in Robby's mouth and in the presence of our parents. This makes for incredible melodrama but completely distorts Robby's nature — Robby was already quiet and withdrawn and would never have said anything to draw attention to himself — and underscores Nizer's false picture of the visits as unnatural hearts-and-flowers sessions that were torture for all participants. My making the request when I did to whom I did (probably a guard) is probably my attempt at the time to show I was not frightened by the prison, and probably very confident that our parents would ultimately win their freedom. I would not have been gauche enough to be flip about the electric chair in front of my parents.

** We never screamed at them to do that or anything else. We didn't sense hostility on their part and didn't show any to them.

that this visit is simply the opening gun in a campaign that will of necessity have to continue over an extended period of time. If we can manage to also give them the impression that we are not unduly upset because we may have to say something to that effect, we will be setting the stage for the proper reaction. The following is a verbal picturization of the kind of thing I have been dreaming up as a sample of the conversation that may take place, only for the sake of brevity here I'm putting it in the form of a monologue, to wit: "Of course it's not easy to know about the death penalty and not worry about it sometimes, but let's look at it this way. We know that a car could strike us and kill us, but that doesn't dispose us to spend every minute being fearful about cars. You see, we are the very same people we ever were, except that our physical selves are housed under a different roof from yours. Of course, we feel badly that we are separated from you but we also know that we are not guilty and that an injustice has been done to us by people who solved their own problems by lying about us. It's all right to feel any way you like about them, so long as your feelings don't give you pain and make you unhappy. What they have done because they are sick, unhappy people who have tried to solve their problems through hurting others is something for them to concern themselves with; that's why we have had you removed out of the reach of their influence, because it isn't right that they should be given the opportunity to continue to hurt you . . ."

ETHEL

She responded to his previous letter four days later.

July 29, 1951

Hello, darling,

I scarcely know how to begin, my mind is in such a turmoil. Fortunately, my scribbling kept me so well-occupied this weekend that it passed much more quickly than I had hoped. Lee's visit, too, was tremendously helpful along these lines; the picture she drew of the children's reactions, however, pleased me none too well and served to dramatize their very real need for proper emotional reorientation.

All the same, dearest, there is a most gratifying upsurge of parental feeling and eagerness to see them which should do a good deal to promote the kind of atmosphere in the counsel room which we so fervently desire. Sweetheart, I shall do all that is within my power to set them at ease and prepare them for your coming; do try to lay aside some of the anxiety, meanwhile. Believe me, I am trying to convince myself, at the same time!

Hah! You can't make me jealous with your boats and trains; I have an envelope full of rare specimens collected with painstaking care by that intrepid hunter of wild insects, namely, your wife! Dearest! Daddy, how sweet and thoughtful of you to have hit on such a splendid plan! It's just the thing, particularly for Robby, who methinks may be a little shy and strange with us . . .

There is a great deal more that will come to me later in the day as I walk slowly about the yard and ruminate, that I'll be simply aching to share with you. Oh, yes, if he neglects to question me as to the form of the death penalty, this lovely job will fall to you, in which case answer him briefly but unequivocally that it is painless electrocution, which we feel, of course, will never come to pass. You can explain it in terms of a highly magnified electric shock that anybody might sustain through contact. Believe me, my loved one, children are what their parents truly expect them to be. If we can face the thought of our intended execution without terror, so then will they. Certainly, neither of us will seek to dwell on these matters, unduly, but let's not be afraid, and they won't, either. I am utterly convinced that that's all there is to it! All my love, darling —

ETHEL

We greeted my mother with observant, identical statements: "You look shorter, mama." Then the four of us (including Manny) spent a while deciding why she seemed shorter. Robby and I had grown, of course, but we settled on the answer that she was wearing prison slippers whereas she used to wear high heels. She wore a gray housecoat which looked like a bathrobe. My father's ordinary prison costume (I was surprised that he didn't wear stripes!) contrasted with her dress, which made us think of a hospital. She appeared weak to me but her psychiatrist's recollection is that she grew stronger in prison than she had ever been during the time she was his patient prior to her arrest.

We saw them separately in the early visits. As the warden noted in his letter of May 21, 1951, to Manny, social visits between my parents were to be arranged by the prison. Although Manny always accompanied us, these reunions could not possibly be passed off as legal consultations. So we were not permitted to see them together.

Often Robby and I hid behind the door while Manny told one or the other parent that we couldn't come that day. Usually our giggling gave us away before he could finish the sentence! I have memories of eating chocolate bars, singing "And those caissons go rolling along," playing a game called Hangman that Manny taught me in which every time a player misspells a word another limb is added to the drawing of a head in a noose until finally the whole body dangles and the game is lost. I mentioned to them that I should be a lawyer to help them with appeals and worried about losing the current appeals. On one visit, probably late in 1952 after there was already a lot of publicity about the "Atom Spies" and ugly personal experiences had convinced me that the vast majority of Americans thought my parents were guilty, I began to wonder if the whole country were crazy or if *I* were the one out of step. Could my parents be guilty? So I asked if they really were innocent. The reply was, "But of course we are," and I was satisfied. Many of the specific incidents alluded to in their letters about visits I do not recall.

The most significant memory Robby and I have retained from the visits was the great feeling of warmth and love that existed in our family. Our parents may have fretted about us and maybe on occasion felt the visits were failures, but our memories are that they were wonderful. The family was united, however fleetingly. Robby doesn't clearly remember these visits, but he does remember them as fun with little trauma attached. It is from these visits that he gets his strongest idea of our parents, of their warmth, good feeling and love.

Manny's memories support ours.

Whenever the children visited them, there was never a tear. There was only laughter. I sometimes sat in there in that room and I was wondering whether I was living in this world or some world of fantasy. To see these four together in that counsel room you would imagine that they were playing in their own living room. They would talk about school. They would sing songs. There would always be laughter and smiles on the faces of the Rosenbergs. Of course what happened afterwards in their respective cells is something else again, but this is one indication of the type of people they were who understood that they must not permit their own children to see their own misery or their own plight or that they were worried about themselves.

Our parents immediately set down responses to the first visit.

August 1, 1951

My dearest love,

My heart is leaden within me; I'm afraid I was anything but calm although Manny probably indicated to you that I was wonderful. And to judge by outward appearances, I guess I was. But as I smiled and kissed the children, I was experiencing such a bewildering assortment of emotions that I don't think I was enough in control of myself to have accomplished anything very far-reaching. Actually, I doubt anyone else could have either; after all, a first visit after a year's separation, can hardly be expected to do much more than "break the ice." Nevertheless, I am unable to set aside my sense of let-down and frustration; nor can I, needless to say, escape the terrible ache and longing that relentlessly pursue me now that the sweet sound of them is no more.

And yet I am also so full of pride and joy . . .

LOVE, ETHEL

August 1, 1951

Dearest Love of my life,

Just a brief résumé of today's occurrences. This morning found me restless, tense and very anxious. All different thoughts went through my mind and now in retrospect I can frankly say that they were products of a terrific desire to do right by the kids. When the sound of your voices singing drifted down to the cell block my tensions began to vanish. Robert's shrieking was music to my ears.

After lunch I went into the counsel room and the kids were hiding behind the door. When I hugged them they seemed so small and far away. I was a bit dazed. I choked up and my eyes teared and Michael kept repeating, Daddy, your voice has changed. After a couple of minutes I was back on an even keel. A round of kissing and hugging and then Robby sat on my lap. His peaked thin face, ringed eyes, looked up at me and he said "Daddy why you no come home." I carefully explained. He replied "Why did you not visit us Sundays at the Shelter"? Again I explained. Naturally the baby could not comprehend. He dashed around the room and played with the chairs.

I gave the boys a bag of hard candies and showed them the drawings of trains, buses and cars. Michael spent most of his time drawing tracks with a pencil. Constantly I kept drawing him out. The big fellow was reserved and shy. He hardly looked at me. Using your suggestions I asked what you discussed. He finally said a few things about Dave, Tessie and Ruth. The only time we really got warm was after explanations about your family. Then he popped out, "was there an amicus curiae in your trial. Who besides Mr. Bloch was a witness for you?" The fact is both children are disturbed. One thing he said stands out, and that is that it would be better if he were here and not I. Of course, I could not develop very many things in this first visit. Some songs and a talk on the play school loosened the kids up. Again I must state that you set a good tone for the visit and it went off better than I had expected. Do you know that your boys insisted that the guards frisk them also. The children said that you look smaller. I showed that boys I am sans mustache and the little one asked, Where did it go? It is evident to me from their answers that they don't play with their blocks, tracks, clay, erector set and other materials. It may be that either the things are lost or just not available for their use. We'll have to go into this in detail. Darling, the children need us and I hope, it is not much longer that we will suffer such anguish being separated from them. Michael told me about our room being ready and about Bubbie shifting to the living room showing that he is all set. I hope you see this before our visit so we can use it as a basis of discussion. After I left them I felt I tore out a piece of heart* —

Love,
JULIE

Aug. 16, 1951

My Dearest Son Michael,

It is indeed very gratifying to hear from those who come to visit me and read from the letters I receive that you enjoyed the visit very much and you want to see us as soon as possible. Your Mommy and I discussed this matter and we're trying to make arrangements for another visit sometime next month. Now that a beginning has been made we'll have a better chance to get reacquainted. This time it will be easier for both of us to discuss all the things you have on your mind. That includes questions about our case and your future. By now you have no doubt begun to appreciate the fact that it takes time to accomplish things and even to discuss and talk matters over. For me your visit was wonderful. It made me happy to hold you in my arms and kiss you. You have grown my darling and even though at times it has been very hard for you, it is easy to see that many improvements have been made. We will continue to strive to see that you are happy and all possible is done to help you and care for you. Again I want to tell you that I am confident in the end we will be set free because Mommy and I are innocent and we will fight in every possible way and through the courts to win our freedom as soon as possible. In the meantime I want you my love to be healthy and happy and know that your parents will be home with you when this case is over. I think about you and love you with all my heart and I'm anxious to see you soon again.

My dearest boy Robert — I am happy that you liked the trip on the train and you enjoyed the visit. It was fun picking you

* A Yiddish idiom in translation.

up and throwing you into the air, giving you a horsie ride on my back and playing games. When I see you again we'll be able to play some more. If you like let me know and I will make more pictures of trains, buses, cars and boats. It's good to see that you fellows get along so nice with Mr. Bloch as he is a wonderful man, likes you boys and is working very hard to win our case. The thing that is giving me a great deal of satisfaction is that you are so happy with the lovely Bubbie Sophie and the lady S———. Word from you and news about you is always welcome. I send you my children, kisses, hugs and all my love. Let me hear from you.

YOUR OWN DADDY — JULIUS

Sweet Mama — please take care of your health as we're depending on you and I'm sure you understand that the children are growing boys and they should be given a great deal of leeway in play and you should take it easy and be calm. I know you are terribly upset but for my sake please try. All my love

YOUR SON — JULIUS — REGARDS TO S ———

3

Clinging to Memories

BOTH ROBBY AND I have clung to the memories of those prison visits. They are the parts of our family's life that are closest to us in time. For Robby, the prison visits are especially important. He has only one solid memory of our parents before their arrest — he's urinating in the bathroom with our father, who comments on what a big boy he's become. The one-hour prison visits provide him only with glimpses: "I resent the government's taking them away from me before I had a real memory to live with. There is no way to build it and no way to recapture it — it's just gone." I am more fortunate than Robby, as I can remember much about the time we lived with our parents.

Our family lived in a low-rent housing project known as Knickerbocker Village, which covered two square blocks, with two complexes of apartment buildings thirteen stories tall. Each complex had an inner courtyard with walkways connecting the entrances to the six buildings in each court, grass plots with KEEP OFF signs, and several flower beds interlacing the walkways. Ivy grew up the walls of the buildings that faced the inner courtyard. We lived on the eleventh floor and my father told us the ivy would reach our windows in about two years. Between the two sets of buildings was a concrete playground where I loved to play. I rode my tricycle in the playground; often my father pitched to me and I'd "bang the ball way over [his] head for a home run." At the corner of the other set of buildings was the K and K luncheonette where I gleefully drank cherry vanilla ice-cream sodas.

I had a tremendous sense of being the center of the universe. Of course most infants have this outlook and gradually and tenderly they are disabused of it by experience. Until 1950, I was catching on very, very slowly — too slowly according to my social worker — and had to learn the cold truth abruptly between 1950 and 1953.

My parents were generally willing to let me have my own way in terms of food and catered to me. My father took me for subway and El rides and played ball with me. We all played cards together — Go Fish, Casino and War. My mother let me type on her typewriter. She taught me vowels and consonants, and I carefully inserted vowels in each set of letters to make them look like words. My typing forays created a character named Grechalkis, whose exploits I dictated to my mother (a rapid typist who kept up with my constant chatter). I used to get a kick out of scrambling the letters in my father's name — Julius, Juluis, Julisu, or with an omission, Ulius. Ulius became a character in the Grechalkis stories. Since my father worked all week, our jaunts to Prospect Park, the Bronx Zoo, Staten Island, etc., were important for him also.

January 31, 1953

Dear Manny,

. . . I just happened to be thinking of our Saturdays of the long ago. They seem so far away I've almost forgotten them. This was my day out with Michael and Robert while Ethel took care of her personal needs, shopped etc. Usually we'd pick out a trip that required every means of transportation streetcars, buses, trains and if possible a ferry ride. We'd leave in the morning with a bag of lunch, a baseball and bat. Sometimes I'd take along a couple of their friends and borrow a camera and we were off to a park, the zoo or to South Beach or some other point of interest. Six to eight hours of fun and frolic with even only two kids would wear me out but oh so pleasantly. We'd always ride in the front of trains standing up and if there were a number of ways to get to our destination I chose the longest, with the most transfer points and if possible those that passed many switching tracks. Even if it rained we spent the time on trains. One of the favorites of the boys was the 3rd Ave El to South Ferry and a ride to Staten Island the train to South Beach. The children and I were so happy together. We'd get home tired and grimy off with our street clothes, on the floor with a game or blocks and relaxing in our play while we listened to the children's records. Then supper with Mommy a bath with boats, floating objects and water pistols. I'd be drenched and so would Ethel in the youthful horseplay that we all indulged in. Ethel took over the boys reading, singing or just being with her fellows and I'd clean up the mess in the bathroom. Then for a little while longer until bedtime we'd all share of each other and it was most satisfying for our family.

This is how it was and this it must be again. With courage and hope. For life and love,

JULIE

Memories both intruded upon and soothed their existence, and it did and does ours.

Feb. 1, 1953

My Lovely Nightingale,

Oh joy of joy I caught a couple of bars of your rendition of Gounod's "Ave Maria" and the "Alleluia." Imagine if only your door were open, what a lovely concert we would have. I reminisced a bit of the many times you would sing my favorite arias and folk tunes. Honey, as I thought of it I just adored you. Too bad you weren't closer. I'm sure I would have conveyed my deepest feelings for you in a way that is very proper indeed for two lovebirds. I send you my tender kisses as messages of my heart . . .

. . . Believe me, Sweetheart, I have to fight not to think about our precious children too often for the longing breaks me up and hurts so badly. Oh darling! how wonderful it would be to once again be together and back with our family. I just thought about the good times we used to have. You carrying Robbie on your back and Michael on my back and the big race was on. Do you remember the procession when it came time for the little one to be put to bed. You led the way holding his feet, I held his shoulders and Michael marched in the middle with his brother's back resting on his head. It was loads of fun and the way we carried on, a little nutty, but happy. Such poor innocent babes suffering cruelly without any cause. This, none of us will ever forget. Let us keep hoping we will someday win this case and help restore the boys' happiness.

I've got a secret to tell you my wife, that I'm very deeply in love with you (as if you didn't know it). Well, what do you say? Enough of this nonsense!

YOUR DEVOTED — JULIE

Sometimes the whole family would go on trips. I always enjoyed the trips to South Beach, but I liked them even more when we swam there. In the summer of 1949, my mother, Robby and I stayed in a cottage in Goldensbridge, New York (my father came up on weekends), and we went to a nearby lake whenever we could. One summer at South Beach I began to swim. Previously I had only waded up to my neck when the water was calm. There I watched one parent swim while the other stayed with me. Sometimes I climbed onto my father's shoulders but I didn't let him swim with me, though he assured me he could swim with one hand. On this particular day I just pushed off and started dog paddling, surprised at how easy it was. I tried it again. "Hey, is this how to do it?" My mother looked and called my father's attention. "He's swimming, he's swimming. Hooray. Hooray." I can hear those words as if they were uttered a minute ago.

Our family was not perfect, however, only normal. Even before my parents' arrests I was a bit wild. One aunt recalls that on vacations she physically removed me from my mother for a couple of hours a day so she could have a little peace and quiet. Dr. —— remembers that my mother considered my incessant demands for attention a serious irritant. Adult discipline and control were difficult, in part, because, in the words of Mrs. Phillips, "You were so clever and you had so many ways of getting around people that you had no one who would stand up to you." The problems with food at the shelter were rooted in my mother's constant willingness to feed me only those foods I liked. She generally dealt with me by giving me what I wanted. If I fussed over meals, she rarely made me leave the table; instead, she tried to make a game out of eating. I was a wild lion and she a lion tamer who danced around me and fed me scraps of meat as I "performed." That was her way of having me eat and keeping my happy.

But sometimes she didn't give in to me and my stubborn persistence must have been very trying.

A particular skirmish stands out. One afternoon I tried, against her orders, to phone a friend who was away at summer camp.* I knew the address so I picked up the phone to get the number. My mother replaced the phone on the hook and spanked me on the butt. The phone rang. The operator said something to which my mother replied, "Cancel it." I must have really wanted to speak with this friend for I braved repeated spankings, and we had at least one more round. Then to make up with her, when she was ready to take the garbage to the incinerator I first taunted her with a threat to phone, then promised to obey when she pleaded with me. I watched her through the peephole in the door and kept my word.

As I demanded more of her time, pushed further against her nonexistent limits, I became a very tense child. Finally, she brought me to the Jewish Board of Guardians, a private social welfare agency. Mrs. Phillips, my social worker, states that my mother was tremendously idealistic in dealing with people. She could not bring herself to treat them as they were, but as they should be (in the humanitarian, generous, unselfish sense). So she always worked to make me happy. Dr. ———— concurs with Mrs. Phillips, though he notes that my mother's problems with me were peripheral to her own personal problems that led her to seek his aid. Mrs. Phillips also states that progress was being made both in my mother's understanding and in my own personal adjustment when the government intervened.

Part of the mythology created by the kept press and the latter-day apologists for my parents' conviction is that my personality problems stemmed from "child neglect." The truth is, our mother lavished too much attention on us. At our parents' trial both Greenglasses testified that in 1943 the Rosenbergs suddenly disengaged themselves from political activities. This has

* As my parents were poor, long-distance phone calls were a luxury.

been frequently repeated in print without attribution as if it were common knowledge instead of the testimony of these two perjurers, and many consider it a damning fact. "They must have been doing something" is the common reaction. My response is, if we accept as a fact that our parents ceased political activity in 1943, the reason is because *I was born.* They were doting parents. Though one might wish to quarrel with such priorities, it is certainly conceivable that they gave up political activity to spend time with their first child. On the other hand, it is a fact that our father remained active in his union, the Federation of Architects, Engineers, Chemists and Technicians (FAECT) until he was fired in 1945.* Many members of this union were being fired for their political activities during the later years of the Second World War, and he was involved in the attempts to reinstate these members.

Our parents were very physical in their affection toward us. Robby was nursed. We were always being carried around. They were uninhibited about not wearing clothes around us. They referred to organs and bodily functions without smirking, blushing or making up silly names. As children, Robby and I preferred the silly names! (Which reminds me of my three-year-old son's reaction to being told, "Urinate." "I'm not a Nate," he indignantly replied.)

I do not recall either of my parents speaking directly about political issues to me. There were fragments of political understanding that somehow were introduced to me by conversations overheard, by records and by current events. I recall a "bridge game" with my father in which I was a bridge and various convoys passed over me. When the fascists came along, I raised my position. My father grinned ecstatically. "Yea! You killed the fascists! Shake hands, bridge!" His smile, mustache, the bump between his eyes directly above his nose, and his clear-rimmed glasses are still strong memories to me. The fact that a political view is such a keen memory might indicate that there were many such messages sent in our household.

I recall the mayoral campaign of 1949 in which Vito Marcantonio ran as an American Labor Party candidate. People in our

* For an account of my father's activity with the FAECT, see Virginia Gardner, *The Rosenberg Story* p. 58f.

apartment building often talked about his race. My parents went out election eve and when they returned I asked, knowing their answer, whom they had voted for. I don't think I found out later that he lost. I had assumed he would win and once the election was over and I heard no more about it, I lost interest. I didn't know who Marcantonio was or what he stood for, or even that he was in Congress.

By some type of osmosis, I sensed that the Russians were our allies in World War II, a war that was fresh in my family's memory. One of my uncles had lost his entire family to the Nazis, and many members of the family had served in that war. Some of them adorned our dressers in their uniforms. "And Those Caissons Go Rolling Along" was a family favorite, which we even sang in Sing Sing. I was unable to understand during the Korean war that the Russians were not on our side. I described to a fellow inmate at the home the wonderful weapon our Russian allies had. When a bomb fell on this weapon it opened up, caught the bomb and shot it back, shooting down the bomber plane.

When all of these memories are put together my general feeling about my parents is certainly not sufficient to fully understand them as people, and I as well as Robby have a great void in my life. However, I do understand their family orientation, their attentiveness to both of us, and I can match the politics I find in their writings with the few political messages that penetrated my consciousness while we lived together. As the visits continued and the time since we had lived together lengthened, I fixed many specific pre-arrest as well as current memories of them indelibly in my mind. Though they are not enough, I do have more to hold on to than Robby does.

4

Life with Grandma Sophie, 1951–1952

BEFORE THE summer was over, Grandma's inability to impose limits on me began to generate conflicts. I slowly began to go wild. Already I was very nervous and sat for hours, it seemed, drawing train tracks on paper. In general, I wanted my own way all the time. S—— tried to intercede and establish a semblance of discipline; naturally, I resisted her. My conflict with S—— fueled an antagonism between her and Grandma which finally led to S——'s departure from the house. I do not recall all the specifics, but the following correspondence, though obviously heavily biased in favor of Grandma, tells part of the story. These letters are also important because they reiterate the opinions given by the rabbi and psychiatrist in their interviews: that our parents were constantly concerned with us and attempted to involve themselves in our upbringing. According to Gloria Agrin, Manny Bloch's chief assistant, no decision of consequence concerning us was made without their participation.

August 20, 1951

My very own darling,

Ever since Lena's visit on Saturday and her disclosure of the widening rift that threatens the very foundation of the relationship we had hoped to build a hundred different thoughts and feelings have been hammering heavily at my brain and heart. It was all the more frustrating then to learn that we should have to postpone a really thoroughgoing discussion of the problems involved until Manny returned next week.

Indeed, I had such a sense of haste and hurry that I forgot

altogether to impress upon you the need to exercise the greatest possible restraint and tact in speaking with your Mother on Wednesday. Whether rightly or wrongly, I know she must be suffering deep hurt and I, for one, don't propose to wound her further. On the contrary, I'm sure you will agree, that every sympathy and kindness must be shown her. It is on this basis, alone that we shall finally win through to the necessary solution.

In the meantime, my heart aches for my sweet pussies; with what joyful eagerness I should set about re-establishing their emotional balance and security. Whatever difficulties their lives might present, the simple fact of our strong desire to understand and guide them would serve to promote their needs and bring about their eventual well-being. Oh, darling, what manner of monster are the so-called humans, who with cold deliberation, brought us to this pass and can now witness our collective distress with no single sign of remorse, no twinge of conscience, no cry of shame! . . .

YOUR ETHEL

Our parents were especially alarmed that the conflict in our home might further affect Grandma's poor health.

August 22, 1951

Dear Manny

It is only because I am terribly worried about my mother's health that I am forced to ask you to do something about this situation at a time when you are deep in work on our appeal. When my mother visited me today I noticed that she had lost a considerable amount of weight and that she had a sickly look about her. In the past she has been under constant medical care for her high blood pressure. For the last three months she hasn't seen a doctor. It is imperative that she see a neighborhood doctor at once as she might have a stroke if her pressure goes too high. Besides this, it is obvious that relations at home are not good. It is necessary that S—— and my mother individually discuss this problem with you and they be made to understand the necessity of accepting each other as a grown individual. There must be an early resolution of this difficulty. A complete listing of duties and responsibilities might help. Please understand that I feel that my mother's health is much worse and she needs medical attention . . .

JULIUS

August 22, 1951

Dear Manny,

I'm hoping you can get here as early next week as you can; after today's visit with Ethel and my mother in-law, I feel that it is imperative to begin straightening out an increasingly negative situation as soon as humanly possible . . .

(In the meantime I have a practical suggestion for one particular problem my sister-in-law mentioned. She claims there is annoyance over the fact that the children rough it up rather noisily together in the early morning before the adults are ready to rise and supervise their dressing and breakfasting. I used to prepare them by a proper suggestion the night before, for them to use certain play materials, specifically laid out for their use within easy reach for quiet early morning play — to materials like plasticene, a couple of particularly attractive books (something large and colorful which they don't get to see as often as their other books —) a magic slate for each of them to scribble on, and nice, large pads of unlined drawing paper with a box of good crayons for each. — you might even say that their Mommy had made the suggestion for them to so behave in the morning and would be happy if they would try to remember to undertake this kind of play — just the same way they used to when Mommy and Daddy were still asleep at home. The adults have to be patient, however and realize they need constant encouragement, and do their part also by making the necessary materials accessible, to start the ball rolling for Michael and a couple of new rubber cars (for their noiselessness) would be fair to get Robby started along these lines.)

Love
ETHEL

August 31, 1951–September 6, 1951

Dear Manny,

. . . due to the particular facts around which our talk revolved and the light it served to throw upon the existent negative relationship, a certain friction has begun to take shape in my mind that I should like to share with you. The fact that stands out most sharply from among the welter of detail and seems to me to deserve the most serious attention, is the imperative need in that household, for a single authority which must operate despite the fact that there will of necessity have to be two sets of people (Julie's folks on the one hand, and the stranger or pair of strangers on the other), that will be guided by that authority. Obviously, in the present set-up the representatives of each of the two sides are very self assertive; S—— very vocally and demandingly so, Julie's mother benevolently and apparently undemandingly but nonetheless so. Now since we agreed for various substantial reasons that my mother-in-law stays no matter who also does not, it behooves us to try to determine just what kind of person or persons would hit it off best with her and yet be capable of holding the reins firmly and enforcing the single authority that is so vital for the provision of the common good.

You see Manny, there is one glaring error in S——'s calculation . . . no matter how important it may be to properly guide the intellectual and emotional development of children, these do not proceed counter to and apart from what S—— (and you, too, to a lesser degree) has chosen to contemptuously disguise and push aside as "mechanics." Unfortunately one cannot behave inconsistently with children gaining their confidence and respect in one area, and exposing our lack of will and love (and perhaps even incidentally jealousy of the people who do have those very abilities we pretend to scorn), on other fronts. The good mother is the key to proper child rearing . . . it seems to me only correct to assume that no matter how sympathetic and understanding we may be about the peculiar difficulties involved on this particular job (Julie's mother, the children's needs, etc.) and no matter how valid these reasons may have been, — I say it would be dodging our responsibilities if we did not unequivocally recognize that S—— was not able to rise above the feelings of personal discomfiture that the job (with all its attendant headaches) engendered and thereby lost a splendid opportunity to command respect through sheer performance. Not only did she fail to take the lead, not only did she complain about the miseries of her lot, but at the same time, she secretly resented the top grade performance of an individual who was clearly inferior to her in many other respects.

Believe me, the foregoing emphasis on S——'s lacks does not by any means set aside my genuine understanding (expressed to you during our visit) that my mother-in-law was herself harboring a similar resentment and jealousy. However it is nevertheless my contention that despite such a natural inclination on her part and despite her other faults, these would have taken a back seat in the face of proper appreciation of her very real abilities and virtues combined with an authority bolstered by the type of initiative and performance as I have already indicated. In other words the complaint was lodged that Julie's mom was not permitting S—— to take the initiative with the kids, but there is no getting around it that S—— was emotionally incapable of taking that initiative when she might have — One of the best examples of this inability on her part (there were a number of similar examples which got lost in the shuffle when you were last here), was her attitude toward bathing the children. Personally I'm all for cutting corners myself and found nothing to decry in the fact that Mike was showered even though after months of showering at the shelter, he certainly could have stood to gain by the luxury of frequent baths in the heat of summer. However, in the case of Robby, whom she saw fit to stand up in a small slippery waste bowl (with the attendant danger of protruding faucets) even after the well-taken suggestion was made that she seat herself near the tub on the ladder stool so as to avoid straining her back (which she had originally given as her reason for not properly bathing him) — I say, this is an example of the kind of thing which forced my mother-in-law to take the initiative willy-nilly, you see, by taking a self-willed and childishly offended attitude when she did not meet the requirements of the job and when they then of necessity, had to be pointed out to her, she actually reinforced my mother-in-law's hand rather than her own.

Let's take a look for a minute at her attitude concerning the children's romping in the early morning prior to the time of her own rising. During one of my sister-in-law Ethel's visits to the house she very pleasantly suggested a possible course of action for the temporary separation of the kids, Robby to stay with her [S——] until the household was ready to begin the day and asked for her own ideas if any on the subject. The only response was a sullen silence; now while it is understandable that S—— was perhaps not inclined to embrace a suggestion which involved the further taxing of her patience just when she wanted most to rest, it is patently clear that her reaction represented not so much an interest in solving the problem her own way as opposed to Ethel's, as a resentment that there should be such a problem to begin with and a resistance to coping with same at all.

Incidentally let me state for the record, that I was mistaken when I said my mother-in-law had not told me of her own sudden exit from the house, when S—— without a word of warning silently prepared to leave. She very defiantly did tell me it and although I reprimanded her for her own lack of consideration, I could not help but feel that she was simply giving her a dose of the kind of unpleasant medicine she had been dishing out herself. After all, it was for S—— to explain her need to go out and to assure her she would be back at a reasonable hour.

Perhaps it will seem to you that I am needlessly belaboring the point and thereby, also unmercifully blaming S——; however there are some very vital lessons to be learned from such a thoroughgoing analysis which we would do well to heed; that is my sole purpose for making it along the lines I have . . .

YOUR ETHEL

Our parents had other concerns as well. They were determined to make our reunions positive experiences.

September 5, 1951

My very own dear precious boy:

. . . Bunny dear, since our visit, I have been feverishly pacing about indoors and out, thinking of the children's coming visit and jotting down possible answers to possible questions. The following will give you some clue as to my mental ramblings, supplementing the suggestions I made earlier to you with regard to our status here as inmates awaiting outcome of appeal.

"The reason I play ball alone except for the matrons is that I am the only lady inmate in a men's prison; you see since Daddy and I stood trial together it was decided that we should not be separated pending our appeal. Of course, it makes us very happy that we are in the same prison; first of all, we are able to see each other once a week and secondly it makes it easier for everybody else to see us. Naturally, we wish we could live together while we are here, but there are certain rules and regulations that must be enforced when there are so many people to be guarded, and although to you it seems mean that we should be kept apart, the authorities have to treat us the same as everybody else — Besides, Daddy couldn't have matrons looking after him any more than I could have guards looking after me. Living alone makes it hard for us but lots easier for the authorities to do their job, which is to keep us well and safe and sound so that when the reversal we are working for so hard comes through, they can produce us in court. Of course, knowing your Daddy and Mommy as you do, you are sure we would never do any foolish thing like trying to escape or doing ourselves or someone else harm. But there are prisoners who do attempt such acts, so they are simply not taking any chances with us." "Question of privacy involved in men taking care of men and women of women. Only when there is an intimate relationship into which the man and woman have entered through deliberate choice is there no need for such privacy."

I don't know what, if any good, the foregoing will do you — I am laboring with an increasing sense of self-consciousness and lack of confidence in my ability to do right by them. I have determined to let Mike help me by first asking him what he figures our answers might be, before I attempt to give an opinion. Probably it will be a lot easier when I have got them in my arms at last, and can really demonstrate how much I love them — Julie dearest, I miss you and them and the beautiful life we led, so dreadfully I am suffocating . . .

Yours always,
ETHEL

Sept. 9, 1951
My Dearest Sweetheart,

The children's visit turned out just perfect. They were in excellent spirits from the time I entered the room and enjoyed it so much that they were disappointed when it was over and Michael said he wants more. Because of the good effect you had on them the atmosphere was like a warm family get-together. The boys were hiding under the desk and Robbie's childlike giggles gave them away. They rushed to me and we embraced. "Oh Goodie" said Michael as I gave him a pencil and pad and he began to draw. I showed them my collection of insects and put a couple of bananas and two Hershey bars on the table. The big fellow said Daddy Please don't stuff us. Robbie however proceeded to down both Hersheys and a banana and romped around screeching and acting mischievous. I held him close kissed him and carried him around so I could talk to Michael. Most of the hour was spent in discussion. It started with a discussion of the death sentence which he said he read about in the paper. I told him we were not concerned about [it], that we were innocent and we had many avenues of appeal and that it was not his job to be concerned about it but to grow up and be well. He asked me how you die and I told him and he asked if there is an electric chair here and I said yes. He kept on asking about the appeals and what if finally we might lose then death faced us. I kept on assuring him but I could see he was terribly upset over it. He then looked at the Sgt. and said you'd better watch me for I don't want my mother and father to die for if they do I'll kill Dave. His determination, sincerity and youthful grave look moved me so. Another time he said Daddy the man in the Guardian says you are innocent too and I'd like to give him the four dollars I saved in my piggy bank because he's for you. He asked many questions of what he read about money, fingerprints the action of the F.B.I. and the jury. I explained as well as I could and Manny helped and told him on the ride back home he'll go into more detail. The boy said Daddy maybe I'll study to be a lawyer and help you in your case and I said we won't wait that long as we want to be with him and grow up together. He wants so to help us, to do something and be assured that all will be well with us. Oh Darling he is burdened with all these grownup problems and he feels them deeply. I asked him how his Bubbie Sophie was and he said not so good because he gives her trouble. You understand he makes noise and the neighbors complain and he has guilt feelings that they'll make them move because of it. A little incident took place that revealed something of Robbie's problem. In his exuberance he spun the tray with the glasses around and one of them fell off and broke and immediately he scooted around Manny to hide and Mike said look what you done. But I pooh-poohed it and reassured him. The baby and Michael are both frightened and only our early return to them will quickly heal all the harm done.

When I see you I'll have lots more to tell you. I'm sorry if I rambled. I miss you terribly. All my love my sweet darling.

JULIUS

Not all their attention revolved around problems, but even pleasanter thoughts hurt.

Oct. 4, 1951

Dearest Sweetheart:

Since my last letter to the children in which I described the activities of the trash I have been observing I find it increasingly difficult to sort out my thoughts and feelings concerning them, and to communicate these with some degree of clarity to myself, let alone to attempt to establish an unbroken line of correspondence with them. There is a commingling of resistance and guilt which is most disconcerting indeed. Perhaps I need the stimulus of a visit from Manny and for Dr. ———, bringing me news of them and the home situation generally to arouse me out of the stupor into which I seem to have sunk. I am most desirous of seeing one of them at least this weekend.

My darling, I had never dreamed I could experience such intense hunger — such bitter longing; I glow with aliveness the better to savor the ashes of death. Yet can the acrid taste accomplish aught but a fanning of the flame, a fiercer burning, a renewed striving to triumph and to live.

Sweetheart, I find myself regretting that we were unable to "exchange" our individual visits with Lee. Neither of us got around to sharing information the other had received about the kids. For example did she recount for you a certain phone call during which Robby assured her he always gave Michael her regards "but what's the use, he never pays any attention to what I say anyway!" She also mentioned that "Pop" had urged her not to forget to tell Ethel that I am fast becoming acquainted with them and they are very bright children! Incidentally Robby, with that refreshing lack of inhibition common to our emotionally healthy normal child, complained to "Pop" about the size of the Hershey bar he had brought him compared it unfavorably (and out loud) to the kind his Uncle Dave usually buys!

Oh, darling, what a wave of wanting washes over me for them and for you; it grows more and more difficult for me to put off my natural human desires, to warn myself of the searing destruction of our hopes that may yet be ours to contend with!

Only love me, my dear husband, only love me; I am your wife with all of myself!

YOUR LOVING ETHEL

Things improved for a time in the fall but the cause of the problem persisted. My mother's "coordinating central authority" in committee form never was implemented as far as I can remember. S—— finally gave up and left. When she did, she made arrangements to meet me downtown promising to take me out to eat and give me a *big thick pad* that I could draw endless miles of tracks on. My grandmother remained so hostile toward her that I canceled the appointment.

I have always felt terribly guilty about S——. I believe that she was right and that my parents, Grandma and, in the end, Manny were wrong. I desperately needed discipline and she had tried to provide it.

Around the time she left, one of our relatives brought us a television set which had a tiny screen and a large magnifying glass to enlarge the picture. I was overjoyed at the arrival of the television. Robby marveled at the box and thought the people inside it were watching us as we watched them. It bothered him that we just sat while those on television did so many interesting things. Though Grandma was criticized for letting us watch too much television, there was really no alternative. She didn't know what to do with us. I was particularly affected by a "Ramar of the Jungle" type show (even at that age I noticed that every chase sequence ran repeatedly over the same jungle path) starring Frankie Thomas as Tim Tyler, the great white hunter's son. A gang has killed Tim's father, so Tim, a teen-ager or younger, sets out with his tame elephant Bollo (whose language he speaks; sample: "Ee-Noo-A-Ha-Ha" which I think meant "Stop"), to track the gang and finally catches them all.

I identified so strongly with the orphaned Tyler that I concocted a fantasy hope — that Frankie Thomas was, in fact, our incognito older brother who had changed his name for fear of disgrace when our parents were arrested. After our parents were released, we would all be reunited and Frankie would reestablish his relationship with us.

Television was like a drug. I watched it day and night. While Grandma fretted on Friday evenings about using electricity on the Sabbath, I was engrossed in "I Remember Mama," "Our Miss Brooks" and "The Schlitz Playhouse of Stars." This last show I watched because I liked the opening: a whirling globe, the bottle of beer appearing on it and the phrase, "The beer that made Milwaukee famous." I also liked the commercials for James Melton's "Ford Festival." A trio of singers urged us to "Buy Ford; Best Buy; Bye Bye; Buy Ford!" The writer of these commercials was Lewis Allan, a Hollywood writer, whose legal name was Abel Meeropol.

The excess of television was a prime example of Grandma's

inability to control me. Luckily I had two other outlets — school, which turned out to be a bad experience, and a family in the neighborhood who befriended me. I went to school loaded with the arrogance that accompanies success. I had a wonderful record from the Bronx school and figured I would duplicate it here. I didn't reckon with my personal problems. I liked the school but my situation quickly slid downhill. As I was a good, fast reader, I often was bored by the slow pace of class. The worst manifestation of my problem was in penmanship. I just could not slow down and apply myself to neat, careful writing. In addition, the teacher was strict and not very sympathetic to children.

December 2, 1951

My Dearest Sweetheart:

. . . My sister and I had a pleasant visit and on the whole the conditions at home are good. But I feel we should ask Manny to look into the situation that has developed at school with Mike. I am interested in any steps that might be taken to reassure our boy of our support and encourage him to have more self-confidence and I'm not concerned with his negativeness and independence. This may be indicative of some difficulty, but I'm glad to see that as yet he hasn't knuckled under and I want him to be strengthened constructively before any damage is done to him. In order for me not to be misunderstood I'll discuss this matter with you in detail when I see you.

Now that I've talked to my sister I'm enthusiastic about your suggestion of rings for the children's presents and you will make the show of presenting the rings (or if possible it will be done in your presence) and then I'll be able to see the boys wearing our tokens of love. My lovely wife how thoughtful you are for our boys and my mother and other people, and all the time it's you who need the gifts and presents as just rewards for the woman that you are. I'll save up my gift to you until the day we go home together and then both can live again. Nothing I say or do can bring our joyous moment close but I am very optimistic. Always your own —

JULIUS

December 3, 1951

My dearest bunny:

. . . Concerning Michael wouldn't you just know that I had already begun to mull over in my own mind the almost identical thoughts you saw fit to set down on paper! As a matter of fact, I have already notified Manny to obtain, through Dr. ———'s good offices, an up-to-date report from Miss ———* concerning the school situation and Michael's development generally, so that we may be the better prepared for our next visit with the child. I also urged him to be here on Friday, so that we might discuss plans for the most enjoyable holiday week for the children that can possibly be organized, in terms of gifts, entertainment events and our own family with them. I have a number of interesting ideas about same which I am simply on tenterhooks to share with you, Wednesday morning! Ethel's visit was so conducive to fruitful reflection concerning our boys and the weather was so marvellously mild and pleasant, that the weekend was marked by very little of the emotional upheaval that is usually my lot . . .

Oh darling, my longing grows intolerable especially when you describe me as your "wonderful person" and "your lovely wife" — dear husband, please know in return that I feel myself wholly encompassed by your love and greatly heartened by your confidence. Gently I kiss you goodnight; sleep sweetly my love, until we next rest in each other's arms once more.

YOUR LOVING ETHEL

Ultimately there was no solution to my problems. The visits to my parents, the articles in the *National Guardian*, the National Committee to Secure Justice in the Rosenberg Case did not compensate for the fact of separation from my parents and the lack of discipline at Grandma's. My grandmother was a lovable and courageous woman, but she was elderly, slightly infirm and very, very unhappy. Her favorite expression referring to David and Ruth Greenglass which I heard countless times (as well as my garbled memory can transcribe her Yiddish curse) was "Brennez-

* A social worker at the Jewish Board of Guardians (not Mrs. Phillips).

elle-zein," which can be roughly translated as "They should burn!" After reading the *Guardian* articles and comprehending what David and Ruth had done, I was prepared to divorce them from my family (I had always found Ruth a cold fish, and David seemed insignificant, nondescript), but Tessie presented a conflict. I already knew she was siding with her son against her daughter, and that my mother had said, "I have only one mother, now." Yet I was torn because she and Chutcha had taken us for weekends from the home while the Rosenberg side had usually come only on Sundays. I had a phone conversation with Tessie during which she asked why I didn't come to see her. I replied haltingly, "I hear you're not on our side." She said, "Your momma and daddy should come home, that's what I'm for." I doubtfully answered, "Oh, okay . . ." I'm sorry I never told her what I came to think of her. When my adopted parents informed me of her death in 1957, my response was, "Oh, good."

Ben and Frances Minor lived about four blocks from us, and they had two sons, the older of whom, Michael, was a year younger than I. Frances had been advised that Robby and I lived in the neighborhood and she thought Mike and I might play together. She introduced herself to Bubbie and invited me over. Mike and I got along immediately. We established our headquarters in the back alley and played there, if the janitor's vicious dog was not about. The alley was a long, concrete yard with concrete walls on both sides save two entrances into the cellar on either side of the stairs. We played punchball, running bases, tag, hide and seek and many games I've probably forgotten. Often Mike's friends joined us, so we played team games as well. I adopted the nickname "Ike," and we used to say in unison, "Mike and Ike, look alike, eat alike," etc. The latter was not really true. I was terrified that the Minors might feed me food I didn't like. Soon, they discovered the foods I'd eat and were astonished at my ability to consume so much and stay so skinny. I was still compensating for not having eaten well at the home and continued to have a prodigious appetite into the early years of my marriage.

In addition to the Minors, I made some friends on my block,

specifically Phil and Lawrence. My "acceptance" reached its zenith at Yom Kippur — I knew it was Yom Kippur because Grandma walked down to the river with Robby to empty her pocket of sins — when I was invited to play in a punchball game. Soon after that I shared with Phil my knowledge from the *National Guardian* that my parents had been framed. I reasoned that the best way to save them was to inform people of their innocence. Phil's mother seemed sympathetic when I discussed the case with her. Phil warned me not to tell Lawrence because he would blab the news all over the neighborhood. I thought that would be beneficial because then people would read the *Guardian* and be convinced. Phil and I told Lawrence. My idea was tested in early October at Lawrence's house, where we were watching television. His mother asked me my name, and when I answered her she asked, "Are you Julius Rosenberg's . . ." I didn't let her finish as I triumphantly launched into my speech. "Yes, and if you read the *National Guardian* and the . . ." She cut me off. "Don't talk to me about it." I resumed watching television, conscious of negative vibrations from the adults in the room. Lawrence's brother, who had been so friendly and supportive in the punchball game, started working on Lawrence. "Look, Lawrence, are you an American?" Lawrence wanted none of it. "Mommy, he's bothering me." Seeing by their clock (fifteen minutes fast) that the show was over — though it was still going on in front of our noses — his parents told me it was time to go. As I turned to leave, Lawrence's mother, who was beginning to look and sound like Tessie Greenglass, admonished him. "That's the last of your Communist friend." I walked down the hall, and she called after me, "Don't let me catch you hanging around Lawrence again." I think that was the first time I'd heard the word "Communist" and heard it contrasted with "American." I was to hear similar phrases in school as I grew older. I ran home crying and S—— and Grandma comforted me. Their attempt to make light of "a few ignorant people" succeeded for the moment, but over the next few years I became aware that the whole country was as frightened and vicious as this madwoman in our neighborhood. My parents were informed of the incident:

Oct. 14, 1951

My Dearest Sweetheart:

. . . I don't know if Ethel told you of a disagreeable incident that happened to Michael. He had gone to the house of a boy he met and told this kid's mother about us and she chased him out of the house and made him feel terrible. When he got home he cried but S—— explained that some people are ignorant and prejudiced and reassured him. After a while he got over it and was himself again. From all indications he's getting along nicely at school. He likes his teacher and the work. Now that friends are taking an interest I'm sure they'll see to it that he is surrounded with enough decent people to offset the bad effect of low lifes. How I miss the children and long to share the sweetness of our own family life. Now that a committee is being formed I'm sure we'll be able to have them look after our boys' welfare . . .

. . . All my love —
YOUR OWN JULIUS

Oct. 15, 1951

My sweet,

I am sick at heart for our dear innocent Michael; oh, the savage cruelty with which he must perforce become acquainted so soon, so soon. There will be enough rebuffs of the same sort which will warrant the most clear-sighted efforts on the part of our well-wishers to insure the kind of self-esteem that will enable the child to withstand the emotional shocks involved. You see, it isn't enough to make certain that he has positive human relationships (imperative as these are). There must also begin to be recognized Michael's inner needs which tend to drive him to unconsciously "set up" situations which will eventually end by inflicting suffering upon him. When his internal problems begin to receive careful, sympathetic consideration, he will have the necessary confidence to take rejection in his stride. In the meantime, I weep bitterly and reflect sadly upon the sort of inhumanity that can bring itself to so brutally punish an unprotected little boy who has never done any harm to anyone. Small wonder, however, when you consider the steadily mounting and alarming tide of callous disregard for elemental human rights that is inundating our country today!

Love you,
ETHEL

October 21, 1951

My Most Wonderful Woman,

Now many people know who you are and how much I think of you. It seems to me that there are now many people who know what a swell person you are (reading my letters and yours). To be sure I'm pretty proud of you, my wife. Speaking of how well you write and express your true feelings some day when this misery is past history, I hope you'll find it in yourself to write a book so that large numbers of readers can get mental nourishment from your creative talent. Were I to enumerate the wonderful virtues you possess, I'd run out of glowing adjectives, however, besides being an excellent writer and singer, you're a good sweet, warm, socially-conscious human being, humble, understanding and have a lovely personality and above all, you're my girl. I am very glad it's understood that you're all mine because I'm extremely jealous of such a great prize. Oh how glorious it would be to enjoy the sweetness of being with you in the comforts of our own house. Sweetheart, I'm madly in love with you.

Thank goodness, tomorrow is Monday and we'll be seeing the two prides of our union. I suppose Lena filled in the messy details of the incident with Mike as they were even worse than I had feared. I hope to be able to speak to Manny about the situation with Mike and the social worker. I'm sure that this visit will be as fruitful as those in the past. Did my sister tell you about how Robbie enumerated all the people he loves and left us out? When he was asked about Mommy and Daddy he replied, but why they no come home? Naturally he was happy to know she's going to visit us and asked Lena to bring us home with her. It isn't necessary for me to tell you of the ache in my heart for the pain our boys suffer. As their mother I know

LIFE WITH GRANDMA SOPHIE

you're beside yourself in torment. Oh my darling even though I'm confident and know we'll eventually be set free, for the sake of our children and our innocence I hope our going home happens fast. Also, because of what I know of you and how I feel about you, I go through all kinds of hell thinking of how you're suffering. Please good people do right by yourselves and us and make an end to this brutal frame-up. I'm keeping my eyes peeled for letters from people and activity in our behalf. Saypol didn't know what he started and his name will be mud for the miscarriage of justice he helped perpetrate.

Of course I'm looking forward to our Wednesday hour. It is always the brightest hour of the week. Honey Bunny things are picking up and it is a good omen for us.

Your own lover,
JULIUS

After the Lawrence debacle, I didn't play with anyone on Laurel Hill Terrace. I was afraid of all of them. I have one memory flash of an encounter that may or may not have happened: Robby, Grandma, S—— and I are walking home; as we near the front door of our building, two older boys playing ball pause in their catch. One throws the ball at the curb; it ricochets, hitting my grandmother in the head. She catches her glasses in her hands. The other says, "Good shot." "What do you mean, 'good shot'? You almost broke my glasses." They give her a fresh answer without a trace of remorse. S—— blisters them with words, and as she was an imposing woman who no doubt could take on both of them, they remain silent.

I now walked to school by going north on Laurel Hill Terrace, rather than taking the logical route past Phil's and Lawrence's buildings. Once while coming home with Grandma and S——, I glimpsed Phil and Lawrence ahead of us. Without a second's thought, I raced by them toward the apartment house. They caught me as I was trying to make it up the stairs. They didn't hit me, and, in fact, were not hostile, but I was terrified and struggled to get free. Maybe I even screamed. S—— and Grandma arrived and separated us before they had a chance to say more than,

"Wait a minute, we just want to . . ." I wonder if they wanted to be friends. I was too scared to find out.

Grandma had taken our parents' piano, and I began taking lessons, walking clear across Manhattan to my music teacher's. On the way I imagined the lines in the sidewalk were outlines of tracks that switched into each other as I went along. The lessons were in the evenings, so often my entire trip was in darkness. (Then no one thought it dangerous to send a child on such a long walk by himself after dark in upper Manhattan.) Frances says I found refuge in the piano just as I found an outlet in making tracks. Guests visiting at Grandma's were constantly regaled with "renditions."

The piano, the tracks and the television were my means of relaxation. School and life at my grandmother's house were sources of tension. Even being with the Rosenberg family was not a release, because whenever they came — they visited regularly on Sundays — they did not take us out. It was a tight squeeze — the entire family, with two sets of cousins in addition to Robby and me, in that tiny apartment.

After S—— left, Frances became more involved with me. She took me to see my social worker a couple of times. Though my parents had high hopes for the success of the social worker, I think the time I spent with the Minors was far more significant for my well-being. I spent countless afternoons after school in the back alley and in their apartment and was very comfortable around them. The bad scene with Phil and Lawrence did not cause me to withdraw entirely from the effort to free my parents. I asked Mike to pass out committee leaflets with me. I'm sure if the committee or my family had known they would have been horrified. They probably had left leaflets lying around the apartment, and I appropriated them to help my parents. All we did was walk around the neighborhood shoving the fliers under peoples' doors. I can still picture Lawrence's door as we quickly ran by it. I'm not certain I wasted a leaflet under it, but I was scared his mother would open the door and discover me. I talked openly around Mike's friends. I've since blocked out two occurrences until the interview with Frances. P——, a schoolmate of ours, suddenly stopped playing with us. Mike remembers that P——'s parents forbade him to come over because I played there. A neighbor's son was a pretty close friend of Mike's, and the two families got along well until the day T——'s parents refused to allow Mike and me in their apartment. We both knew why. We returned to Mike's apartment. He was crying. Very tense, I sat down and drew tracks. Mike asked his mother why T—— couldn't play with me. As Frances started to explain, he interrupted, "But even if they believe that about his mother and father, Ike didn't have anything to do with it. Why should they blame him?" He was receiving a political baptism by fire at the age of eight.

Despite my problems in school, my lack of discipline at Grandma's and my own recollection that I was turning into a wild man, Frances does not have especially negative memories of me. She admits I was

> . . . hyperactive. You couldn't sit still. You got your hands into everything. You were a jittery kid. Your voice would get very shrill. It was very hard to get you to sit down and listen to a story, for example. There were times, but it was hard for you.

I used to twirl my hair around my finger among other nervous habits. However, "You weren't disrespectful, not in my house you weren't disrespectful." I am quite surprised by her assessment. Though she admits I didn't know how to relate to adults, because I was so frenetic in my reactions, she remembers me as an agreeable child.

> We were very fond of you. You were a nice kid essentially. A very intelligent child. . . . This period was a kind of interim where the pressures were not so great. You could feel more at ease that it was a temporary situation.

I gave the impression that I'd be living with my parents in the future and that I had complete confidence in their innocence. The social worker corroborates this point. "You were still with the family." Even though the pressures on Robby and me were building, I was

> able to play and get enjoyment from that from which kids got

enjoyment. Whatever it was, I think it speaks well for your folks, because something was there that was good, that was sustaining. Where did you get it? You got it from them.

Robby and I, ordinary kids with problems in 1950, were in the process of becoming severely disturbed by 1953. Yet, in 1951 I was not the difficult, unpleasant child I would become.

My relationship with Mike Minor was usually friendly. Our squabbles were few, though he and I did engage in the vicious games kids play — gang-up time, let's everyone ignore Mike (or Ike or Johnny, et al.). All in all, the Minors' household for me was an island of normalcy in my increasingly abnormal life.

The National Committee to Secure Justice in the Rosenberg Case was formed in late 1951. The initial appeals were argued in that same period. Our parents continued to cope with the pressures of separation, hoped for justice from the Circuit Court of Appeals with its well-known liberal, Judge Jerome Frank, and were cheered by the *National Guardian*'s series of articles and the formation of the Committee.

Sept. 20, 1951

Dearest love,

It seems that I have "fallen upon evil days" even the ardor of your weekly wooing, spiked with those quaint pet names you so inevitably and endearingly call me, fails to dissipate the gloom that hangs like a pall over me nor to dispel the sense of doom and foreboding which dogs my footsteps as I drag myself unwillingly about the quiet desolation of the yard. In desperation, I forcibly turn my thoughts to the anticipated gratification of a thorough legal discussion with our brilliant attorney, only to realize with dismay that his visit will be an all-too-temporary respite from the cold bitter, inhuman loneliness of that camouflaged vault politely known as the "Women's Wing" to which I shall subsequently have to return. And then the grim warfare that I must constantly wage (oh the barbaric horror of my living interment must surely engulf me) goes forward relentlessly. All hail to the CC's, venerable College of Cycles; the wheels of chance spin round and round with never a resolution. One leaves the familiar setting for a short space in order to come back to it, in order to leave it again, in order yet once more to return. Good God, is there only this one groove upon which the wheel of my life must forever spin in endless torment! . . .

Always lovingly
ETHEL

Oct. 22, 1951

My dearest darling,

I have done all the crying tonight, I hope, that I'm going to; my end of the visit with the children was all but a complete fiasco! And I am in the most wretchedly unhappy state I have yet been.

First of all, Lee brought me a piece of information on Saturday which had me frantically casting about hours after her visit for some way of avoiding a meeting between Michael and my mother. Realizing that I might not have the opportunity to discuss it with any degree of privacy on Monday, I finally decided to write Dr. ———, expressing my anxiety and disapproval and instructing him to phone Manny first and to and then, if necessary, to get in touch with the J.B.G.

Bernie's coming was another disturbing factor; both of us labored under terrible tension and were mutually relieved when the bus arrived. I am hoping that Lena gave him the earful that I, for some strange reason, contained within me for a solid hour!

So it was in a kind of resigned stupor that I awaited the children's arrival; and now, no matter how sensibly I try to reason with myself that Robby's truculence and Michael's anxiety were the necessarily logical outcome of a set of circumstances over which I had no control, I am rife with a sense of personal failure.

Darling, I shall have no peace until I have poured out my anguish and chagrin to you on Wednesday. I trust that the description you give of the hour you spent, will serve to somewhat allay my own suffering.

Sweetheart, I love you, tummy and all!

YOUR MIS'ABLE WRETCH OF A WIFE

In response to the *Guardian* series, many people wrote offering to help.

November 4, 1951

Love of my life: How thrilled I was to hear such splendid news from Manny's lips. I was moved to tears to hear such tender and compassionate letters from good people with humane feelings. The lawyer consultation was a stirring and emotionally satisfying experience. When I'm happy and see you in such good spirits I feel like I'm floating on air. I feel so close to you and I love you with all my senses. It is indeed inspiring in this hour of our greatest need to see the visible evidence of a concrete support from many ordinary people. We are truly not alone. There is a tremendous reservoir of good people in our land and they will see to it that the facts are made known and that we will get the justice we're entitled to. There are so many mixed feelings I have and most of all I want to be able to share them with you. How my arms ached to hold you! How lucky I am to have such a wonderful precious woman as you for my wife. I am proud of you and for your sake I want us to be home with our children. The difficulties we face are many and the torment great, but the successful termination of this mess we're in looks more promising as time passes.

I read the brief and I wrote Manny telling him what a stupendous job he did and how everlastingly grateful we are for his tireless efforts for us, both his legal work and the humane acts of devoted friendship he has performed for us and our boys. I love the guy . . .

JULIUS

November 15-16, 1951

My sweet, my dearest love,

Since my last precious glimpse of you, as you waved goodbye at the door, I have run the gamut of emotions. At the moment I am comfortable, relaxed and contented as a student in good standing of the College of Civil (CC's to you) possibly can be, except that I feel like I've been put through a wringer. At first I was so unhappy, I collapsed and sobbed uncontrollably, after which I spent a miserable afternoon and evening, alternately tense with apprehension and calm with the determination to stand my ground. My head ached and my stomach knotted, but I made it; for a change, I spent a fairly decent night and awoke close to 9:00 A.M. elated to realize that by dint of sheer will and intelligence I had turned the tables once more. Indeed, I experienced such a sense of profound relief, I became almost hysterical with delight and whooped it up all morning, laughing and singing gaily. At 2:30 P.M. of course, the curtain of silence was lowered as usual, but then I was no longer interested in conversation anyway!

Sweetheart, I am so grateful, to you for being all that you are to me. We are apart, it is true and yet I feel myself growing always closer to and more at one with you. The love and understanding you pour out to me is a fountain of refreshment upon which I may draw unceasingly. My dearest, I am more and more in love with you, as time inches its dreary way onward! . . .

Mail call, honey,
ETHEL

December 16, 1951
My very dearest love:

During the week, it seemed to me my feelings had congealed like the very ice out in the yard; your warmly expressed words had such a thawing effect, I am only just now realizing what kind of a hard crust had formed across my heart. Of course, while I wrote you on Friday morning I felt a stirring within me and if there had been a little extra time before the pick-up of mail, I think I might have loosened up considerably more. As it turned out, it fell to your last letter to me to break through the deep freeze into which I seem to have settled.

Darling, I am looking at my writing through a blur of tears. I miss you so badly! It is indeed fortunate that this lonely, visitless weekend was bright. With sun instead of darkness or gloom that might so easily have prevailed after such a snowstorm. All togged out in my "CC" finery, and looking like a small, roly-poly in my visor hat and military coat I trudged determinedly through the snow (by now there's very little left that doesn't bear my footprints). Come what may, be it fair weather or foul my feathered friend runs to be fed!

I am apprehensive about the weather, however, insofar as the children's traveling here is concerned, and am hoping they can be brought here with a minimum of difficulty. Sweetheart, I am so delighted whenever your thoughts coincide with my own. How did you know that I had been planning to let Robby more or less set the pace and give him as much of the attention he needs as I possibly can without depriving Michael altogether; and that in the event that such did happen, it had already occurred to me that you should have to make it up to him.

You are absolutely right; If I could learn to set less store by what does or does not get accomplished in the short time that is allotted to us I should gain tremendously thereby, and certainly the children wouldn't suffer any more because of it. It is easier said than done, however, my friend, and tension is bound to build up in me until I actually lay eyes on them. I'm sure your own nail-biting activities have not exactly let up and you have all my sympathy, dearest, believe me —

Mail call, honey
LOVE YOU — ETHEL

December 20, 1951

Most Precious Dear: . . . I must let you know again that the children's visit was most excellent and all of us enjoyed it to the utmost. Oh dearest you have given us two wonderful children to brighten our lives and make living so worthwhile. Remarkable improvement must be noted in our children . . .

The Chanukah services last Tuesday brought back many pleasant memories. Vividly do I recall two years ago when we celebrated the festival of lights in our own home with our two boys. Little Robbie would not let matters proceed until he had his own kepal on his head. Then Michael sang the benediction in his shrill high-pitched soprano and the kids trooped around singing. As at our services we played the same records at home and we certainly made it a memorable occasion for our youngsters. At the time I particularly recall your preparations for the occasion by thoroughly informing yourself on the full meaning of every day and the careful selection of toys and gifts to mark the holiday in its true spirit. To us this holiday signifying the victory of our forefathers for freedom from oppression and tyranny is a firm part of our heritage and solidifies our determination to win our own freedom. How paradoxical it is that at the same time that I feel such a sense of satisfaction at the full life we've lived can I at the same time feel the terrible pangs of pain, illimitable sorrow and furious loneliness. Soon, soon my sweetheart we'll be in the New Year and I am optimistic that 1952 will be much better for us . . .

YOUR OWN JULIUS

January 3, 1952

My Dearest Ethel,

. . . In the immediate period we will probably read quite a lot concerning our case since the D.A. will be submitting his brief on Jan. 7, then there will come our reply brief and finally the oral argument. This will of course, be the parting shot at the circuit court of appeals and then our fate will rest in the hands of three men. I hope they are in a good frame of mind and receive our appeal in a calm and judicial attitude and a fair judgment can only bring a reversal. I am hoping for a strong opinion in our favor to help us beat this case hands down if we do have to go on trial again. From here on in I'll keep my fingers crossed. Darling we've got the facts and law on our side what we need now is public opinion and mazol.* Again I repeat I'm optimistic and I have high hopes.

Lately because of the sedentary existence I follow and the fact that my normal intake of food is more than that which is required by my body for energy. I'm beginning to get a rubber tire about my midsection. Since I'm beginning to feel sluggish and uncomfortable I resolved to control the amount of food I eat and I'm going on a limited diet. As yet I'm not exercising but I believe I'll have to apply myself as I've got to consider my better half and I don't want your man getting so out of shape. Now after such thoughtfulness on my part don't you think it is

* Yiddish word meaning luck.

about time that you invited me to your house. Oh my sweetheart I miss you terribly and it's ages ago that I've held you in my arms and enjoyed the sweetness of your lips and was warmed by your love. The agony, endless emotional strains, fearful torment cannot be equated but for us it represents untold misery and only the exultant joy of our reunion at home will be able to salve the wounds and do away with this nightmare. Let us find in each other the additional strength to overcome the approaching crisis of this next hurdle. Be strong my wife so that I may get some sustenance from you. Confidently — Love —

JULIUS

Jan. 10, 1952

My dearest Julie,

Time continues to beat out its merciless measure composing a savage theme that winds through my life seemingly without end. Oh, the unspeakably horrible, monotonous, senseless waste of it; as you will doubtless be able to imagine, only too well, I am fed to the teeth with it! . . .

Love you dearest
ETHEL

My Sweet Mother,

. . . As for us we've been more than holding our own and no small measure of the credit belongs to you my beloved mother because you have taken a great burden of worry off our minds by taking care of our children and giving them the care, comfort and love that only a devoted grandma can give her own family. The visible evidence of the physical and emotional well-being of the boys was so apparent to us at their last visit. To me your son, who is proud of his understanding mother, it is a great personal satisfaction that in spite of all the physical and mental difficulties you nevertheless are selflessly and tirelessly giving your all for our children and for us.

Mama I know you find some happiness in once again seeing the smiles on Michael and Robert's faces and knowing that they feel secure with you and we too have had our morale lifted and have been encouraged to keep our chin up. Just take care of yourself we are counting on you and depend on the strength of your mother love. Since we know exactly how you feel it isn't necessary for you to strain yourself too much to visit us.

We have seen so many heartening signs. Conditions at home have measureably improved. Many good decent people are working in our behalf and making the facts of our case public knowledge. This will make known to all the nature of our case and the fact that we are victims of a political frame-up and that we are completely innocent. We can also be thankful that we have excellent legal counsel. No matter how long it takes we will never lose faith. We are confident of our final vindication and happy reunion at home with you and the children.

All my love —

Your Son —

JULIUS

During the arguing of the appeal, their meetings were dominated by legal considerations. This preoccupation often caused them to shortchange their emotional needs with unhappy results.

January 17, 1952

My Sweetest Dear,

I have been in such an emotional dither since Manny left, especially since there were so many things my heart longed to say to you, darling, as we parted. Julie dearest, of course, I'm not angry! Yes, I am, at that; I'm angry to a point of boiling fury for our helplessness in the face of our enforced separation. The injustice of the misery we have had to endure fills me with a righteous indignation that will not be denied.

Sweetheart, expect me to pull a couple of boners now and then; perhaps I pull them merely to test your attitude toward them and me. Not that your temporarily sharp reaction exactly cramped my style outwardly, or even caused me to lose any sleep over it; still it does make me feel I haven't, genuinely, your acceptance of my right to, yes, make an ass of myself, if you will —

Whatever might be involved, I love you dear one, as I love my very own life. And speaking of life, what an appetite for living our Manny arouses with his thrilling account of the activity on our behalf. All honor, say I, to the People — and to the People's Advocate!

All my love —
YOUR ETHEL

January 17, 1952

My Sweetest Wife,

At this moment I feel quite disturbed because we didn't have enough time to finish our discussion at our legal consultation and I believe because of it I left you with the wrong impression and also did not have sufficient time to make amends for my brusque conduct. First of all, darling, I was terribly keyed up until our counselor put in his appearance and I was so completely set on hearing as much as possible about the legal argument and the briefs in the allotted time that I was a bit hasty and impatient. Then, too, I feel so strongly that we must discuss these two matters you brought up privately and I intend to dwell in detail on this point at our next visit. Please sweetheart understand me, I know you must feel that I didn't give you enough consideration when you were presenting your viewpoint and to an extent you are right but if we were able to thrash this out I wouldn't feel so bad about it. Drop me a note as soon as you can and tell me all is forgiven . . .

I love you with all my heart,
YOUR OWN JULIUS

Feb. 15, 1952

Most Precious Heart of Mine,

With the turmoil and excitement of the children's visit and the rushing developments of events in our case I didn't have time to tell you that your face was beaming, that you looked very lovely, and that I love you very much. Considering the circumstances we managed beautifully and acccomplished a great deal. The contribution we made to the cause of our fight was considerable and it continues to be a source of personal satisfaction.

Ah; dearest, it was wonderful despite the anxious atmosphere to live together again as one happy family and this is worth any sacrifice for it is true love of family and the real dignity of human life. The boys are making progress. Michael is doing much better and I am convinced our little baby needs a great deal of help. Also they are both physically run down and I get the feeling there is too much of a burden on their minds. The sweet memory of the smile, the kiss, the gay laughter and the young voices still pleasures the hours of my loneliness. Can people really understand that our hearts, sincerity and conscience go into what we write say or do and to those who see the truth it is good and right and to those who hate it is defiant and arrogant. We have experienced unbelievable rottenness because of this case but in our wildest dreams we never could comprehend such base knavery. All the world knows that the perpetrators of this latest fraud are monsters and I am confident they will come to know the entire story of this terrible miscarriage of justice. It's a very rough fight and a most difficult one but I still feel confident. I'll just never give up to lies, to indecency and unjustness. And if I repeat too often, it is because I have to express my feeling or I'll burst for I adore you sweetheart. I admire you for all that you are Ethel and my love for you is undying. As long as we do the right thing by our children and by the good people of the world nothing else matters. We will have to call on the great strength of the solid union of our hearts and souls to find the stamina to face what is in store for us, with courage and dignity. If I may say so myself I think we ought to be proud that we didn't weaken to any blandishments that would leave compromised any of our principles. Fears cajoling and threats don't bother me but we must be very careful of the cunning tricks of vicious madmen.

I've been quite busy reading and writing and I haven't had much time to think about putting necessary things on paper that will have to be attended to without too much delay. Soon as I catch up on my writing I'll tackle the job. See you soon my dearest and I invite you to know that you are always in my heart and mind and the mere thought of you is solace enough for my aching heart and builds up my morale. Always devoted to you

YOUR JULIE

Judge Frank wrote the unanimous opinion that ended (as it turned out) all judicial review for our parents, who were naturally extremely bitter.

7:30 A.M. Feb. 26

My dear one,

Last night at 10:00 o'clock, I heard the shocking news. At the present moment, with little or no detail to hand, it is difficult for me to make any comment, beyond an expression of horror at the shameless haste with which the government appears to be pressing for our liquidation. Certainly, it proves that all our contributions in the past regarding the political nature of our case, have been amazingly correct.

My heart aches for the children, unfortunately they are old enough to have heard for themselves, and no matter what amount of control I am able to exercise, my brain reels, picturing their terror. It is for them I am most concerned and it is of their reaction I am anxiously awaiting some word. Of course, Manny will get here just as soon as he puts in motion proper legal procedure for our continued defense, but meanwhile, my emotions are in storm, as your own must be.

Sweetheart, if only I could truly comfort you, I love you so very dearly.

. . . Courage, darling, there's much to be done.

Your devoted wife,
ETHEL

February 28, 1952

My Loveliest One,

. . . I'm still terribly shocked by the horrible and shameless affirmation of our conviction in such apparent haste. The more I think of it the more an idea jells in my mind and to help effectuate my purpose I hope the clerk of the court sends me a copy of Judge

Frank's "opinion." Ethel I intend to carefully go over all he said and pick out all his distortions, omissions, placing of facts in the records that are not true, building up straw men and knocking them down, presenting his personal views of what took place at our trial in short exposing his legal chicanery. Your husband intends to write an opinion of this "distinguished" jurist's propaganda treatise. It is impossible for me to conceive the far-reaching effect their decision will have on furthering the judicial attack on the American people but I can't help but see the crass deceit and sophistry used by a so-called "liberal" and honorable man to continue this political frame-up and use all sorts of rhetoric to camouflage the fact that our lives are being sacrificed in the interests of keeping non-conformists in line. Honey now more than ever it is necessary for us to exert all our efforts in the only manner we have left to us and that is to write what we know and feel about this star chamber procedure and expose it . . .

Always yours,
JULIUS

In their letter to us they attempted to hide their bitterness over the latest setback.

March 4, 1952

Dearest children,

Did Aunt Lena tell you of her visit to me and of my messages of love to you both? Darlings, I am so sorry you had to be disappointed; I am just as unhappy about it all as you are. However, if you think we're licked, you just don't know your Mommy and Daddy! So do the best you can to get used to waiting all over again, but give yourself time because it's very hard not to mind. Daddy and I understand only too well just how hard it is and we're slightly bigger and stronger than you are. Nevertheless, let's not forget the old team cheer: "The Rosenbergs are re-e-a-l hot!" And more and more wonderful people are beginning to realize this and are pitching in to help send us home to you where we belong.

The snow is whirling outside my window as I sit at my writing table and wonder what my pussies might be doing at this moment. The other day when I was outside in the yard, the snow that had fallen the night before looked so much like the icing on a birthday cake, that I couldn't resist "printing" letters in it with my right foot. By the time I was through, all our initials were outlined clearly, M.R., R.R., E.R., and J.R. Do you remember how we used to tease Daddy by calling him, "J.R. the wonder dog"?

Speaking of birthday cake reminds me of a certain date, (March 10) when my dear Michael will be nine years old. I wish I could really tell you how happy I should be to celebrate the day with you and Robby in person. But since this is not possible I can only say that I shall be thinking of you both and loving you with all my heart.

Mike dear, what a perfectly wonderful picture of you I received; you know, the one that was taken in school. Since Robby doesn't attend school yet, I told Aunt Lena to make arrangements to have a good picture done of him outside, so that I can see my boys just as they are right now whenever I get hungry for a glimpse of them.

Robby dear, how do you like the drawings Daddy made for you? I didn't see them but I bet they must be swell. I am hoping you have fun on Mike's birthday. When you are five on May 14th, he will enjoy yours, too.

Again, all my love, my very dearest children.

MOMMY —

They then settled down for the long wait for a possible Supreme Court review.

April 13, 1952

Darling woman,

. . . Dearest many are the pitfalls that face us and the enemies we have are very powerful but we are right and are conducting a principled fight and that is the guarantee that we will win! The possibility of peace in Korea and a loosening of world tension will contribute materially to us obtaining a review of our case in the Supreme Court on its legal merits and our chances for a reversal will be enhanced. Sweetheart I'm more confident than ever as we enter the last major round to reverse this travesty on justice that has been perpetrated against all Americans in our case. Yes my love hold on to your seat as we're in for some rough times. However we know the score. We've got the courage of our convictions. We're confident the people will not let us down and we've got our perspective on our complete vindication. Keep your chin up Ethel if we must suffer through this nightmare then in the manner we conduct ourselves we will contribute to the general welfare of the people by serving notice on the tyrants that they can't get away with political frame-ups such as ours. The common men in our country when they know the facts will fight for a just cause. It takes a lot of time and hard work to get them to overcome their inertia but now that grass root sentiments are aroused public opinion will have its effect . . . We've left a big chunk of suffering behind us these last two years and we are coming closer to our emancipation from all this torture . . .

Always devoted to you,
JULIUS

Increasingly, they drew courage and sustenance from the work of the Committee in the court of public opinion. They also sought to fight back when attacked by press columnists. One such attack came from Max Lerner in the New York *Post* of June 19.

June 21, 1952

[to Emanuel Bloch]
Dear Friend,

. . . I read Max Lerner's column appearing in the June 19th issue of the New York Post. I will not dignify this demagogic disgusting baseless attack by entering into any polemics with this so called "liberal," apologist and hireling of the American Judenrat. However I'll just make a few pertinent observations.

The basis for Nazism was laid by the Goebbels technique of propaganda. Attack the communist and Jew and then everything goes: lies, brutality genocide and destruction of all opposition, socialist, labor unions, catholics, free-masons and democrats. Today in our country this trend is yet at the early stages and the hysteria is raised and created with the persecution of communist and all those accused of communism. The "eminent" columnist is guilty of the very things he accuses the Committee to Secure Justice in our case. He presents no facts but he shouts red. No mention is made of the undemocratic act of denying the Academy of Music for a Public meeting, nor does he answer all these questions: the lack of a fair and impartial trial, the lack of even one shred of evidence to substantiate any charge against us only the obvious motives of the self-confessed spies for doing the bidding of the prosecution as their part in a deal to frame us. The gentleman asks us to prove we are not guilty neglecting to state this is not the way our system of justice operates for it is the duty of the district attorney to prove beyond a reasonable doubt by use of *hard facts* that we are guilty. Remember dear Sir [Lerner] only recently you were denied the right to speak at a university because it was alleged you were a red. You cannot buy immunity by joining the conformists in their political programs against the left and the progressive. You howled because you saw the visible evidence that the American people, the Jews of Flatbush who learned the lessons of Hitlerism are rallying to support the Committee in its fight to rectify this miscarriage of justice and are rejecting your poisonous propaganda. Today my wife and I are innocent victims of the political climate beware Mr. Lerner the Justice Dept. has concentration camps all ready. Tomorrow you too may be one of the many victims of growing neo-fascism. Tell the Committee to keep punching they're getting results — Let me hear all that's taking place. I'm feeling fine and very confident.

Regards to all — As ever —

JULIUS —

My mother offered the following letter for possible use in the struggle.

May 14, 1952

Dearest Ethel,

The cards were simply exquisite, the rich roses of yours presenting a weird contrast to the delicately soft coloring of your children's. It was their simple yet deeply sincere expression of concern for my health that wrung the unwilling tears from my heart. I wept then unshamedly for our collective pain and bitterly assailed the fate that had befallen your innocent brother through the unspeakably foul lies of my guilty one. For myself, I have disclaimed from the beginning of this fantastic frame-up, and shall continue to disclaim, any knowledge of or share in espionage activities of any kind whatever. Indeed, though I wish dearly to live, disclaim it I shall with the last tortured breath I draw! . . .

How I should love to personally thank the "two expectant parents who fight for a better world for all children"; the "unknown friend" who assured me that "we are many who believe in you"; the sister who admired "your courageous stand"; the couple who pledged "to make the bravest mother in America the happiest"; and the individual who penned the short but tremendously inspiring words, "We struggle on!" This does not omit of course all those others who expressed a heart-warming wish to see me reunited at last with my husband and children, and offered their enduring love. Greetings to you all, good brothers and sisters, I am humble before your cherished gifts!

While I must spend my hours among the shadows, I am unyielding in my belief that the American people will not tolerate our legal murder and will find the means to bring the real conspirators against the peace and progress of us all to justice! Verily, the prophets of old spoke truly when they said, "Resistance to tyranny is obedience to God!"

Always lovingly,
ETHEL

P.S. . . . The foregoing letter is to be used for Academy rally or for East Side rally.

With the end of summer and the Supreme Court decision drawing near, they continued to rely on the Committee for hope and morale.

Sept. 7, 1952

Dear Manny,

In between sneezes brought on by my hay-fever allergy, I got to think about your health. After all I find it's very difficult to function on all cylinders mentally and spiritually when one is afflicted with bodily ailment. Ethel and I are concerned about you and we insist you take care of yourself. Remember sweet guy besides being our devoted friend we're counting on you to help save our lives. We hope by the time we see you that you will be feeling in the pink again and are not neglecting your physical condition. The best intentions and strongest will power have been frustrated by illness. Pretty please for our sake do take care . . .

Ethel will be writing you on the children's visit and I hope it won't be too much of a strain on them. From some of the news my brother brought me I can begin to discern a maturing of the campaign into a broad movement of all sections of the people who understand the deeper implications of our case and are working to secure justice for us as an important step in turning back the attack against civil liberties and the fight for peace. The political nature of our trial and sentence is evident to all who are acquainted with the facts and it's imperative to reach the public with this message. You have given us the best legal defense possible but only the court of public opinion can assure us the freedom that is rightfully ours. The effectiveness of the fight to save us will depend on the support we can get during this period while the high court is reviewing our petition for certiorari. I have confidence that our friends will not let us down with "too little and too late." Clarity of purpose and perspective will help guide those who are leading the campaign to take timely action. In the meantime we need news of progress to fortify our morale and strengthen our determination to keep on a high level our principled fight. You know make it a little easier for us, it's tough enough here.

Don't forget to give my best to your wife and to pop. Send my regards to all. I guess we'll be seeing you and the boys soon . . .

As ever,
JULIE

P.S. I don't mean to sound discouraged only I miss my boys and Ethel very much and at times my heart aches for them because I'm lonesome and worried about their welfare.

5

A New Home

LONG BEFORE ROBBY AND I were informed about it, Manny and others, including our parents, had decided to find another home for us. Certainly the growing publicity, the upsetting experiences I'd had in the neighborhood and the conclusion that our grandmother was not equal to the task all contributed to this decision.

Robby and I were given a trial run at the home of a nice woman whose name I've forgotten. We spent a pleasant weekend with her. She said that lots of children were around during the summer, and I immediately envisioned so many kids playing Cowboys and Indians that they could fall down dead (as happened on TV) and "stay down" until the game was over. True to form, I imagined myself the coordinator of the entire group. But we did not spend the summer with her.

Another weekend we stayed at the home of a New Jersey doctor who had a family of at least three kids. We kicked a soccer ball (probably a volleyball) around and saw the movie, *Bells on Their Toes.* I enjoyed that visit also. We wound up staying near Toms River, New Jersey, with Ben, a chicken-feed salesman, and Sonia Bach, personal friends of our parents. They had two children, Maxine, a college student, and Leo, a year younger than Robby. They told us that before Robby was born, my parents and I spent a summer at their cottage. A railroad track ran past my room; every morning the train sped by and woke us up. When Ben, Sonia and my parents entered my room, they found me standing up on my bed looking out the window at the train.

July 11, 1952

My Dearest Sons,

I was very much pleased by the nice letter I received from Michael. It warms my heart to know that you are having fun and getting along nicely. Just as your mother and I told you at our last visit and which you yourselves know we have many dear friends and there are lots of good people who are decent and are doing all they can to help us. Now my boys you are experiencing and understanding affection and love of two fine people Ben and Sonia who are not strangers. Therefore you should feel free to ask them for answers to any questions that are troubling you and I am sure you will get the right kind of response.

Since you are going to be busy having a good time going places and doing things and you may not find enough time to write to both Mommy and me I suggest you write to your mother and Wednesday when I visit with her she will be able to read me all the news you send her. Of course, I want you to know I am most interested in learning about the day camp, the swimming and all the activities that you and Robbie are indulging in. I'd like very much to be with you boys and your mother on vacation but that will have to wait until we win this case. In the meantime I want to assure you my children that I miss you very much and I love you with all my heart and we your parents will keep in touch to make certain that you are doing alright. Bubbie Sophie was up to see us and told us how you managed at home and I am very confident that you will have a wonderful summer vacation.

Don't forget to send my regards to Ben, Sonia, Leo and Maxine and all our other unknown friends. Remember sweethearts your job is to play, be happy and have fun and we your parents, Manny and other grownups will continue to work on our case to win our freedom. You have seen how confident we are so don't worry because many people are learning the facts of our innocence and are coming to our support. Before I forget I want you to know that we enjoyed our last visit very much and the next time I see my two dears we'll both have many good things to talk about. So let's hear good reports of your progress. As for me I'll keep on reading, writing, and working on our case and I am very confident that in time we will be reunited as one happy family as we have lived in the past. I'll talk to your mother and arrange with her for us to take turns writing you. Have fun kids the country is a wonderful place to be in the summertime. Perhaps it will be hard to recognize you what with all that sun, good food and nice people. So long for now —

DADDY — JULIE

Ben and Sonia were warm people who lavished physical affection on us, which we needed and responded to fully. Robby especially would climb into the lap of any woman even remotely hinting at such an invitation. Generally we were happy at the Bachs'. We had space to run, playmates and the security of attention from adults obviously stronger than Grandma. Also, the knowledge that Ben and Sonia were our parents' friends helped us to feel we were still surrounded by family. Leo, however, presented a source of conflict. Robby and I wanted *all* their attention, we didn't want to share it with anyone, even their son. In addition, Leo was just learning coordination. Robby, now five, began to play in the baseball games, but Leo was more often a spectator, a role I'm sure he resented. Thus, except for the times Robby and Leo were together without me, the relationship was distant. Robby and I were so close that whenever I left him to visit someone, see a Little League game or a movie, he waited up for me, worried that I might not come home.

But problems did not assert themselves until the pressure of events overwhelmed us. Our experiences with the Bachs in general were very happy. That summer we both went to a day camp in Lakewood. This time Robby was not too frightened to go, and we had a wonderful summer, though the first several days were unpleasant. I had an ordinary accident that happens to lots of kids. I pitched a softball to a counselor, and he slammed it back at me, hitting me on the forehead. I screamed in pain. Placing the tiniest circular Band-Aid on the offended section of skin, a doctor pronounced my head harder than the softball. Unfortunately, Robby's incident was more disquieting. Somehow he had gotten the idea that eating cold chicken would make him deaf. At the first lunch, cold chicken was served. He panicked, fearing he was being poisoned, and flung his fork the length of the table. At the other end of the table a three-year-old sat in the path of the fork. Luckily, the assistant camp director deflected it. Robby very quietly said, "The chicken's cold." The owner of the camp spanked him, not understanding that Robby suspected he'd been poisoned. Later, informed of the incident, I collared Robby out behind the softball field and brought him in to apologize to the director and assistant.*

During the summer our states of mind improved, though I reflected how I was feeling much more obviously than Robby did. He carefully concealed his anxieties, assuming it was simpler not to bother adults with his fears. It never really helped. He had asked many adults to bring his parents home, but they were never able to. The only thing they did was make an embarrassing fuss over him. If he didn't complain, everybody would think he was fine and leave him alone.

Gradually, Ben and Sonia introduced us to their friends in the radical Jewish community, all of whom supported the struggle for clemency in our parents' case. I'd learned my lesson in the Phil and Lawrence incident and didn't try to proselytize my neighbors' parents. Steve was my best friend in Toms River, and I didn't have to convince him of my parents' innocence, he being an ardent supporter. His brother was Robby's age, and we often visited them on their chicken farm. Robby was mesmerized by their egg sorter, trying to guess as the egg traveled down the conveyor belt which category — small, medium, large, jumbo — it would be. Sometimes we helped box the eggs after they'd been sorted. Steve was held up to me as a model to emulate. He ate heartily, weighed ninety pounds, while I limped along in the seventies. His parents allowed him to stay up much later than I could. A better, stronger athlete than I, he spent hours teaching me to field as we threw grounders and fly balls to each other. He could ride a two-wheeler, which I was never able to master, and he used *curse words*, which seemed very daring.

* He never explained his fear of cold chicken, and I never thought to ask. Many years later, he brought it up, and then I remembered his remark when he threw the fork.

After a summer of making friends, enjoying swimming, visiting our parents at least once and endlessly playing ball, Ben and Sonia popped a question that must have already been answered by Manny and my parents — would I like to stay with them and go to a Toms River school? I wanted to, but felt a little guilty about leaving Grandma. Searching for a specific reason to stay, I asked if basketball was played at the school. The Bachs replied in the affirmative. That did it. "Oh boy, sure I want to stay. I'd just love to throw the ball into that hoop." I'd never played basketball in my life; I just needed an excuse to assuage my conscience about Grandma.

While we were adjusting to the Bach family, our parents continued to wait for the Supreme Court, cheer on the Committee, and continue the family relationships.

Sept. 18, 1952

Sweetest Bunny,

I must say that your last epistle was a gem and moved me very much. Fundamentally so because of its keen insight in our situation and what the future holds for our case. You have an important gift that you must bring forth for others to see because you have now become integrated in a "case." This is a duty we owe to mankind for we possess the ability to poignantly present our cause in its most dramatic way especially as it affects the lives of our fellow Americans. This contribution to our fight we can make and we ought to work hard to do our part as we see it and as we are able to translate for all to know the facts. Of course we must do it at our own speed and in our own way but we have the stuff and the Committee can do a swell job with it.

The samples of the literature Manny sent us shows that the Committee is doing a splendid job and I'm feeling a lot better after seeing some of the results. In the last two days I've received two beautiful New Year's Cards, chosen in very good taste, that expressed all the typical warmth of my family wishes on this special occasion. There also was a letter from Lena and the wonderful letter from the boys. If we want to get these letters often we'll have to answer them as soon as possible. If you can see your way clear, after our boys visit us, drop them a line . . .

I'm well prepared for our visit with the boys this weekend and I've done as you suggested to insure that things will go off smoothly. As the day approaches my anxiety increases especially since I am hoping for a very positive and constructive visit for our two precious dears. Anyway we'll be able to celebrate the New Year by being together, even though it is under these difficult circumstances. Let us look forward to a year, when we will be delivered from all this misery and take up again the sweet family life we know and love so much. Our wishes and hopes are for a peaceful world because only in an atmosphere of calm can justice really triumph and can people enjoy a free democratic life. The coming year will be an important one of decision for us and many other people and we can enter it full of confidence knowing that we have progressed well in our campaign to win our freedom . . .

JULIE

September 25, 1952

Sweetest children,

You are exactly that, you know; since Saturday, I've been walking on air, remembering how you looked and what you said. How wonderfully satisfying it was to squeeze you in my arms and exchange loving kisses. As a matter of fact, I plan to have all the Rosenbergs, short and tall, fat and skinny, spend one solid week doing nothing else but, sometime in the near future, the nearer the better, of course! When Daddy was in to see me on Wednesday, we babbled like a couple of kids ourselves, marveling first over one of you and then over the other, and we dearly wish for you to know how proud we are of the fine job both of you are doing, each in his own individual way, just the most worthwhile job anyone, be it adult or child, *can* do — that of growing and changing and developing, into healthy, happy people . . .

All my love —
MOMMY —

Sept. 28, 1952

Dearest children,

What a glorious day it was to celebrate a birthday. I awoke to find a gold sun bright in a clear blue sky. A mild breeze wafted in gently from the Hudson and it was heavenly good to fill the lungs with sweet, fresh air. Overhead the sea gulls floated by on indolent, gray wings, and only the sound of the starlings, possibly scolding, broke the all-pervading stillness. I walked quickly about the peaceful yard, stopping every now and then to inspect the bits of green stuff struggling up through the cracks in the concrete, and trying to imagine what you two might be up to, this fine morning! My goodness, I thought, that's right; I am 37 years old today, old enough to have chalked up to my credit a grand family, a worthwhile life, and a host of wonderful friends; old enough also to realize why I must spend my birthday alone, but strong enough, too, to know without any doubt whatever, that those artificially induced storms about which Ben told you, will at long last no longer be permitted to rage at the expense of decent mankind. This day I spend apart from loved ones is all the proof I need that there is no loneliness too great to withstand, no task too difficult of accomplishment, for the establishment of that kind of world that will give all peoples the opportunity to live and work and grow together, in love and in dignity and in peace! Know then, my two dearest dears, that bitterly as I missed you, (and there's no two ways about it, I'll have to go on missing you until we're all together at last), know then that I was gladdened because I understood the necessity to accept my responsibility for your dear sakes, just as it warmed me to remember all the other countless parents who are standing up for their families! Our precious children deserve no less than that! . . .

Robby, darling, would you please make a few pictures for me? I should like very much a drawing of the "wolfie" and the bear with the long nails, and the one of the doorknob and the two bell buttons. And you, Mike, honey, compose a poem — or if you'd rather draw something, too, I should be delighted. Such presents would bring you closer to me and make me ever so happy!

Your Daddy is fine and sends all his love — And so does your Mommy! — X X X X X X X X X X X X X X X X X X X X

The school year was a good one for me. Robby had a half-day introduction to it in kindergarten, though his experience wasn't very positive. He felt out of it, a stranger in the class, and spent a great deal of time assessing which of his classmates were bullies, whom he should avoid, and which would be fun to play with. He napped and finger-painted with them, but didn't feel a part of the class.

As the year progressed, I took pride in excelling in my studies and was gratified that the teacher seemed to like me. I wasn't having "talking out of turn" problems. It occurred to me that the odd school years — first, third and fifth grades — were exceptional for me. (My discipline problems began in the second grade, when our family was still together.) The most important lessons I learned in fifth grade were the value of keeping my mouth shut and the pervasiveness of anti-Communism in America. My friend Steve was a vociferous class participant. He invoked the ire of the teacher, who put him down, calling him "Big Mouth." The teacher good-naturedly kidded me with names like Herman and Murgatroyd. I enjoyed the friendly attention but wondered if he were poking fun at me.

He explained the Soviet dictatorship and its one-party system. "Stalin could vote for himself; even if nobody else did, he'd win." Surprisingly, the specifics of the Korean war were not discussed in school. (The son of the Bachs' landlord was killed in the war, and the family sat shiva for the required period. I wondered if they believed Judge Kaufman's sentencing speech blaming my parents for the war — and, consequently, their son's death.) To illustrate the superiority of the American political system, the teacher drew a ballot on the board, using four party headings — Republican, Democrat, Socialist, Communist — demonstrating that we gave the voters choices. He did not mention that the Communist Party was all but illegal in the United States and was not allowed on the ballot. From personal experience I knew too well that Communists were hated. Ben was once harshly questioned by one of his business associates about his efforts on my parents' behalf, "Now

Bloch, hasn't he got Communist affiliations?" Assuming a Socialist was less offensive than a Communist, I interrupted the interrogation with a question of my own. "Ben, you're not a Communist, you're a Socialist, aren't you?" I'm sure I didn't help. In fact, some time during or after our stay with the Bachs, Ben lost his job.

During the 1952 presidential election I rooted for the Progressive Party candidates, Vincent W. Hallinan and Charlotta Bass, who I was certain would grant clemency, but I also knew deep down that they didn't have a chance. So my next hope was Stevenson, who I thought would be more willing than Eisenhower to grant clemency. In school, while publicly supporting Stevenson, Steve and I whispered conspiratorially for "Vinnie and Charley."

In addition to school, Robby and I attended Shule* which stressed Jewish history and culture, and Yiddish. We even performed Yiddish plays. Our Shule was radical, our teacher having marched in the May Day Parade. She once lectured us on the terrible new law — the McCarran-Walter Immigration Act — which threatened mass deportations. Mostly, however, we learned about the Maccabean Rebellion and sang World War II resistance songs, such as the song of the Warsaw Ghetto uprising. There was no formal religious indoctrination about the existence of a Supreme Being, and my irreligious tendency, submerged at Grandma Tessie's and Bubbie's, began to reassert itself. In this context I was ambivalent about morning Bible reading in school. Each morning one of us read a passage, usually from the First, Twenty-third or One-hundredth Psalm. Once a substitute teacher came in and requested a reading from the New Testament. It was my turn, and I found myself reading from the Gospel according to John. Some friends violently signaled me as if I were doing something wrong. When I finished reading, they explained that Jews shouldn't read from the New Testament because we don't accept Jesus Christ as the son of God. I didn't know what they were talking about, but by the next day our teacher had returned and we went back to reading from the Old Testament which belonged to Christians and Jews alike.

* A Jewish cultural school.

Through the Shule our circle of friends widened. Robby and I visited at other people's houses; friends, relatives and Committee supporters from New York called on us at the Bachs'. We considered ourselves part of a community.

Nevertheless, despite our generally happy lives, whenever Manny Bloch showed up, we clung to him from the minute he arrived until he left. Manny was our strong link to our parents, practically an extension of them. We could sense their warmth and love transmitted through him to us. We also continued to enjoy the visits to Sing Sing, though we have no particular memory of the one which prompted this letter:

October 2, 1952

Dear Michael & Robert,

Your Mummy and I have made a sort of arrangement to try to alternate in writing you letters in order for you to be informed as to how happy we were to visit with you and we certainly enjoyed talking to you and playing games. Mike please keep us informed of how you are doing at school with your studies and how you spend your time. Of course it was fun doing the arithmetic problems and discussing history and geography. I like your singing Robbie and had a good time playing mousie and pussy cat with you.

Please thank Sonia and Ben for the lovely New Year's card. I was very pleased to receive one from them. These past two weeks I've been very busy reading the trial record. At this time I'm making thorough notes in order to discuss pertinent questions with our dear friend and distinguished counselor Manny Bloch. The Committee made a very good move in printing copies of the entire trial proceeding. An impartial reading of the facts in the case will bare the monstrous miscarriage of justice that has been perpetrated as a political frame-up against the freedom of the American people. This is a threat to create a paralyzing fear throughout our land so that the evil forces, who would do away with us can have a free hand. Since we want you our sons to live in peace, to play, learn and grow in security we continue as always even in this very difficult position, to fight for these principles. Because it is in the interests of all people mankind is rallying in its multitudes to secure the peace and the democratic ways we hold dear and since our case is an integral part of the bigger fight they will also come to our aid.

The Committee has outlined an ambitious program which if successful can insure a victory in this campaign. The coming months are the most crucial ones and only vigorous, relentless, concerted activities now will be timely in helping us get public support to win our freedom. It is imperative that the record be gotten into the hands of public leaders in all walks of life and that the facts & issues of this case reach millions of people. We are optimistic that with this kind of support we'll get *certiorari* and be able to prove our innocence and eventually be completely vindicated. I am sure Ben and Sonia will be able to explain all this to you in a way you will be able to understand. Let us keep on hearing good reports from you our precious children. Don't worry we your parents will be together with you again when this is all over.

All my love —
DADDY — JULIE

About this time, we became very friendly with Emily and Dave Alman, who had been instrumental in creating and spreading the National Committee to Secure Justice in the Rosenberg Case. The Almans had not met our parents and never would, in spite of repeated efforts to obtain permission to visit them in prison. We saw a lot of them, when they weren't working their heads off for the Committee. Their two daughters, Michelle — I called her Shelley — and Jennifer, were roughly our ages. Shelley became my girlfriend — she was an excellent ballplayer — and I would always give her a big kiss when she arrived and when she left. There are other visitors from the Committee with whom we have remained friendly.

As fall turned into winter, we were restricted in outdoor playing, so we crammed in as much baseball as possible before dark. I noticed Robby's peculiar habit after catching the ball of precariously balancing it in his glove and trying to throw it. I couldn't drum it into his head that he was supposed to toss the ball with his bare hand, not his glove. Then it dawned on me that he was a *lefty,* and was wearing a right-handed mitt on his left hand. I taught him to catch the ball in the glove, throw the glove down and then peg the ball with his unencumbered left hand. The following summer the Bachs bought him a lefty's glove.

Indoors now most of the evening, we needed to keep ourselves occupied. "Monopoly" got tiresome but not playing chess with Ben. I also read books and Classic Comics. Inevitably, perhaps, I began to ask for a television set. (The miracle is that my addiction had not produced withdrawal symptoms when we moved to the Bachs'.) They conceded; soon we were immersed in "Howdy Doody" and "Captain Video." TV quickly conflicted with our routine, as they had had us going to bed early, which now meant *before* "Captain Video" was over. If we had no other plans, Robby and I sat glued to the set in the face of Ben and Sonia's disapproval. Observers noted that we watched TV clinging to our penises for dear life. Obviously, despite living with a fine family, all was not well.

Throughout 1952 and 1953, I was well aware of the progress of the appeals and the step-by-step realization of my nightmare prediction. I followed the *National Guardian* as avidly as my parents did, even writing the *Guardian* a letter to thank them for their aid, pleading, "Don't let my parents die." I was less communicative by mail with my parents. Actually, Ben wrote most of the letters over my signature, though a few were real, handwriting and all. Our visits were most important. During one of these reunions, with publicity mounting about the case, we noticed the photographers. Though Manny did not cover our faces, hustle us into the car, etc., and though Cedric Belfrage, editor of the *Guardian,* along for some of the visits, remembers that I used to shout and yell at the reporters about my parents' innocence without any apparent fear, both Manny and I were afraid. We hoped nobody would recognize us. (Robby detested the photographers to the extent that he has blocked out the memory of their presence.) I was scared of being found out. After all, I was Michael Rosenberg and Bernard Bach was signing my report card.

In class the teacher had once asked me where my parents were.

On the spur of the moment I lied, saying that they were on a world tour and would be away for more than a year. Ira, a neighbor and classmate, asked me to have them send a picture postcard. One day I asked to keep my report card long enough to show my parents who were "passing through." The teacher agreed and I took it to Sing Sing to show it off.

The school-bus driver recognizing my photograph in the paper reported me to the school authorities. The Superintendent of Schools called Ben in. When Ben showed him my report card, he remarked, "Very bright boy." That seemed to be the end of it, except now I was afraid of admitting my last name. Also, the special teachers (music and art were taught by roving teachers who came into class several hours each week) now called me by name, distinguishing me from the rest of the class whose names they didn't know. Steve thought this was sinister, and I fought to brush away his fears. I couldn't ignore Ira's question about my parents' names. "Esther and Julie," I answered. (At birth my mother had been named Esther Ethel.) He would have none of it. "They call her Ethel, don't they?" Another friend inquired, "Hey, Mike, any relation to those two spies?" That was tough. I answered, "No," reasoning that they weren't spies, so I was not related to spies. But I realized that I was denying them and hated myself for it.

Throughout this period my parents were still waiting for justice — more than eighteen months had passed since their trial. Dr. ———— mentions that our mother greatly worried about what would happen to Robby and me during her long incarceration. Also, they recognized that the government might exploit their executions politically — "to show the world that they're the masters, they're unyielding and will not listen to world opinion because they feel that might be a suggestion of weakness." Somehow they remained optimistic.

June 2, 1952

My Adorable Darling,

. . . Rain! Rain and more rain and after reading newspaper all day I fell into a drugged sleep. It has been my experience that after a visit with Manny, the family or you I reach such an emotional peak that when I lie down on my bed to rest for a few minutes I doze off. The funny thing about it is that after I wake up I feel so tired as if I've done a hard day's work with a pick and shovel. Since I am so emotionally starved when I do get my satisfaction it is at such a rapid rate that I feel completely drained when it's over. Anyhow I'm awake now and feeling good that in a couple of days I'll be seeing your beautiful face again. . . .

Sweetheart I looked up at the picture of our little Robbie standing in front of his sweet Grandma. Ethel what I saw moved me so. There was my beloved Yiddish mother full of compassion, aged with experience pain and hardships and yet a symbol of courage and strength. We have so much to look forward to and it is so important for our loved ones and all Americans that we win a decisive victory in our case. I'm optimistic and with each passing day I feel more certain that we'll get the justice that is rightfully ours because many people are rallying to our support. It is gratifying to see how enthusiastic my brother and sister become as they become aware of the great extent of help the public is giving us. The positive result is in itself the precursor of more and greater progress in the campaign to win a new trial and eventual freedom. We must take new courage from our new-found friends because they have made the issues clear to the public and the frame-up is exposed and all around people will fight for decency and right. —

ALL MY LOVE   YOUR JULIE

"With criminals it's quite different. They expect to be executed. I don't think your mother expected to die." With these words, Dr. ———— dismissed the "martyr" theory of my parents' unwillingness to confess to lies as the Greenglasses had done. Despite their optimism, the long separation from family and friends weighed heavily. Sometimes they succumbed to depression.

Sept. 15, 1952

Sweetest Julie,

I expect what I wish to say in reply to your letter of the 14th, shall require but a very few lines and shall therefore make it less difficult for you to receive before we meet on Wednesday. My darling, more and more I tend to withdraw into the deepest recesses of myself, stimulated to emerge fully only when you are with me; and yet I am moved by your poignantly expressed need, to attempt to communicate with you, even in the absence of your physical being. Day by day our separation grows the more bitterly intolerable; day by day, the assault upon mind and spirit grows the more viciously insistent. The fact that no degree of pressure will ever cause us to repudiate those principles of democracy that sit beleaguered with us behind these repugnant bars, does not in any way mitigate the heartbreak we suffer nor render less culpable the refusal to alleviate it to some more comparable degree. Wait, wait and tremble, ye mad masters, this barbarism, this infamy you practice upon us, and with which you regale yourselves presently; so gleefully, will not go unanswered, unavenged, forever! The whirlwind gathers, before which you must fly like chaff!

Sweetheart I love you with a strength that defies my pain —
Still, hold me close, my heart is so heavy with wanting you —

Always,
YOUR OWN WIFE

6

Waiting for Justice

ON OCTOBER 13, 1952, the Supreme Court denied *certiorari*. This did not imply the Court affirmed the conviction. As Justice Frankfurter wrote at the time, "It means, and all that it means, is that there were not four members of the Court to whom the grounds on which the decision of the Court of Appeals was challenged seemed sufficiently important when judged by the standards governing the issue of the discretionary writ of *certiorari*." In other words, denial of *certiorari* is a denial of the review, *not* a review and denial on the merits of the appeal. Judge Kaufman then fixed the execution date for the week of January 12, 1953. The intensity and length of their letters reflect the increased pressure after the Supreme Court denied a rehearing in November. In truth, one might say that they were all but executed in January and February of 1953.

Oct. 13, 1952

My very dear one, my darling,

The plot stands exposed at last in all its ugly nakedness, in all its pusillanimous rottenness. Again political necessity has overruled due process!

My sweet, understand me well; there grows within me now a deep calm a power such as I never knew I should ever be capable of possessing. Only I was in such a state of shock and daze that my brain only began to function clearly too late to do full justice at this time to the barrage of ideas and words that demand expression. Suffice it then to quote just these lines from a letter I am sending Lena:

"The bow is tempered, however by the knowledge that there is yet time for much to be done. And so I write to earnestly beg you not to squander this time in too many useless tears, not to permit yourself to be stamped by anything you might hear or read. The hate-mongers, you know we have always with us: please know that they leave me quite unimpressed. Mark my words; you will now begin to see an avalanche of protest! You see, Lee, strange as it may seem to you, it is "they" who are afraid, it is *we* who have the powers to dismay *them* if we will but believe in ourselves and mass our full might for decency and justice!" My deepest, strongest love,

Your Wife Always
Ethel

Oct. 16, 1952

Beautiful Woman,

Unfortunately you do not see all the newspapers that I have access to, for if you were able to read them you would note that just as you said, that an avalanche of protest already has begun to materialize. From a line here a bit of statement there one can gather that we are receiving a considerable amount of support in our efforts to get a hearing before the Supreme Court. It is important not to lose heart for one moment because as soon as the volume of public clamor reaches sizable proportions they will be forced to grant us our day in court. I am not dismayed by the weakness certain so-called liberals and progressives show because at every crucial point where they must take a determined stand and act on it they take a defeated position. Again they deluded themselves with the false idea that it is possible to buy immunity by being against certain key progressive issues and claim look we're against the communist, the progressives, the Rosenbergs and they even equivocate when it comes to the question of peace and war. Strange as it seems I too feel calmer and more determined because I have my self-respect and I feel stronger knowing that we have consistently conducted ourselves with dignity according to the principles of decency and democracy. The job of getting the facts and issues of our case before the American people is a very difficult one but the latest action of the highest court in our country will make it easier to get the facts before the public . . .

JULIE

They both sought to calm our fears as well as their own.

Oct. 16, 1952

My dearest, darling children,

Forgive me for not having written you at once, but my heart simply rebelled at the thought of breaking your innocent ones. Gradually, however, I have come to the realization that since we have all been living with this situation for some time, and since the devoted people around you must certainly have assumed full responsibility for handling your disappointment with tenderness and understanding, my continued silence in the face of tidings of which you were already fully aware, would accomplish nothing so much as to heighten your anxiety. Besides, once the first shock had worn off and I was my usual calm self again, I wanted ever so much to speak with you and to reassure you about us both.

Daddy was in to see me on Wednesday, the same cheerful smiling Daddy as he ever was, and was delighted to find that my spirits matched his own. He did not waste any of the precious time, you may well believe, but settled right down to map out the next phase of the campaign. In a day or so, we shall have ample opportunity to exchange plans and ideas with Manny Bloch, who, and you may rely on it, will leave no stone unturned, no legal avenue unexplored, to see that justice is truly done.

Your mother, (I hope you have gathered from the above) is in a fighting mood; and while some tears must be shed (and you should feel perfectly free to relieve yourselves in whatever way you need to), I'd like to be able to feel that I have conveyed if only in some small measure my own confidence, and have lent my children some small degree of comfort and encouragement. Nor am I faking this confidence; trust me that it is wonderfully real and strong!

Only one thing bothers me; I am never able to fully express in words, how very, very much I love you. And Daddy agrees that he, too, has that difficulty! Please know that we are both fine and will continue to keep in close touch with you.

Again, let nothing dismay you; there's much to be done, and we are rolling up our sleeves to do it! —

Our best regards, our deepest love —

Always,
YOUR LOVING MOMMY

Oct. 23, 1952

Dearest Michael & Robert,

. . . Ethel told you the news of what is happening in her last letter to you and like all things the news isn't always good. Up until this point the legal results, that is in the courts, have been against us but as you know the important part of the fight, winning the support of public opinion is beginning to reach such proportions that it will force the courts to review our case.

It is not good to burden you children with problems that are not yours and are beyond your comprehension and therefore when Manny visits you next he will read you parts of my letter that you will be able to understand and explain as much of the situation as possible.

One thing must be crystal clear and that is that our case if allowed to stand is a very great threat directed at the heart of the progressive movement and it is an integral part of the conspiracy to establish fear in our land. The political nature of the frame-up is obvious and the facts must be presented to expose to public attention the danger that this holds to those who fight for peace.

You my precious sons must continue to study, play, have fun and keep well. The news of your accomplishments and your doings warms my heart and makes me happy to know that you are in very good hands.

Even though the autumn breeze, blowing from the Hudson River keeps our exercise yard quite cool I sure miss my fresh air. I still manage to play a vigorous game of handball or boxball every day. From the scores of the games I can say in all modesty I do well for myself. The signs of the changing season are all around us. The wind blows leaves and seeds over the wall and it's interesting to watch the maple tree seeds spinning down slowly because the attached half wing gives it lift, making it look like a helicopter. All around us are the freshness and vigor of life and we sense it here but above all we are closest to the world we know and love, when we hear from you, and see you, and read the National Guardian and visit with my family.

I see Ethel regularly and I can say we are both well & calm. You know your Mommy and Daddy and we repeat to you we will not let you down and we will continue to discharge our responsibilities to you our precious children and to our brothers and sisters, who are fighting for peace, decency and justice. We are confident we'll be set free and be together with you again. So be patient and let's each of us do our job and keep smiling darlings. All my hearts love —

YOUR DADDY — JULIE

Then the Court refused to reconsider its original ruling on November 17. My father wrote my mother that day.

Dearest Ethel,

The Supreme Court failed to redeem itself but persisted in acquiescing to this growing madness. Mass pressure is the only thing that will restore the bill of rights, maintain the constitutional liberties and save our lives. Take hope darling the avalanche of protest we predicted will come now. We are not alone and the significance of our case is being understood by ever increasing numbers of people. Their actions in our behalf will be the answer.

After I heard the news broadcast I reread your letter of the 13th of Oct. and found your analysis very appropriate and applicable to the instant action. Then I read the letter from France again and together they gave me new strength . . .

I am calm, confident and prepared to contribute my all to the campaign to win us justice. Keep your courage up sweetheart the toughest part of the fight is here now.

Since the pressures will become greater as time passes I

propose we give all of our visit over to our personal problems. I've prepared my few remarks in concise form to give you most of the time.

I am sure that my family will devote their efforts working to save us and therefore I am not going to write them at this point. Before the week is out we should get some indication of how the wind is blowing . . .

You are ever present in my mind and my heart is all for you. Every night when I go to bed I hug you close to me and feel at one with you. Although we are apart I am positive we are one in mind and spirit and that is what really counts. Remember sweetheart I am completely devoted to you and I love you more than anything else in the world because you symbolize so much that is good.

We are not deluding ourselves for we are still to go through more agony and greater kinds of hell before this nightmare is over. I have no doubts that we will come through in flying colors. The enemy does not know the source of such determination and strength. We however understand and are confident.

Keep your peace of mind my love and that pretty smile on your beautiful face and I know all will be well —

Your husband and greatest admirer
JULIE

Nov. 23, 1952

Dearest Ethel,

You already know that the "honorable" Judge has ordered that we remain alive for only 50 odd more days. I'm sure we'll confound him again for before the ink was dry on his order our lawyer began to fight back with the various legal steps we've talked about. . . .

Now that the issue is being drawn in its crucial stage the hirelings of the Hearst press have spewed forth some additional fabrications, products of whiskey-soaked brains, to hurt our fight. It seems to me that there exists in our country a "phantom" Goebbels type general staff with representatives on major newspapers whose purpose it is to act as the theoretical section of neo-fascism and use its technique, anti-communism distortions, professional stool pigeons and constant repetition of big lies. . . . They are not alone for they often receive editorial support from their papers . . .

. . . Again I'm hesitant about writing our boys and I'll have to let it go until I think I can do justice to all that I want to tell them . . .

YOUR JULIE

Beginning on November 28 and continuing for a full month my father wrote many long letters to Manny Bloch that he hoped would be the basis of a "personal statement," an analysis, a picture of what he is like. These letters are much too long to be included in their entirety.

Dear Manny,

I know I have a heavy responsibility, a duty to the people to contribute my all to the common struggle for peace and decency. But, I have been held back because I feel inadequate to the task, for I want to be worthy of the faith and support of my fellowmen.

It is very difficult for me to know just where to begin. Therefore, I've decided to write a running account of my thoughts as I get them. Note, the date will be based on the remaining days that are left us as decreed by the death sentence of our Government.

This will be no polished manuscript, rewritten with an eye to grammar, style or even completely coherent. Therefore, please consider my weaknesses and human frailties and I'll just put down my ideas as they occur.

I'd like this to be a conversation between me and the reader, whoever he or she may be and as I go along I'll tell you dear person why I take the liberty to communicate with you.

Our Government through the instrumentality of one of its Federal Judges Irving R. Kaufman has decreed that my wife and I be put to death in 45 days . . .

Suppose we look into this espionage business.

On P. 19 of Martin's book* is found the following:

"In 1940, 1941 and 1942 ships leaving American seaports had had the same security measures to protect their departure. Yet many of their broken hulls and water-soaked cargoes had washed up onto the beaches of New Jersey, Virginia and the Carolinas, where German submarines had spotted them within sight of shore. In case after case, every man on board had been marked before the Captain opened his orders. Though they may not have known it, the cargoes they carried were reinsured with Munich. The routine system of placing insurance had put precise information on their sailing date and destination in the hands of the Germans before the ship left port."

All industrial plants were reinsured and full reports by insurance inspectors including blueprints of the installations, description of the fire hazards and risks, and inventory of the contents of the buildings, room by room. One example cited of plans for a large new magnesium plant with one of the blueprints having an arrow pointing at a valve with the legend "Under no circumstances must this valve be closed while the plant is in operation, an explosion would result."

All these activities during war and peace time come well within the scope of the Espionage Act. However these gentlemen were fraternity brothers, "honorable" men, they were never indicted. However, on no documentary, we were charged with conspiracy to commit espionage because we always spoke and worked for peace and exposed these plutocrats.

What about the death sentence?

I think you should read Brig. General Telford Taylor's book "Doctors of Infamy." He was the chief prosecutor of the leading representatives of German medicine during a war crimes trial. I know you will find it very difficult to keep from retching when you read of these revolting, barbaric, monstrous atrocities. There were a number of very lengthy and famous trials such as the Nuremburg war crimes trials that documented the facts of their overwhelming guilt. However, only a minute number ever paid fully for their crimes. The members of the

---

* *All Honorable Men*, by James Stewart Martin, on the role of the German cartels in Hitler's regime and the failure of de-cartelization after World War II.

fraternity did not allow justice to take its course. Under their aegis slight legal technicalities were found to stop the trials of war criminals. Then they commuted the death sentences of these convicted criminals, released them from prison because thousands of these individuals were needed once again to take their places as errand boys doing the dirty work of the "honorable" men.

This is the kind of equal justice under the law our Government metes out. And we have only 43 more days left to live.

During the course of my testimony I stated in court that I believed the Russians carried the brunt of the war and that the allies should open a second front. This didn't go well with the court but if a second front had been opened sooner the Nazis would not have had time to exterminate 6,000,000 Jewish people and millions of other victims of fascism. At Page 1079 of the trial record I gave the following testimony. "and in discussing the merits of other forms of governments, I discussed that with my friends on the basis of the performance of what they accomplished, and I felt that the Soviet Government has improved the lot of the underdog there, has made a lot of progress in eliminating illiteracy, has done a lot of reconstruction work and built up a lot of resources, and at the same time I felt that they contributed a major share in destroying the Hitler beast who killed 6,000,000 of my co-religionists, and I feel emotional about that thing.

Q. Did you feel that way in 1945? A. Yes, I felt that way in 1945.

Q. Do you feel that way today? A. I still feel that way."

The court didn't like this they wanted me to confess to crimes I did not do, to bear false witness against innocent people and to allow myself to be used as a tool to create anti-Soviet and anti-Communist propaganda to add to the hysteria and the cold war. I would not allow myself to be used even for propaganda purposes to increase the tensions between the United States and Russia. Only better relations between these two countries can benefit the peoples of both lands and insure world peace.

The only documentary evidence produced by the Government to tie us up with this case was a tin collection can. "Save a

Spanish Republican Child" and our lawyer in summation said hollow, hollow like the case against the Rosenbergs for in no way can anyone infer any connection to espionage.

This can was supposed to be used to collect funds to aid the innocent victims of the fascist butcher Franco. We admit we are ardent anti-fascists. Not only did we donate money to help refugees but we collected funds and signed petitions to aid the Republican cause.

I remember when the rebellion broke in Spain and my wife and I decided to help them. Ethel had studied voice. She is a coloratura soprano and she sings beautifully. Since I studied Spanish in college I taught her the words to two songs. Tango de las Rosas and Ay-ay-ay. Then together with a few of our friends we went to Times Square on Saturday night. Ethel sang these two Spanish songs and No Pasaran and the rest of us held the corners of a Spanish Republican flag. The people contributed generously, coins and dollar bills. The public was overwhelmingly in favor of the Republican Spanish cause. However, the fraternity brothers were on the side of Franco while we fought fascism. For this we are condemned with 42 more days left to live . . .

The going was very rough and our father interrupted his writing to send the following note of hope to our mother on X minus 43 days.

Nov. 30, 1952

Dearest Ethel,

Ever since Manny's last visit I've been going through a state I am sure you are very familiar with. My conscience and my mind tells me it's my duty to write and very often at that but here's the rub even though I know it, I feel inadequate to the task. I've begun and stopped at least three times daily since Friday and at the same time I've denied myself the pleasure of going into any new books. Over and over again I tell myself I'll do the best I can but it is coming harder than pulling teeth . . .

. . . I must say that I'm elated that our affidavit was successful in getting Kaufman to disqualify himself from hearing the motion. This is our first victory in 2 and ½ years of legal efforts and is only an indication of how far we've come already to have this motion granted without going to a higher court. Even more important at this point is the kind of support we're getting at home and abroad. The Committee is doing a terrific job and so is Manny. It was just wonderful to read this week's National Guardian a storehouse of comfort and inspiration. So principled a policy and clear in its efforts to mobilize public opinion behind the campaigns that are of cardinal importance to the people's interest. I was particularly moved by the poem that appeared about the children. For it was exactly like it happened.

Darling wife the avalanche you predicted 19 months ago is here and they have taken us to their hearts and are going all out in our behalf because they are awake to the great danger to all if this miscarriage of justice is not rectified. We can take heart because this is the true barometer of the people's feelings and this will guarantee that we live and win complete vindication.

Of course, there is still a long fight ahead with the most important hurdles yet to be overcome but I have more confidence than ever that we'll succeed no matter what the obstacles are. Too bad my love I had to seek inspiration by proxy from you when you in the flesh, right here beside me is the best kind of stimulant. I am impatiently awaiting our next tête-à-tête at our favorite screen . . .

. . . Devoted as ever —

JULIE

Three days later he resumed his opus to Manny Bloch, and through him to the public.

. . . On this 40th day left to live I want to talk about some of the servants of the abattoir such as the pen hirelings of big business. As you know it takes large sums of money to own a newspaper and it depends on advertising for the revenue needed to keep on operating. Though control of the technical means in the newspaper business such as; newsprint, paper, the large news services and by the very practical lever of paid advertisements, which is tantamount to a mortgage, the fraternity brothers control and in the main dominate the editorial and news slanting policies of the so-called "free" press. For practical purposes it is not necessary to be too rigid nevertheless, finesse is needed to hoodwink the readers.

To effectively determine just where the press stands we have to know what its position is on the key issues of the day and the main orientation of its program.

Where do they stand on the cartels? Are they fighting the policies of imperialism that up to date has been responsible for the shrunken bodies, the swollen bellies of children, poverty, disease and hunger, short stunted lives devoid of all but the most meager means to maintain body and soul much less the ability to raise the moral, mental and cultural standards of the colonial people? Are they supporting every moral for their national liberation so that these men and women can determine for themselves their own form of government can appropriate to themselves a larger share of their national wealth and above all walk with human dignity as free people masters of their own destiny? Or do they support the robber barons in their merciless exploitation, degradation and racist policy against the interests of these people. No amount of prettied up high-sounding phrases about the need for raw materials, numeral wealth and strategic positions against the bogey man communism can justify imperialism in any form.

Where do they stand on peace and coexistence? Are they fighting militarization, alliances with every fascist and reactionary regime, superweapons that are only of an offensive nature, jingoistic programs and bellicose statements that are made in the guise of national security while preparing and concentrating massive means of aggression? Are they supporting "agreements" that only mean surrender to the program of finance capital? Are their policies only based on anti-communist belligerent propaganda?

Where do they stand on the living standard of the people? Are they fighting the policies of big business that imposes increasing burdens on the common people and in effect lowers their living standards? Or do they under the cloak of patriotism use witch hunts to harass labor unions and decrease the purchasing power of the people?

Where do they stand on Liberty and the Constitutional Rights? Are they going along with the hue and cry that the legal rights of communists can be breached because of their politics? That those accused as reds not be allowed to teach in the schools, speak on the radio, write in the press, earn a living, because they hold unpopular views. The law of the land is that everybody must be protected equally by the Bill of Rights and if not it is only a worthless piece of paper.

The truth is that practically the entire press does the bidding of the fraternity brothers of the cartels on these key points. The so-called liberal New York Post occupies the left flank of this group and prints weasel philosophical excuses for the need to go along with the tide. Of course they raise pious voices on some revolting reactionary measures but never on a principle of fundamentally deep basis because their job is to influence the liberal, labor and progressive people to support the government policy that is leading to war.

We'll discuss this paper's actions on our case after we talk about this topic on this 39th day we have left to live.

It has been heralded by our enemies that we claim we were convicted because we were Jews and that we are raising a false issue of anti-Semitism to win support for our cause.

Here are the plain hard facts:

1) From the very beginning, starting with our arrest and going through the trial, the various appeals, reading the trial record and all our letters and statements it is crystal clear that we never said nor intimated that we were selected out and convicted because we were Jews. No amount of semantic gyrations, distortions, or words out of context can change this truth.

2) After our sentence the *National Guardian* a progressive weekly through a series of articles by William A. Reuben brought to public attention the background facts and reviewed the case. This led to the formation of the National Committee to Secure Justice in the Rosenberg case. They were convinced we are completely innocent and then went to work; presented the facts and held meetings.

3) Prior to the organization of this committee this was the chronology of the actual origin of the charge of anti-Semitism. The first and basic charges of anti-Semitism appeared in the anti-communist Yiddish press.

(a) *Jewish Daily Forward* — April 5th editorial and article by Hillel Rogoff in April 12, 1951 and *Jewish Day* editorials April 6 & 8. These papers voiced disapproval of Judge Kaufman's unprecedented death sentence that he handed down on April 15, 1951.

(b) M. Danzis — *Day* editor on April 12, 1951 said "One cannot overlook the Jewish element in this unfortunate tragic Rosenberg trial."

Hi Leivik — a poet in an article in the *Jewish Day* on April 16th said, "the Judge should have been free from the Jewish complex." In the same vein a column was written by Dr. G. George Fox, Chicago-Rabbi columnist for the Sentinel.

(c) Therefore, the Rosenberg committee did not create this issue or first note anti-Semitism in the case. They only brought to public knowledge the existence of these statements and pointed out the appearance of anti-Semitic strikes and literature about the Rosenbergs as "Jew-Communist-atom-spy." * For they as well as Jewish leaders realized that the case has potentialities not only for a dreadful anti-Semitic wave, but also for grave danger to the elementary liberties of the American people as a whole.

4) When it became evident that the public and especially the Jewish community were waking up to the implications of the case and were reacting to this gross miscarriage of justice, some self-appointed leaders of Jewish organizations took on the role of an American Judenrat to disrupt and abort the growing movement. To do this a great myth was created. Oliver "Pontius" Pilat, New York *Post* reporter planted the germ.** He made the

---

* Even in 1974, Attorney General Saxbe publicly made the identification of Jews with left-wing activities. Also, Richard Nixon, in ordering his 1972 presidential campaign not to try reaching people connected with the arts, said, "They're Jews, they're left wing." Anti-Semitism is not dead yet.

** Oliver Pilat wrote many vicious and false articles about my parents for the New York *Post* and then put them together in a book published in 1952 called *The Atom Spies*. Later, when some papers stolen from David Greenglass' lawyer were sent (from France) to Manny Bloch, it was discovered, among other things, that Pilat was a secret public

accusation and tried to establish his lie, prima facie, as a fact, that we claim we were convicted because we were Jews and because of anti-Semitism. The egg was then laid in a New York Post editorial to add credence to this non-existent invention. A febrile attempt to further clothe this illegitimate offspring with some semblance of fact was made by S. Andhill-Fineberg paid bureaucrat of the American Jewish Committee by stating again this charge with some added twists. The fabricator based his "objective research job" on reports in the New York Times and on Pilat's book. This was published in a 9-page single-spaced memorandum $9/10$ of which was a diatribe against communists and was not based on the actual source material the trial record, our letters and statements but on oft repeated anti-communist charges . . .

I'll tell you about our relationship with our children. Just one incident will serve as an illustration. At night before I used to leave my machine shop I used to call home. My three year old little Robbie would answer the phone and I heard his happy exclamation. "Is that our Daddy" — "Yes baby" I replied. "How's my big fellow," and he went on, "Bring home cherry o'nilla ice cream and one milk." Later as I came through the door with my arms laden down with purchases the boys would give me a boisterous affectionate welcome and Ethel would peek out from the kitchen smile warmly, beaming with pride in our wonderful family. While she prepared the supper I'd quickly change into some work pants so we would play together on the floor.

My lovely wife and I we shared everything together and gave our all to help our boys develop as healthy, socially concerned human beings, holding dear the principles of democracy, liberty and brotherhood. In our behavior, in our play with them, in the stories we told them and by understanding and devotion to them

---

relations man for the prosecution. Some of the most illuminating of the "Rogge papers" (named after Greenglass' lawyer, O. John Rogge) are reprinted in Wexley, pp. 637–44. The information re Pilat is contained in the following quote: ". . . I had lunch with Ruth [Greenglass], Pilat, and HJF [one of Rogge's partners]. We looked at Pilat's articles. They look O.K., but HJF as a precaution, told Lane [one of the prosecutors] previously he would insist Pilat, who already had 2 Conferences with Saypol, show the draft of the articles to Saypol or Lane." From an interoffice memorandum of the Rogge law firm on August 23, 1950. Quoted in Wexley, p. 642.

we gave them more than just parental love. Through them and in them we mentioned a love for humanity for its basic goodness and its inherent creative genius.

You can understand how desolate and barren our existence is since we have been forcibly torn from our boys. We can't hear the sound of our sons. The shouts, the joy, the cry of pain when hurt, the quizzical seeking questions, the thin singing voices, the even breathing when they slept in the stillness of the night all gave richness and warmth to our home. Our family growing, developing secure as a harmonious unit cemented with understanding and love. Nothing is more precious than complete acceptance and devotion between parents and their children. I have to stop now for my heart aches too much for they have been denied their birthrights. But even this we must bear to help stop similar and greater tragedies from being visited on other children, and innocent parents. The imperialists must be stopped in their mad plans that will bring terror and destruction to families . . .

On December 4 (X minus 39 days) he again interrupted these letters to write to Robby and me.

Dear Mike & Robbie,

We have been kept very busy. I am spending almost all of my time writing to our lawyer Manny. Many things are happening in court that need our cooperation but also more important than that is the growing fight by the people to help us win this case. Since we are a vital part of this struggle I've been concentrating on giving a running account of our views on the trial, the issues in our case and any ideas I think might be of interest to readers who want to know more about us. When our counselor is able to extricate himself from the legal jungle I'm sure he'll read some of these letters to you. Therefore don't worry because you don't hear from me directly for we are in the thick of a terrific battle. This much I can say we are very confident, we are pleased with the kind of campaign the committee is waging and the support we are getting seems like it will be successful in eventually setting us free.

As for us we're both healthy and well and just raring to get home and be with you fellows. Now just because we haven't written is no excuse for not letting us know how you are doing. It is the little details that we are most interested in. The books you read Mike. The toys you play with Robbie. Your friends. How do you spend a typical day? What goes on at school? Tell us news about Sonia, Ben and Maxine and Leo. Anything you do or say is precious to us. We treasure every word you write. Please boys continue to keep in touch with us regularly. We'll make up for it sweethearts. Even though we haven't been writing we've been talking about you, making plans and discussing various items with our lawyer and with our family — concerning you boys. Also Mama and I now see each other twice a week on Tuesdays and Fridays and we're able to accomplish more this way and many is the time we exchange stories of our pleasant experiences with you our sons. I'd like to know if you've improved your chess game Michael because in here I'm champion. It is a little more difficult for us to play the game than usual. Each player has a complete set in front of him on a numbered board and he shouts his moves from one numbered square to another to his opponent in another cell. Don't worry son you and I are going to play some good games . . .

You know kids when you're in a situation like us and you are positive that you're right then you are able to fight all the harder for your cause and no matter how difficult it looks you are sure it will come out alright —

All my love and kisses.
DADDY JULIE

On December 22, 1952, the execution papers were served. It was X minus 21 days. My father returned to his efforts.

. . . Today my mind went back to the year 1933 when we lived in the midst of the great depression. I was a High School senior at Seward Park H.S. and it was very difficult for me to decide whether to continue my schooling or take a job for the family was in a very tough financial situation and the future for young people like myself didn't look so good.

Although only fifteen years old I was fully aware of conditions around me and felt a deep social responsibility to do something about them. To earn a little money I used to peddle penny candies on Sundays. The profit went from a low of 40 up to 80 cents for a good day.

Now one day on my way home from school I stopped to listen to a speaker at a street corner meeting on Delancey St. in the lower East Side. His topic was the campaign to win freedom for Tom Mooney labor leader who was imprisoned on a frame-up. The same night I read a pamphlet I had bought, from the speaker, that presented all the facts of this case and listed how the reader could help free this innocent victim. I was determined to do my part and since I had saved up $1.10 and the cost of a box of candy was 60¢ the very next day I went and contributed 50¢ to this cause. Then I began to distribute literature and collect signatures on a petition from the students at school and from my neighbors. This is the way I implemented my convictions to fight for right.

There is an incident that occurred which is still very fresh in my mind. It happened during my first year at City College in 1934 in the Great Hall where I had to attend freshman chapel with all other freshmen. The student council was then responsible for the programs during this hour and usually invited guest speakers. This particular time, over their strenuous objection, the president of the school Frederick Robinson (boo) usurped this right and on his own invited a delegation of foreign students from fascist Italy to be guests and help make good will for that regime among us students.

When the prexy got up to speak he was greeted by a chorus of boos. He was forced to sit down without being able to speak but he managed to state that "our conduct was befitting guttersnipes." After all the heinous deeds of the fascisti was not palpable to Americans with democratic instincts and everybody present booed lustily.

To re-establish order the authorities allowed Eddie Alexander, president of the student council to speak. The hall was perfectly quiet when he began. "I was given permission to speak if I don't say anything derogatory against fascism. But I want to convey a message to our enslaved and tricked brothers under Italian fascism." The truth cut too deep and the fascisti students dragged him away from the microphone and a free-for-all began. 3000 voices thundered in the Great Hall, "Abasso il fascismo" "Demuerte de Mussolini."

At this point the prexy called in New York City's finest and the college student body was treated to a lesson in nightstick civics. The entire metropolitan press printed distorted accounts of what took place and heaped abuse on the students. Within a week almost the entire student body wore buttons that read "I am a guttersnipe. I hate fascism." Subsequent events such as: Il Duce legions bringing "civilization" to Ethiopia via bombs, flames and death to innocent defenseless natives proved we were correct in our position of fighting fascism. But 21 students, including Alexander, were expelled . . .

At school I took a very active part in the campaign to free the Scottsboro boys. My extracurricular time was devoted in this constant work for these good causes. Together with thousands of other young people I studied, read, participated and learned.

I took a part-time job as a clerk in a drug store on Lenox Ave. near 125th Street in order to earn enough to make ends meet. Daily I walked through the Negro neighborhood from school to work. I saw what discrimination meant. Overcrowding in slums, 25 to 50% higher prices than those charged in other neighborhoods for the same items and higher rents. The store employees in the neighborhood were all white. There were many incidents where the police were charged with brutality.

One night while I was working in the store there was an accident, on Lenox Ave. A speeding bus ran over a middle-aged Negro man and he was brought into the store bleeding profusely from his leg that was almost completely severed off. It took the ambulance more than ¾ of an hour to answer this emergency call while this man bled to death. I had to mop up this man's life's blood and I'll never forget this crime that permits such a thing to happen to a human being.

Then there came a time when all the resentment against these accumulated abuses that were seething in this boiling cauldron overflowed into the Harlem riots.* The public sat up and took notice and the Negro people of this area won some relief for their justifiable grievances. Stores hired Negroes. The police let up on some of the rough stuff and committees of investigation went to work. Of course, not enough was done to solve the problem.

What I'm getting at in reciting some of my experiences is that there are things you don't learn at school or from reading but you must see. All this I integrated in my store of knowledge; the truths I saw with my own eyes together with my formal education so that I could understand the world I live in and function better as a social human being.

There was a strike of auto workers who were locked out. This took place near our campus. A number of us helped them with their picketing and once when we went to their union hall we noticed that the strikers' families were in very bad financial straits. A student committee to help them was set up and funds were collected to buy food for these needy families. I remember well the feeling of brotherhood when we turned over crates of food to the strikers' welfare committee.

This is part of my background and goes to make up the person that I really am a progressive individual. Is this the reason they have given us only 3 more weeks to live? They tell me in many devious ways you can save your wife and yourself. Make a deal: Do what the Government wants . . .

It is Christmas eve now and 16 years ago this week the most important thing in my life happened to me. I met my wife then. Looking back now I am sure it was the best thing that occurred to me in all these years. Although I had decided to quit school and go to work because conditions were bad and the future didn't look good Ethel convinced me to finish my studies. She helped me with my work, typed all my engineering reports and lent me moral encouragement. Of course, we did our share of smooching and believe me that was very inspirational. By the way, I miss that now. You see I fell in love with her very soon after we met.

* 1943.

You must know my Ethel. I cannot sing her praise too highly to you. She is sweet, gentle and generous. Very warm hearted, understanding and possesses a keen and analytical mind. Her virtue is a fine character and all who are acquainted with her know her true goodness. This situation gives me a chance to see her real worth and I am sure I have a great woman for my wife.

We can be so happy together. We want to be reunited with each other and our two sons. Our will to live is strong and that is the reason we fight so hard in this principled way to win our case. We have faith that the people will see to it that this will not be our last Christmas eve.

Let me tell you from the bottom of my heart we are working to make this a Merry Christmas and a Happy New Year for all the people.

Deeds of goodwill and deeds that make for Peace that is what the world wants . . .

December 27, 1952

It was cold in the yard this morning. Winter was asserting itself. Gusts of icy wind blew across the yard, stinging my ears and carrying to my nose the pungent fishy odor of the Hudson River. A soaring seagull was sailing upward in wide circles lifted by the strong wind and gracefully, without effort, covered the expanse of the wide open sky that my eyes could see. Yes, my spirit, too, took wing with that bird. Suddenly with a roar, man's invention, the jet plane, intruded into nature's scene but the white puffs that were bunched like an endless chain into clouds hid it from my sight.

Then as I took another turn around the yard my eyes glanced at the white streaks of calcium that seemed to make odd shapes as they ran in broken lines from brick to brick along the wall of the death house. I began to think of the chemistry of the building materials. Through my mind flashed a picture of coal and iron ore being dug from the bowels of the earth, trucks bringing it into the mills, iron and steel pouring from the furnaces, fabricated parts making their way to Sing Sing, skilled mechanics building all these parts into a strong structure using all the science of modern industry to make a death house. Just as this panorama imprinted itself on my brain, the exercise guard gently reminded me my fifteen minutes yard period was finished. I breathed once more deeply of the fresh free air and then I went to my cell. The steel door closed, a key turned in the lock, the padlock snapped and I was once again shut in my cubicle of concrete.

Day and night, pacing back and forth, lying on my bed and endless thoughts crowding through my mind. So little time left so much to say and live in a couple of weeks. What should be put down first? To Whom? How?

Please listen, look, see, hear, feel. Learn the truth and get at the facts. Each for his own defense must defend right and life.

Over and over again I began to write to my sons. I wrote a few lines and tore up the paper. Then I put it off again and sent Ethel a letter and again I couldn't make it and I continue to write you dear friend. It is futile to tell a mother not to grieve for her children. Well do we realize the terror and emotional hardships our two bunnies are going through. We, their parents, see the terrible hurt visited on our boys and know the mark that has been made on their lives. And when I look through the screen at my wife in her cell and see the tears streaming down her face and her body straining with all its might to contain the sobs of pain, I try to quiet her, while inside of me I'm crying all over. It's the damnable injustice and horror of it all. We feel and love so strong. Because we are so sensitive we must do right by our children and for others like them we must do what we can to prevent a similar catastrophe a product of hysteria and cold war, from being visited on thousands of other innocent parents.

Dec. 28, 1952

Dear good Manny,

In everything I've written and all that I've said I try to explain to my sons the meaning and reason for this situation. A great part of the job and responsibility will be yours to help them understand. One thing I feel sure of that when they are older and read the trial record and all that took place they will know that all the way through we their parents were right and the knowledge of this truth will buttress their feelings and confirm their confidence in themselves and in us their parents. We are still optimistic but we are alarmed that madmen in their haste to conceal this rotten frame-up will snuff out our lives. This must never be . . .

On December 31, the Court of Appeals affirmed the denial of the motion for a new trial filed on December 10. Though the court used harsh language to describe the prosecutor's conduct, it denied the motion for a new trial because Manny Bloch had not moved for a mistrial when the prosecution's misconduct occurred. Our father responded:

Jan. 1, 1953

Hello Bunny,

Happy New Year to you Ethel darling. May this year see events take place that are more to our benefit than those that have happened in the old year. The Circuit Court of Appeals ushered out the old year with another piece of hair splitting in an opinion that continues to help bury us. Just as we expected the cards are stacked against us. However they are forced to write opinions and from the fragments that I read in the newspapers they recognize the prejudice caused to us by the publicity as handled and have so stated.

Both courts are of the opinion that despite the prejudicial conditioning of complained of publicity the *defendants' failure to take timely corrective procedural steps,* now forecloses the courts from giving us relief as prayed for. To all this I say bunk.

I believe that true justice is concerned with substance — not forms or modes of procedures. If it is recognized that the publicity complained of served to deny us a fair trial and due process of law then failure of counsel to make timely objections, or passage of time, *in no wise corrects the unfairness of the trial.* In other words if to begin with, it was an unfair situation, the situation did not later become "cured" because of passage of time.

If the court's opinion is to be squared with an ordinary common-sense interpretation of whether or not their holding is good law, we come to the absurdity as follows: That because of negligence, laxity, inexperience, of ineptitude of a lawyer his clients can be deprived of life even though the courts admit that their trial was infected by prejudicial unfairness. Of course, mature reason dictates the rejection of this. Enough, it just galls me to think of this terrible injustice.

Honey I missed you terribly New Year's Eve and all day today. I spent the hours ushering in the New Year reading the material published on our behalf and rereading your letters. Naturally, I was terribly moved but I felt so close to you sweetheart . . .

JULIE

Before returning to Toms River for the beginning of school in 1953, we paid another visit to Sing Sing.

January 3, 1953

Dearest Manny,

. . . Today our precious boys came and our own family lived once again for two hours. I could see the trust in little Robbie's eyes, and the sweet, warm tender feelings of love that passed between us, in all that he said and in our play together. I carried the baby on my back, giving him a horsey ride. We looked through the barred window at the sea gulls and the tugboat pulling a string of barges on the Hudson. He zoomed through the room pretending to be an airplane as I held him in my arms tightly pressed to my heart. The pictures he drew and the drawings I made for him were interrupted while he kissed my cheeks as he circled my neck with his little arms. My son was happy with his daddy. Julie was a big pussy cat chasing the little mousie, Robbie, and we had fun. Our baby got our true feelings.

Michael was troubled and disturbed and the burdens on him were obvious to us, his parents. My darling wife did so well by him. She explained patiently, carefully, firmly, but all the time with a complete acceptance of him and showed such wonderful understanding. It was really a most positive visit for all of us.

I promised to play Michael chess. I hope to someday.

Then they had to go and as I helped Michael with his coat he suddenly clutched me with his hands and stammered as he lowered his head, "You must come home. Every day there is a lump in my stomach, even when I go to bed." I kissed him in a hurry for I was unable to say anything but "everything will be all right."

When I was in the solitude of my cell once more and the door clanged shut behind me I must confess I broke down and cried like a baby because of the children's deep hurt. With my back to the bars, I stood facing the concrete walls that boxed me in on all sides, and I let the pains that tore at my insides flood out in tears. The wretched beastliness and inhumanity of it all. Take heed, tyrants, you will answer for your misdeeds . . .

Time is short. There is but ten more days left to live. I will do my best to crowd in as much work as possible. I am raising a warning for I believe this is a test case of threatening fascism at home. Don't let them murder us.

As ever
JULIE

Our father again interrupted his "statement" with the following letter on January 4.

Dear Manny,

. . . Gosh, Manny, I'm concerned about Ethel, it's terribly hard for her. Because I love our children so dearly I love their mother so much. My wife is a diamond and no amount of lies, filth or vilification can scratch her honor or mar her dignity. I believe she has risen in stature as an individual, in spite of the misery even within the confines of this slaughterhouse, while we face death. This to me is the singular proof of her novel character, good conscience, and yes of our innocence. I hope I were able to give her more comfort and ease her great pain, but all I can do is write.

Because I love to build, to create with my hands and mind I studied to be an engineer. My professional opinion as the crisis approaches and as the issues are sharper and clearer is that we are closest to the absolute truth and right. I am not dealing with the matter in a subjective way but refer to it objectively, the reality in nature. Perhaps I am confusing because this is too much like a physical or mathematical concept. However, I believe that the idea I am trying to get across, at least the substance of it, is the ultimate truth.

No matter what happens you must continue to work until you prove to all that we are innocent as indeed we are . . .

The next day our mother echoed our father's reaction to the Court of Appeals' decision.

Dear Manny,

What price perfidy! I have just read the excerpts of Judge Swan's opinion* carried by the New York Times on New Year's Day. All legal considerations aside, I am sick for the unconscionably sneering attitude, the snide insinuations you have had to suffer on our behalf. It is a shockingly deplorable level indeed to which morality has sunk when public servants of such exalted position find entirely acceptable the questionable technique of the slur and the smear. With what extraordinary aplomb, with what high-handed unconcern for fact, with what cool disdain, your carefully organized, thoroughly documented, soberly stated arguments were dismissed!

Perhaps I am naive, but it doesn't seem possible that a responsible governmental body should stoop to subject to jeers and jibes one whose selfless devotion to justice and inspiring nobility of purpose merits only the most boundless admiration, the most affectionate thanks. Please know that we honor and love you, as indeed do all lovers of truth and decency, beyond any measure!

ETHEL

On December 30, there was a reduction of sentence hearing before Judge Kaufman. He truly displayed his bias in that hearing and the record of it should be given out to everyone. His opinion denying the motion received wide publicity in an obvious attempt to counteract the Committee's successes, particularly abroad. In the opinion, he reiterated that he still believed

* The Court of Appeals December 31 decision.

their crime worse than murder. However, he did reduce the pressure somewhat by staying the January 14 execution date so a clemency petition could be filed with the White House. But there was a catch.

January 6, 1953

Dear Manny,

. . . Kaufman's magic hamstrings us as follows: *First* — He effectively prevents us from ever seeking a Supreme Court review of our motion for a retrial on newly discovered evidence because no other legal moves are to be in process while making this final executive appeal. *Second* — Our lawyer has less than 4 days in which, to secure forms from the President's pardon attorney in Washington, D.C. to prepare all necessary paper and petitions for relief, to have us at Sing Sing sign them before a notary and then file all these papers in Washington, D.C. All by this coming Saturday . . .

. . . It is now obvious to all that Kaufman's "opinion" which could be entitled "Alleged Communists or pro-Communists are Better off dead" was deliberately conceived to use this distorted judicial pronouncement as the case for political propaganda: 1) By the State Dept. to offset mounting foreign indignation against this monstrous frame-up and brutal sentence that shocks the conscience of Mankind. 2) Through the instigation of the Justice Dept. at home a high pressure press and radio campaign is in full swing to oppose and stop the growing protest movement against the horrible death sentence and above all to present the spread among the entire people of the grave doubts that many already have about our guilt . . .

As ever
JULIE

January 9, 1953

Dear Manny,

It strikes me that Judge Irving R. Kaufman's immortality is at last assured; future generations will cite his decision denying us clemency as the epitome of that artful double-talk and intellectual dishonesty so prevalent in the "Age of Hypocrisy" (more conventionally known as the 20th Century) and bestow upon him with refreshing candor, the eminently fitting title of "Master of Sophistry"!

Full of the most extraordinary inaccuracies and omissions and the kind of specious reasoning that lends credibility to distortion, it strains so hard to be profound and fails so dismally to be anything but puerile. Striking a pose worthy of Thomashefsky and Barrymore combined, and drawing a revoltingly respectable solemnity, calculated to represent himself to the gullible as a saddened but serenely dutiful guardian of the nation's "security" he is actually at great pains to conceal the inherent moral bankruptcy of his position. Hence the shrill and officious trumpeting of a pigmy, whose cowardly violation of the true worthiness of the human spirit, must be expiated by the "slaughter of the innocents"!

In this wise, it even becomes necessary to traduce the noble lines of a George Eliot* whose entire life, ironically enough, is a monument to those very ideals a Kaufman sees fit to slander and subvert. Surely, this is plagiarism on a signally low level; for while it is true that authorship is duly acknowledged, the cynical use to which this fine literary expression was put — a use that clearly could never have been intended by a great-souled woman who herself rebelled at the falsity that "saves the form while damning the spirit" — such a use I say, constitutes a travesty and a defamation of a very repulsive sort indeed.

Enamored of quotations as the good judge seems, however, I would hazard the guess that a study of the following excerpts from Shaw's "Saint Joan" would not have inclined him to press them into service against the Rosenbergs! As you will recall, John de Stogumber the English chaplain, who had been one of the most bloodthirsty advocates of Joan's proposed burning, comes rushing in from this "glorious" spectacle, overcome with remorse and sobbing like one demented. "You don't know; you haven't seen; it is so easy to talk when you don't know. You madden yourself with words: You damn yourself because it feels grand to throw oil on the flaming hell of your own

---

* Kaufman had quoted the following lines: "There is a mercy which is weakness, and even treason against the common good."

temper. But when it is brought home to you; when you see the thing, you have done; when it's blinding your eyes, stifling your nostrils, tearing your heart — then — then — Oh, God, take away this sight from me — Oh, Christ! deliver me from this fire that is consuming me — She cried to Thee in the midst of it: — Jesus! Jesus! Jesus! She is in thy bosom, and I am in hell for evermore!" And there shall you be, Judge Kaufman, for a crime "worse than murder"!

ETHEL

On January 12, our father returned to his statement.

Dear Manny,

The stupendous propaganda campaign against us is reaching unprecedented heights. Why the sheer weight of newsprint staggers the imagination, but it sets one thinking. They are doing a selling job. The authorities are adamant on going through with this madness or is it because they are having a difficult time convincing the public? This weekend alone each and every newspaper carried extensive news stories and feature articles on our case. Now they have presented the prosecutor's side of the case only and since they have to repeat and reiterate it so often, it shows that they are not meeting with too much success. This is the favorite Goebbels technique — continuous repetition of pronouncements that they hope will become to be accepted by the people as the facts. Methinks they protest too much. But they cannot and they must not be allowed to hide the truth, the record of the trial and all the facts in the case.

The only means we have of defending ourselves is to write the facts as they are and we have authorized you to use our letters to make available this information to the public in order for them to know us as we really are. We must find some way to break into that impenetrable barrier that keeps our side out of the great newspapers of our country. Experienced and more competent writers than I could do a much better job than I ever hope to be able to do but I must make every effort. Help me all you can dear friend to get this across.

I would like you to prepare with our cooperation an open letter to the American Press answering all the lies and the common misconception that the newspapers are feeding the public. We should base it on the trial record and only include such personal items that are of interest and that would present us in our true light.

Since they disseminate public information and news it is their duty and it is in the interests of fair play that they don't black out our side of the controversy and allow us the opportunity to place paid advertisements in their papers. I'm not naive but I believe it's worth a try. In a short time we'll know the decision of the President that will either doom us or spare our lives and we have a right to insist that in some small measure we be allowed to present our story. It won't be remiss to show their bias and distortion of the facts in our case.

Always it is the most rabid witch hunters that are leading the pack and driving the weak to silence. It is, therefore, no mere coincidence that at the hearing before Judge Kaufman and in the Jan. 9th Victor Riesel column in the Mirror a new line of attack was opened this time against our legal defense, the selfless very competent attorney counselor Emanuel H. Bloch. He is too effective in defending our rights, exposing the frame-up and performing his legal responsibilities exposing the frame-up in the highest professional standards of legal advocacy in the most ethical and moral way possible. That is the reason for their subtle and dangerous attacks. It is still another step in the *tactic — fear,* the *method — coercion,* the *objective — conformism* and orthodoxy spelling out fascism that brings with it racialism and leads to war. This is a warning sign and we must be alert to combat this before it deprives people of the chance to defend themselves against charges as is their right under the Constitution. The only manner we can maintain our rights is to fight for them.

Obviously, the situation is fraught with grave danger. Not only are our two lives in jeopardy of being snuffed out but the safety and security of our fellow countrymen is threatened. If there is no reason or sanity left in Washington then in desperation they may allow the executioner to pull the switch and murder us. Then who knows that tomorrow the authorities may turn around drop an atom-bomb or some other means of mass destruction and set off a world war that would end civilization. It is precisely because the people are aware of this danger that we have won such popular support in Western Europe, Asia, the Americas and even in our country, in spite of the overwhelming press barrage of lies and distortion. The cry of Communism is not working and all that they accomplish is to continue to fumble and pile mistake upon mistake.

The need of the hour is vigilance and action to let the Government know the true feeling of the people. I sincerely believe our chances have improved to live to fight to prove our innocence but the possibility still exists for an adverse decision. But I remain confident and I continue to hope that we will succeed in our common efforts for this worthy cause . . .

All my love,
JULIE

On January 19, my mother commented in retrospect on the pressure she had just been through.

October, 1952

Dear Manny,

Fortunately, you had prepared us so well at our last consultation we took this latest hammer-blow with admirable dignity and self-control. I think we have every right so to characterize our behavior, for while it is no easy matter to contemplate one's own imminent demise, it is far more horrifying to watch the cauldron boiling and the plot thickening right out in broad daylight, while the people flee, hysterical with fear headlong down the path to their own destruction and the liberals flounder about pathetically atop their synthetic fences!

On Monday, Oct. 13, the Supreme Court, with the praiseworthy exception of Justice Black, used its proud office to write "justice" off the statute books. By its refusal to review a case that involved two decent young parents and questions of law vital to the democratic well-being of the entire citizenry, they clearly sanctioned the scrapping of due process and the incidental scrapping of human life. They also demonstrated a reluctance to pass upon a record that exposes all too effectively a creaking makeshift of a case and a hollow mockery of a trial thereby revealing a quite astonishing lack of that independence of thought and action we had come to associate with such a venerable body as the United States Supreme Court!

January 19, 1952

Much water has flowed under the bridge since I wrote the aforementioned words, a national election of unprecedented importance has taken place . . . and the Rosenbergs' calm prediction that the people would refuse to acquiesce in legal murder, has been borne out a thousand times over . . . On Sunday, Dec. 21, 1952, I sat quietly in my cell, "listening" to the songs that close to 1000 people were singing in a heavy rain at Ossining Station (although I couldn't actually hear them) and feeling a calm and a safety and a spiritual bond that no deprivation, no loneliness, no danger, could shatter!

. . . Jan. 14th, came and went, as did those hectic ones just prior to it when officials of one kind or another were giving us the familiar run around and the scribes were nobly assisting with a campaign of slander that daily assumes the characteristics of the sewer. Sweet essence of putrescence!

There are, however, memories not listed in any calendar, memories of emotions that flashed by meteor-like, in bewildering succession, and that now in retrospect, are so many burned-out stars, identically pale and colorless and forgotten. Again, casting a glance backward over the shoulder of the swiftly speeding present, I remember vividly that each day then seemed to me to be stretching out long and endless and golden with promise. I wrote my husband, "The battle rages, but I am serene!" And to my children, I sent a charming, light-hearted little poem clipped from the Sunday Times by way of Chanukah Greeting.

All, all past, and decision close at hand; for us, sitting here and fighting for breath in an ever narrowing circle of tightening time, it looms large and unknown, color-blurred and shapeless upon the gigantic canvas of a furious age. And yet, essentially, it is a simple decision, predicated as it is upon a few simple propositions.

. . . Whatever the merits of the case, millions of people throughout the world today, numbering among them some of the most outstanding figures of our times, view the refusal of the courts to grant the Rosenbergs relief as an affirmation of the couple's insistence unshaken after nearly two years in the death-house, that they are political victims of the cold-war. Accordingly, these millions have registered the most vigorous kind of opposition to the execution of the sentence . . .

. . . While the entire world storms, thunders, exhorts and pleads, we are witnessing the astounding spectacle of the most powerful nation on earth bound, helpless, powerless to reverse itself because it is always so much easier to commit new errors, than to right old ones! . . .

As I have already stated, it is a remarkably simple decision, for all the hysteria that is being deliberately fomented, for to "lose face" by granting clemency to the Rosenbergs is to demonstrate in the most palpable manner possible that Justice is something more than a ruthless treadmill, which once set upon a certain course must like some horrible Frankenstein, grow stronger than the controlling hand upon its throttle and run blindly amuck! . . .

ETHEL

Grandma Tessie did not visit our mother in Sing Sing in 1951 or 1952. As the clemency decision neared, she appeared to try and induce her daughter to falsely confess and back David's story.

Jan. 21, 1953

Dear Manny,

This is to let you know my mother was here on Monday; the following transpired among other things, which I think may interest you. 1) I expressed pleasure at seeing her, but inquired why she had expended the time and energy to travel to Sing Sing (and alone to boot), when she might better have saved some for a trip to see Davy . . . Now, brace yourself for a shock; fact is, I am still in a state of stupefaction over its bold-faced immorality. Above point, while verbalizing the emotional factors she could employ in speaking with Davy, I pointed out to her that whatever unfortunate fear of reprisal Davy might be harboring, it was my life that was in peril, not his — and further, if I, while awaiting electrocution, was not afraid to continue to assert my innocence and give the lie to his story, why couldn't he, in a far more advantageous position, be man enough to own up, at long last, to this lie, and help to save my life, instead of letting it be forfeited to save his face! Our conversation follows, and I quote almost verbatim. Said she, "So what would have been so terrible if you had backed up his story?" — I guess my mouth kind of fell open. "What," I replied, "and take the blame for a crime I never committed, and allow my name and my husband's, and childrens' to be blackened to protect him? What, and go along with a story that I knew to be untrue, where it involved my husband and me? Wait a minute, maybe I'm not getting you straight, just what are you driving at?" Believe it or not, she answered, "Yes, you got me straight; I mean even if it was a lie, all right, so it was a lie, you should have said it was true, anyway! You think that way you would have been sent here? No, if you had agreed that what Davy said was so, even if it wasn't, you wouldn't have got this!" I protested, shocked as I could be, "But, Ma, would you have had me willingly commit perjury?" She shrugged her shoulders indifferently and maintained doggedly, "You wouldn't be here!" . . .

Love —
ETHEL

The government's campaign continued to focus on pressuring our mother. Her arrest and severe sentencing, her transfer to Sing Sing (in virtual solitary confinement) were supplemented by more direct public acknowledgment of her status as a hostage.

February 9, 1953

Dear Manny,

In recent weeks an ugly development has been gaining ground. It is being casually bruited about by our less than wholesome brethren that I am to be spared by commutation out of a humanitarian consideration for me as a woman and a mother while my husband is to be electrocuted. Further, it is hopefully confided, in such an event my "spy secrets" would not die with me and the possibility would still exist for my eventual recantation. Lastly, the responsibility for the decision concerning my husband's life would be shifted squarely onto my shoulders and his blood would be on my hands if I willfully refused to make him "come across"!

So now, my life is to be bargained off against my husband's; I need only grasp the line chivalrously held out to me by the gallant defenders of hearth and home and leave him to drown without a backward glance! How diabolical, how bestial, how utterly depraved! Only fiends and perverts could taunt a fastidious woman with so despicable, so degrading a proposition! A cold fury possesses me and I could retch with horror and revulsion, for these unctious saviors, these odius swine, are actually proposing to erect a terrifying sepulchre in which I shall live without living and die without dying! By day there will be no hope and by night there will be no peace. Over and over again I shall see the beloved face and fancy I hear the beloved voice. Over and over again, I shall sob out the last heart-broken, wracking good-byes and reel under the impact of irrevocable murder!

And what of our children, noble testament to our sacred union, fruit of our deep and enduring love; what manner of "mercy" is it that would slay their adored father, and deliver up their devoted mother to everlasting emptiness. Know then, you warped, gross, eaters of dust, you abominations upon this beauteous earth, I should far rather embrace my husband in death than live on ingloriously upon your execrable bounty.

Be under no illusions, either, magnanimous sirs, that I shall besmirch and dishonor my marital vows and the felicity and integrity of the relationship we shared, to play the role of harlot to political procurers. My husband is innocent as I am myself and no power on earth shall divide us in life or in death. Trust me, I shall remain faithful, trust me, I shall not revile him! My shattered life shall be his immortality and his memory shall be safe from your wicked debauchery.* But the savage reprisal you visited upon me shall pursue you to the edge of your graves and beyond, and your names shall be anathema wherever love is the First Commandment!

Take heed, reckless speculators in human misery, lest History exhume your rotten carrion and solemnly charge you with cold-blooded** killing! Take heed, despoilers of all that is good, lest you create a new and more flaming "Joan"!

ETHEL***

Then, on February 11, the pressure resumed in full force.

February 12, 1953

My Darling,

The Great Emancipator is whirling in his grave while the phoney crusader is acting like a knave. Just as we had been informed by our lawyer that it would take at least another week for Eisenhower to get the record the newspapers let the cat out of the bag and said that the Attorney General brought over the file to the President's office at 4:00 P.M. and at 5:07 P.M. the prepared statement was ready.**** Of course, he did not read the record nor did he see our petition. To cover up this apparent discrepancy they say on his own he's been brushing up on the case. I guess in between playing golf, playing footsies with all his big business cabinet members and playing around with the Formosa issue. Such bald hypocrisy. The man's just a plain liar. Why, he doesn't even make sure that he's accurate in his haste to use shopworn platitudes — stating the obvious fallacy that the Supreme Court reviewed our case. It is true that the initiative and the heavy advantage is at present with the smiling General but he did not reckon with the people for instinctively the military mind had only contempt for them. He may be successful in that we will be put to death but he has

* Corrected to "cowardly slander" the next day.
** Changed to "vengeful" or "wanton" (the decision was left to Manny).
*** In this and other letters their recognition that by publishing their letters they could take a hand in their own defense shines through. The process of getting the letters published had already begun and in the following months they anxiously awaited the first edition of *Death House Letters*, which was finally released in June.
**** Denying clemency.

shocked the conscience of the world and revealed himself a perfidious reactionary who is ready to embark on risky adventures that may bring on world war 3. He will find that this move of his administration is a terrible mistake. I feel certain that the people will do everything to change this decision . . .

Like you, my beloved, I find it most difficult to think about what this new development will do to our precious sons. The heartache is just too much for it is impossible to do anything to protect them from the horrible consequences of our execution nor can we assuage the deep hurt that they will have to bear. I will have to find the strength to suffer through the torment and begin to write our children a long letter. This, we must do and we'll talk about whether it would be best to send it to Manny to hold until such time as he feels it is appropriate to read to our children. At this time we'll have to seriously make preparations to finish up a number of items in order that everything necessary is done and is not left to the very last minute . . .
Always devoted to you forever,

YOUR JULIE

On February 17, 1953, the pressure abated. Three weeks before the newly-scheduled execution, after Judge Kaufman had denied a long enough stay to appeal the December 31 ruling of the Court of Appeals to the Supreme Court, the Court of Appeals itself, mindful of its earlier criticisms of the prosecutors, stayed the March 9 execution until a petition for *certiorari* could be filed with the Supreme Court.

Judge Learned Hand rejected the prosecution's arguments against a stay saying

People don't dispose of lives, just because an attorney didn't make a point . . . You can't undo a death sentence. There are some Justices on the Supreme Court on whom the conduct of the Prosecuting Attorney might make an impression . . . Your duty, Mr. Prosecutor, is to seek justice, not to act as a time-keeper.

In the late winter and early spring of 1953, the case continued to fall apart not only in the minds of those courageous and open-minded enough to read the trial transcript, but also through the discovery of new evidence.

In April of 1953 the *National Guardian* published a story about the discovery of the console table that David and Ruth Greenglass had both testified was a gift from the Russians — Ruth even asserted it had a hollowed-out portion for microfilming. I easily remembered this table as the small drop-leaf telephone table in Grandma's house, and at the next visit with my parents I eagerly discussed this with them. I must have seemed hazy about the table's having been in our apartment before the arrest, until my father reminded me of his difficulty with the swiveling braces that supported the two drop leaves. "Yes," I excitedly recalled, "and you used to push toothpicks up into the screw holes so you could make the screws tighter." They smiled at my memory.

The table was a most important discovery, because it was one of the only two points at which the testimony of David and Ruth Greenglass, which was the basis of the entire government case, could be checked against the repeated denials of my parents. At the trial, the jury had believed David and Ruth. Anything that would have convinced the jury that the Greenglasses were lying might have led them to acquit my parents.

Mr. Leon Summit, the *Guardian* reporter who'd located the table, set to work rounding up corroborating evidence that the table in Grandma's apartment was indeed the table mentioned at the trial. Aside from obtaining affidavits from family members about the transfers of the table from our parents' apartment to our grandmother's, he sought a prosecution rebuttal witness, Mrs. Evelyn Cox, the cleaning woman in our home from 1944 to 1945 (I have no memory of her). She had testified that the table was often kept in a closet. The prosecution had made much of the table being "hidden" in the closet, though it was in the living room the night the FBI arrested our father and raided the apartment. When Mr. Summit and the Reverend H. S. Williamson called on Mrs. Cox, she readily identified the table. When Mr. Summit pressed her, she said, "See that scratch; I made that once when I was cleaning. I was upset that Mrs. Rosenberg would be mad at me, but she only said, 'Don't worry about it, it's just a cheap piece of wood.' " Mrs. Cox also remembered that my father had done some repair work underneath to reinforce the rickety table. When they turned the table over, the work she had described was visible. At the trial Prosecutor Saypol had introduced furniture catalogues as evidence and challenged my father. "Don't you know, Mr. Rosenberg, that you couldn't buy a console table in Macy's . . . in 1944 and 1945 for less than $85?" *

Mrs. Cox refused to sign an affidavit, though she offered to ". . . swear in any court in the land that that looks like the table . . ." They wouldn't take no for an answer, returning three times with an affidavit, only to be turned away finally by Mrs. Cox's daughter, who claimed that her mother was ill. However, she did relate to them the following story paraphrased for me by Mr. Summit:

When the FBI brought Mrs. Cox home from the trial they had admonished her to keep her mouth shut. Until Summit and Williamson had arrived with the table, she had not even told her family about the testimony. The daughter said she wanted to be left alone. Her husband was a policeman, she a school teacher. Every day after Summit and Williamson left, the FBI came in and grilled them about what had been said. If the men were to return again, she would call the police.

It is very possible that the daughter would today deny this story, but I believe Mr. Summit. The awesome power of the FBI, the hysteria of the times, had frightened away a potential life-saving witness.

The hysteria of the time had also kept the Rosenberg family away from the trial. Nor were they called as witnesses to corroborate our parents' testimony about the console table. Thus, they were unaware of the importance of the table as evidence. Manny Bloch had assumed the table had been sold to a junk dealer when the apartment had been abandoned. He did not know that an aunt had saved the table since it was the best piece

---

* A Macy's employee signed an affidavit stating that a Macy's code found under the table showed a price of $19.97. My father had testified that the table cost approximately $21 and that he bought it in 1944 or 1945, which the Macy's code also confirmed.

of furniture in the house and that Grandma was using it when Robby and I moved in with her. At the time, Manny had no researchers working with him to trace the table.

Then Mr. Summit uncovered another new piece of evidence. On February 16, 1953, our father made a potentially major contribution to his own defense.

February 16, 1953

Dear Manny,

In the small printed booklet containing the record transcript page 510–511 Dave said "Julius told me he had stolen the proximity fuse when he was working at Emerson Radio. He told me he took it out in his briefcase. That is the same briefcase he brought his lunch in with and he gave it to Russia." This is supposed to have been done as a Signal Corps Insp. at Emerson Radio. That would fix the time somewhere during 1944.

1. We could get positive proof from Emerson Radio that no proximity fuse was missing or stolen at any time and specifically during the time I worked there. (All information pertaining to this matter, security, set up of plant, can be verified by ———— ————, President of Emerson.)

2. ———— ————, man in charge of Signal Corps, Lt. Col. ———— ————, Officer in Charge of Newark Signal Corps, Lts. ———— ————, ———— ————, two area officers who were in charge of Emerson Radio could verify all pertinent information.

3. During my assignment at Emerson my briefcase was always kept in the bottom drawer, right hand side of my desk in the Signal Corps office. It never went anywhere else in the plant. It contained a complete Signal Corps Stampkit about 3″ wide 6″ x 8″, extra inspection apparatus, (micrometer, paint, additional stamps, cross flags, etc.). Two thick files of memoranda each about 2″ thick. Inspection regulations booklet and a couple of booklets on Government regulation pertaining to the job. Quantities of different forms needed in my inspection work like vendors, shipping documents, acceptance forms, time sheets, expense forms, inspection reports and quantities of franked envelopes. There were three compartments in the

briefcase and it was always packed full with all these items and this was the only briefcase I used when I worked for the Signal Corps. I only took it from the desk when I had to go on an inspection trip to another plant where I needed all the materials to do the inspection job. Also, whenever one came into the plant or left it, armed security guards inspected the contents of the briefcase and any packages.

When I did bring my lunch from home I always brought it in a paper bag.

4. The proximity fuse was a bulky item in size and shape and, even if my briefcase were empty of the other material, and it never was, and if the fuse were put in one of the pockets of the briefcase, it would bulk it out quite a bit. It would be difficult to secure from the production line (without it being noticed or missed) a proximity fuse, pass through a number of armed security guards without being detected, conceal it properly in my briefcase in the Signal Corps off. (always full of other Signal Corps employees, over 20 of them, and a secretary and Emerson personnel had access to it also), pass at least two more security checkpoints containing armed guards with this conspicuously bulky briefcase, without being detected. In short, even if someone wanted to commit the crime the setup at Emerson ruled out the possibility and besides none was stolen or missing all the time I worked there.

5. Nor was I in direct contact with the inspection work of the proximity fuse but I supervised those inspectors under me who did the actual work on the production line, on the testing and in the packing.

6. The office is on the 2nd floor and in the beginning the pilot never was made on the 6th floor and when material went between floors they passed close scrutiny of armed guards and foremen. The same was true when the production line on another side of the 2nd floor went into operation. Besides I never carried a proximity fuse between floors.

7. Every unit entering the production line was accounted for, even the parts. Line five kept a running account at start, during and end of the day at many points in the line and at each new process. Every subassembly and especially each complete

assembly was accounted for and even the rejects were recorded and kept. I believe the contractor was even paid for the rejects. Never while I worked there were any units missing, lost, stolen or unaccounted for.

A real thorough job can be done on this one single item that Greenglass slipped and said something specific. It appeared prominently in the Circuit Court of Appeals 1st opinion in our case. We can discuss this in detail and really go to town here.

As ever, JULIE

Mr. Summit immediately contacted two supervisory employees of Emerson Radio Corporation, who — contradicting the Greenglass testimony — agreed that the only way our father could have stolen a proximity fuse was by piecing together rejected parts that he might have accumulated on a garbage detail. No company records revealed a missing fuse, and he was never on any such detail when he could have taken one. Next they volunteered the clincher — the FBI had never even inquired at Emerson if a proximity fuse was missing.* This is an extremely relevant point, because the Greenglasses maintained they always told the whole truth. The failure of the prosecution to check this piece of testimony is one reason why my brother and I have charged prosecution officials with suborning the perjury of David Greenglass among other things.

Mr. Summit asked for affidavits, but both men refused. The lack of subpoena power severely hindered Manny and his colleagues in proving my parents' contentions on these issues. Finally, a week after the Supreme Court denied *certiorari* for the second time (May 25), Manny filed whatever affidavits he had received and sought an evidentiary hearing under Section 2255 of Title 28 of the Federal Criminal Code. (This provides for an evidentiary hearing if the defense can construct a *prima facie* case for substantial fraud having been perpetrated upon the jury so as to deprive the defendants of a constitutionally fair trial.) Seriously raising doubts about — rather than disproving — the Greenglass

* A secret Justice Department report in 1957 states that the FBI interviewed an engineer at Emerson who said no whole proximity fuse was missing. If this is true, they evidently dropped the investigation there.

testimony on the console table and other matters, our side hoped to gain that all-important subpoena power. With subpoena power, our side would have been in a position to prove David and Ruth's perjuries as well as governmental subornation of perjury and suppression of evidence favorable to the defense. The FBI agents who searched our apartment could have been compelled to testify about the presence of the table and the fact that they weren't even suspicious enough about the table to mention it in their written report, much less to take it.

The government knew their fraudulent case could have blown up in their faces. (Their refusal to release the FBI files on the case after twenty-three years indicates a continued desire to cover up that fraud.) But Judge Kaufman was there to rule in their favor. In a decision written before he had heard the oral arguments, after a hearing in which he had refused to even look at the table, Judge Kaufman denied the motion.* Because Harold C. Urey was one of the scientist witnesses listed for the prosecution's case, it was falsely conveyed to the defense and jury that Urey approved the government's position (actually, he was never even contacted).**
He came to the hearing with some doubt in his mind as to the guilt of our parents. During a recess a *New York Times* reporter asked Urey's opinion. He responded:

> Now that I see what goes on in Judge Kaufman's courtroom, I believe the Rosenbergs are innocent. When I look in that courtroom I see no Kaufman but McCarthy . . . What appalls me most is the role the press is playing. The judge's bias is so obvious. I keep looking over at you newspapermen and there's not a flicker of indignation or concern. When are you going to stop acting like a bunch of sheep?

The next day the *Times* reported Kaufman's denial of the motion without mentioning a single detail of the new evidence or reporting Urey's reaction.

The press blackout of the substance of our parents' appeals, the tremendous play allotted to prosecution arguments, angered our

---

* The judge spent fifteen minutes in his chambers after the oral arguments and then read an opinion which took thirty minutes. See Schneir, p. 212.
** Among the others were George Kistiakowsky, J. Robert Oppenheimer and General Leslie Groves.

parents even as they comprehended the reasons for it and sought to reach the public as it were "over the heads" of the press.

March 22, 1953

Precious Bunny,

I'm going around with that faraway look in my eyes. You guessed it. Just some more of that spring fever. Now that I've read . . . the latest issue of the National Guardian I can understand the reason for the New York Times giving such prominence to something that is only a rehash, that Greenglass asserts he did not lie! You will note that now they are finally forced to fall back on the weak premise that he says so and ergo it must be so! Sweetheart, the public is questioning, and very strongly so, the verdict in this case and they have reason to believe that it is corrupt . . .

YOUR, JULIE

April 16, 1953

My darling wife,

. . . In today's New York Times I read that the New York County Lawyers Association is looking into the growing evil of "trial by newspapers" that effectively prevents the accused form obtaining a fair, impartial trial. They could start off their work by looking into our case, and studying these egregious features that point out the terrible burden placed on an accused facing a passion-arousing charge. Is there any better proof of the complete bias of the press against us, than by noting their complete silence on the exposé of the so-called Russian "gift" console table? Obviously the kept press is corrupt and will not print the truth in this case. Of course whenever politics or special interests enter into the picture, honest reporting and writing true facts gives way to transient political needs. It is therefore of primary importance that the truth be made available to the greatest number of people that can be reached and that is the reason for the crucial need of the National Guardian and the Committee in this situation . . .

YOUR DEVOTED HUSBAND

April 23, 1953

My dearest wife:

. . . You probably will recall the last scene of Maxwell Anderson's "Mary of Scotland." Elizabeth tells Mary that she has seen to it that the history of her reign will be written as she orders her writers to put down the events although in fact they are untrue. Also in our case and even more so at this time, we see a similar situation in the way the newspapers are reporting the events in Korea. Of course, if you follow eight papers daily as I do you too would be able to immediately recognize contrived news reports to mislead the public. The way I see it, the "free press" is conditioning the people in order to blind them to the truth and confuse them and prevent an effective rallying behind a correct program. This is done because in spite of the efforts of the most reactionary forces in our government the people of the world are forcing a peace in Korea now and to continue their evil efforts they are pushing for a fascist domestic policy under the guise of anti-Communism. Since there is an interrelation between domestic and foreign policy each of these trends will effect the final outcome of peace in the world. It is therefore imperative at this time that the people help us win a victory which will contribute to advance the political trend of opposition to a police state at home and war abroad. It seems to me that spreading the facts about our case will insure that history will record the truth about this miscarriage of justice and give the public a chance to right the great wrong done us . . .

. . . I am confident we will win —

All my love,
JULIE

Until the Supreme Court's decision of May 25 denying *certiorari* for the second time, my nightmare prediction was pushed into the background. Nothing could happen to our parents until the next court decided, and the next court might even decide in our favor. Meanwhile they were still alive, and Robby and I could be together with them as well as hear from them in Sing Sing.

March 12, 1953

Dearest Ethel:

From both Michael's and my sister's letters I hear a note of greater confidence and it is indeed remarkable how people working for a good cause which is based on their convictions, can be fired with spirit, enthusiasm and courage. Actually, the most fruitful results are obtained from actions motivated by a thorough understanding of the situation and a knowledge of the purpose of what one wishes to accomplish. First I must say we are honored by the solicitude shown our children and my family by the good people the world over. Most important is that great numbers of people are aware that peace and freedom are the primary goals and they are alert to all issues such as our case that are an integral part of the major problem facing the world. We cannot ask any more than that we continue to work for this just cause as we fight to save ourselves . . .

Oh, darling, I feel so frustrated. I would like to stop the ordinary man on the street and talk to him for I feel sure it would be easy for both of us to agree on our joint interest. Then I begin to worry that I'm not writing and putting my thoughts down and use this means to get my views across. However, somehow it just doesn't always work out as easy as it should and do not for one moment think it is because I'm worried or downhearted that I'm not very productive, on the contrary, it is precisely because I want to be crystal clear in formulating my thoughts that it requires such great efforts on my part . . .

Always devoted to you —
YOUR HUSBAND — JULIE

April 26, 1953

My dearest wife,

Each succeeding time I see the children the parting becomes more difficult. .It is taking a terrific toll and I've been terribly heartsick since they left. The baby's crying and Michael's parting expressions were very painful and if it affects me this way I'm much concerned for the great hardship it visits on our beloved little ones. Truth is they are growing nicely and getting along well but definitely they are disturbed about our situation and their innocent young lives are being badly marked by this brutal tragedy. I'm beside myself in anguish impatient to help them and to assuage your own suffering somewhat. I'll try to console myself with the knowledge that I am acting in their best interest by defending our honor and maintaining our principles for a decent life with dignity. We really have a wonderful family, and I love you all so very much. Both of us can feel proud of our sons' personal accomplishments and it is important that they recognize themselves and are more confident in themselves as people. When will our government begin to recognize the great disgrace this case is bringing on its good name. Humanity is revolted by the cruelty involved in this case. I feel confident that the good people will be able to save us and set us free . . .

It is appropriate on this anniversary of the Warsaw Ghetto to recall the words: "May you on the outside be blessed. Where are our deliverers?" The American people must fight the creeping fascism that would destroy us all and the issues involved in our case require that we be freed to prevent the massacre of political opposition in our country. Resistance must be mobilized before the forces of darkness gain momentum against the people's interests. To the extent that the public is rallied to defend the causes of freedom, liberty and decency, to that extent will they defeat fascism, maintain peace and save our lives . . .

All my love,
YOUR JULIE

May 12, 1953

Dear Children,

Today was my birthday and I started the morning off with a very wonderful visit with your charming mother Ethel. She looked very pretty and welcomed me with a Happy Birthday and a big sweet smile. I told her, I sent our good friend and lawyer Manny a letter congratulating him because he happens to have a birthday on the same day.

Of course then we talked about our precious sons and how in

this one week when we were home together we celebrated Mother's day, my Birthday and last but by no means least our Robbie's Birthday. Brother Michael was a birthday boy last March, which is sort of a preview to you Robbie and now you yourself will be six years old. You must know son I am very happy on this day because we had the good fortune to have such a swell boy like you as one of our children and you can rest assured that I'll find ways even here to make this day more joyful. I suppose by the time you get this letter you will already have received our presents and we hope you like them.

I remember very well and I believe Michael remembers too, the day both of us went to the hospital and took Mommy and you home. Your brother was only 4 years then and he helped hold you while we rode in the car and I am sure that he is today proud of you Robbie as he was (on the whole) glad those days to have another baby home. Of course, today when one feels secure and is respected as an individual each one of us leans on our own worth and even as 6 & 10 year olds we are able to be much happier. Therefore my greatest pleasure is to have seen with my own eyes the very marked progress both of you have made this last year and at each birthday son we are proud of our achievements and mean to better ourselves to get more out of life. It goes without saying that learning to be social beings, getting along with our neighbors and understanding the world we live in are part of growing up and in this manner our dear friend Sonia and Ben have done a splendid job.

As for us your parents we are working to give you fellows the best present we know of and that is to win this case and come home to you. Growing up we are able to realize that at times good things that are really important require great sacrifice but difficulties must not deter us who are your mother and father from working for the best interest of you our children and all children.

I am aware that our good friends will try to make this day a joyous one for you boys and I want to send all my love, kisses and best wishes. Happy Birthday Robbie. We will look forward to spending the next one home with you. In the meantime I am glad to know that you our precious boys are busy doing your job, being boys and growing up and we your parents will work hard to do our part to win this case and come home soon —

All my love —
DADDY — JULIE

May 14, 1953

Dearest Ethel:

Congratulations, Mommy our baby is 6 years old today. It seems only yesterday he was only a tiny fellow and now he's going to school, writing, doing the things little boys do and growing up. Not only have they falsely accused us but they have robbed our little one of his babyhood and early boyhood and denied him the comfort and love of his parents that are his birthright. This crime against our children is the most dastardly part of the frame-up against us. When decent standards no longer exist and humane considerations are destroyed then all civilized people have much to fear from those political vicious men who rule the destinies of our lives. . . . It must be obvious to all that only positive mass action by the public will be successful in redirecting our country toward peace in the world. Also our future depends on this same fact.

I had not intended going into this type of a discussion but only to talk about our sons and the meaning of their birthday but we can't kid ourselves the most important need they have is for us to win our fight for freedom. . . . You know that I am terribly proud of our children and believe me when I say that I never loved them more dearly than I do now. The strong family bond and paternal feelings I have for Michael and Robbie give me my greatest incentive to do right by them and uphold the honor of our name. Of course, you, my darling are aware of the deep affection and profound love I have for each and every member of our fine family unit. To me this has always been the most vital factor in my real understanding of the life force. Understanding fundamental human relations and promising this bulwark of strength permits me to stand fast to the principles we hold dear and to defend the truth in the interest of honesty. Surely this position is a difficult one but at the same time the most rewarding one for my self-respect and dignity. I guess after 35 years I should be more modest in what I write, but in all sincerity and humbleness this is the true estimate of the way I see myself and my actions.

The afternoon after I saw you I had a pleasant ride through the prison as a birthday present. The lush green lawns, rows of tulips, all of the signs of spring, the wide river and open spaces were wonderful to see and then they spoiled it all by yanking out a molar. Imagine spoiling my birthday by pulling a tooth! There just ain't no justice.

The wonderful birthday cards I received were well chosen and expressed the right kind of sentiment and they moved me deeply. I just can't help loving my family and friends.

Always your own —
JULIUS

May 21, 1953

Ethel Darling,

At this moment I'm very lethargic and in a romantic mood. I guess it is the combined effect of a nice long spring day and a natural desire to be with my beloved. The constant longing is a powerful force that makes me ever conscious of my deep need for you and spins me on to renewed endeavors to be reunited as in the past. Everything seems so unreal and out of focus. Our weeks are marked off by the two short visits we have and the months, the years an endless period of torment and yet no sign of relief. It seems like we suspended somewhere, far off seeing everything that's being done and not being able to do anything even though we are the center of the controversy. A realization of the situation reveals the magnitude of the horrible dilemma. The initial attempt to stifle the life force and sterilize life of all its beauty and magnificence are after all the issues that are involved. Only understanding these things is it possible for the mind to comprehend the full meaning of our case and the fiendish death sentence against two innocent people. Perhaps what I am saying sounds a bit disjointed but you can believe me I am writing just as I feel about these things and getting them off my chest. I know I'll have a sympathetic listener in you. You will note that I think the most crucial attack against the American people is the psychological offense against a free and reasoning mind that frightens the individual into conformism, via hysteria. No self-respecting person with pride and dignity will be able to flourish under this situation and history has proven that the only answer to this autocratic anarchy is forthright defense of freedom, democracy and peace.

Therefore, my love it is not only a matter of life but also the most worthwhile attributes of civilization that we fight to maintain when we struggle to keep our principles of decency and the sacredness of our honor. With all this honey girl I am able to withstand the great pressures that force me to cry out for satisfaction because the mind and heart have added strength to the will. Sweetheart I hope you are able to translate these words into the deep honest feelings I have about this matter because then I am able to commune with you and it is my sincerest desire that we share these emotions and thoughts. Of course in my mind I've been thinking about our relationship and sometimes I am able to get across to you some of my intimate feelings in a letter even more so than through the screen and bars when I face you at our visits. It is that if we were really together there would be no obstacles to prevent our complete sharing as we have in the past. Silly me, you know there is only one answer to the problems I pose. I wanna go home with you dearest and enjoy life together. It is important that we continue to have faith and I know we'll both continue hoping. Always devoted to you —

YOUR OWN JULIE

During the summer of 1952 Robby and I had attended our first Rosenberg meeting, a picnic rally at a place called Friendship Farms Camp. There I was introduced to Helen Sobell, told that her husband, Morton, was a co-defendant of Julius and Ethel's and because he did not lie like the Greenglasses he was sentenced to thirty years in prison. Although I'd read the *National Guardian* regularly, I'd never heard of him. In her speech, Helen referred constantly to "Ethel and Julie and Morty." Momentarily I resented this "new" person for stealing some of the limelight from my parents. Recognizing how stupid this was, I went out of my way the next time I saw Helen to say (pompously), "Remember Helen, we're also fighting to free Morty." Only recently with the benefit of hindsight have I come to understand Morton's incredible courage through his long nineteen years in prison. While my parents feverishly tried to save their lives, Morton had only the endless prospect of "Doing Time" to look forward to. His incarceration prevented him from participating in the struggle to save them.

At the rally I insisted on taking the stage for the first and only time; against Ben and Sonia's wishes, I practically dragged Robby on stage. They urged me to quickly walk off without saying anything. All we did was wave to the crowd.

The major address was delivered by William Patterson, a black Communist and a leader of the Civil Rights Congress, which had sought to overturn the convictions of Willie McGee, the Trenton Six and many others in jail on trumped-up charges.* He struck a note of sober pessimism in his exhortations to the crowd: The Trenton Four was a victory but the Trenton Two remain in jail. Willie McGee was a defeat; the Rosenberg case was a defeat . . .** I asked someone why he called the Rosenberg case a defeat. The response was that at this time it's a defeat. I guess he hoped to exhort the crowd to make greater and greater efforts. I would have preferred a more optimistic speech. I didn't want to think of our parents' case as a defeat. They referred to that rally in their next letter.

July 27, 1952

To Our Most Precious Sons Michael & Robert,

Your mother and I were very happy to receive such a nice letter from our sweet boys. After Mr. Bloch and his wife visited you he came up here and spent a couple of hours with us. Most of the time was used in discussing his report on your living with

---

* For the story of the remarkable William Patterson, see his autobiography, *The Man Who Cried Genocide* (New York: International Publishers, 1971).
** For Trenton Six, see Belfrage, p. 142. I later found out that one of the Trenton Two, Colliss English, died in prison before his third trial. He had been in jail since 1948.

Sonia and Ben and on the day camp. From all that he said we know that you like it and are really enjoying every minute of the time.

You must understand that it took a great deal of planning until we were able to work out an arrangement with swell people like Sonia and Ben for you fellows to spend the summer there. They are warm-hearted people, good and kind and above all are doing all they can to help set us free and see that you our children are well taken care of. From your last letter I can tell you are comfortable and are able to relax and be yourselves. I know no better two people who can act as your temporary mother and father while we your parents are forced to be separated from you fighting to win our case. You went to the picnic boys and with your own eyes you could see many of the people who are behind us and you were able to hear with your own ears answers from strangers to some of the questions that are troubling you . . .

In the meantime dearests be patient and continue to play and have fun and leave it to us grownups to take care of our problems. I suppose Robbie and you Mike have found new playmates and friends and are enjoying the outdoors, swimming, games and new places. When you have an opportunity write us more about the day camp how you two are getting along and of course we want to hear more about Ben, Sonia, Leo and Maxine. Don't fail to give them our warmest greetings and love. To any friends who ask you tell them we are confident that we will win this case.

Your sweet mother and I are very glad that you are learning new things and are receiving the best possible care, understanding and love. There are very many wonderful people in this land who are doing their best to make this a better and happier world for all children to live in. We too are part of that and we are looking forward to the day when we will be reunited in our own home.

Your Dad — JULIE

One April Sunday in 1953, we accompanied Ben and Sonia to a big Rosenberg rally at Randall's Island's Downing Stadium in

New York City. They warned us not to call attention to ourselves
by talking with anyone or going on stage. This time I followed
their instructions to the letter — to the point of brusquely
rejecting Mike Minor whom I hadn't seen in almost a year.
Perhaps I didn't want to hint at my identity by fraternizing with
Mike. In any event he was hurt. (I'm glad we met again later and
renewed our friendship.)

The console table was displayed on stage. One of the only
speakers I remember was Grandma Sophie, who said, "That's the
table that I took" — in her accent, "Dat-ze de table; what I
took-it." With these words, the case should have collapsed
around the nation, but the press never printed the substance of
anything our side said.

During these spring months my grandmother and others in the
family labored long and hard on our parents' behalf. Grandma
was pretty effective with reporters. Asked about money from the
Russians, she dismissed the allegation: "I had to bring fruit to the
house they were so poor! The children should have fruit!"
Reporters commented to members of the Committee that
Grandma should have been speaking from the beginning. Her
direct, common-sense answers had impact. (Of course, until 1952
she was busy with Robby and me.) Several relatives sought
personal audiences with key officials and pleaded face to face with
Judge Kaufman (though he covered his eyes when Grandma
demanded he look at her). My uncle David Rosenberg extracted
from my mother's brother Bernard the affidavit corroborating our
parents' testimony that David Greenglass was in trouble for
stealing uranium from Los Alamos. These relatives provided a
major morale boost as the Supreme Court decision grew closer.

On May 25 the Supreme Court denied *certiorari*. The tension
present in our parents' letters of December and January reasserted
itself.

May 26, 1953

Dear Brother,

    . . . You will notice again the unseemly haste to deny us a
hearing to prove our claims. The only answer is that the Justice
Department is afraid to let us prove in court that we are indeed

innocent. It is obvious that this latest psychological campaign is well planned to brainwash the American people in our case and throw up a smoke screen so that they can get away from answering our new evidence by using self-serving statements and a false issue of talk to save our lives. Here we see the modern application of the rack and screw to coerce innocent people into false confessions and to use them with the threat of death. Many people now are convinced and all the world will come to know the plain truth that we are completely innocent.

I realize the pressures on all of us are tremendous and threats and fear cow many people but we must not falter to save our lives in a decent and honest way. At this time my heart goes out to Ethel, the children, Mama, the girls and you and I want our bond of flesh and blood to draw us close in love, comfort and understanding. Dave as brothers we have shared much together and what I treasure most is our close relationship as two separate individuals who respect each other and practice the tenets of real brotherhood. Ours is a most difficult task to prove the worth of the dignity of the individual and of human integrity in spite of a brutal sentence facing us. Take strength and help Mama and the girls stand up in the days that are ahead. I can tell you that Ethel and I will remain faithful to our children and our self-respect regardless of the outcome. You must continue to help us and don't for one minute ever allow the lies and threats to frighten you. I am sure our family will do all it can to save us. Send all my love to them.

Tell our friends to work hard the crucial hour is here now. I am confident the court of the people will still have a chance to prevent this miscarriage of justice . . .

. . . Your devoted brother,

JULIE

May 27, 1953

Dear Manny,

. . . Heil McCarthy! Imagine! Two impudent and imprudent heretics had the audacity to challenge the line laid down by our "gauleiter" in order not to deprive two lowly citizens of due process! Seriously, this is political persecution, shameless, blatant, cynical. But it must not be a cause for pessimism: the appearance of health often merely masks a rotting organism. The bravado, the display of strength must not be mistaken for victory itself; quite the contrary, it is only through a correct evaluation of the purely psychological nature of the attack that it will lose its power to cripple and immobilize the defense.

It is the relentless struggle to live life that defeats death! To put it in classic terms, "There is nothing to fear but fear itself." Tell the Bachs they must feel this great truth themselves, so that they may infect our children with their courage and ours. If we, the parents, dare not permit ourselves the luxury of emotionalism neither may they. More difficult yet, but unavoidable, they must be our voices, our strength and our love. On the rock of such proudly assumed burdens, the hate that would cruelly damn two innocent children must surely batter itself useless. How wonderful that the sacrifice brother must make for brother, and sister for sister, requires no apologies, no scraping, no bowing. Only an answering humility, an overpowering appreciation, unsolicited but freely forthcoming, wells up out of the depths of one's being. And it is suddenly a tremendous thing to acknowledge oneself human. Only comfort my kids; I can't help it, it hurts dreadfully for them.

All my love and all my devotion,
ETHEL

Judge Kaufman fixed the execution date for June 18.

May 31, 1953

Ethel Darling,

What does one write to his beloved when faced with the very grim reality that in eighteen days, on their 14th wedding anniversary, it is ordered that they be put to death? The approaching darkest hour of our trial and the grave peril that threatened us require every effort on our part to avoid hysteria and false heroics, but only maintain a sober and calm approach to our most crucial problems . . .

Dearest, over and over again, I have tried to analyze in the most objective manner possible the answers to the position of our government in our case. Everything indicates only one answer — that the wishes of certain madmen are being followed in order to use this case as a coercive bludgeon against all dissenters. However, I still have faith that the more responsible elements in the administration will let sanity be the better part of judgment and save our lives. It seems to me that at this moment it is still touch and go, and therefore we must see to it that the maximum is done in our behalf . . .

Sweetheart, I know that our children and our family are suffering a great deal right now and it is natural that we be concerned for their welfare. However I think we will have to concentrate our strength on ourselves. First, we want to make sure that we stand up under the terrific pressure, and then we ought to try to contribute some share to the fight. To my way of looking at the problem, this is the way we can look out for our children's interests best . . . All the love I possess is yours —

JULIE

On June 2, James V. Bennett, the Director of the Bureau of Prisons, visited my parents as a direct emissary of Attorney General Brownell. He made a flagrant "talk or die" offer which our parents reacted to with a press release condemning the offer and insisting upon their innocence. The Justice Department responded by claiming the visit was "routine," no deal had been offered.

June 5, 1953

Dear Manny,

. . . After reading the bald lie of the Justice Department that Mr. Bennett's visit was routine and that they intimated no deal was offered, I feel it my duty to present the facts as they took place last Tuesday.

First, let me tell you that the mental torture Ethel and I went through took a very great toll and has revealed the naked, ugly brutality of police state tyranny.

On Monday, June 1st, Mr. Carroll and Mr. Foley, U.S. Marshals were up to serve us with papers setting down our executions . . . Their visit was routine.

Tuesday at 11:00 A.M. after my visit with Ethel, I was ushered
into the counsel room and there was Mr. Bennett. Mind you,
this was the first time I was alone with anyone without an officer
or Sing Sing official present (I believe it's against the regulations
here) . . .

Mr. Bennett opened the conversation and said:

"Mr. Brownell, the Attorney General, sent me to see you and
he wants you to know that if you want to cooperate with the
government you can do so through me and I will be able to
make arrangements for you to talk with any proper officials.
Furthermore, if you Julius can convince the official that you
have fully cooperated with the government, they have a basis to
recommend clemency."

You can realize how shocked I was, but I didn't want to lose
my temper or my self-control and I said that in the first place,
we were innocent, that is the whole truth and therefore we know
nothing that would come under the meaning of the word
"cooperate." By the way, I asked, did you tell our lawyer that
you were coming to us about this matter?

He said no, your lawyer will see you tomorrow. I told him to
get in touch with you as it was the only proper thing to do. He
said he would, later on.

You mean to tell me, Mr. Bennett, I said, that a great
government like ours is coming to two insignificant people like
us and saying "cooperate or die?" It isn't necessary to beat me
with clubs, but such a proposal is like what took place during
the Middle ages. It is equivalent to the screw and rack. You are
putting a tremendous pressure on me.

He said, "Why, do you know that I didn't sleep last night
when I knew I had to see you and Ethel the next day and talk to
you about this matter? I was terribly worried."

How do you think we feel sitting here waiting for death for
over two years when we are innocent, I asked. My family has
gone through great suffering. My sister had a breakdown; my
aged, ailing mother is tormented; our children have known
much emotional and mental agony. Then you talk to us about
this! Remember, Mr. Bennett, we love our country, it is our
home, the land of my children and my family. We do not want

its good name to be shamed and in justice and common decency, we should be allowed to live to prove our innocence.

He then said, "No, not a new trial. Only by cooperating will there be a basis to ask for commutation. Look here, Julius," he said, "you didn't deny that you do not know anything about this espionage." I certainly did, I answered, and furthermore, did you read the trial record, sir?

He said he had not, but continued, saying, "you had dealings with Elizabeth Bentley."

I never did, and if you read the record, she said on the witness stand that she did not know me and never met me.

"But you had dealings with Gold, didn't you?"

Of course I didn't. Gold also said on the stand he never met me or knew me. You should have read the record to be familiar with the facts.

"Oh, I read the newspaper accounts of it." (It is interesting to note how they become convinced of their own lies and will not stick to the trial record of the case.)

"Listen Julius, I was just sent here, but if you agree, I will bring someone to see you who is thoroughly familiar with the case and you will try to convince him you have cooperated with the government."

What do you want to do, I asked? Have him convince me I am guilty, when I am not. You want him to put ideas in my head. You will only be satisfied when I say the things you want me to say, but I will not lie about this matter.

"Look Julius," he said. "Gordon Dean, the head of the Atomic Energy Commission, is a very good friend of mine and if he is convinced that you have cooperated fully and told all you know about espionage he will see the President and recommend clemency."

I don't know anything about espionage, since I am innocent and I think you should tell the Attorney General to recommend clemency because it is the just, humane and proper thing to do in this case. Our country has a reputation to maintain in the world and many of its friends are outraged at the barbaric sentence and the lack of justice in this case.

"I know there has been a lot of publicity in the case, but that is not germane. What is the point is that you have to convince the officials that you have cooperated. Well, Julius, why did your brother-in-law involve you?"

I believe he did it to save his own skin, also to try to make himself out to be a minor, innocent dupe dominated by someone else so that he should not be held accountable for his own actions. Besides, the government had caught the Greenglasses with the goods and they had to find some way to mitigate their own punishment. With my background of being fired for alleged communism from the government service, because I was a union organizer, and since he was a relative and knew me intimately, and we had violent quarrels and there existed personal animosity between us, I was falsely involved. Also the prosecution saw a chance to make great political capital out of "communist-spy-atom-bomb." My wife and I became scapegoats and were straws tossed around by the political controversies that raged in the cold war. Why not go to the Greenglasses and get *them* to cooperate to tell the truth about this family?

You yourself, Mr. Bennett, as head of the Prison Bureau, know that Greenglass and Gold were together in the Tombs for nine months discussing the case, studying notes from a big looseleaf book, rehearsing testimony, talking to FBI Agents, the prosecution, and their attorney. You know this because the records of the Tombs will show it, and yet your department refused to give us an opportunity to subpoena these records to prove this. You know that Greenglass was coached on the A-bomb sketch testimony, both verbally and from notes. You know the prosecution permitted the Greenglasses to perjure themselves. You know the prosecution caused Schneider to perjure himself. You know the government is preventing my wife's family from coming forth with exculpating evidence that they are withholding from the court. In short, we did not get a fair trial and we were framed. Now you want us to admit that this big lie is the truth. That we can never do.

Sure Mr. Bennett, we will cooperate fully. Give us our day in court and under oath from the witness stand, we will repeat the truth and at the same time, we will be able to subpoena witnesses to prove our claims. That is the way to give us justice.

"Oh no, Julius. No new trial — only by cooperating can you help yourself."

But you can have the district attorney agree to one of our motions? Then we will put up or shut up, and I am sure we will be vindicated.

"No. That is not germane. You have to cooperate with the government."

How about the death sentence? Certainly, even if the verdict were a true one, which we vehemently deny, we never should have gotten such a severe sentence. The history of our country in freeing war criminals, Nazi and fascist, in not putting to death traitors and spies, and yet, for the first time making the Rosenbergs the worst criminals in all our history — You know, as a reasoning man, this is not right. All the facts in the case, the trial record, and the sentence prove it was a means of coercion. The humane, just and proper action would be for our lives to be spared. We are a leading, powerful country with a great prestige in the world and we must consider what the people will think about the fact that our government says to two people, "Cooperate or die." Remember, it would be in the best interest of our country to commute our sentence of death.

"But Julius, I am giving you the opportunity to cooperate," he said. Sure, Judge Kaufman made a terrible blunder with this outrageous sentence and he has the bull of the tail and he can't let go.

"That's right, Julius. He needs you to help him change this sentence and you can do this by telling all you know." I cannot bail him out for his mistake, for we never should have received this sentence and in fact, we never should have been brought to trial.

"Julius, all the courts upheld the conviction many times and all the officials in Washington believe you guilty. Why most everybody believes you guilty."

You know that only one appeals court upheld the verdict of the original trial and the denial of *certiorari* does not pass on the merits of a case. At all other times, we didn't get a hearing, but only the right to file papers. This is the form of the law, not its spirit. Always such haste — because they are afraid we will prove our innocence. Also people like Dr. Urey, Professor Einstein, scientists, lawyers, men of letters have grave doubts about the case after reading the trial record. The Pope, three thousand Christian Church leaders, prominent rabbis and millions of people have asked for clemency.

"No, Julius. The Pope did not ask for clemency."

Yes he did. And I have the articles from *L'Osservatore Romano* to prove it. We had the record printed — the one that records the entire proceedings of the trial and people read it and they came away with grave doubts about the justness of the verdict. This record is available and will be read. The only way to cleanse this damning record is to let us live so we can prove our innocence.

"Julius, the trial not being fair, the sentence being too severe, and all the publicity are not germane to the issue. The only way is for you to cooperate and convince the officials in Washington. Then, they will have a basis to ask for clemency."

All these three years, you say, I am not telling the truth. Then if I say what you want me to say, that would be "cooperating," and then it would be the "truth." In good conscience, I would not lend myself to this practice and I must say in effect, this pressure on us is cruel and unconscionable. The only decent thing to do is to tell Mr. Brownell to recommend clemency.

It was twelve o'clock when he went in to see Ethel for a half-hour, and then they brought me into the women's wing and he continued to try to browbeat us for another half-hour until one P.M. Ethel will tell you about what took place during this hour.

At the end of our session, the Warden walked into the women's wing and asked, what is this all about? I told him Mr. Brownell sent Mr. Bennett to tell us if we cooperated with the Government he would recommend clemency to the President. You will note that the Warden was not present when the offer was made.

After I was in my cell again after one P.M. Mr. Bennett came over and he tried to convince me again to let him bring people who are familiar with the case and "you would submit to answering questions of what you know about this." Then I said, why this would be like brain washing, Mr. Bennett! He then asked if he could come to see me again and I said yes, if he brings good news. Ethel and I resolved not to see anyone except when you are present also . . .

JULIE

June 7, 1953

Dear Manny,

. . . I must say for Ethel that she is indeed a gem, a most marvelous and heroic woman. Although the strain has been very severe, I am proud that we were able to resist the mental torture successfully. It is good to know that all of us are doing our utmost. When, oh when will our agony be over and how soon will we see some daylight? We are waiting and hoping to hear the good news soon.

As ever, JULIE

Our mother wrote in painful detail of Mr. Bennett's "talk or die" offer.

June 8–9, 1953

Dear Manny,

. . . As you may recall, on Tuesday of June 2nd always hereafter to be remembered as "Deal Day" Mr. James V. Bennett, Federal Director of Prisons, paid us a "routine" visit at Sing Sing and we wired you at once, concerning same. To fully comprehend the true significance of this incident it is necessary to examine a number of salient factors.

Ever since the imposition upon us of a manifestly savage and vengeful sentence we have been periodically advised via newspaper, radio and television, that the opportunity to save ourselves rested upon our willingness to "cooperate" with the Government and "confess" our guilt. Often, these unofficial "invitations" to "talk" had risen in pitch and intensity to such an extraordinarily well-timed and collective clamor, as would have indicated a definite purpose on the part of the Government. Indeed, hot upon the heels of the Supreme Court's latest refusal to review, it was deliberately and falsely reported that an offer had been made us; and when you, as our counsel, roundly and publicly denounced this "news item" as an unethical fabrication, the Government was forced to show its hand. Subsequent events hear me out, to wit. After Judge Kaufman had, with his usual indelicate haste, fixed the week of June 15th for our joint execution, two U.S. Marshalls in the presence of the Warden, personally served me with official notification papers . . . That was Monday, June 1st. The very next day, just as I was sitting down to lunch, Mr. Bennett entered the women's wing of the Death house and announced himself. Contrary to all established practice, he was alone with me . . . Mr. Bennett came right to the point. Attorney General Herbert Brownell, Jr. had directed him to inform me that he could make available to me any official to whom I might care to divulge espionage information I had hitherto withheld. If I cooperated in this fashion, the Government stood ready to invalidate the death penalty. He had been visiting with Julie for an hour — since my husbands personal visit with me had ended at 11:00 A.M. as a matter of fact and now he was anxious to get my viewpoint.

I made it short and sweet. I was innocent, my husband was innocent, and neither of us knew anything about espionage. And if the Attorney General were to send a highly placed authority to see me, I should simply reiterate what I had just stated and urge that clemency be recommended to remedy a shocking situation.

Gently, Mr. Bennett prodded me to "cooperate." "Surely you must know something," he coaxed. I picked him up quickly, "Well, now, how could I when I did not participate in any way? In order to cooperate as you desire, I should have to deliberately concoct a pack of lies and bear false witness against unoffending individuals. Is that what the authorities want me to do — to lie?" He was properly horrified. "Oh, dear, no, of course we don't want you to lie. But now take a family, for example. One member might not be actively engaged in certain activities, but still have the knowledge concerning another member's activities." I was exceedingly polite but firm. "The fact still remains that I don't know any more than I knew during the trial. I told the full and complete truth then, and I don't intend to start lying now." He tried another tack. "I am a perfectly honest individual myself, yet my experience in these matters has shown me that for one reason or another, a person will sometimes plead innocent, knowing full well that he is guilty. Wouldn't you agree with that?" "I will be just as frank," I replied evenly, "and grant you that there have been such instances. Nevertheless, I couldn't possibly concern myself as to the motives involved in such cases. I do, however, know my own mind and heart, and I tell you in all conscience that I continue to maintain my innocence for the sole reason that I am simply not guilty of the charge."

"Well, the Government claims to have in its possession documents and statements that would dispute that, so if only you were willing to cooperate, there might be a basis for a commutation." *

I remained entirely unimpressed. "To begin with, I couldn't possibly know, nor do I care, what they have or don't have. Whatever it might be, it has nothing to do with me. Besides, if what they have is so damaging, why do they need me to confirm it, at this late stage? If you are persuading me to confess to activities concerning which I have solemnly sworn I have no knowledge, on the basis of evidence with which I was never confronted in court, then obviously the validity of this evidence must be strongly questioned, if it in fact exists at all. I will tell you this very bluntly. The most powerful Government on earth has sent its representative to approach two insignificant little people with a disgraceful proposition, because it is fully aware that the convictions were illegally procured, the sentences vindictive. And rather than risk exposing their participation in a rotten frame-up, and with a double execution they are anxious not to carry out only days away, they have the effrontery to try

* This claim endures two decades later. Prosecutor Saypol told the jurors after the conviction that he hadn't used over half the evidence. Yet when independent researchers and others have asked to see the files, the government has refused. (One secret report, prepared by Justice Department official Benjamin Pollack in 1957, supposedly was based on all the government's information. Researchers have since seen this report and it contains nothing new.)

to forcibly wring from us a false confession, by dangling our lives before us like bait before hapless fish! Pay the price we demand, or forfeit your lives, is that the idea?"

At this juncture, Mr. Bennett hastened to stem the rising tide of my indignation. "Come, come I have not said anything of the sort, you are misinterpreting me." "On the contrary," I retorted, "I have understood you far too well. Of course, you are not quite so cold-blooded, but I have interpreted to you, and correctly, the Government's intent. So here is our answer. We will not be intimidated by the threat of electrocution into saving their faces, nor will we encourage the growing use of undemocratic police state methods by accepting a shabby, contemptible little deal in lieu of the justice that is due us as citizens. That is for Hitler Germany, not for the land of liberty. A truly great, honorable nation has the obligation to redress grievances not to demand tribute of those who have been wronged. For grudgingly sparing their lives — lives that should never have been placed in jeopardy at all!!"

"But we are trying to help you by seeking your cooperation," he pleaded, beginning to flounder in earnest now. Somehow, he was not managing things as he had doubtless intended, and the mask of nonchalant authority was beginning to slip, revealing his very real discomfiture. "Say, what you will," I declared unmoved, "camouflage it, glamorize it, whitewash it, in any way you choose, but this is coercion, this is pressure, this is torture." I pointed to the clock that was cheerfully ticking away my life. "Let me say to you in all sobriety you will come to me at ten minutes of 11:00 P.M. on Thursday, June 18th and the fact of my innocence will not have changed in the slightest" . . .

Throwing up his hands in despair, finally, he requested that Julie be brought in. For another half-hour he fairly entreated us to "cooperate," even promising to enlist the aid of his good friend, Gordon Dean, Chairman of the Atomic Energy Commission. My husband was wonderfully poised and forthright. "How can America stoop to such tactics," he demanded, "and hope to command the continued respect and affection and support of our friends. It is simply unthinkable! Frankly, as one human being to another, can you offer me one reason that might possibly justify the unheard of barbarity of the sentence? And don't you feel at all called upon to recommend clemency to the Attorney General as a matter of plain, ordinary decency and common sense? How can this nation afford to let such villainy go unchallenged and be indelibly recorded to the everlasting shame of incoming generations! Wouldn't it be the better part of valor to grant Mr. Bloch the opportunity to prove our contention that the entire conduct of the case was marked by passion, prejudice and perjury? Just imagine! Even if it were true, and it is not, my wife is awaiting a horrible end for having typed a few notes! A heinous crime, "worse than murder," no doubt, and deserving of the supreme penalty, while the most atrocious and wanton killers known to civilization, the Nazi war criminals, are being freed daily . . ."

Mr. Bennett began to look a little distraught. "What you're saying is not germane. Please, if you would only agree to cooperate, something could be worked out. There just won't be any other way." (sic!) "Of course," I interjected, "a hearing based on new evidence is not germane; after all, we might actually be able to prove our claims. But it is germane for the government of a great nation to victimize two helpless people just because a world controversy has developed as to their guilt, and to tell them in effect, to knuckle under or die!"

Oh, I neglected to mention that a good bit after Julie's arrival the Warden had finally come hurrying in. Now the visit was beginning to draw to a close. My husband was speaking, "Consider carefully, wouldn't it be more advantageous to the United States to let us live? Wouldn't it be a real proof to the peoples of the world that this country is genuinely concerned with human rights? Doesn't your coming here at the behest of the Attorney General indicate that the handling of the case has cost us a good deal of prestige on the other side? Obviously, it would be much less costly in terms of this prestige to give us the opportunity to prove our innocence!"

"Oh, oh, there's been so much politics made of this case — too much — and it isn't germane. You say you have never hurt your country, do you?"

As we vigorously assented, he said, "Well, then, cooperate

and give us the information we need to enable us to recommend a commutation!" We stared at him, appalled; then Julie said slowly: "You see, Mr. Bennett, we love her so much we will not permit her good name to be dishonored by entering into an immoral arrangement!"

He shrugged his shoulders wearily . . . As he turned to go, I made a final plea. "Grant us our day in court, Mr. Bennett. Let us live that we may prove our innocence. That's the decent way, the American way!"

Afterwards I learned that he had followed Julie back into his own corridor and had attempted yet once more to convince him that his only hope lay in "cooperation" . . .

ETHEL

With the executions less than two weeks away, Manny filed the motion for a Sec. 2255 evidentiary hearing on June 5. The console table and other new evidence were introduced.

June 7, 1953

Ethel Darling:

I must say I had an excellent visit with my sister and it is most gratifying that my family are all busily working on our behalf; confident of ultimate victory instead of being paralyzed with fear engendered by the latest nefarious actions of the prosecution in this case. I think the spirit that has raised their morale is indeed indicative of a trend for the better. Of course, after my sister told me about the new evidence that has been uncovered I too, was heartened. It seems to me and I believe I know a great deal about our case that the latest motion for a new trial is beyond any doubt our strongest legal action and besides it contains some devastating stuff that can break this case wide open. The only reason I have any reserve about it is that we must go before Kaufman and by past performance he will not let the law govern in our case. However, if the information contained in the new evidence motion papers is widely circulated, the courts will be forced to give them some consideration. At any rate, I am still hopeful about our chances in the courts. Especially since the public campaign in our behalf is gaining strength and also because the political situation in the world is changing for the better. Considering all the angles I feel that we can still be optimistic about winning this case at this late hour.

Of course, I don't want you to get me wrong. I am under no illusions about the benignity of certain of the officials who run the country but I have to hope that reasonable and practical minds will govern and determine the final decision of our government if and when it does come down to the question of life or death. At the moment nobody can tell what the exact solution will be but in a large measure our analysis of the case has always been found to be correct and I am confident that we will live to prove our innocence.

. . . I have faith that we will live to be in each other's arms again — love you always —

YOUR JULIE

June 11, 1953

Dearest Manny,

No wonder you are confident, the latest stuff is terrific. Reading it has given me a good deal of comfort.

Nevertheless, I am under no illusions and am preparing myself for the worst, while remaining just as hopeful and working hard for the best. Since, however, I am a grown woman, I have to figure there might be last goodbyes to make. In this respect, I am fairly beside myself because of the tiny amount of time left in which legal matters must take precedence over personal ones. You know what's bothering me; how can you possibly be expected to continue making the necessary moves (and they will be made right up to the last), and still manage to bring up the children. Tell me, magnanimous sirs, have we grown so calloused, so inured to kindness and simple human decency, that we unconcernedly plan to re-unite a couple in death on their 14th wedding anniversary, after having deprived them also of a last bit of happiness with their children. After all "justice" might not triumph if too much time were frittered away on such frivolous amenities! I say mercy must also have "its day in court," lest law become a jungle beast prowling for prey.

Besides, I remember very distinctly reading an article in the "Times" which quoted Justice Vinson as saying he was denying a stay because he didn't think the government would set a date before June 15 — Furthermore, you yourself told us he hadn't passed on the merit of your request but that the request was made too soon and therefore denied it. Doesn't it strike you as odd that ever since the date was set, everybody (press and radio alike) has been harping on the same old theme of June 18th as though nothing could possibly happen to upset the "proper" functioning of the well-oiled machinery! Doesn't it help to pressure the Supreme Court into making a hasty decision because there's a "deadline" to meet!

I should feel so relieved if there were a stay, so that come what might after it was used up, I should know at least that our affairs were completely in order and that we had had ample opportunity to visit with our children.

Do something, Manny, try, won't you. It is inconceivable to me that they will permit such a piece of crudity as our execution on our wedding anniversary. But then, I am an incurably soft individual who just can't understand how men may sound and look like men and be only sadistic devils in disguise!

In any case, plan to see us next without the children. We deserve your exclusive legal attention, emotional deprivation or not. If your back-breaking efforts yield fruit, there will be plenty of time to visit socially at our leisure. We serve the children's needs much more for the present by concentration on our defense . . .

Love,
ETHEL

June 10–11, 1953

Dear Manny

It is encouraging to hear that you are confident and most comforting to receive your sincere greetings. The latest legal papers came with your note and I read them over carefully . . .

These papers should, and conceivably could shock and perhaps will *shame* the august court to take definitive steps in initiating a review which will allow the stinking mess to be aired, and in time correct the hypocritical parody of justice which has been palmed off on us as being a "fair trial" . . .

However, Manny, in an intelligent and adult appraisal of our grave situation, and of the many other worthy legal showings made to the courts, what can I tell myself as assuring that this too will not go out the window? That as applied to us, the law has absconded into the never-never land of politics and maybe by vigorous tactics as these latest, you our lawyers may shock or shame the judiciary to forsake the executive branch of government and *act* as a judiciary branch! Mind you I say this studying our legal situation in the most objective manner projecting myself into the position of those responsible officials who must calmly weigh what is truly in the best interests of our country and justice.

I realize full well that the political situation is the determining factor in our case. Therefore considering the growing world opinion in our behalf and the easing of international tensions and the proximity of a truce in Korea, our execution at this time will be looked on as an act of madness and a reversion to barbarism. Because of this I am able to hope that the Court will decide one of our legal actions on its merits on the basis of law.

At this point we have completed a record that for all time raises grave doubts about our guilt and the government can rectify this miscarriage of justice very simply if we are allowed to live. Our many legal actions give them an opportunity to give us our day in court . . .

The simple truths and the issues as they are drawn in and around our case demand a vigorous and determined fight for justice and life. It is now Thursday morning June 11th as I finish this letter and our date is set for next week. Will the people deliver us to celebrate our wedding Anniversary or will they let us go to our doom? The answer is in their hands.

. . . All my love — As ever —

JULIE

On June 12, 1953, the last day of school, I looked forward to three full months of leisure time with my friends. But the summer had to begin a week later. On June 14, we got up early to catch a chartered bus to Washington, D.C., filled with our friends. In the capital we joined our grandmother and the Almans. I promptly acted the lover by racing into Shelley's arms, kissing her and holding her hand as we walked up to the White House. A week before, I had written a letter given me to copy to President Eisenhower.

I think this tactic was a mistake. Though I vaguely understood the reference to Oatis, a more patient approach, drawing out my own formulation of a letter to Eisenhower would have been more effective. In any event, whether it was my letter or not, Eisenhower probably never would have seen it.

Now I carried the letter to the White House gates and handed it to the guard. Unlike the prison visits in which I sensed the reporters' hostility to my parents, here the reporters seemed to belong to the large clemency picket. I had been told to say nothing to the reporters other than what I had to say was contained in the letter. But I was excited about being photographed and interviewed. In various news programs and movies I had been impressed by the phrase, "No comment," which I desperately wanted to say; yet I respected Dave and Emily Alman and so I wanted to obey their directions. After I handed the letter to the White House guard, I achieved a compromise when a microphone was thrust into my face, a friendly voice asking if I had anything to say. Dave Alman began, "The kids are pretty tired . . ." but I happily plunged ahead: "Everything I had to say was in the letter. I wouldn't wish to comment further."

Robby's recollection of the trip is not so pleasant, as he sensed desperation and was offended by the adults cooing over him. We did not participate in the picketing, but I do remember the signs — "Michael Rosenberg [or Robby Rosenberg] says 'Please save my mommy and daddy.' " — which I would gladly have carried.

On Monday, June 15, the Supreme Court refused a stay of execution which would have permitted Manny breathing room to file a brief outlining the new evidence. The five-to-four vote was upsetting. Justices Robert Jackson and Felix Frankfurter joined Black and Douglas. I previously calculated to myself that since the Supreme Court had decided eight-to-one and seven-to-two against us, the five-to-four vote meant the arithmetic was improving. The next time we'd win. I also thought that the five-to-four vote might induce Eisenhower to grant clemency.

The next day Robby, Ben and I were driven to New York City

Dear President Eisenhower,

I saw on television on Monday, Mr Oatis is not in prison anymore because the President of the country let him go. It said his wife will write a letter to the President over there and she told why Mr Oatis should be let on. I think it is a good thing to let him go home because I think prison is a very bad place for anybody to be.

My mommy and daddy are in prison in New York. My brother is six years old his name is Robby. He misses them very much and I miss them too. I got the idea to write you from Mr Oatis on television. Please let my mommys and daddys go and not let anything happen to them. If they come home Robby and I will be very happy we will thank you very much

Very truly yours
Michael Rosenberg

to meet Manny, who rode with us to Sing Sing for the visit our mother had asked for. I knew that there was an application for a stay before Justice Douglas. If that failed, Eisenhower was the last hope. We saw both parents together, they sat at opposite ends of the table. Robby and I wandered around the room, hugging them and listening. I took heart when Manny said, "Douglas won't grant the stay but I'm sure Eisenhower will grant clemency." Our mother read aloud a "mercy" letter she had written to Eisenhower. Though I heard only snatches of it, my ears pricked up at the mention of the Oatis affair cited in my letter.

354 Hunter St.,
Ossining, N. Y.

June 16, 1953

President Dwight D. Eisenhower
White House, Washington, D. C.
Dear Mr. President,

At various intervals during the two long and bitter years I have spent in the Death House at Sing Sing, I have had the impulse to address myself to the President of the United States. Always, in the end, a certain innate shyness, an embarrassment almost, comparable to that which the ordinary person feels in the presence of the great and the famous, prevailed upon me not to do so.

Since then, however, the moving plea of Mrs. William Oatis on behalf of her husband has lent me inspiration. She had not been ashamed to bare her heart to the head of a foreign state; would it really be such a presumption for a citizen to ask for redress of grievance and to expect as much consideration as Mrs. Oatis received at the hands of strangers?

Of Czechoslovakia I know very little, of her President less than that. But my own land is a part of me, I should be homesick for her anywhere else in the world. And Dwight D. Eisenhower was "Liberator" to millions before he was ever "President." It does not seem reasonable to me, then, that a letter concerning itself with condemned wife as well as condemned husband, should not merit this particular President's sober attention.

True, to date, you have not seen fit to spare our lives. Be that as it may, it is my humble belief that the burdens of your office and the exigencies of the times have allowed of no genuine opportunity, as yet, for your more personal consideration.

It is chiefly the death sentence I would entreat you to ponder. I would entreat you to ask yourself whether that sentence does not serve the ends of "force and violence" rather than an enlightened justice. Even granting the assumption that the convictions had been properly procured (and there now exists incontrovertible evidence to the contrary), the steadfast denial of guilt, extending over a protracted period of solitary confinement and enforced separation from our loved ones, makes of the death penalty an act of vengeance.

As Commander-in-Chief of the European theatre, you had ample opportunity to witness the wanton and hideous tortures that such a policy of vengeance had wreaked upon vast multitudes of guiltless victims. Today, while these ghastly mass butchers, these obscene racists, are graciously receiving the benefits of mercy and in many instances being reinstated in public office, the great democratic United States is proposing the savage destruction of a small unoffending Jewish family, whose guilt is seriously doubted throughout the length and breadth of the civilized world! As you have recently so wisely declared, no nation can chance "going it alone." That, Mr. President, is truly the voice of the sanity and of the leadership so sorely needed in these perilous times. Surely you must recognize then, that the ensuing damage to the good name of our country, in its struggle to lead the world toward a more equitable and righteous way of life, should not be underestimated.

Surely, too, what single action could more effectively demonstrate this nation's fealty to religious and democratic ideals, than the granting of clemency to my husband and myself.

Such an act would also be a fitting reply to a small boy's desperate appeal. His bright young mind and homesick heart prompted him (even as his mother's was prompted), to see in Mr. Oatis' release, a hope for the release of his own dear parents. I approach you then as he did, solely on the basis of mercy, and earnestly beseech you to let this quality sway you rather than any narrow judicial concern, which is after all the province of the courts. It is rather the province of the affectionate grandfather, the sensitive artist, the devoutly religious man, that I would enter. I ask this man, himself no stranger to the humanities, what man there is that History has acclaimed great, whose greatness has not been measured in terms of his goodness? Truly, the stories of Christ, of Moses, of Ghandi hold more sheer wonderment and spiritual treasure than all the conquests of Napoleon!

I ask this man, whose name is one with glory, what glory there is that is greater, than the offering to God of a simple act of compassion!

Take counsel with your good wife; of statesmen there are enough and to spare. Take counsel with the mother of your only son; her heart which understands my grief so well and my longing to see my sons grown to manhood like her own, with loving husband at my side even as you are at hers — her heart must plead my cause with grace and with felicity!

And the world must humbly honor greatness!

Respectfully yours,

(signed)   (MRS.) ETHEL ROSENBERG #110-510
WOMEN'S WING — CC

When it was time to leave, I faced the denouement of my nightmare prediction. The day after tomorrow our parents would die. I had never contemplated death, would not fully comprehend the horror of either death or capital punishment for many years; nevertheless, I knew that their dying was something terrible. Yet they didn't seem to consider it as such. I wanted them to *do* something. This was not an ordinary visit — "see you next time" — this was it! What could I do to stress that fact? I started to wail, "One more day to live. One more day to live." I was not crying. I was not so much disturbed for myself as I was disturbed by their nonchalance. They tried to assuage my fears as they kissed us goodbye. Of course, I didn't know about Bennett. Breaking down in front of us was a luxury they could not afford; they were engaged in a tremendous act of will, with the "deal" there for the taking. My mother understood exactly what I was trying to say, and quickly penned a letter to us. I doubt I would have understood it if I had received it, but now her insight comforts me.

June 17, 1953 *

Dear Manny,

Please send this letter to the kids or phone it in to them or send by messenger in as short a time as possible as I don't know where they are staying now.

My dearest darlings,

This is the process known as "sweating it out," and it's tough, that's for sure . . .

Maybe you thought that I didn't feel like crying too when we were hugging and kissing goodbye, huh, even though I'm slightly older than 10. And maybe you thought I was just too matter of fact to stand, when your outraged feelings demanded acknowledgement in kind. Darlings, that would have been so easy, far too easy on myself; and I had to resist a very real temptation to follow your lead and break down with you. As I say it would have been only too easy, but it would not have been any kindness, at all. So I took the hard way instead of the easy, because I love you more than myself, and because I knew you needed that love far more than I needed the relief of crying.

Instead, I reassured you, as well as I could, in the minutes we had, and promised to write. There is one thing among many others I'd like you to know. The kisses are there between Daddy and myself even though we may not exchange them presently.** And while it would be sweet to be able to do so, it is only to the degree that parents are able to give each other and their children the strength and encouragement to cope with their problems and to "sweat it out" if need be, it is only to that degree, I say, that people really love.

I know, sweethearts, an explanation of this kind cannot ever substitute for what we have been missing and for what we hope

* This is misdated. She wrote it on the 16th.
** At one prison visit I had said, "I never saw Mommy and you kiss" (obviously referring to them not kissing in prison).

to be able to return to, nor do I intend it as any such thing. Only, as I say, we need to try to remain calm and free from panic, so that we can do all we can to help one another to see this thing through! . . .

All my love and all my kisses —

MOMMY

We returned to New Jersey, Manny to Washington. The next day, June 17, Robby and I were playing Monopoly. Sonia and Maxine were in the kitchen. All of a sudden there was an incredible commotion, Maxine yelling what sounded like, "Ma! Ma! I almost broke my neck!" More screaming, but oddly they sounded happy. They burst in on us and started hugging us. "The Douglas stay! The Douglas stay!" I couldn't believe it; Manny had been so sure he wouldn't grant it. As the news sunk in, we became wildly happy, Robby included. He had noticed me listening to the news a lot, but had been keeping to himself the fear that our parents would die. He had even imagined that Manny had to list ten reasons why they should be allowed to live, and because Manny had succeeded, the stay was granted.*

Throughout the afternoon, we sang "William O. Douglas for President." The same day Congressman Wheeler of Georgia introduced an impeachment resolution against Douglas. Before the afternoon was over, we learned that Attorney General Brownell was requesting a special Supreme Court session to overturn Douglas' stay; by the evening Chief Justice Vinson recalled the Court for the following morning. We didn't know that officials at Sing Sing were ordered to continue their plans as scheduled, in case the Supreme Court overturned Douglas' stay in time for the 11:00 P.M. execution.

In New York, lawyers conducted a frantic search for a District Court judge who would accept jurisdiction over the motion that had impelled Douglas to grant the stay. If a court accepted jurisdiction and set a date for a hearing, then in all likelihood the

* In fact, Manny's application for a stay had been turned down. Douglas accepted an application from two lawyers, Fyke Farmer and Daniel Marshall, who were filing a "next friend" brief on behalf of Irwin Edelman who was strongly critical of the defense strategy. For a summary of Farmer's and Marshall's point and Douglas' reasoning for granting the stay, see Schneir, pp. 237–243.

Supreme Court would not vacate Douglas' stay. As it happened, though they rousted many judges, none of them would touch the case. On Thursday morning, lawyers working with Manny prepared a new strategy, drawing up papers, elaborating the point Justice Douglas had ruled on. These were to be filed with Judge Kaufman with a demand for a quick refusal in the event of a decision to vacate the stay. Upon his refusal they planned to appeal to the Circuit Court of Appeals which was based in New Haven, boasting the liberals Jerome Frank and Learned Hand, both of whom had voted for the stay in February, all but begging the Supreme Court to grant *certiorari* so they could decide whether the prosecution's reprehensible conduct had been grounds for a new trial. As Manny, his associates, and Fyke Farmer and Daniel Marshall prepared for the first oral arguments before the Supreme Court, three lawyers in New Haven — Marshall Perlin, Samuel Gruber and Arthur Kinoy — prepared the arguments they hoped never to make.

Robby and I tried to go about our lives as before. I figured we had a five-to-four decision against us before; maybe we'd at least get five-to-four *for* us this time. Then there was always Eisenhower. I don't recall details of June 18. Our parents spent the day drawing up wills and writing their final letter to Manny.

Dear Manny,

I have drawn up a last will and testament so that there can be no question about the fact that I want you to handle all our affairs and be responsible for the children as in fact you have been doing. Ethel completely concurs in this request and is in her own hand attesting to it.

Our children are the apple of our eye, our pride and most precious fortune. Love them with all your heart and always protect them in order that they grow up to be normal healthy people. That you will do this I am sure but as their proud father I take the prerogative to ask it of you my dearest friend and devoted brother. I love my sons most profoundly.

I am not much at saying goodbye because I believe that good accomplishments live on forever but this I can say, my love of life has never been so strong because I've seen how beautiful the future can be. Since I feel that we in some small measure have contributed our share in this direction. I think my sons and millions of others will have benefited by it.

Words fail me when I attempt to tell of the nobility and grandeur of my life's companion, my sweet and devoted wife. Ours is a great love and a wonderful relationship it has made my life full and rich.

My aged and ailing mother has been a source of great comfort and we always shared a mutual love and devotion. Indeed she has been selfless in her efforts on our behalf. My sisters and my brother have supported us from the start and were behind us 100% and worked on our behalf. We can truthfully say that my family gave us sustenance in the time of our great trials.

You Manny are not only considered as one of my family but as our extra special friend. The bond of brotherhood and love between us was forged in the struggle for life and all that it means and it is a source of great strength to us. Be strong for us beloved friend and we wish you long life to continue your fruitful work in health and happiness for without doubt you are a fine man, dear friend, and sweet advocate of the people. I salute you and caress you affectionately with all my heart.

Never let them change the truth of our innocence.

For peace, bread and roses in simple dignity we face the executioner with courage, confidence and perspective, never losing faith.

As ever,
JULIE

P.S. All my personal effects are in three cartons and you can get them from the warden.

June 19th — Ethel wants it made known that we are the first victims of American Fascism.

ETHEL and JULIE

The Supreme Court did not reach a decision that day; our parents were not executed on the scheduled date. The AEC and Justice Department pressured Eisenhower to refuse clemency, while the State Department continually informed him of the broad-based political support overseas for clemency, adding that the executions might hurt America's image. Eisenhower no doubt summarized his own attitude in his reaction to Brownell's importuning at a Cabinet meeting: "My only concern is in the area of statecraft — the *effect* of the action." Guilt, innocence or mercy were absent from his calculations. Congressmen who supported clemency told members of the committee that given the pressures on Eisenhower, the clemency decision would be very close. Several more days of world-wide protest, the twenty-four-hour picket line around the White House and the flood of telegrams urging clemency (21,500 arrived between June 16 and June 21)* might tip the balance.

The government knew they had to kill the Rosenbergs then, or the case would backfire. Had clemency been granted, our parents would have been in jail fighting to expose the fraud for the rest of their lives. In fact, a U.S. Attorney admitted that under a precedent established in the Grunewald case our mother's prejudicial cross-examination would have entitled her to a new trial if she had been alive. The Supreme Court had been convened for its extraordinary special session to take the case out of the courts and out of the public eye before such irresistible pressure could build up. As James Kilsheimer III, one of the assistant prosecutors later remarked, "We were taking a propaganda bath in the world." Also, there was speculation that Chief Justice Vinson had been encouraged to believe that if he reconvened the court, clemency would be given.

On Friday morning, June 19, the Supreme Court vacated Douglas' stay. Bloch and his associates filed separate petitions for stays with a few individual justices but to no avail. The New York action began with a prompt refusal from Judge Kaufman, and the telephone rang in the New Haven Federal District Court where Perlin, Gruber and Kinoy waited. They rushed to present an appeal of the motion just rejected by Kaufman to Judge Learned Hand. If their action produced a stay of even three days, a three-judge panel would meet to hear a full appeal on Monday. Any one of the Appeals Court judges held the power to grant such

* This number was not exceeded until the firing of Archibald Cox and the so-called Saturday Night Massacre by Richard Nixon produced a "firestorm" of protest telegrams.

a stay. The official clemency petitions, in the hands of the Pardon Attorney, were to be immediately transmitted to the President. Manny and Grandma sought a personal meeting with him as well. In New York, another lawyer asked Judge Kaufman to stay the executions scheduled for Friday, 11:00 P.M., long after sundown when the Jewish Sabbath begins, so as not to desecrate it. Kaufman replied that the Justice Department was taking care of the matter.

At the Bachs' the lawn was swarming with reporters. As Steve and I played catch, pictures were constantly snapped. Steve cautioned me not to call him by his last name and not to throw the ball past him. If he turned around the photographers might take his picture. I thought of a photo of me swinging at a pitched ball and missing. The caption would read, "Michael Rosenberg strikes out in play, as his parents were striking out in Washington." Soon we were called inside. We watched a baseball game on TV which was interrupted with news bulletins throughout the afternoon.

The first blow, the Court vacating the stay, was magnified by the fact that they voted six to three against us. Justice Robert Jackson had switched sides. Probably he did this so he could urge clemency in the written majority opinion. He concluded with the words:

> Vacating the stay is not to be construed as endorsing the wisdom or appropriateness to this case of a Death Sentence. That sentence, however, is permitted by law, and, as was previously pointed out, is therefore not within this court's power of revision.

Legal hope still existed in New Haven. The three lawyers attempted to find the prestigious Learned Hand in his chambers, only to be informed he was not present. They later found out that he had secluded himself in the next room. Judge Swan was available. He took the position that he alone would not grant a stay; however, if they could round up two more judges, he'd consent to be the third and hear their motion for a stay that afternoon. He took them to the home of Judge Jerome Frank, spoke privately with him and then left. The lawyers were ushered in to present their motion.

The second blow came when Eisenhower denied clemency, coupling his decision with a statement which read in part: ". . . by immeasurably increasing the chances of atomic war, the Rosenbergs may have condemned to death tens of millions of innocent people all over the world."

Unaware of the proceedings in New Haven, I thought our only possibility now was my mother's "mercy" letter. At Sing Sing Rabbi Koslowe was consulted about the desecration of the Sabbath were the executions carried out after sundown. He consulted with some of his teachers and then reported to the authorities that extending life three hours from 8:00 P.M. (approximately the time of sunset) to 11:00 P.M. would not desecrate the Sabbath. They ignored his opinion and bulletins flashed their decision to the nation.

Manny heard it in Washington. I heard it on TV. It began to seem as if I weren't watching a baseball game at all, but a newsreel of our parents' death. The news was broadcast as drawings of their faces filled the screen. I was riveted to the TV. I couldn't move: I couldn't turn it off. "Warden Denno of Sing Sing prison has advised reporters and staff that scheduled executions of Ethel and Julius Rosenberg, convicted Atom Spies, have been moved up to 8:00 P.M. so as not to interfere with the Jewish Sabbath. Repeat . . ." Robby has no recall of these events. Later, we went to Steve's house and I was sent outside to play ball.

In New York City, my father's brother Dave and his wife drove to Sing Sing hoping for a last visit with our father. As it was obvious Eisenhower would not see her, Grandma flew back to New York. Manny's telegram to Eisenhower asking for a personal meeting, and pointing out that the Supreme Court had never reviewed the case, was ignored. His decorum and courtesy and adherence to the "rules of the game" had been stretched beyond the breaking point by Kaufman's snideness, Saypol's arrogance, Brownell's cruel machinations, the head-in-the-sand behavior of the courts and their most liberal judges, and finally Eisenhower's unwillingness to even read the clemency petitions. He erupted. His education of the nature of the political tiger he had uncritically grasped by the tail more than three years previously* pushed the words out of his mouth: "WHAT KIND OF ANIMALS AM I DEALING WITH!!"

Daniel Marshall flew to New York in midafternoon to file another application with the Federal District Court in New York. In New Haven the sun was shining brightly as Judge Jerome Frank informed the three lawyers before him that he had tried to take his mind off the terrible events soon to transpire by working in his garden. He agreed to hear their motion, remarking that they were acting in the best tradition of lawyers and that if he were still practicing he would be doing the same thing. They began to present their argument. He agreed that their points had merit. "I'm sure if this had been presented earlier, your clients would have gotten relief." However, when they begged him to grant a stay, he refused. He said that in the light of the Supreme Court's action that morning he could do nothing. He became very emotional and tearful. As far as he was concerned, the Rosenbergs had already suffered cruel and unusual punishment by having their last-minute stay vacated after only one extra day of life. If he granted a stay, the Supreme Court would probably be called back again to override it, only increasing our parents' agony. At length he agreed to sit with Judge Swan if another judge could be rounded up.

Time was running out. The lawyers arrived at the home of Judge Clark. They knocked on the door, but no one answered. While Kinoy and Gruber kept knocking, Perlin repeatedly telephoned from a booth across the street. After a half hour of knocking and calling, somebody inside the house picked up the phone and informed Perlin that the judge was playing golf. A phone call to the judge at the course produced the following response: "I've never been involved in this case; I never want to be involved in this case." Perlin entreated him to sit with Judges Swan and Frank on a three-judge panel. He said he would confer with them and call back.

---

* In a speech given in September 1953, Manny described his first thoughts on our father's predicament: "I assumed quite naturally at the time and quite incorrectly as events turned out that this was going to be one of those typical situations where a person suspected of Communism, Communist affiliation or beliefs, associations would be hauled before some Grand Jury or Congressional Committee and he would probably take refuge in his rights against self-incrimination and whatever constitutional rights were available to him. I told him to go home and not to worry. I didn't consider that his liberty was in jeopardy."

In Sing Sing, my parents were permitted to spend the afternoon together, separated by the usual wire mesh. The accelerated schedule for execution forced the prison to dispense with the traditional "last meal." My father merely asked for an extra pack of cigarettes. They wrote Robby and me one final letter:

Dearest Sweethearts, my most precious children,

Only this morning it looked like we might be together again after all. Now that this cannot be, I want so much for you to know all that I have come to know. Unfortunately, I may write only a few simple words; the rest your own lives must teach you, even as mine taught me.

At first, of course, you will grieve bitterly for us, but you will not grieve alone. That is our consolation and it must eventually be yours.

Eventually, too you must come to believe that life is worth the living. Be comforted that even now, with the end of ours slowly approaching, that we know this with a conviction that defeats the executioner!

Your lives must teach you, too, that good cannot really flourish in the midst of evil; that freedom and all the things that go to make up a truly satisfying and worthwhile life, must sometimes be purchased very dearly. Be comforted then that we were serene and understood with the deepest kind of understanding, that civilization had not as yet progressed to the point where life did not have to be lost for the sake of life; and that we were comforted in the sure knowledge that others would carry on after us.

We wish we might have had the tremendous joy and gratification of living our lives out with you. Your Daddy who is with me in the last momentous hours, sends his heart and all the love that is in it for his dearest boys. Always remember that we were innocent and could not wrong our conscience.

We press you close and kiss you with all our strength.

Lovingly,
DADDY AND MOMMY
JULIE   ETHEL

P.S. to Manny: The Ten Commandments religious medal and

chain and my wedding ring — I wish you to present to our children as a token of our undying love.

P.S. — to Manny

Please be certain to give my best wishes to ———.* Tell him I love and honor him with all my heart — Tell him I want him to know that I feel he shares my triumph — For I have no fear and no regrets — Only that the release from the trap was not completely effectuated and the qualities I possessed could not expand to their fullest capacities — I want him to have the pleasure of knowing how much he meant to me, how much he did to help me grow up — All our love to all our dear ones.

Love you so much —
ETHEL

The phone rang and Judge Clark told Perlin, "I have conferred with Judges Frank and Swan and we will not hear your application." Defeated, the three lawyers headed back to New York. Now there was only the final argument by Daniel Marshall in New York, and perhaps one final chance for Manny to see President Eisenhower.

In Union Square, New York, a mass meeting, originally scheduled to celebrate the stay, turned into a grim Death Watch as the Almans and others reminded the crowd of all the doubts in the case. At 6:00 P.M. Manny appeared before television cameras to quote from Justice Jackson's opinion and concluded, "That makes nine Supreme Court Justices opposed to the death penalty." With our mother's mercy letter and the opinion in his pocket, he walked to the White House. Though permitted to leave the letter and opinion, he was prevented from entering or using the telephone in the call box. In the New York office of the *National Guardian,* James Aronson, Cedric Belfrage and John T. McManus prepared two front pages — ROSENBERGS EXECUTED and ROSENBERGS SAVED.

Back at the hotel, Manny and Gloria Agrin hung on the phone for forty-five minutes trying to get through the White House switchboard. The pickets marched; the New York crowd cried.

* Our mother's psychiatrist.

Playing baseball, I wondered about Eisenhower's reaction to the mercy letter.

When Grandma arrived home, a doctor and rabbi attended to her as sundown and the Sabbath approached. David Rosenberg was not permitted to see our father, as the deadline for final visits had long since passed. In her Queens home, Aunt Ethel was frantically trying to contact somebody important who might influence Eisenhower. She kept crying and looking at the clock. Her twelve-year-old son stood on a chair and turned the face of the clock to the wall.

At 7:30, Eisenhower claimed to have read the mercy letter and still declined to intervene. Daniel Marshall arrived in New York and was referred to Judge Kaufman. At 7:20 our parents were separated — my father returned to his cell. At 7:45, in his final moment of triumph, Kaufman denied Marshall's application. All legal and political opportunities had been exhausted. My mother wrote the following short notes:

Dear Manny,

These are some notes I want you to give to ———*. They are attached to this letterhead. There are also a few last notes for you — the one beginning with quote from Geo. Eliot. Dearest person, you and ——— must see to my children. Tell him it was my last request of him. They must have professional help if needed and he must see that they are tested to find if it is needed.

All my heart I send to all who held me dear. I am not alone — and I die "with honor and with dignity" ** — knowing my husband and I must be vindicated by history. You will see to it that our names are kept bright and unsullied by lies — as you did while we lived so wholeheartedly, so unstintingly — you did everything that could be done — We are the first victims of American Fascism.

Love you,
ETHEL

* Our mother's psychiatrist.
** At one of her last meetings with Manny our mother said she shivered from head to foot when she thought of getting into that chair and having the current run through her, but "I will die with dignity."

Geo. Eliot said "This is a world worth abiding in while one man can thus venerate and love another —"

Honor means you are too proud to do wrong — but Pride means that you will not own that you have done wrong at all —

I cry for myself as I lie dead how shall they know all that burned my brain and breast —

The fat's in the fire to say nothing of the books — (my best to Pop Bloch)

When it grew too dark to see the ball, Steve and I trooped back to the house. Hoping against hope that the mercy letter had succeeded, I asked what had happened. They didn't answer directly, "We listened to every station; they all said the same thing." I didn't respond. I didn't cry. I just sat on the couch and stared at my hands. I couldn't react. I was not to cry emotionally for six years. Steve piped up, "You're taking it just like a man, Mike." Sonia cried and hugged me. She said, "You'll stay here with us." Yes, I thought, I guess I will. They suggested I not tell Robby, who was probably asleep already. He retains a memory of my being very beside myself for missing some of the news about the case. He recalls adults consoling me. He pretended ignorance about the execution, which relieved everyone. In fact, he understood very well — Manny had failed to think of an eleventh reason.

7

Orphans of the Cold War

A WEEK LATER Robby was talking about Mommy and Daddy coming home when I impatiently said to Sonia and Ben, "Oh, let's tell him. Robby, Mommy and Daddy are never coming home; they're dead." Once again he pretended not to understand.

The Almans stopped by on their way out west. They had knocked themselves out for two years trying to save our parents. Now they were taking a family vacation and wanted us to come with them. Even though I was "in love" with Shelley, I was scared to leave the Bachs, who decided against the trip. Before they left, Shelley and I talked about getting married. Our problem was that since we were minors we needed parental permission. I thought of a plan: I would kill myself, go to heaven and get my parents' permission, then ask God to send me back to earth so I could marry Shelley. In the end, we decided to wait until we were older.

The summer settled down to just what I'd planned when school let out on June 12 — an endless summer of playing ball, visiting friends, going swimming, going to amusement parks at the shore. I watched the Dodgers demolish the National League and win the pennant. I learned the line-ups, followed the box scores, and thrilled to the team that boasted Rookie of the Year, Jim "Junior" Gilliam, who teamed up with veteran Pee Wee Reese around second base, Most Valuable Player, Roy Campanella, sure-hands Billy Cox at third, the big hitters Gil Hodges, Duke Snider, Carl Furillo (who won the batting championship), and of course, Jackie Robinson batting clean-up; he had been pushed out of his second base position by Gilliam and finally found a regular position in left field. The pitching staff of Carl Erskine, Preacher Roe, Billy

Loes, and Johnny Podres with Clem Labine in the bullpen more than compensated for the loss of Don Newcombe to the army.

When the next issue of the *National Guardian* came, with the appropriate banner headline, I was not permitted to read it. Nor was I permitted to read the *Guardian* after that. Sometime after the execution I received an anonymous postcard:

> Of course you feel for the loss of your parents, but when you think of all the boys they killed in Korea, you should realize that they deserved to die. Why don't you change your names and become Christians?

The Bachs took the card and made sure I never went to the mailbox again.

Robby makes no distinction between that summer and the previous one. It seemed to him filled with the same games and the same people. Early that spring Robby had begun to learn how to write his name. During the summer Sonia practiced with Robby on the blackboard on their sun porch. She said he was very lucky because he could spell his name so many ways: Robert, Robby, Robbie, Bobby, Bobbie, Bob or Rob. It took a long time to master all of this, and he was proud of his accomplishment.

As school approached, I looked forward to getting back into the swing of things. Forgetting about my "every other year jinx," I expected school to be a snap. Unfortunately, my restlessness in class and boredom with certain subjects, led me to fidget, talk out of turn, secretly read books during the class periods. My teacher graded students on how well they measured up to their potential, rather than on an "objective" scale vis-à-vis other students. Thus, I found myself with no A's on my report card and a number of bad marks. Robby was nervous about entering the first grade. This was no longer kindergarten, not baby stuff anymore. On the last day of summer vacation before first grade he fell asleep mumbling, "Reading and writing and 'rithmetic; that's the way to do it, Dick." The entire school adventure — the older, taller students, the identical school buses — intimidated him, inculcating a sense of total powerlessness.

For me, the fall was disastrous. School was not the success that I'd anticipated. Life at the Bachs' deteriorated, conflicts with Leo intensifying. In fact, antagonism was so prevalent that one day when Leo and I played Monopoly together and I was polite and considerate, Sonia went out of her way to compliment me. I built up a feeling that Ben and Sonia were too strict, not letting me stay up late enough or watch enough television. I longed for weekend visits to other families, tried to weasel invitations to join friends at the movies. Ben saw my long faces so frequently that once he hugged me in exasperation saying, "Please behave yourself." The same pattern that had developed at Grandma's was repeating itself. No one was sufficiently strong and skilled to deal with me consistently, calm me down and at the same time communicate the sense of warmth and love they obviously felt.

School was tedious. I read lots of baseball books, and my main participation in class consisted in giving oral reports about them, wildly acting out the drama of the final games portrayed in the stories. Leo was a pain; Robby a burden. Ben and Sonia began to strike me as ogres. I write this now with a great sense of shame, because they gave themselves so fully in that year and a half. The positive contributions they made when no one would take Robby and me in, and consequently the personal difficulties they faced because of the climate of the times, cannot be overestimated. My ten-year-old self lacked the understanding and sensitivity that would have permitted me to return their love so selflessly given.

Not long after school began, the Superintendent of Schools decided to exclude us from the district on the spurious grounds that we were not residents. Manny personally confronted him but in vain. Ironically, the last assembly program I remember at Toms River praised the state of New Jersey and the local school system.

On the bus home from school one of those last days before vacation, a friend whispered to me that he'd known my last name ever since my parents' execution. I asked him not to tell anyone. On the very last day before Christmas vacation, when a guy tried to pry my last name, Bunky (a neighbor and friend who knew who my parents were) interceded, getting into a fight. The friend who had promised secrecy then slowly and with great pleasure began to explain my last name and what had happened to my parents. The bus ride was interminable. Later, at home, when I thanked

Bunky, he told me of his other fights in my behalf. I'll always be indebted to him for these attempts to help. I wish I could find him and thank him. The combination of the bus incidents and the problems at the Bachs' made me wish for a Christmas vacation with Grandma in New York.

While my life slid downhill, and the eviction from Toms River inexorably drew near, Manny undertook the responsibilities our parents had entrusted him with. The published letters in the States were followed by editions overseas, and he set up a trust fund for Robby and me. Next, Manny toured the country making speeches to raise money for the trust fund. He hoped, as he made clear in one of his speeches,

> that the tragedy through which these children lived will not leave its everlasting stain. I don't know yet. What we'd like to do for the children is give them a fighting break in the world. We want to give those children an opportunity to live without financial worry. We don't want them to live like wealthy children, because they came from plain ordinary poor people. I don't want those children to ever forget that they belong with the people and they don't belong with the snobs. But I do feel that we ought to give those children an education, and college education and professional education and maybe a little money to open up an office or whatever they might do.

Concerned about giving our wounds time to heal, Manny never mentioned the trust fund and deflected a number of well-meaning pen-pal offers of correspondence from sympathetic children.

Alice Citron, a frequent visitor at Ben and Sonia's, was involved in the process of deciding where Robby and I should be placed. Manny had received a number of adoption offers, besides those from the obvious people like the Almans and the Bachs. There were even adoption offers from foreigners. (A kibbutz in Israel offered to take us.) Alice had known Abel and Anne Meeropol from the days when Anne and she were both active Teachers Union members in the New York City public school system. In 1952, the Meeropols had offered to provide us a temporary home until our parents were freed. After our parents' execution, they expressed to Alice their eagerness to adopt us. Alice felt they would be wonderful. In addition, Anne and Abel had lost two children at birth, and so we would be filling an important need in their own lives. Anne had directed a nursery school, been an incredibly effective teacher with the neglected "latch-key" children of Harlem and was strong enough and sure enough in her understanding of children to deal successfully with me. Abel was an intelligent, artistic, gentle, humorous person who admirably complemented Anne's strength. In short, Alice told Manny they were the ideal couple for us. On the strength of her recommendation, Manny arranged our tentative home with them.

The first day of Christmas vacation Ben drove Manny, Robby and me into New York for a Christmas party at the home of W. E. B. Du Bois. Dr. Du Bois had attempted to file an *amicus curiae* brief on my parents' behalf in the Supreme Court. His wife, the writer Shirley Graham, was one of the five trustees of the Rosenberg Children's Trust Fund. (Besides Manny, the others were James Aronson of the *National Guardian*; Yuri Suhl, the author of works on Jewish immigrant life in America; and Malcolm Sharp of the University of Chicago Law School who joined the defense for the last desperate appeals.) At the party I tweaked Dr. Du Bois' beard a couple of times and made friends with a kid my age named Billy. Together we poked fun at a magician calling himself "the amazing Manny" (not Manny Bloch), claiming he was a fake. Manny Bloch explained that Robby and I would be picked up by a couple named Allan; then he and Ben left.

After the magician's act, kids clustered around the piano, singing. By the end of the party, a blond, ruddy-faced woman was playing the piano. She turned out to be Anne Allan. On the way to Grandma's house they told us their names were really Abel and Anne Meeropol — Lewis Allan was Abel's professional name — and that soon we would be living with them. The next day Manny and the Meeropols came to Grandma's to insure that the transfer went smoothly. Grandma cried, accusing Manny of "taking us away." We left quickly; I was disturbed at Grandma's reaction. That was the beginning of a sense of distance from her that we came to feel as the years passed.

After a few days of settling in at the Meeropols', we drove to

New Jersey to collect some clothing and toys. I greeted Ben with the announcement, "Since we've been railroaded out of this town, we're moving to New York." He and Sonia seemed dazed by our swift departure. Guiltily, I cannibalized the electric train set, leaving them with only two of the six switch tracks. Ben plaintively concluded, "Well, I guess I can fix something up for Leo." Robby and I didn't stop to consider the heartache they were experiencing. Years later Robby and I met them at a play. Leo proudly introduced Robby to a friend as "my former foster brother." Flustered, Robby didn't know how to respond, wanting to keep it all behind him. Ben greeted me with, "You'll excuse me if I'm speechless, understand?" We hugged each other. Still later we corresponded a bit. Neither Robby nor I can ever fully express our gratitude and we hope our inability to communicate was not hurtful to them.

Anne and Abel lived in a small apartment at 720 Riverside Drive, corner of 149th Street, in a largely black neighborhood. As we walked in the park during the Christmas vacation I made a remark about living in Harlem. Sensing my uneasiness, Abel gently indicated that my prejudice was showing. I was horrified that he'd think me biased, though on the first day of school I admitted that I had been afraid. The school was 90 percent black, but everyone was so friendly toward me, the new kid in class, that I came home to announce that Negroes were really great! That must have sounded awful to them, and they shushed me for saying it so loudly.

What pleased me most about moving in with the Meeropols was using their last name, a terrific asset. There would be no need to deny my parents, because no one would ask me. We would not be embarrassed by having different names from the people we lived with. Because I still wasn't sure which name was the real one, Lewis Allan or Abel Meeropol, I took out a library card as Michael Rosenberg Allan.

Robby and I shared a bedroom. The Meeropols slept in a sofa-bed in the living room. One of our first activities was to organize "meetings of the united family." Anne was president, Abel veep, Robby sergeant at arms (whatever that meant) and I was secretary. We also enjoyed making family tape recordings, which introduced us to Abel's gift for comedy. I can still remember the first tape. I could barely contain myself because I wanted to do a race-track announcer calling a race where Beedle-Bomb won after being last most of the way. Anne started the tape, "We are making this tape with Michael and Robby as part of our family." Robby went first, "I am happy that I am living here. Today is December, Tuesday the 27th." I had to say something, interjecting a quick "shut up." Anne complimented Robby and added, "except for that voice that came in and said something." "I'm sorry. I'm sorry," I apologized, happy to be able to say something else. I launched into my Beedle-Bomb routine but was cut off because it ran too long. Then Abel spoke, "I'm duh horse" (in a gruff voice). "I was running duh race." (Hysterical laughter from Robby and me.) "That boy was only watching, but I'm duh one who knows how it feels. The jockey weighed five hundred pounds, and I only weighed one hundred pounds. And when I went up that track, Bruddah, it was rough." (Our laughter continued throughout his spiel.)

At the second taping, Robby took a page from Grandma's book and in a fit of hysterical laughter proclaimed, "Dave Greenglass should burn! He should burn in the trashcan!" Struggling to contain himself, he added, "That voice should stop saying shut up; but this horse, he's a neigh-neigh horse, he's . . ." Robby's monologue dissolved into uncontrollable hysterics, ". . . too much of a neigh-neigh horse . . ." The Meeropols must have been shocked out of their minds. I was somewhat amused but felt Robby was treating a serious matter lightly.

During a later tape recording, Abel introduced Rocky Rocky Head, the heavyweight champion, who ate only hard-boiled eggs (we were already arguing over food; my eggs had to be hard-boiled all the way through, and Anne thought that was nonsense), and Squishy Squash, the flyweight champion, who ate only soft-boiled eggs.

In mid-January, Manny visited us and joined our recording session. His cross-country fund-raising trip, though he didn't speak to us about it, had exhausted him, and he was currently fighting a disbarment proceeding instituted for his "intemperate remarks" against Attorney General Brownell and President Eisenhower. He mentioned that he had called Eisenhower a murderer, which struck me as a little too extreme. I would reserve my venom for David and Ruth Greenglass. Later, I came to accept Manny's characterization, agreeing with Grandma's contemptuous epithet, "Puss-face," whenever Eisenhower graced her television screen. Manny sang with us and then talked into the microphone as Medium Boiled Head, a moderate position between Abel's two characters. He offered to fight the winner of the bout that I was preparing to announce. Amid whoops from Abel (in different voices) of "Throw me the towel but don't hit me with it!" and my incoherent patter, the fight ended when Rocky hit Squishy in the stomach — "Here come the soft-boiled eggs. They're flooding the ring. Everyone's drowning. Blub, blub." Manny was cheered by our progress. A friend of his recalls the day after this visit Manny couldn't take the grin off his face. He was so happy that we were doing well and kept saying, "It's wonderful! It's wonderful!"

A week later Manny was dead. Robby and I loved him for his quiet warmth, his overwhelming devotion to our parents and us. We still miss him.

Manny died before the formalization of his guardianship. This would have caused no confusion had we been ordinary citizens, because Grandma was the next of kin. In our case, several influential persons sought to "kill" us by removing us from people who shared our parents' politics. This goal was blatantly spelled out in a letter or position paper written by one of the chief anti-Rosenberg propagandists, S. Andhil Fineberg.

A few weeks after Manny's death, Alice D. Ferrer, an Officer of the New York Society of Prevention of Cruelty to Children, filed a petition alleging neglect:

. . . since their discharge from the Department of Welfare [in June of 1951 — erroneously stated as July in the document] and particularly since their removal from the custody of their grandmother, these children have been exploited and made the subject of propaganda by persons seeking to raise funds, using the names of these children publicly for this purpose. That such exploitation has been and is contrary to the best interests of the children and prevents them from developing normal and healthy attitudes and from leading normal and healthy lives. That in their present environment they are further exposed to such exploitation.

She claimed that we were discharged from the shelter only with Grandma's assurances that she would keep us in her home, and that the Welfare Department didn't know Robby and I had left New York City until October 1953, at which point they demanded of Manny that we be returned to New York. This latter assertion is surely a lie, because the social worker from the Jewish Board of Guardians, which complied with this effort to "save" us, had visited us in New Jersey in 1952.

Whatever the merits of this petition, Judge Jacob Panken of the Children's Court Division of New York County immediately ordered that we be produced in court. On the evening of February 17, at 7:00 P.M., when Robby was in bed and I was already in my pajamas, city officials accompanied by my old social worker (not Mrs. Phillips) from the Jewish Board of Guardians knocked at the door. They wanted to take us to court right away. Anne and Abel tried to reason with them that an abrupt seizure would traumatize us. They also started frantically calling lawyers. Uncompromising, the officials threatened to carry us out by force. Confronted by two New York City policemen and with more outside, Abel declared they would take us over his dead body. One of the lawyers called contacted Judge Panken who advised the officials that he hadn't intended them to summarily bring us to court; tomorrow would be soon enough. Before the officials retired for the night there was a charade played out for my benefit. I came out to say good night, and, to prevent my being frightened, Anne introduced the cops and officials as family friends. I recognized the social worker but didn't think anything of it. I even played the piano for them.

Throughout the night police guarded the street, the corridor outside the apartment, even the roof. The next morning a phalanx of police escorted us to court. Robby and I were separated from the Meeropols and kept waiting in a room. We knew something terrible was up. After a farce that Panken sought to masquerade as a hearing, we were "remanded" — neither our lawyers, Grandma, nor the Meeropols were told where. Anne pleaded with the social worker to let them accompany us, but she stiffly said, "We're taking care of it." (In 1974, when I interviewed the social worker, she confessed to me that the incident was so distasteful that she probably had blocked out her memories of specific events.) Her personal role was to be someone whom we were used to. Her agency saw its role as protecting us from the horror of our lives, from being made political footballs. Fineberg and other political string-pullers, I am convinced, were trying to murder Ethel and Julius again by transforming their children's love for them into hate. They intended to place us with "patriotic Americans" so we'd grow up despising our parents and honoring their murderers.

Once again we were institutionalized. Fortunately, those who'd struggled to save our parents rallied again, including Attorneys Alexander Bloch and Malcolm Sharp, and Gloria Agrin, Grandma, aunts, psychiatrists, including Dr. ———. Within 24 hours they filed for a writ of *habeas corpus* in the New York State Supreme Court. At the initial hearing, Friday the 19th, Justice McNally ordered that Robby and I be produced on Saturday morning, the next day. The lawyer from the agency where we were staying tried to stall.

MISS SCHWARTZ: Your Honor, tomorrow is the Sabbath and these children are in a Jewish agency up in Pleasantville and it isn't possible to bring them down tomorrow.

THE COURT: What about that?

MR. BLOCH: That is a problem, too.

THE COURT: Sunday is a legal holiday and Monday is a legal holiday. What about it?

MISS SCHWARTZ: I think that the children can't be harmed by letting them stay where they are until a determination here on Tuesday.

THE COURT: That is not for you to decide, that is for me to decide . . .

THE COURT: Where is your client, the grandmother? . . . You tell me, are you a very religious woman?

SOPHIE ROSENBERG: Yes, but I keep it now and I want the

children should be here because I am very anxious to see the children, your Honor.

THE COURT: You say that it wouldn't cause any undue disturbance to these children to have them brought here on Saturday?

SOPHIE ROSENBERG: No, it wouldn't anything happen to them. I never ride on Saturday, but now I ride because I want to see the children because I love the children, because the children are not happy.

THE COURT: Because the children are what?

SOPHIE ROSENBERG: Not happy there.

THE COURT: What did they do on Saturday when they were with you? Did they go out and play and everything?

SOPHIE ROSENBERG: Yes, they go out and play.

THE COURT: Play with other children?

SOPHIE ROSENBERG: Yes.

THE COURT: Go to the movies on Saturday?

SOPHIE ROSENBERG: Yes, sometimes, yes.

MISS SCHWARTZ: Your Honor, the agency is an Orthodox agency and they are officially closed.

THE COURT: I have that in mind. I understand that. When you say it is an Orthodox agency, that is one thing, but there must be some people there who can bring the children down.

MISS SCHWARTZ: They don't travel on Saturday. Their offices are closed; they don't do any work on the Sabbath.

THE COURT: All right, they will do this work. I order you to produce the children here tomorrow at ten o'clock. You heard the grandmother. She says she is a religious woman and it wouldn't disturb her at all to have the Jewish Sabbath broken. If it doesn't disturb her, I don't see why it should disturb anybody else.

Produce the children here tomorrow by ten o'clock.

While Justice McNally was listening and deciding, Robby and I spent a miserable day at Pleasantville Cottage School, the institution to which Judge Panken had secretly "remanded" us. Before we'd been spirited away, the Meeropols entered the room with forced smiles telling us we'd be together soon and not to worry. The same kind of anger I'd felt that last afternoon in Sing Sing welled up over their unwillingness to acknowledge the gravity of the situation. I moaned during the entire car trip to Pleasantville. It occurred to me to jump out of the car and run when we stopped for a red light, but I couldn't desert Robby. At one point to make me feel better, he smiled. I tried to convince him of the seriousness of our plight, though I didn't cry.

At Pleasantville we were placed together, thank God, in one of the cottages and never left each other's side, prompting some of the boys in our cottage to comment, "They even go to lavo together" (Pleasantville slang for the toilet). While we got ready for bed, they talked about seeing us on the evening news show. Excited they talked over each other. "Are you Julius Rosenberg's . . . ? You were wearing that same hat . . . Your brother didn't have his hat on . . ." Ignoring my feeble attempts at denial, one kid giggled, "Hah! Your mother's a spy!" only to be chastised by some of his friends. Regardless of the fact that they weren't hostile, Robby and I were scared of them. They cursed, fought with each other, acted tough. The next day we were sent to school. That afternoon, an official of the home told me we were riding to New York early the next morning for a hearing. I hoped against hope that we would not come back.

Saturday morning we were driven down to New York, where we were hustled in a side entrance before the photographers could snap pictures of us. Newspapers, coats were flung over our faces. In the courtroom Justice McNally had us approach the bench and asked with whom we wanted to sit. "The Meeropols," I answered. "Your grandmother?" "Yes, both."

We hugged Abel and Anne and sat beside Grandma. A friend of theirs, Harold Loren, had driven them down to the court. A thrill of hope shot through me when he leaned over and said, "The other judge was a bastard, but this guy is on our side." Due to the fact that Harold was employed by the New York City public school system, his chauffeuring of and being photographed with Anne and Abel imperiled his job in that period of loyalty oaths and teacher purges. We have never forgotten this important act of courage and friendship. Others of their friends were not so brave.

Basically the hearing consisted of the Justice's sympathetic direct examination of Grandma followed by a very short, half-hearted cross-examination by the attorney for the City Welfare Department. The most impressive exchange occurred when one lawyer for Welfare protested that the Department's only aim was to shield us from publicity. Here we were, anonymous at last, with a new name, a stable home, regular visits to family, the beginnings of therapy with a psychiatrist, and in one day of dirty work, the Welfare Department, assisted by the Jewish Board of Guardians and Judge Panken, had destroyed it all. Gloria Agrin responded magnificently.

> Now, as to this wide publicity, this was caused by nothing done on the part of the family or the people who are in control of these children. It is this unfortunate and, if I may characterize, barbaric seizure of the children that has brought about all of this publicity which was totally unnecessary. They had been, before they were seized, in a home where they were well cared for, happy and adjusting, and there is no reason to assume that the Grandmother or any one who, like a maid or a servant, who is brought in to aid or assist her, will in any way refuse or fail to neglect to protect the children from this publicity . . .

Neither the lawyers for the city nor the Jewish Board of Guardians could persuade my social worker to testify that, judging by standards of health and competence, Grandma was not fit to provide a home for us. She thought that it obviously appeared better for us to stay with Grandma, though she believed her unfit. I doubt the Justice would have been swayed; he was on "our side." Nevertheless, he was confronted by a ticklish situation. Children's Court (Panken) had claimed prior jurisdiction; as a State Supreme Court Justice he did not presume to have the right to *overrule* Panken. To solve the dilemma he merely stated he was conducting the hearing that Panken had not held on the issue of the "parole" of Robby and me pending disposition of the basic issues of guardianship and the neglect petition in Surrogate's Court and Children's Court. (Surrogate's Court had jurisdiction over guardianship matters, while Children's Court heard only neglect, abuse and related cases.)

During a recess McNally called us into his chambers, handing

out candy bars. He listened to my complaints about Pleasantville,
my reminders that the Meeropols were the people Manny Bloch
had placed us with and my evidence that "Bubbie has high blood
pressure." Still, since Anne and Abel were not related to us, he
very correctly ignored my gratuitous "testimony" and "paroled"
us in her custody.

> I find on the facts that the paternal Grandmother is a God-fear-
> ing woman, practices the Jewish religion, which is her religion. I
> believe that the interests of the children would best be served by
> paroling the children in her custody, pending the outcome of the
> litigation in the Children's Court, and I so order.
>
> Mrs. Rosenberg, you may take the children, and I am depending
> on you to hold these children in your custody pending the outcome
> of the litigation . . . Send the children back to school. Teach them,
> as you believe, the tenets and principles of your ancient and
> honorable religion.
>
> Teach them out of the Old Testament. Never let anybody talk to
> these children in derogation of this country or its principles. You
> teach these children to love this country; it is their country. It is a
> very sad and distressing circumstance.
>
> These children are entitled to the same chance as any other
> children. As far as I am concerned, they are going to get it . . .

We'd won a great victory — the first victory our family had ever
won in the courts. We were overjoyed. Robby and I raced up to
the bench to thank Justice McNally. "God bless you, Judge," I
said. We walked out of the court — across from Foley Square
— and down a long, broad staircase. Crowds cheered when
Grandma appeared with us in tow, cameras clicked. One headline
the next day read, "Spies' orphans go to Grandmother." By now
Robby knew what an orphan was. For the first time he had to
realize that our parents were never going to see us again.

Panken had been outflanked. With the basic guardianship issue
pending before the Surrogate's Court, he was faced with a petition
from the City Welfare Department to drop the neglect case, and
he had to acquiesce.

Resisting pressure to appoint the head of the Jewish Board of
Guardians as co-guardian to guard our "property" (the trust fund)
to protect it from "political misuse," the Surrogate appointed as

co-guardians (unrelated to the Trust) Grandma and Kenneth D. Johnson, the Dean of the New York School of Social Work, formerly a Family Court judge and a personal friend of Eisenhower's. Until we knew his position regarding our future, we held our breath.

A while before he died, Manny had approached Dr. Frederic Wertham about examining and prescribing whatever activities and life-styles would be necessary to heal the scars of the recent past. He accepted us into his clinic and began giving us very thorough examinations. With the return to Grandma's house, we completed the testing.

When we examined and treated Michael and Robert at the Lafargue Clinic we found that both had been severely traumatized. This was due not only to the unnatural loss of their parents but also to the subsequent disarrangement of their life circumstances by a hostile environment. This resulted in all-pervasive feelings of uncertainty based on the objective conditions and hard to overcome. At the same time we found that both had definite positive emotional resources which warranted a good long-range prognosis.

According to examination, observation and tests Robert suffered from a diffuse anxiety state. He only half knew what had happened to his parents. He remembered his mother being upset when he saw her in Sing Sing, but he did not know why. He was an alert and imaginative child. Robert was badly in need of understanding delicate supportive psychotherapy, which was given him by me and members of the staff. He responded remarkably well.*

Michael was more seriously affected. He knew exactly about the fate of his parents and also understood what happened later. He suffered from what was classified as a reactive depression, with anxiety features. Tests even indicated suicidal tendencies. He was very lively and quick of comprehension. He suffered from a sleep disturbance with nightmares in which he would cry out "Mommy" or "Daddy" in his sleep. He needed more prolonged psychotherapy and guidance, given him by me and members of the staff under my guidance. That led to a good adjustment.

I remember the long series of tests and the couple of years of weekly visits to the clinic, but my memory of the specifics of our

* Robby believes he was just carefully covering up — that he knew very well what had happened.

discussions or the nature of the psychotherapy is almost totally dimmed. My recollection is that as soon as we were back with Grandma, I began to feel better.

Dr. Wertham and his staff had recommendations for Dean Johnson, who turned out to be a wonderful man. They recommended adoption, legal change of name, avoidance of all publicity, and admission to special private schools. Dean Johnson concurred in all the recommendations. He was tall, ruddy-faced, and spoke with a funny (Boston) accent. He and Grandma became good friends and he also established an immediate rapport with the Meeropols. He was obviously concerned with our personal well-being. We took to him immediately.

Until the summer of 1954, we lived with Grandma, who was helped by a governess, Margaret, and spent every afternoon with the Meeropols. We were enrolled in Hebrew school and remained at the public school near Abel and Anne.

I had already adjusted very well to school and my return was very smooth despite the publicity. Some classmates told me, "You're lucky we love you here." (Harlem remained a sanctuary for radicals, black and white, throughout the 1950s.) For some reason, the parents in that school had not absorbed the frenzied fear of contamination by "reds" characteristic of that decade. Several times I was teased in the school yard, and consequently always ate my lunch indoors, but I never was afraid when with my classmates or friends. Academically I had a good year, too, finally banishing my "jinx" in the second half of the sixth grade. Toward the end of the semester I was told I was selected as a candidate for the "S.P." (Special Progress) classes in junior high school, enabling me to do three years in two. I was very proud of this achievement.

In addition to Margaret, Grandma was assisted by friends who took us to school, by visitors who entertained Robby and me every evening in order to woo us away from the television set. A man named Lefty was a frequent caller. Robby and I took great pleasure in pulling on the few hairs left on his bald head and hiding his glasses on his forehead. He spoke German, French, Spanish, a little Russian, and used to fake accents "Sid Caesar style" for our benefit. His talents and sense of humor rivaled

Abel's. An incredibly intelligent man, he took the time to talk world events with me, answering my questions about Indochina, a country I'd heard about that was much in the news in 1954. We played chess between conversations and kidding around; he beat me, but not badly, and was careful to throw a few games. Three years later when he married a woman with a young daughter, we lost touch. Five years after that I was a counselor at a camp in which his daughter was a camper. I regaled her with stories about him before she'd even met him. One day late in the second summer there, she said to me:

> When my father adopted me, I really didn't know how to behave with him; I'd never had a father. Your stories about him and the love you had for each other showed me a side of him I never knew. I feel I can relate to him more fully now that you've told me these things.

Since I had been extremely grateful to Lefty, I was happy to in a small way repay him.

Dean Johnson arranged for us to live full time with the Meeropols after the summer of 1954. In February of 1957, he helped finalize the adoption in Surrogate's Court. Surrogate Collins, who originally appointed Johnson, signed the papers. The plans encouraged by Fineberg, abetted by the Welfare Department, the Jewish Board of Guardians and Judge Panken had been scuttled. This victory is an immensely significant one for us. Robby and I still shudder to think what would have happened if those bastards had succeeded.

Part II
A New Life
by Robert Meeropol

If We Die

You shall know, my sons, shall know
Why we leave the song unsung
The book unread, the work undone
To lie beneath the sod.

Mourn no more, my sons, no more
Why the lies and smears were framed
The tears we shed, the hurt we bore
To all shall be proclaimed.

Earth shall smile, my sons, shall smile
And green above our resting place
The killing end, the world rejoice
In brotherhood and peace.

Work and build, my sons, and build
A monument to love and joy
To human worth, to faith we kept
For you, my sons, for you! *

Ethel Rosenberg

* She later changed the last line to "For our sons
and yours," but the change was never implemented
and the poem was published in this original form in
Death House Letters.

8

From Rosenberg to Meeropol, 1954–1958

FROM THE START our relationship with the Meeropols was special. It's not that Grandma Sophie or the Bachs did a bad job so much as that these two people were really committed to us, had storerooms of energy, planned for and thought about our needs and had no children of their own. Anne had always been excellent with children, and both of them handled us beautifully. Michael was headstrong, loud, nearly impossible to deal with. His behavior didn't seem abnormal to me since I was accustomed to his strong feelings about getting his way. I was judged to be the more normal of the pair, largely because I concealed my problems and fears so no one would fuss over me, resulting in my being rather quiet and withdrawn. I let Michael grapple with the dilemmas of the external world, so he shouldered a great deal of responsibility. While the Meeropols' principal job in the beginning was calming Michael, they had the opposite task with me. At six my shell had not hardened (I still made many slips), and it was possible to coax me to open up.

In fact, considering our experiences, Michael and I were in remarkably good shape. The mythology surrounding our parents paints them as fanatics who neglected their children for politics. This is simply not true. Our relative sanity reflects the strong base they provided for us. After their arrest, the Committee to Secure Justice for the Rosenbergs did not manipulate us for political purposes; rather, we were shielded from publicity by loving adults.

Our most difficult years fell between 1950 and 1953, when we lived with a number of different people or in institutions. Yet, despite our traumas we were salvageable, and the only conclusion I can draw from this is that adults concerned about our welfare were careful with us. The Meeropols, too, sheltered us. They did not continually refer to our parents though they did reinforce our great love and respect for Ethel and Julius by portraying them as courageous people who died for their beliefs. I never doubted our parents. We grew up with the knowledge that the government had lied and framed them even though the Meeropols didn't encourage us in this direction.

Generally, we talked about the present — school, playing — rather than the past, which suited me as I didn't care to dwell on the past and soon forgot much of it. Those who had befriended us in those difficult years did not come to see us, since the Meeropols thought they'd remind us of the past. The Meeropols made no special to-do over us, achieving normal family relationships with remarkable rapidity. Abel recently mentioned an incident which occurred in those first few months. As our last name had not yet been changed, Michael worried that his new friends would uncover his identity. Abel, flipping through a Manhattan directory, showed Michael page after page of Rosenbergs, including listings for Michael Rosenbergs. He was considerably relieved. Similar simple, concrete acts quickly soothed our fears, which were never completely banished, of course, but receded into the background.

The Meeropols kept us occupied. In addition to family tape recordings, Anne played the guitar and led family sings. Abel was a terrific storyteller, joker and cartoonist. Aside from Rocky Head, he invented characters like Tomato Nose and a dog, Hungry Soup Bone, who howled whenever the word steak was mentioned. When another character, a miner said, "I'm going to stake my claim," the dog howled, soon we'd all be howling. General Custard forever tracked across the waterless expanse of the chocolate desert. Abel's stories went on and on. The Meeropols took us on many excursions in their old, black 1948 Pontiac. The radio didn't work, and Michael and I pretended to control Abel's driving by pushing radio buttons signifying slow or fast or stop. Somehow Abel managed to maintain this illusion without driving dangerously though at times he had to ignore our commands. Michael and I needed an abundance of warmth and love which we certainly received. There was plenty of hugging and kissing, affection we hungered for. The Meeropols were the best thing that had happened to us in more than three years.

Regarding myself an outsider, constantly changing homes and hiding my past, I had to have my confidence restored. Anne drove me to the school yard one day toward the end of first grade. There we met a classmate who challenged me to a race, but I declined, thinking I'd lose. Usually I didn't take chances or push myself. Anne urged me to accept. We ran across the yard and back and, much to my surprise, I almost won. Such incidents helped me make friends as I grew confident I could perform well and became more willing to extend myself.

In the summer we were sent to a "Y" camp in Pennsylvania. This was another move for me, and I disliked leaving the Meeropols. When I reached camp I came out of my shell enough to cry and was traumatized to the point that I couldn't shit for five days. The counselors checked off bowel movements on a BM check list, and another camper and I watched the rows of checks lengthen while ours remained empty. At last the dam broke, and we were fine. Michael, too, suffered a bout of homesickness. The division leader, on the lookout for such campers, allowed him to call home. Abel's voice reassured him. Arrangements were made for me to see Michael over rest hour. I remained introverted. The kids in my bunk, who were a year older, intimidated me. My counselor had to write letters home for me as I refused to write, pretending I didn't know how. Unwilling to learn to swim, I stayed in shallow water, though I did participate in nature activities and other sports. The counselors, teen-agers who liked to scare the campers, didn't help me much. One of them told the story of the white witch of Brooklyn who ate little boys. We all had nightmares but, unlike the others, I repressed mine. Another counselor delighted in telling us that the noises emanating from the woods were made by wolves. After Abel and Anne visited us on Parents' Day I felt more secure. By the last week I was savoring camp life, which freed Michael from the chore of looking after me.

Michael continued to fear discovery, suffering silently while his bunk mates wondered aloud if a guy named Marty Rosenberg was related to the dead Rosenbergs, who, in the words of Michael's counselor, "deserved to die." He began addressing postcards to "Mommy and Daddy," and was soon using these names naturally. It took me nearly a year to call them Mommy and Daddy.

On Saturdays we visited Grandma. She soon grew to resent our attachment to the Meeropols, calling them strangers, telling Michael they were being paid to keep us, questioning us at length about whether their home was kosher. She refused to come see us. We largely ignored her questioning. The Meeropols played down the situation, preventing it from developing into a major conflict. Grandma was getting old and had been irrevocably stricken by her son's death. She cried frequently and during the last ten years of her life descended into senility. I didn't forget my parents or the events surrounding their trial, though generally these thoughts did not surface. But Grandma was a living reminder of the destructive nature of our government. When thinking about her I'd also fantasize about the revenge I'd seek, at the same time recognizing that I couldn't put a price tag on depriving children of their parents.

In order to please Grandma and the court, the Meeropols sent us to Sunday School to learn about Judaism. The classes weren't uninteresting, but I could conjure up more tantalizing ways to pass a Sunday morning. After we were Bar Mitzvahed, we stopped attending classes. I was a nonbeliever; religion never made any sense to me, and I found no rationale for believing in a force greater than visible power and the environment.

Michael enjoyed learning the prayers, reciting them with enthusiasm at his Bar Mitzvah. He had gotten so carried away that in an unguarded moment a few hours before the ceremony he said, "This is the happiest day of my life." The rabbi overheard and made that remark a central part of his "charge" or closing speech. Michael was embarrassed, but Kenneth Johnson was moved to tears. Michael balked at writing his own speech because of all the family references usually contained in it. The rabbi was taken into confidence and proved extremely sympathetic. When David Rosenberg rose to give his "brucha" or blessing, the rabbi conveniently got a frog in his throat in the middle of pronouncing David's last name. The rabbi also wrote Michael's speech.

In school I was one of the best students, though I did not excel at reading aloud or spelling. Part of my reading problem was shyness. Anne tutored me on and off for years, teaching me vocabulary, imparting a love for books. Michael and I continued to demand attention from the Meeropols. We had no sense of internal discipline and indulged in unproductive, time-wasting habits. They interested us in projects and in initiating hobbies.

During the fall of 1954 we moved into a bigger apartment. I was unhappy about another move, making new friends. Fortunately, we stayed in this apartment for six years. An entire section belonged to Michael and me. When given the choice, we always shared a bedroom, so we converted our second room into a playroom. By closing the door at the end of the hall, we formed our own little apartment. Having so much space was quite a luxury. However, within a few months we graduated from the apartment as we'd found kids to play with on the street. The school I attended was not very different from the one I'd left, the teachers being memorable for their mediocrity. Anne aided me in math, and I became fascinated with numbers, adding long columns, doing long division and multiplication — skills the rest of the class hadn't been taught. One afternoon after school, I showed my talents to the teacher, who complimented me, but intent on sticking to her lesson plans gave me no further encouragement or guidance.

Michael and I discovered that if we talked quietly at night in our bedroom, the Meeropols couldn't hear us. We planned "talking nights," abbreviated to "TN." They had to be scheduled since I went to bed an hour earlier than Michael and it wasn't easy for a seven-year-old to stay awake for an extra hour. Then Michael came to bed and we joked for an hour before going to sleep. Naturally, I was often tired the following morning. Our TN's lasted for six years, almost every other night, and we were caught less than a half dozen times. The walls were well insulated.

Few of our friends or their parents knew our identity, but life was not without its reminders of the past. We still saw Grandma as well as some of our father's sisters and brothers although we never visited our mother's family. We traveled to family Passover Seders with mixed feelings about these reunions. I looked forward to being with the family; at the same time, they refreshed my memory of the turmoil I sought to put behind me. After a while, I began to feel like a stranger around my family. This was partially due to the Meeropols, who as outsiders were not relaxed around my more religious and politically conservative relatives. Gradually we saw less of them. In the meantime, Anne's large and close-knit family supplied us with numerous cousins to play with.

Anne usually taught drama at camp during the summers. Abel stayed in the city to write, driving to camp on weekends. Harold and Bea Loren bought a large tract of land with an old resort house and farm area, opening a teen-age camp in the Catskills in 1955. Michael, twelve, was one of the youngest campers; I was a "counselor's brat," left on my own. Sometimes I pounded nails into houses and weeded the garden with the older campers. Generally, my time became unsupervised, and for hours I wandered the hills, developing a deep love for nature. After all, I was a city boy — the forest presented a new world to me. I spent three summers at that camp. During those years I must have been incredibly patient; watching the baseball team practice two hours every afternoon, I wasn't asked to play once. Michael's being on the team drew me to practices. That summer a hurricane hit the camp and it rained for days in the mountains. I played on the dirt road, redirecting the streams, damming them to form large puddles. The plants, customarily seared in August, were a deep green as if spring had returned.

By the fall of 1955, the worst of the anti-Communist hysteria in the country was over. Even at the Meeropols' house I was conscious that we had lived through dangerous times, that people had been willing to point accusing fingers. Books by Lenin and Marx were hidden, particular newspapers such as the *National Guardian* not mentioned. I kept silent, knowing somehow that this discretion was bound up with the fate of my parents, rarely discussing politics with my friends. Michael went even further. In a class taught by a right-wing social studies teacher, he volunteered the opinion that anyone not believing in God was a bad

American. Even though I was only eight, I could easily see through the school rhetoric about freedom and democracy under these circumstances. One day as I walked home with a classmate, Alfred, we talked about the newspapers our parents read. The safest statement would have been that my folks read the *Daily News*, because everyone read that paper, but I knew it was terrible and didn't mention it. They subscribed to the *New York Times*, but few others did, so I was afraid it was better left unnamed. Finally I compromised by saying they read the *Post*. To my relief, Alfred admitted his parents did too.

For my friends on the street, excelling in sports was crucial. They judged a person's character by how well he caught or hit a baseball, whether he made big plays. Ethel and Julius, Julius especially, taught us to root for the underdog, that the quality of the individual effort was more important than winning. Being a good sport and having heart were more essential than natural ability. Luckily, I played well enough to avoid being the scapegoat. At ten and eleven I often joined Michael and the older kids if one of their regulars didn't show up. This was quite an honor, and if I played well I'd be happy for days.

At Christmas, the anniversary of meeting the Meeropols, we started the tradition of eating out in order to celebrate. This year we went to the restaurant owned by Gloria Agrin's husband, Gloria being one of the few from our pre-adoption days we continued to see. Afterward, we rode up Fifth Avenue to see the Christmas decorations.

Harold and Bea Loren dropped by with two goldfish in a bowl, and by December we boasted about our five-gallon tank of goldfish; soon we were also caring for a tank of tropical fish. We began selling as well as cross-breeding them; the sign in our window advertised, "Mike and Rob's guppies." Michael did most of the work but involved me in his plans. (The last fish died in 1962.) One spring night I woke at three in the morning to sneak a look at the fish, quickly turning on the light to see what they looked like when asleep. My father, a light sleeper, came in to find out what had happened — he thought the episode funny.

My mother started teaching weekend drama classes, including a teen-age class in which Michael participated for many years. He loved acting, performing for people. Another woman taught a younger group which I belonged to. I liked the group but dreaded the moment when I had to perform. I also signed up for art classes at the Museum of Modern Art. These classes were stimulating though I couldn't overcome my frustration at not being able to put the image in my head on paper. The teachers thought I was extraordinary because of the colors I chose. Not until high school, when a doctor diagnosed partial colorblindness, did it become evident why I painted with secondary colors. When I did produce a painting that appealed to me, I redrew it with minor variations, trying to perfect it. I just couldn't think of new subjects to paint. The Meeropols were very artistic, giving me numerous opportunities to express myself, none of which bore fruit. Michael, on the other hand, was musically inclined and did a fair amount of acting.

In the summer of 1956 I watched my mother direct rehearsals for a play, *The Valiant*. I became fascinated by the plot: a man awaiting the electric chair convinces his sister he is really not her brother so no disgrace will fall on the family. At the performance, as the execution approached, I couldn't stand it any longer and left, saying that I had to go to the bathroom. Abel followed me, admitting that he doubted I had left for that reason. For a while I was silent, then I hugged him and asked, "It won't happen again?" He replied that it wouldn't and held me for a long time. Such reassurance and understanding eased my tension considerably.

The third grade was my last in the New York public school system. That spring my mother took me for an interview at a private liberal-left school in Greenwich Village. They accepted me, and the next fall I entered the Little Red School House. Michael enrolled as a ninth-grader in Elisabeth Irwin High School, the affiliate of my school. Many show-business personalities, artists and leftists sent their children to the Little Red School House. Norman Mailer and Arthur Miller's children attended this school; Angela Davis and Mary Travers were students there. We called our teachers by their first names. There was but one class of thirty children per grade. Most of my classmates had known each other for several years, so it was difficult to break into their crowd. I made friends rather quickly with another new student but remained on the periphery of a cliquish and socially sophisticated clan of nine-year-olds.

Michael too had to adjust though he was one of the better students in his class. The first day he entered the classroom, he heard some of the basketball-conscious boys exclaim, "Oh no," not wanting any competition. Also, it took him much of the year to adjust to the informality of the classroom. He was often admonished not to stand when addressing the class. Unfortunately, in a class with the reputation of cut-ups, Michael stuck out as a "goody-goody" whose high grades must be due to "brown-nosing." In his sophomore year a teacher criticized him for being too wrapped up in himself. One of his classmates was the same Billy he'd met at Dr. Du Bois's party, but Michael didn't acknowledge their previous acquaintance until their friendship grew during junior year. Billy told Michael he sometimes wondered if Michael even knew he was the son of Julius and Ethel Rosenberg. Billy was not unfamiliar with McCarthyism—his father had been removed from his Brooklyn pulpit for his left-wing opinions.

I continued to play on the street. By this time I realized my personality was composed of several layers. The most superficial layer was that of a street kid, very much like any contemporary, though I abstained from the racist jokes the other white kids laughed at. The second layer was that of the left-winger. Politics and political debate intrigued me, and I became vocal in class, shying away from physical combat but thriving on verbal combat. I couldn't share this interest with my pals on the street and doubt that they had the vaguest notion about my far-out politics. The third layer was my core — I was the son of Julius and Ethel Rosenberg. I never talked about them with any of my friends. Even with Michael, Abel and Anne, I had the briefest of exchanges about them. In fact, I suppressed most of my memories.

In 1957, Abel and Anne asked us if we wanted to be legally adopted. My strongest desire was to skirt the entire issue so I hastily agreed. In February we went down to a courthouse to quietly sign the legal documents. We felt secretive, as if at any moment a reporter might materialize to expose us. He didn't and life returned to normal.

For me the past was painful to remember and easy to forget,

but Michael continued to be tormented by his memories of having denied he was a son of Ethel and Julius Rosenberg. From the time we adopted the Meeropol name, he tried to set his sights on a year when he would assume his real name, feeling he had to "atone" for his cowardice and "take his medicine." During our TN's, he sometimes reminded me of our identity. If, thinking Anne or Abel might overhear us, I asked where Mommy and Daddy were, he responded, "They're dead." I shrugged this off, often continuing to talk as if nothing had happened.

Most of the kids I played with came from lower-class homes. In lengthy bull sessions we idolized the older juvenile delinquents (JD's), gangsters and the FBI. Local cops were the lowest of the low — they confiscated the sticks we played stick ball with — but the G-men were heroes. To us the G-men and gangsters were similar in that they carried guns and were not bound by the same societal constraints governing the rest of the public.

The end of the 1950s brought on my first political activity.

9

Early Politics and New Camouflage, 1958–1965

MY FIRST PEACE MARCH in April 1958 was part of the Ban-the-Bomb Movement organized by SANE. A few hundred marchers, largely between ten and twenty years old, gathered at the George Washington Bridge and walked through Manhattan to the UN Plaza where older marchers who weren't up to the long hike joined us. The march was such a pitifully small affair; people were still apprehensive about demonstrating. Hecklers screamed, "Go back to Russia," as we passed by. (These marches have always frustrated me.) Listening to adults and watching TV, I knew how revolutions evolved in other countries — small demonstrations were followed by larger demonstrations which were succeeded by strikes and riots, culminating in a general strike and a takeover by the workers. The classic Marxist model in childish terms. So I anticipated that these marches would comprise the first link on the chain of events leading toward revolution. However, the people involved were largely pacifists, and few shared my vision. Several friends and I considered ourselves more daring. Even at nine or ten we wished for direct action, dismissing the older leaders as frightened and old-fashioned. This was the seed of our New Left attitude. Even I, who had experienced firsthand the way in which power crushed people, chafed at ambivalence. In the fall of 1958 and again in the spring of 1959 I picketed Woolworth's in Harlem — part of the NAACP's campaign against the store's segregation policy in the South. I shared the Meeropols' belief in civil rights and human dignity.

That previous May while Michael and I were playing Monopoly someone knocked on the door. Our parents instructed us to be quiet, not to open the door. Earlier the phone had rung, and when my father picked up the receiver the caller hung up. The House Un-American Activities Committee was holding hearings in town. In the late 1930s, he had been called before the Rapp-Coudert Committee investigating left-wing activity at City College. Now HUAC was looking at his record to determine if he had Communist affiliations. He was certain the caller at the door was delivering a subpoena. Anxious about our being subjected to adverse publicity again, the Meeropols decided to avoid a subpoena if possible. The following morning Michael and I ran to the subway, looking over our shoulders for the little man with the subpoena who might be chasing us. On the way home from school, a man trailed me from the subway and knocked on our door after I closed it. We didn't answer. Dad hastily moved us into a friend's apartment near Yankee Stadium; we became the "Pearlmans." Since he had a few more days of school, Michael stayed with Gloria Agrin. There he engaged her in long sessions concerning our parents' case. She admitted how isolated Manny became when he first assented to take the case — she said even left-wing lawyers crossed the street if they saw her or Manny approaching. Also, she explained that Manny hadn't cross-examined Harry Gold because he was a monstrously pathological liar and they were grateful he hadn't claimed to know the Rosenbergs. On cross-examination he might have gone so far as to assert that he'd inspired my middle name, Harry. Rereading the book of prison letters, Michael was terribly distraught and moved to discover that for our protection we had not been given the last letters, in which our parents contemplated their deaths. Michael continued to shield me from even these discussions; his contact with our past was far stronger than mine.

For example, Michael had seen the movie *Knock on Any Door* in 1955, and read the book in early 1959. He was unprepared for the ending of the book, the activities and thoughts of the hero presented in excruciating detail as he prepares for and goes to his death in the electric chair. Michael was as riveted as he had been five and a half years earlier when television blared the announcements of our parents' death schedule. Feeling a strange emotion building up, he flung himself on his bed and started to cry for all the years since 1953 he had remained dry-eyed. Abel heard him and entered the room. Seeing the novel on the desk, he realized what had happened. They hugged each other for a few minutes, then Michael wrote this entry in his journal:

> I read the end of *Knock on Any Door* which describes a man's feelings as he goes to his death in the chair. It shook me, and it broke me. I realized that the two dearest people in the world to me had gone through that agony and more. They probably worried about their "babies" and what would happen to them. My God was it awful. I cried and cried and cried so much. I feel terrible. Oh to be half as courageous as those two wonderful people — Ethel and Julius Rosenberg. MY GOD

This emotional release was significant. Repressing his sorrow, "taking it like a man," had been debilitating.

Having no acquaintances in this neighborhood, I grew bored, but Michael soon joined us, and we romped on the street. I was somewhat scared, but we seemed to have escaped successfully, outsmarting the system. Supposedly, the Pearlmans came from Rochester, New York, so Michael and I adopted the roles of hicks. Standing in the building's elevator, we'd gaze at the ceiling with mock curiosity; when alone we giggled in a countrified accent, "Ain't nothin' like this in Raw-chester." We received the extra treat of attending several Yankee baseball games, the Meeropols correctly judging that baseball would take our minds off other matters. A few weeks later we went to summer camp, but Dad didn't return to the house until midsummer, after the committee had packed up and left town without locating him. Such events increased my fear and tension, although I had learned to live with worse circumstances.

I was gaining confidence, becoming outgoing, speaking more frequently in class. By the sixth grade I had a small group of friends and no longer suffered the indignity of being left out of the in-group parties; we threw our own parties. Politics became my springboard. I read the *New York Times* and history texts, and took part in debates.

That summer I went to a left-wing camp with an international perspective at which my mother was the drama counselor. Camp competition was organized in an Olympics rather than team week or color war. Most of us chose to represent Russia or Ghana or India, not the United States. For the most part campers were proud to be American though they hesitated to represent a right-wing government. Morton Sobell's son, a few years younger than I, was also at this camp though I didn't have much to do with him. I enjoyed camp, was something of a leader, having caught on to the fact that if you sang loud and took command, campers looked up to you. I was almost a teen-ager and personality was becoming very important, preoccupying our crowd with judgments about who was phony and who was not. I guess I was somewhat phony, consciously acting to attract people to me, working at appearing to be easygoing. Self-control had been learned at an early age, so I rarely got into any but political arguments and was pleasant to almost everyone. I continued to be absorbed by nature activities and hikes. This summer was an important one — the first time that I belonged to a group of kids my own age and didn't feel like an outsider. Having all started from the same point at the beginning of the summer, we had no pre-established groups to contend with as at school. It dawned on me that I relished being with people; they didn't seem to mind my hanging around.

Michael traveled to one of the early Washington civil rights marches in May 1959. I desperately wanted to go along, but my parents said I was too young. In vain, I argued with them, one of the few times I was adamant. I think they eventually felt guilty about not letting me go.

That fall I entered Elisabeth Irwin High School. Michael and I rode the train to school together. The previous spring I'd had my first taste of E.I., as we called it. The high school staged a moving-up ceremony in which the seniors sitting near the auditorium stage left their seats and moved into the seats in the balcony. Then the eleventh graders filled the seniors' seats and so on down the line. The sixth grade (me included) sang a song and occupied the seventh-grade seats. This ceremony embarrassed me, as Michael and I had composed a parody of the song and he was trying to make me laugh by mouthing the words to our version. The song had lines like "Summer is a coming in, merry sing Cuckoo, Bullock starteth, buck to verdeth, merry sing Cuckoo. Cuckoo, cuckoo, merry sing cuckoo." We changed these lines to "Summer is coming out, shitty sing Cuckoo, Bullock starteth, buck do farteth, shitty sing Cuckoo. Cuckoo, cuckoo, I think I'm going cuckoo." I managed to keep my composure. Michael was glad we attended the same school. He had become an accepted member of his class by junior year, and he confidently anticipated being a senior.

Seventh grade meant increased academic pressure. I couldn't bring myself to study, telling my parents there was no homework so I could play on the street. Finally, the teacher called my mother for a conference; she was angry when I got home that day. I think I felt worse about being found out than about not doing the work. I told countless small lies to cover up my not studying, not practicing the violin, not going to bed on time.

I was still fairly introverted, bothered by residual feelings from the early 1950s that I should repress my thoughts, that others wouldn't like me if they really got to know me. Politics was an area in which I could be relatively honest because my teachers tolerated my opinions. I countered arguments that the Soviet Union didn't allow free elections with the line that the rich controlled the two-party system, that two presidential candidates didn't offer a substantial choice, that in any event the average citizen didn't have much influence over the selection of nominees.

Though I felt obliged to achieve, instead of pouring more time into improving my school work I devised complex schemes to avoid it, indulging in new hobbies such as compiling a weather chart of high and low temperatures. Statistics intrigued me and I drew complicated precipitation charts. These solitary hobbies suited me. (I still track the weather, keeping charts in the winter.) Also I read books on dinosaurs and human evolution. This interest subsided but was rekindled in college, attracting me to anthropology.

My brother and I remained close, stayed up late talking, played together on the street. Michael was forever trying to build me up with flattery — I was the better athlete, better around people, better at getting my way with our parents. The latter was certainly true. If they opposed him, they had a big fight on their hands; he often quarreled with them over curfews and his girlfriends, and until he left for college he was constantly champing at the bit. Our parents were stricter than most of the E.I. parents. Once, while they squabbled, I pretended to cry; when my mother asked why, I answered, because everyone was fighting. It worked like a charm. Michael apologized to me, they promptly stopped yelling. I prided myself on being able to manipulate those older and wiser. Unlike Michael, I acquiesced to our parents' wishes, then surreptitiously did what I wanted. Since this deception worked only if I didn't get caught too often, I frequently obeyed. I wasn't getting away with much.

Although Michael was forever complimenting me, I felt totally inadequate beside him. For the last few years he'd been studying the guitar and played it quite well. (Our parents had to force him to go outside instead of practicing so much.) He was very popular in camp, had a girlfriend, was invited to many parties. As a senior at E.I., he'd finally made it into the "in" crowd by winning the election for president of his class. He was a top student, a Merit Scholarship finalist, and had been accepted into Swarthmore, one of the best colleges in the country. Michael was a big man in high school, and I was nothing. I couldn't play the guitar, the very idea of finding a girlfriend thoroughly intimidated me. I was an underachiever carrying a B average. There was no question but that Michael was infinitely superior. We both tended to look up to each other; in truth, I was merely following in his footsteps, unable to win the recognition he had.

On Sundays Michael and I hung around Greenwich Village — he played his guitar in Washington Square Park. He'd been playing blues with a clarinetist, and with Michael's guitar teacher's younger brother, they had formed a trio. The clarinet is a B-flat instrument, and this inspired the group's name, the "B-flat Stompers." Playing in Washington Square regularly, they acquired a small fan club. Michael's success impressed me, so the next summer at camp I tried to learn the banjo but couldn't stay with it.

One of my favorite activities was taking long walks with my father. We'd go to Riverside Park frequently and climb on the huge rocks. We both loved the river and admired the George

Washington Bridge. In the 1930s, before he'd become a professional writer, he'd won a prize for a poem he sent to a magazine describing the bridge. For many years we continued these walks and rode our bikes long distances along the river.

A new kid, Danny, entered the seventh grade, and we became fast friends, listening to blues records, such as "Lightnin' Hopkins Country Blues," discussing politics — Marx, Lenin, revolution, though we talked without much comprehension — and girls.

My social standing in the class was improving, and it didn't hurt to have the senior president as a brother. His class had jelled into a spirited, interesting and interested group. They discussed existentialism in French class and induced the school to permit seniors to substitute an independent study program for a course. Michael found a good friend in Doug, whom he roomed with in college. At one point Doug, not knowing about our first parents, had raised a question about the Rosenbergs, and someone rebuked him because the question might have upset Michael. At once Doug called Michael to apologize, effusively praising him for not losing his sanity during those nightmare years. From that time they were close friends.

David Greenglass was released in 1960. I noticed his picture in the newspaper but didn't have much of a reaction to it. Michael responded more vehemently, fantasizing a confrontation with him. Whenever an incident occurred such as Greenglass' release, the case back in the news, a new motion filed on behalf of Morton Sobell or a book about the case published, we grew apprehensive about losing our anonymity. However, I was able to put such worries out of my mind and luckily was never forced — until recently — to face the situation of publicity about the case.

In 1960, I was Bar Mitzvahed, after which Grandma Sophie moved to Queens to be near one of her daughters, and we rarely saw the family. For my Bar Mitzvah I had to recite a forty-minute set of prayers in Hebrew and give a speech. Since the birth of the State of Israel and my birthday coincided, I gave a political speech urging peace in the Middle East. Hating to perform in front of a crowd, I was extremely nervous. The rabbi commented that I was a gifted, extraordinary boy for composing my own speech. Michael was proud of my speech. Ever since his Bar Mitzvah he'd been waiting to say the brucha of the older brother over me in Temple. He loved to perform. After the service my parents threw a big party during which I managed to evade my mother's request for another recitation before assembled relatives, friends and tape recorder. Several camp friends and I played musical laps in the back room. The only event of note was Grandma Sophie's backing her chair into the fish tank, cracking the glass, spewing water and fish everywhere. Frantically, Michael and I cleaned up the mess, scooping the fish into auxiliary tanks before they died.

Michael was very earnest, anticipating events years in advance of their occurrence, agonizing over the time remaining before they happened. During our TN's, he described in detail a cross-country car trip our family expected to take "sometime in the future," adding information about the cities, rivers, deserts and mountains we'd see, when we'd reach which place. I appreciated his comprehensive travelogue. (These days he looks forward to his monthly poker games. Sometimes when I call, he reminds me, "Robby, only ten more days." I bite. "Till what?" "Till the poker game, I can't wait." I respond, "You can and you will.")

Michael was also tremendously self-assured, could never imagine changing his opinions. Taking advantage of his self-confidence, I negotiated a series of five- and ten-dollar bets with him to be payable when I reached twenty-one or one of us was proven wrong. Our first bet when he was fifteen was that he would marry the girl he'd been dating; he didn't and I won. The second bet was that he'd be a lawyer; more recently, I won that bet. (Michael had intended to become a lawyer and clear our parents' names as well as defend others against similar travesties.) Our third bet was that he'd get married when he turned twenty-one, and he almost won. One of my presents to him that year was canceling his debts to me.

The day before Michael left for college, he solemnly predicted that we'd probably never be so close again, emphasizing the significant turning point in our lives. Uncomfortable with this emotion, I laughed at his seriousness. I always checked my emotions. Michael took his responsibilities as an older brother to heart, and he was correct — we never were as close again. During the next decade I saw little of him.

My eighth grade year was excellent socially. Also, I began to understand politics and didn't simply repeat what I heard from adults. Since Fidel's revolution the previous January, I had become a fanatic Cubaphile, catching all the televised accounts of his triumphal entrance into Havana, clipping the *New York Times* articles on him. Whenever someone referred to the refugees fleeing Cuba, I whipped out a *Times* report, showing that the list of refugees read like the membership of the Havana Yacht Club; naturally the rich fled when the poor came to power. I did two major research projects in school — one on Cuba, the other entitled "Negro Slave Revolts" — these being the only work I seriously pursued. As an action-oriented thirteen-year-old, with distinct ideas and a passion for politics, I preferred doing to studying.

I was gratified that my political attitudes were not so different from my teacher's. As he reinterpreted the history textbook for the class, American history became fascinating, especially when read through critical glasses. He taught us that southern historians had written many of the history texts, watering down the Confederacy's essentially treasonous act of secession. I was struck by the fact that the same southerners who publicly waved the rebel flag at football games and supported the Confederacy — which fought the United States government — were advocating that all left-wingers should be thrown in jail or worse for their beliefs. I came to realize how manipulative the educational system is. It's usually not easy to recognize the distortions in a historical text. Relying on the research of W. E. B. Du Bois, our teacher demonstrated that often historians soft-pedaled the reality that blacks got screwed in the Reconstruction era.

Eventually, our class visited Du Bois at his home in Brooklyn Heights. We sat around his living room looking out across the East River to the docks of lower Manhattan and listened as he talked about his education. Gifts and artifacts from dozens of countries were scattered around the room. I was entranced; he was one of the most impressive people I've ever met. I couldn't imagine how this man could be the focus of so much hatred, and guessed that most people had no idea how quiet, gentle and humorous he was. I was outraged by the unfairness of the world around him.

I harbored a strong sense of justice, was bothered when someone was picked on and for the most part avoided the teasing that went on in school, thinking how badly I'd feel if I were teased. These feelings spilled over into politics, especially the issue of injustice to minority groups. My friends and I blamed the captains of industry, the government and the military who together conspired to exploit the public. This conclusion seemed so obvious that I was puzzled over the fact that it hadn't occurred to everyone, although the distortion of history was providing me with clues. Danny and I fantasized about lining the capitalists against the wall, then mowing them down with machine guns. No pacifist, I was really angry about injustice. Karl and I stayed up late one night to originate the student revolutionary party, enlisting three members — Karl, a young camp counselor with whom he'd fallen madly in love (he was thirteen, she was twenty-one) and me. The party didn't accomplish anything other than showing the direction of our fantasies.

Now that I had the habit of critical analysis I could easily perceive that Soviet policies were often misguided. Political events weren't as simple as I'd expected. I was growing up with the same critical attitude that freed a lot of red-diaper babies from Old Left mind-sets and prompted them to join an independent New Left.

I participated in the electoral campaign of 1960 by sporting a button: "Jack and Dick are no answer. We demand peace, civil rights and jobs." Our school held a mock election, which Norman Thomas won with seventy-three votes; Kennedy came in a close second; Nixon garnered one vote and was thus outpolled by *Mad* magazine's candidate, Alfred E. Neuman, who received two votes. The day before the election I swapped my button for one backing Kennedy. When I asked my father why he voted for Kennedy — there seemed little difference between the candidates — he replied, "If the Devil ran against Richard Nixon, I'd vote for the Devil."

Our social group in school expanded into a sizable counter-clique, making it harder to distinguish who was "in" from who was "out." Parties soon encompassed almost the entire class. We developed a nice sense of community, much of which centered around our first romances. At most parties the lights were quickly turned off after parents left — and couples began making out. I was shy around my girlfriend, lacking the courage to be as obnoxiously aggressive as many of the other boys. I wasn't even bold enough to ask for a date; we just happened to meet at parties or in school.

Most cliques formed around one or two good, outgoing athletes. Not the best in sports or extroverted, I combined forces with two or three others who together were as attractive if not more so than any one individual. Rather than trying to be supercompetitive, I shaped social alliances, collecting more and more friends. During the second term I was elected president of the class.

My political attitudes tended to swing too far left for the school. After a particular debate, a classmate warned me if I didn't watch out I'd turn into a Russian spy. By this time my past was so well submerged I shrugged off his remark, never dreaming it might indicate his knowledge of my background. Occasionally, minor incidents occurred but most were so subtle that even now I'm not sure they reflected knowledge of my past. For instance, one very popular boy invited me to his summer house though we were not especially good friends. For his twelfth birthday, Arthur Miller's son invited me along with five other boys to see his stepmother, Marilyn Monroe, in *Some Like It Hot*. As I hardly knew anyone else there I wonder if Arthur Miller knew who I was and if my invitation was extended at his suggestion. Once my mother and I went to a rummage sale on Broadway around 185th Street. The store turned over its profits to the Sobell Committee, a group headed by Helen Sobell, who worked tirelessly for fifteen years to free Morton. An old woman in the store ran over and hugged me. If people were sympathetic, I didn't mind their being informed about my parents, but I still got annoyed and embarrassed when they carried on over me.

This was my last year at E.I. For quite some time, my parents had been looking for a house in the suburbs, and they finally bought an old, big, beautiful house on Broadway in Hastings-on-Hudson. Though I was sorry to leave my friends on the block, my school friends were more important to me, and my folks promised I could commute to school. We moved to Hastings in May 1961. Each morning my father drove me to the end of the subway line seven miles away where I boarded the Grand Central train. The drive was well over forty minutes round trip, a drain on my father. Taking the train into town, switching to a second train to school constituted a long, expensive trip, so eventually my parents reneged — the following year I would have to enter the ninth grade at the local high school. This was a major blow to me as I was flourishing in a protected, supportive environment. The reversal so shocked me that I didn't mention it to my classmates or my girlfriend. On the last day of class the teacher announced the names of all those departing; my friends were astonished, and I was mortified about not having admitted it. At home I sulked, reminded my parents of their promise, swearing never to forgive them. Their decision traumatized me, and I was powerless to improve the situation, ultimately treating it as I did other problems by repressing it. I concentrated on the summer months at camp, ignoring the fall as if it weren't going to happen. Also I spent a lot of time with Danny; we took long walks during which we discussed girls and politics. Danny read the first twenty-three pages of one of Lenin's books; I started reading a biography of Marx but didn't get beyond the first chapter. We talked of revolutionary heroes, eulogizing the anarchists of the IWW. Supporting the Soviet Union, having been reared with that perspective, I idolized the anarchists as well without recognizing the contradiction.

Summer camp was pleasant. The guy sleeping below me in our cabin of five came from an Old Left family, and we spent the summer debating with another kid about whether the House Un-American Activities Committee should be abolished. We also discussed nuclear disarmament and various Cold War clashes. I struck up a rapport with a girl sharing similar ideas. The camp's organized discussion group was entertaining if frustrating; when I objected to the discussion leader's assuming the existence of a supreme being, he shut me up by reiterating that there had to be a being greater than man. I disagreed with him but made no headway. We argued about the Congo, he claiming the Communists were happy Lumumba was dead because he was more useful to them as a martyr; that irritated me but I lacked the proof of later years to rebut him. By the end of camp about a dozen of us had united behind left-wing politics and semi-beatnik folk music. Suddenly the summer was over, and a few wonderful weekends in Washington Square Park with my beatnik, commie pals didn't delay the start of school one day.

While I was at camp, Michael studied for six weeks at the University of Vera Cruz in Xalapa, Mexico. He met a girl there who had a good friend, Jerry Markowitz. After summer school, the three of them traveled together, and Jerry and he grew very close.

I didn't feel totally alone trotting off to become a freshman at Hastings High School. Michael would not be returning to college for ten more days, so at least I could come home to his sympathy.

But even Michael couldn't help me at school. So much of my social personality was based on politics and beat culture, and my new school tolerated neither. Hastings was an old Westchester community, mostly WASP, Republican, although Jewish professionals of a liberal or left bent lived there too. Anaconda Copper had built its main plant along the Hudson River, so there was a sizable working-class minority as well. I found no one to identify with and withdrew into myself. In the first weeks I quarreled with another kid in English class who offered to fight me after school. I had never been a fighter, planning ahead to avoid such encounters before they sprang up. Not only was I scared "chicken," I had no stomach for hitting anyone. I managed to back out of the fight, but the experience startled me, and I soon discovered that if I argued heatedly in class, my opponents were apt to "take physical action" after class, and the teacher was liable to be aggravated. Silence was the best policy.

So my first year at school was lonely, though I ate lunch with a couple of out-of-it, nebbishy ninth-graders. Our chief pastime was shooting craps after lunch. I could think of little to say to them.

After school I went straight home to my solitary hobbies. The social change was drastic. My room looked out across the Hudson to the Palisades — a wonderful room for tracking the weather. The large willow tree in the front yard served as my wind direction and speed indicator. I kept temperature and snow charts. Often I retreated into numbers. One window overlooked Broadway, and, sitting on my bed, I figured out what percentage of cars going by were made by each manufacturer. On weekends I traveled to the city for my old schoolmates' parties — the highlight of the entire year. However, as I was no longer a part of the life at E.I., we began to drift apart, losing touch with each other by the beginning of sophomore year.

Before Michael came home for Thanksgiving I was nervous that his new-found maturity at college would make it more difficult for us to have fun together. When he entered the house and yelled up to me, I anxiously raced downstairs. He met me halfway, grinning, his hand behind his back. I didn't have any idea what to expect. He whipped his hand toward me and squirted me in the face with a water gun — washing away my fears.

In the advanced biology class, I slowly made acquaintances of the intellectual types, and came to know Alex pretty well, a conservative Republican and a religious Jew who was quiet, pleasant and wanted to be my friend. Our bonds were sports and folk music. In this intimidating setting, I couldn't compete in sports. The streets were too hilly to play on, and the games I excelled in were unknown to these suburbanites. When Alex and I talked politics I toned mine down to liberalism; fear and common sense hid the rest.

It was hard to submerge my political ideas, because I was differentiating mine from my parents'. Our first disagreement concerned the new Moscow line, "peaceful co-existence," ushering in the Russia-China split. Although I was naive about Stalinism, China's defense of the current third-world revolutions appealed to me. Peaceful co-existence implied that the U.S. and the U.S.S.R. divided the world into spheres of influence, a policy which sacrificed third-world interests to more firmly secure the Soviet Union's economic growth and prosperity. Michael and I consistently sided with China against Russian foreign policy.

Aside from feeling intellectually right, these discussions were particularly stimulating as I enjoyed debating with my parents. Around this time I began to see the flaws in many adults, especially my teachers. To my amazement, some did not appear to be that intelligent, and I felt that I could top them.

The summer of 1962 I copied my brother's idea, enrolling at the University of Vera Cruz to study social anthropology, Mexican history and Spanish. My mother, a seasoned organizer and go-getter, financed the trip by leading a teen-age group on a tour. I was going along, and so were my old bunk mate and my camp girlfriend, so I looked forward to the trip. Unfortunately, the tour did not run smoothly, the kids naturally rebelling against my mother from time to time, leaving me in an impossible position. Wanting to live more like the Mexicans, one friend grew progressively angry over our fancy hotels. Again I was torn — the accusation of being bourgeois stung but I couldn't side against my mother. Then my bunk mate and I quarreled over the details of the tour; we rarely saw each other after that summer.

I was too aloof to get acquainted with the Mexicans. I hung around with the other North American boys, doing foolish things such as dropping water balloons from the hotel roof in Mexico City. I became friendly with John, a political ally, and we disputed with Eric, who wasn't. At one point the Rosenberg case came up, Eric claiming they were guilty traitors, John contending they were framed, Eric arguing they were hanged, John countering that they were electrocuted. I remained silent but was deeply affected. My impulse was to excuse myself and get out of the room, but my feet seemed rooted to the floor. I can't recall what happened next. Perhaps they changed the subject; somehow, I managed to stop thinking about my parents after a while.

The rest of the summer passed quickly. As we boarded our jet for home a guard advised my mother that her luggage was fifty pounds overweight. Belligerent, she contended that we were all students and therefore deserved special treatment. The attendant threw up his hands in defeat. "All right, lady, you win. But if the plane crashes, it's your fault." This warning made me nervous; fortunately, the extra weight didn't hamper the plane. At Kennedy Airport we passed through customs without a hitch.

Not until we arrived home did I find out that my mother had smuggled in four straw pocketbooks loaded with silver knick-knacks to be sold by the Sobell Committee. I was grateful I hadn't known beforehand. The thought of being nabbed by the authorities terrified me as much as getting away with things delighted me.

I became even more withdrawn my sophomore year, having lost track of my camp friends and not eager to see anyone from the Mexican trip. To fill the void I took up a new solitary hobby — reading science fiction. In less than a year I had skimmed through the town library and started buying paperbacks from local drugstores. My parents soon disapproved of this expensive pastime, so I sneaked the books into the house under my shirt. To encourage me to get outdoors, my father cut the old plywood board that had supported our trains and tracks and nailed a basketball net to the garage door. I played basketball by myself.

In high school I was still having trouble with spelling and grammar. Luckily, my father was a professional writer and had taught English in high school for a number of years. Together we reviewed my work. Dad was extremely patient and, instead of doing the work for me, had me research the answers and gave me suggestions pointing me in the right direction. He was always willing to drop what he was doing to talk with me. We usually talked about politics or the natural sciences. He mentioned the things they had thought were impossible when he was a kid, and we tried to predict what changes the future might bring. My mother often told the story that in the late 1920s he had predicted that a device such as television would soon be invented, but she hadn't believed him. Having my parents around made it easier to survive with so few friends.

My weather and science fiction interests attracted me to a classmate, Walter. Politically, he was liberal; he was also an atheist. Neither of us dated. With Alex we formed a triumvirate, spending a lot of time together once the junior year got under way. Our friendship put a stop to my increasing introversion and my social life began to improve. Nevertheless, I was very impatient to escape from Hastings and go to college.

During the rare occasions Michael and I were together, he didn't seem to notice how introverted I was; mainly, he told me about his grand time and we played Ping-Pong. He was fast becoming a big man on campus, and had plenty of girlfriends. In fact, Michael experienced many ups and downs in college. Academically, the competition at Swarthmore was stiff. His adviser, Dr. Joseph W. Conard, an economics professor and a tremendously warm person, exerted a special influence on him. He generously gave his time to students and was sympathetic to and open-minded about radicalism. His passion for social justice was evident. Michael decided to major in economics.

He fell in with a leftist crowd. Judicious questioning and humility were traits they slowly, painfully acquired. Their radicalism at this juncture was accepted on faith, and they didn't yet have the knowledge to provide strong rebuttals against opposing positions. Michael's initial attempts to win arguments in which he defended the Soviet Union and emphasized the injustice of American capitalism failed abysmally. Once, upset by friends dumping on Michael's dogmatism, his roommate explained that because Michael was Julius and Ethel Rosenberg's son he could not contain his negative feelings about the United States, nor be objective in political arguments. Actually, Michael was striving to achieve both and finally did also develop the habit of listening to counter-arguments and reacting with the admission that he might be wrong.

Especially in the first two years Michael's crowd was very tightly knit — they partied and participated in demonstrations together. They began a tradition which continued for four years, driving to Washington to hear the oral arguments before the Supreme Court. There before him sat Hugo Black and William Douglas, who'd almost consistently voted for our parents, and Tom Clark, who'd always voted against them. In 1961 the group picketed the federal building in Philadelphia "to protest the Bay of Pigs invasion of Cuba by CIA-trained mercenaries." The onlookers were hostile, some picking fights, others ripping picket signs from protesters' hands. Michael wondered where the cops had disappeared to. Later he discovered that two of the hecklers were cops in plainclothes who summoned a paddy wagon and arrested the demonstrators who fought back. After a particularly vicious remark from a cop, one of the protestors jotted down his badge number; he too was arrested. That night in the dorm Michael got into a shouting match over the invasion and picketing. The next day one of those he'd argued with said, "Wouldn't it be great if the police were here to arrest S——— and Meeropol." As two cops stood nearby while the statement was made, the comment got passed around and consequently misquoted. A few hours later Michael received a phone call saying that he was about to be arrested. Fearful of public exposure, Mike hid while friends called Gloria Agrin for the name of a local lawyer. By the time he met the lawyer, the misunderstanding had cleared up.

As Michael has said, "The feelings I experienced over the possibility of exposure justified to me my parents' jealous guarding of our privacy in previous years. I spent my four years at Swarthmore trying to make contributions as 'myself' — not as 'the son of.' However, I have only recently learned that many of my friends and acquaintances knew about my background."

Michael's grades didn't improve until his senior year, as in his first three years he concentrated on teaching guitar in Philadelphia to earn money, engaging in political activity, and pursuing girls. Finally, in his last year, his courses captivated him to the extent that he plugged hard, passed his honors exams and was accepted by Kings College at Cambridge University in England for graduate studies in economics.

Throughout college he contemplated changing his name and clung to memories of the past, often solidifying them. One day in the library he spent hours reading the *New York Times* account of the case, June 15–19, 1953. In contrast to his response while reading *Knock on Any Door*, he felt a great desire for revenge, to make the guilty suffer, though this emotion quickly passed. After taking a seminar in moral philosophy, he came to believe that the concept of retribution as a justification for punishment is morally indefensible, that justice is only an instrument of prevention or restitution. Killing a murderer of course does not restore the life of the victim, but the criminal should make personal restitution.

At the time though, I didn't know the specifics of Michael's college life. To me he was thoroughly enjoying himself. He had many friends at college and exciting adventures, such as driving to Chicago every year with a bunch of friends to attend the Chicago Folk Festival. During one of his vacations he visited Jerry, who'd become friendly with Mike Minor at Earlham. He and Michael revived their relationship. Mike persuaded my brother and Jerry to work with him at the summer camp a pal of his had started. At camp Jerry met and fell for Adrienne Rosner, whom he later married. In the week that Jerry and Adrienne, my brother and his girlfriend spent on Cape Cod, Adrienne mentioned to Jerry that when she was a baby her mother had frequently wheeled her carriage with Ethel Rosenberg. After Jerry revealed that Michael was the baby in the other carriage, Adrienne and Michael had long talks about life in Knickerbocker Village and other aspects of the past. Adrienne's parents had handed out leaflets during the campaign to save our parents.

Three days after camp, Mike a camp friend, Danny and I rode to Washington for the great civil rights march that attracted 250,000 to the capital. The size of my first Washington march overwhelmed me — Peter, Paul and Mary, singing "Blowin' in the Wind" on stage, looked like dots; I couldn't see Martin Luther King but heard his "I Have a Dream" speech over a public-address speaker. On the way home I kept hoping that now things would be different, and was disappointed that the political climate didn't improve. I had theorized that more than marches were necessary to institute substantial change; this was sobering proof of my theory.

Junior year proved to be a fairly happy one, because of Walter and Alex, a newfound passion for history and camp friends to enjoy on weekends in New York. My parents, respecting my judgment, allowed me to roam unsupervised in the city. No doubt they realized how unhappy I was in Hastings. Three of us — Mike, Hector (another friend from camp) and I — endlessly discussed politics and our unsuccessful attempts to find girl-friends. Always searching for excitement, we rarely found it and weren't sure what we were looking for. We used to say we hung out together because we had such a good time having a bad time.

I couldn't bring myself to mention my parents to Mike, my best friend, and this intensified the pressure which was beginning to build around my identity, to admit my real name; people wouldn't know me until I did. Yet, I couldn't. Although I didn't often feel this way, when it did hit me, I thought I would burst. To relieve the tension, I'd concentrate on another matter.

My grades improved somewhat. I daydreamed about becoming a politician, assuming I could be relatively successful if only my views weren't so much at odds with everyone else's. Briefly, I considered dishonestly altering my convictions, but the memory of my parents, even stronger than my political philosophy, influenced me to discard this idea before it could be fully formulated.

Through the Meeropols and county-wide leftist ventures, I met other left-wing teen-agers in Westchester and at Mt. Airy in Croton, reputed to have had the largest concentration of Communists in the 1930s. We planned national high-school peace walks. In April I joined my first Westchester High School student march. All of us were keenly bothered by the dilemma of keeping silent about our beliefs and being accepted or voicing our opinions and being ostracized. When the Vietnam war escalated in 1964, I wore a SUPPORT THE NLF button to school. I don't know how I got away with it. Possibly the teachers and students had never heard of the NLF or figured it was an acronym for the National Football League. Sanity prevailed the next day; I didn't wear the button. Occasionally, I couldn't resist such outbursts; still, I covered my tracks better than most. From personal experience I was fully aware of the deadly serious side of politics.

The summer following my junior year my brother and I were reunited at camp as staff counselors. In my first job, I appreciated acceptance by young adults and liked the campers but was not much good at disciplining them. Michael became very attached to Ann, also a counselor, and a friend of Adrienne's. While he was at Cambridge, they corresponded steadily, and Michael returned home in April convinced he would marry her. Ann was not familiar with his background, and when they babysat for friends his first evening back in the States, he knew he had to "say it." He'd never mentioned "it" to anyone, as those he'd started to tell invariably interrupted him to admit they already knew.

Michael recalls, "My heart was going like a goddamn bass drum. I closed my eyes and thought, 'I am the son of Julius and Ethel Rosenberg.' Then, taking a deep breath I repeated it aloud. At first, the name meant little to her; her recollections of the case were vague. I began to talk about the past. She was shocked and read whatever books I gave her about the trial and was convinced of their innocence."

Relying on logging skills learned at a previous camp, I thinned out a pine forest. Not that I was an expert by any means, but I could make a tree fall in the desired direction — away from the campers — which qualified me for the job. At seventeen, with a heavy beard, I had no trouble getting into bars with the older counselors. I rarely got to sleep before 1 A.M., and one morning, to everyone's amusement, actually fell asleep in my cereal. Earlier in the year I had vaulted off a mini-trampoline, dislocated a shoulder and wore a sling for two months. During the third week of camp, I dislocated that shoulder playing basketball. Again in a sling, I was unable to chop down trees. To make matters worse, I stepped on a nail a week later and hobbled around for days. The final week of camp, during a camper-counselor baseball game, I slid over a bat while coming into home plate, dislocating my shoulder a third time. Though I had always avoided physical violence and hard contact sports, this string of mishaps greatly increased my dread of injury.

Most of us at camp were left-wing, our politics evident in the songs we sang — Dylan's "With God On Our Side," Phil Ochs' "Medgar Evers," etc. That summer the gravity of politics was again brought home. Andrew Goodman, one of three civil rights workers murdered by Mississippi deputies, had been a schoolmate and friend of one of the counselors. The killings enraged me, but there was nothing to be done. Many in the growing New Left were attempting to change the system though we felt few perceived as we did the totality of its destructive character. Nevertheless, with the Vietnam war escalating, there was a noticeable increase in the numbers demonstrating, and this raised my expectations for the future of the left.

During my last year at Hastings High, I was finally assimilated into an intellectual crowd, although socially I had a long way to go. Several classmates were obviously more alienated, particularly the girl in my homeroom who was often the butt of sexual jokes and teasing. We never spoke but I felt a bond with her because I realized how close I came to being in a similar position. Two years later, reading *Newsweek* in the college library, I stumbled across an article describing her death from an overdose of heroin. Her body had been found in the trunk of a car belonging to a promising young composer. Her death again reminded me of the lethal character of society.

In England, Michael was fairly impatient to return home while the New Left took its first tentative steps as an up-front radical movement. Beginning with the Port Huron Statement,* SDS with uncharacteristic humility for a left-wing organization proclaimed its search for a new society more humane and democratic than the United States. SDS responded with honesty and courage to the events of the early 1960s, Kennedy's support for Diem and huge military budgets, the pervasiveness of black oppression one hundred years after the Emancipation Proclamation. These facts pushed SDS beyond the anti-Communist consensus that included even the Socialist leader Norman Thomas, and to its credit it did not shrink from such a move. In 1966 it broke with its anti-Communist parent organization, removing the anti-Communist membership clause. Advancing beyond the vague liberalism of its founding statement, SDS began seriously exploring imperialism, racism and monopoly capitalism. Reading the debates, supportive of its groping for an alternative society, Michael felt at home in the movement. In addition he was impressed with the autonomy of local chapters which more truly represented the diversity in America than centralized parties, as existed in Old Left groups.

In my senior year, Arthur and Vic, two boys my age from Croton, and I created the Westchester Viet Cong, dedicated to painting anything we thought an appropriate anti-war target.

* Sale, Kirkpatrick, *SDS* (New York: Vintage, 1974), pp. 290–97.

After plotting for a month we spray-painted the guard house at a nearby army base. Spraying "peace" on an army building may not seem very dangerous in retrospect, but in 1965 we were well ahead of our time, regarding ourselves as a more daring generation of radicals, dismissing the Communist Party and the old progressive movement as outdated and soft, joking about the Communist Party being two-thirds FBI agents. We exchanged Old Left anecdotes like the one about the bystander at a Philadelphia demonstration who cried to a policeman clubbing him, "Don't hit me, I'm an anti-Communist." The cop answered, "I don't care what kind of Communist you are," and hit him again.

A bunch of us were active in forming the "Westchester Students for Peace and Civil Rights." In addition to helping with the spring peace marches, we chartered a bus to a Washington demonstration in February and filled four buses for the huge SDS-sponsored Washington rally in April.

Since Michael had roomed next door to one of its first national secretaries and had been active in its early organizing campaign in Chester, Pennsylvania, I had been aware of SDS for a couple of years. Michael had been arrested while picketing a segregated school which was also the target of a civil disobedience protest, the cops not differentiating between "legal" and "illegal" demonstrations. After a boring day in jail, during which he talked himself out of his fear of discovery, he was released. As part of the package deal to persuade the local black activists and Swarthmore students not to disrupt the city, the government dropped all charges.

To me the left consisted of Communist and Communist splinter groups operating in a stagnant, often irrelevant way. Anti-Communist reformist groups like SANE and the Student Peace Union just weren't radical enough for me. SDS seemed truly radical: that is, dedicated to changing the entire American system rather than patching up a portion of it. So I joined SDS as a member-at-large, carrying my membership card proudly but secretly in my pocket. At that time, SDS had an anti-Communist clause in its bylaws. Red-baiting was terrible, but I rationalized that I wasn't sure what kind of Communist I was; at any rate, I didn't belong to an organized group. And my brand of Communism was based solely on current events, as I hadn't read much by Marx or other theoreticians. Anita, a classmate, and I rode to the SDS rally together and began to see each other. Michael also attended that march, happy that so many turned out to protest the Vietnamese war, impressed that SDS refused to ban "pro-Communists" from the march, concentrating its criticism on the United States. The speeches of Senator Ernest Gruening and I. F. Stone thrilled him as they uncompromisingly laid it on the line — we were intervening unilaterally and should get out the same way we got in. Disturbed about the American escalation in Vietnam, Anita and I were afraid that the Russians would enter the war, not allowing us much more time to live. Rarely have I been so frightened. Even the Cuban missile crisis had not disturbed me this much, as I suspected the crisis would somehow be resolved — but the war did not appear to be solvable. Now that I was eighteen, I was forced to register for the draft.

Politics deepened my involvement with classmates, many of whom I worked with in the Young Citizens for Johnson Committee. Despite the fact that I despised Johnson, Goldwater seemed more evil. Besides, it's fun to work for a winner once in a while. Thinking of all those dollars I collected for Johnson still embarrasses me.

The final term was a rather happy one for me. As my parents were busy with a dramatic review which my father wrote and my mother directed, I was on my own. Like any teen-ager, I assumed I was mature enough to make my own decisions; my parents' presence seemed retrictive at times. When they worked they left me the car keys, so Walter and I had wheels for heading north toward more scenic country. We shared a love of woods, camping and weather. We ate a lot of Dairy Queen and plastic burgerstand food, talked about college, politics, God and people.

A lively debate ensued among several of us after the class trip to the county penitentiary. At one point we walked through a cell block, staring at the prisoners. I was appalled. In class the next day I objected to the display of the inmates like animals in a zoo; I was also affected on a gut level. The students seemed to enjoy peering at the curiosities behind bars — their response sickened me. That my parents had been in jail might have strengthened my reaction, though that didn't occur to me then.

Although I was having a good time at school I counted the days until college. I was turned down by Swarthmore, my first choice, despite good college board scores. No doubt this rejection was fortunate; it would have been difficult to live up to my brother's image. Earlham College, a small Quaker school in Richmond, Indiana, with a liberal reputation and an excellent history department, accepted me. Some of my camp acquaintances were students there and liked it. My four-year wait was ending.

The summer was dull. I worked at a day camp and learned to play tennis. Anita was in Europe, as was my brother, who paid his way across the continent by street-singing with two friends. The final weeks at home were taken up with old pals and parties. Then my father and I drove out to Indiana. College would be a great adventure. I was nervous but confident that the worst was behind me.

10

College and Politics, 1965–1967

I HAD A VERY STYLIZED PICTURE of what the Midwest was like. Having never read *Babbitt,* I didn't characterize that section of the country as politically conservative, socially puritanical and culturally sterile, as many easterners did. New Yorkers pay the price for their provincialism and wind up being suavely naive about the rest of the nation. My image came from the Penrod novels I'd read in junior high school. I expected the college to be surrounded by quiet, tree-lined streets where friendly residents invited me to dinner on Sunday. I anticipated an animated Norman Rockwell painting. Yet, as I'd never been south of Washington, or west of Elmira, except when 35,000 feet in the air flying to Mexico, I was apprehensive driving into downtown Richmond on a hot day. The city seemed somewhat dirty, run-down and unattractive.

After registering with the orientation committee, I was handed a beanie to wear. The college utilized the standard technique of subjecting the freshman class to minor indignities, motivating them to rebel and in the process develop cohesion and class spirit. The beanie was foolish but I put it on, already beginning to feel like a foreigner in Rome. An orientation leader showed my father and me to my room. I opened the door; plastered on the opposite wall was a large poster of the Kremlin and Red Square. I was amazed. I had hoped that I wouldn't get stuck with a conversative roommate, but this was something *I* might have done. Still, a picture of Red Square was a bit uncool. My father, after meeting my roommate, Arthur, complained about the poster, passing us off as conservative Republicans. Apologetic, Arthur offered to remove the offensive art work. We goaded him until he actually started to untape the picture; then I admitted to being against the war and agreed with his preference. Arthur had recently converted to Quakerism. He was a pacifist, a vegetarian, and no great admirer of the Soviet Union. The poster was a souvenir from his summer trip to Russia. I unpacked and my father left, relieved that my roommate was congenial. Lately I have wondered if our rooming together was sheer coincidence or if Earlham knew from my school records that I was Julius and Ethel Rosenberg's son. Perhaps they matched me with a confirmed pacifist for just this reason.

We walked to the gym to hear the president address the class. In his opening remarks he mentioned that some freshmen were under the mistaken impression that Earlham College was a "Quaker Antioch or midwestern Swarthmore"; the class stood up and cheered. Having presumed both to be true, I was taken aback, but soon learned the difference between midwestern Quakers and the liberal, service-oriented American Friends Service Committee. The midwesterners regarded the AFSC as Communist, were proud of their favorite sons, Herbert Hoover and Richard Nixon, conservative Quakers, to say the least. Afterward, I went to vespers — not knowing what they were — for the first and last time. I had one jolt after another, though still convinced that at college my radical views would receive a fair hearing in an intellectual setting. Wrapped in a cocoon for so long, I was ready to blossom in a burst of political activity. Promptly I got into an argument about God with a prospective philosophy major whose father was a minister. He would have fared better had he been able to overcome his surprise at meeting an atheist.

One of the more painful shocks I absorbed was that Earlham enrolled only a few token blacks, otherwise proclaiming its conservatism to the world. The town considered the college red-tinged, loaded with race mixers. Sixty percent of Richmond voted for Goldwater in 1964. A Klu Klux Klan meeting had been held in a neighboring town the previous year. In its population of 50,000, Richmond had over fifty millionaires yet encompassed a black ghetto in which a large proportion of the people had substandard housing. The college reflected this racism by reporting to the parents of students involved in interracial romances. Obviously this was not a hospitable atmosphere for my radicalism, but I was determined to make a go of it.

Finding no anti-war group already functioning on campus, Arthur and I tacked up posters and called a meeting of interested students. Most of those who showed up were lowerclassmen. We didn't know at the time that senior peace activists would spurn a movement cooked up by half-baked freshmen. Without their aid we formed the Earlham Committee to End the War in Vietnam. Among the thirty or forty pacifist activists on campus I thought of myself as the only radical. For me it was essential to change the basic nature of the system in order to solve the problems of war, racism, unequal distribution of wealth and other ills. Also I carefully examined my political philosophy. The terms Communist and Socialist confused me, and in the last year I'd grown disenchanted with the Soviet Union, which was too tightly controlled and failed to provide underdeveloped countries with sufficient economic and military aid to resist the United States. I no longer fully backed Russia but chose not to admit it for fear of playing into the hands of any anti-Communist propagandists. After questioning Arthur about Russia I was even more uncertain.

The first activity scheduled by the Earlham Committee to End the War in Vietnam was a demonstration in downtown Richmond to coincide with the international days of protest against the war organized by the National Coordinating Committee to End the War in Vietnam. The moment we announced the march we ran into trouble — the town refused to grant us a permit to demonstrate, and one councilman reasoned that our activities might be construed as the official position of the U.S. government. The president called us into his office to inform us that for four years Earlham had been striving for solid relations with the town; finally the college was making headway and our type of activity would destroy that precarious balance. Later I learned this was his standard speech. (He used it on us again the next year to stop a demonstration.) He convinced most of the committee they should suspend the march. Seniors fell all over themselves to say they preferred not to hurt the college, which had been threatened with vandalism if the march continued. Arthur, several friends and I rebelled against the alternative proposal of a silent campus vigil; at the same time, we realized it would be unwise to march downtown only five strong and disbanded the march. Furious at this turn of events, I pinned a letter on the opinion board in the administration building:

You will have to forgive me for I am angry. You will also have to forgive me for being a New Yorker who doesn't know how society functions in this part of the country. However, one thing I do understand. The thinking and actions of the people of this area are foreign to everything that democracy stands for. When a group of people want to protest a policy of our government they are told they are insincere by town officials because they have protested before. Of course, if you are sincerely against something, then you can only protest once and then forget about it. When a town official is heard to say that a respected institution of higher learning like this college is a mess and when the police question the protesters as to whether they are soliciting Negroes, where is there freedom in this town? The one newspaper is so biased that it is not taken seriously by many intelligent people. College students are threatened and subjected to insults because they are strangers and view things from a slightly different angle. What is "home town USA"? What has happened to the four freedoms in this town?

One: the freedom of speech. Who would dare to stand up downtown and disagree with our policy in Southeast Asia or even demand negotiations without fear of losing his job, being beaten up or being thrown in jail? The first freedom is nonexistent.

Two: freedom of religion. This also includes those who do not believe in God. Who would dare to proclaim he was an atheist in the middle of town? How much true freedom of religion is there?

Three: freedom to assemble. In this town you have to obtain a permit to use this freedom and the town official can deny you this right for such illogical reasons as the protest might be construed as the official line of the United States government. You are free to assemble as long as you assemble for an approved cause.

Four: freedom from fear. This town is in a bind of fear. We, who merely ask for a reappraisal, were warned that we were in physical danger and that the college might be subjected to various acts of vandalism if our protest is carried out. There is no fourth freedom here.

What has happened to the process of thinking in this area? People are so fixed in their views that they will not even listen to an opposing opinion. What kind of a democracy is this? It is no democracy; it is a dictatorship of ignorance. This is our great free nation, a leader in democracy and thought? I am disgusted with this country; it is rotting externally and internally. All demonstrations and protests I participate in are my own pathetic attempt to remedy this situation. All I ask is that people look around them, sincerely examine all sides of an issue, and act in a way that they feel would truly benefit all of mankind, not Republicans, not Democrats, not Protestants, not white people, not the western world, but mankind. No man is any better than another; every man has the right to his opinion and a right to say what he feels without fear. This is truly democracy.

This letter not only reflected the pent-up political energy accumulating for four years, it also contained some of the major strands of my political philosophy, including elements clearly inherited from the political style of the Rosenbergs, who believed that America took a democratic form but was not a democracy. I truly believed in democracy, had a strong civil libertarian perspective, a respect for intellectuality and an internationalist outlook, yet this is far from being openly revolutionary or socialist. At any rate, I could not have been more successful at achieving instant notoriety. My letter started a furor which soon died down, but not before I had gained a reputation as a wild-eyed radical with a sharp tongue and pen.

As the term moved on, fewer and fewer students attended meetings, the administration having co-opted most of them by convincing them that protest tactics must be toned down. Arthur and I spent a lot of time talking and had enough common ground and diverging opinions to do so fruitfully. For him the major political contradiction lay between the forces of war and peace. He had concluded that President Kennedy had been assassinated because peace was about to break out, while I countered that Kennedy's death was a CIA plot to which Johnson or Nixon might have been connected. As he filled out his conscientious-objector form and straightened out his philosophy of the nature of the supreme being, I argued that there was none. We turned a close friend, Hernán, a Kennedy liberal from Chile, into a radical.

I rarely thought about my real parents. Anita informed me in a letter that she'd found out my identity, but none of my friends at Earlham knew. Sometimes I had the urge to tell Arthur but couldn't. Even though I kept my secret, my personality was much better integrated now, as I no longer had to sustain the liberal veneer of high school or the apolitical attitude of the street. Also, my policy of forgetting the past had worked; much of it was now lost. I had separated my life with my parents from the present, imposing a new background upon the old one. I wasn't even certain how much of my personality reflected the Meeropols' upbringing and how much should be attributed to earlier experiences.

I went out with girls a couple of times but wasn't really attracted to anyone until I meet Dee and Elli one day at lunch and became infatuated with Dee, who was going out with an upperclassman. So I pined away for several months. Eventually I married Elli, who at the time was also going out with an upperclassman. Reasonably outgoing and rarely lonely, I was determined not to repeat my high school experiences and prevented myself from withdrawing. I was really into being a leader, conducting myself in a style I later recognized to be very macho and self-serving. I went so far as to regard one woman member as my secretary — it's no wonder she soon stopped attending meetings. Elli told me that when I chaired a meeting I was hard and impersonal.

At Thanksgiving, the anti-war committee chartered a bus for the big rally in Washington, D.C. A few of us drove down ahead of time to attend the convention at which the National Committee to End the War in Vietnam was created. There I witnessed my first sectarian infighting in the movement, though I had little idea of the factions and what they represented. The Trotskyites were attempting to take over, some members warned. From high school I remembered that the "Trots" seemed willing to use and sacrifice larger organizations for their own, more narrow ends, so I joined the independent delegates in voting against almost every one of their proposals and helped establish a left-wing, nonsectarian umbrella group. It was exhilarating to find so many people to agree with. In belonging to this group I also stressed my independence which was partially a defense mechanism to make it difficult for the right wing to label me, and as well it kept me from having to continually defend China and Russia. Amazingly enough these factions agreed about many issues, yet they wasted their time attacking each other. We returned to college at 6:00 A.M.; after our frenetic weekend the quiet campus was too much to bear. A few of us yelled, "Wake up, Earlham, the world is passing you by." Invoking no response we went to bed.

As in high school I got through my freshman year with B's and C's. About once a month I wrote to Michael, still in England; the distance between us was more than geographically great. We had lost touch with each other. Most of his attention he devoted to Ann, whom he was coming home to marry in December. The previous summer they'd hitchhiked around Europe and were both in Cambridge that fall.

In December I was glad to be back in what I felt was the more liberal, scintillating East, seeing Anita and Walter in Hastings, Mike and Hector in the city. Ann and Michael were married in a small Ethical Culture ceremony witnessed by several good friends and family members, many of whom I hadn't seen in years. Having to deal with two sets of relatives in the same place made me uncomfortable.

Mike and Ann had a wonderful year in Cambridge with its lovely canals, old buildings and bicycles. Lacking a car, a television, a telephone, they lived a simple life. Regardless of his eagerness to become active in America's political struggles, he luxuriated in that country.

January was cold and gray; the anti-war committee was barely functioning. I became disgusted by the pacifist nature of the Earlham Committee and dropped out of organized political activity, an abrupt turnabout for me, but after the hard work of the first term I was thoroughly disillusioned. My circle shrank considerably. To make matters worse, Elli was in New York on an off-campus study program, and Dee was still seeing her upperclassman, leaving me quite a bit of time to watch TV.

My mediocre academic performance continued. Even when I studied fairly hard I couldn't pull better than average grades. From the time I was thirteen, I had intended to get a Ph.D., be a college professor. Despite my background I imagined myself living a peaceful life, married, with children, teaching at a small college. (It didn't concern me that this dream contradicted my emerging plan to some day reopen and win my parents' case.) Now I questioned this assumption as academic pursuits were a minor attraction, and I was upset that I might not find a satisfactory niche in society. I had never considered alternatives, except politics, and the halls of Congress were no doubt forever barred.

My friend Mike hitched out from New York, and we traveled to Antioch for the weekend — the highlight of the term. Since we were in the same boat, we had a wonderful time relating our misadventures. At a friend's house we met a somewhat older guru-type who deeply influenced us, introducing us to the hippie movement, rapping with us about dropping out of society and alienation. Unless the New Left redeemed society, we'd have no alternative but to drop out, in Leary's sense of the phrase, leave the mainstream of America's consumer-oriented society in order to relate to people in new ways. For the next several years I flirted with hippiedom, vacillating between intense involvement in political organizations like SDS and in the youth culture. In spite of the fact that the hippie movement was apolitical, young people presented a constituency numerous radicals thought we could reach. So many of us had been social and political outsiders that we jumped at the chance of being part of the youth and drug cultures to bridge the gap between us and thousands of high school and college-age kids, presuming that the alienation of dropouts could be harnessed to build a massive anti-war, anti-capitalist movement. The lure of belonging to a mass movement was impossible to resist. I returned to Earlham suspecting that a new dawn was upon us, the Age of Aquarius was here at last.

Spring term was a vast improvement over the winter term. I began to see more and more of Elli but though committed to her, I scarcely confided in her, unable as I was to mention my parents. As a result, I didn't reveal much of myself to her.

The Committee stirred into action again, planning a mini teach-in featuring Mike Locker, an ex-Earlhamite doing anti-war research for SDS at the University of Michigan. Locker addressed a hundred students in the auditorium. The hawkish jocks on campus staged a counter-demonstration in anticipation of a fiery radical speaker. Locker, low-keyed, did not harangue the crowd about the war; instead, he talked about organizing techniques. The jocks stood around the room with their pro-war signs, unsure of how to respond. The teach-in did not transform the campus, but it may have given me the idea of transferring. Things were happening politically at Michigan as well as on other campuses. Four friends and I started an SDS chapter which remained dormant, and we didn't pick up the pieces the following year.

The last week of the term was heartbreaking. Elli could no longer tolerate my remoteness and stopped seeing me. I was crushed and only partially succeeded in forgetting her though I was happier by the time I arrived home to arrange for a summer in Europe. Ricky, an old friend from Westchester, and I hopped a slow, overcrowded student ship to England. In July we traveled through France, Denmark and Holland, living mostly with families who had sympathized with my parents. I was rather anxious about using these old connections. In August we attended the Cambridge University summer school then went to London where we boarded with a woman who'd worked on the Rosenberg Committee in the 1950s.

Aside from the people who housed us, we had little contact with Europeans. Instead, we hung out with other wandering student hippies. The families we stayed with taught me valuable political lessons. I gained a deeper understanding of the horror of World War II which still preoccupied them, as they'd lost their relatives during that war. It occurred to me that Americans would be alert to the danger of fascism, less eager to bomb Vietnamese villages if their own country had been invaded, their own cities destroyed. I learned that while Communist and other left-wing parties were in the minority, they nevertheless were regarded as legitimate political forces. Communism frightened most Americans though they had little comprehension of that ideology. Americans appeared so provincial that even long hair irritated them.

On the fourth of July, Ricky and I had participated in an American Anti-Vietnam War Rally in front of the American Embassy in Paris. It was a typical demonstration — a lot of talking and standing around. Two protesters in the back of the crowd burned an American flag, earning headlines in newspapers back home. For me, this was another confirmation of distorted press reporting. Out of 700 Americans, two burn a flag and receive major coverage. When a handful of French students tried to cross the street and approach the American Embassy, the police charged them, swinging lead-weighted capes. Then screaming in French they turned on us, kicking at us to speed our departure. Several of us circled behind a stone wall in a nearby park from which we looked down on the melee. The police systematically separated individuals and beat them before arresting them, six or seven cops to one. This enraged me — a policeman had no right to mete out punishment before a trial. The unnecessary violence, the excessive brutality disturbed me, impelling me, once I was home, to become even more dedicated to the campaign against similar perversions of justice. In addition, supporting just causes was the most effective way I could honor the memory of my parents. A drive to right the world and perpetuate my parents' work kept me involved in politics.

I was far more confident in myself than a year ago, and jumped into my sophomore year full of energy, raring to "knock 'em dead," happily, no longer a freshman male at the bottom of the social totem pole. I was also looking forward to sharing a hall with my buddies. To compensate for the lack of fraternities, Earlham allowed friends to reserve halls. Our crowd of nine freaks and politicos won a relatively prized hall in the semi-basement of a building. The college was in for a new experience. True, beatnik halls had existed in the past, but Earlham was about to witness its first hippie freak radical-activists' hall. We aimed to change peoples' heads.

Entering my room I immediately walked into Arthur's bear hug. We moved down to Hernán's room collecting others along the way. Scanning the crew, I remarked, "With us all here together, it's just gotta be a good year." We trooped over to the snack bar and within half an hour were bored. "This place is dead," I announced. "I'm transferring." Most of the others concurred — only two returned the following year. The college environment stifled us, the rules a constant source of irritation.

Over the summer I'd become more knowledgeable and candid

about my radicalism and learned the distinction between communists — with a lower-case 'c' — and those supporting the Soviet Union. To be radical I didn't need to identify with a foreign power; I could be a home-grown American radical. Being in a tight, supportive group emboldened us. About this time a crucial shift in mind-set occurred in the fledgling New Left across the country. The segment which grew up as red-diaper babies were now openly proclaiming their politics, no longer defensive about their philosophy. We felt part of the wave of the future. We did not bother to minimize our differences with the establishment's set of values, declaring to all who would listen that we represented a strong political alternative, that our way had substantially more to offer than the previous generation's. Furthermore, all of us should be free to dress and look as we wished, to engage in whatever sexual pursuits turned us on. Race should not form a barrier among people. The concept of patriotism should not be manipulated to transform citizens into automatons. Admittedly, we were obnoxious to a degree, assuming we knew all the answers, acting superior to those who rejected us, as if we were infinitely more alluring than the rest of the student body. Having read Richard Farina's book, *Been Down So Long It Looks Like Up to Me,* we fancied ourselves lesser Farinas. Women were treated as appendages, hangers-on; they were cool if they dressed the right way and upheld our anti-Puritanical position. A few women were respected for their intellects, but generally our attitudes were sexist and exploitative.

A clash with the administration was inevitable. The first run-in, a minor incident, occurred when Bob, the anarchist across the hall, and others were caught drawing hammers, sickles and ANARCHISTS UNITE signs in wet cement. The second collision caused a bigger stir. Our windows were half above, half below ground, and women often sat in the window wells talking to us. As women were not allowed in the mens' dorms we were obviously bending the rules. The men's housing council was called into session and quickly passed a rule that no women were permitted to sit in the window wells of any men's hall. Having the only hall on campus with window wells, we reacted by storming into the office of the director of men's housing. He in turn conferred with the dean, who maintained that the rule was unavoidable — one thing would lead to another, and he didn't want any pregnancies on campus. We responded that his rules were stupid so we had no intention of obeying them. The administration was unable to cope with our "mass" action. Students were supposed to be rueful when caught, not defiant. Responsible to the very conservative Quaker board running the school, the authorities could not pretend to sympathize in this controversy as they had with the war protest and thus were prevented from co-opting the more liberal protesters. Consequently, they were forced to adopt a hard-line stance which alienated larger and larger numbers of students. Many who did not side with us admired us for standing up to the administration. The weather got colder so the window wells were uninhabitable, but the battles continued.

I became involved with student power issues and worked with the revitalized anti-war committee. We put on a regional AFSC anti-war conference, bringing Phil Ochs to the campus for a big concert. That weekend was truly amazing — the longhairs in the majority, the administration and jocks greatly upset. Phil Ochs gave a rousing concert to a packed auditorium that included Antioch students. (Usually Earlhamites traveled to Antioch for entertainment.) Ochs caused a flap by telling the story of W. C. Fields' last words for which the punch line is "On second thought, fuck 'em." We cheered while the administrators blanched. The next morning the president of the college was on his hands and knees picking cigarette butts off the floor near the auditorium — the rule prohibiting smoking on the front campus had been ignored. Notes appeared on the opinion board denouncing those long-haired, filthy hippies, as well as the dean's note concerning foul language. Gratified by these responses, six of us tacked up a reply to the effect that we were so appalled by the dirty hippies, so persuaded by the notes that we would shower and shave for the first time in years. The reply ended, "On second thought, f**k 'em," causing a bigger stink and another dean's conference.

After that weekend I again split with the anti-war committee, which changed its name to PEACE — Peace, Education and Action Committee of Earlham — reflecting the schism between their politics and mine. They preached that all factions in Vietnam should stop their senseless killing; whereas I distinguished between offensive and defensive violence, and so considered the NLF's position valid. Hernán and I checked the *National Guardian* every week for the number of American planes shot down.

Michael and Ann moved to Madison where they'd both enrolled in graduate school. Jerry and Adrienne, now married, and preceding them by a year, found an apartment nearby for them, and the two couples were inseparable over the next four years. When Ann became pregnant they all rejoiced; when Adrienne did not, they all discussed adoption. Jerry and Adrienne adopted twin boys; Ann and Mike adopted a son a year later. The children have grown up together like brothers and sisters as their parents sustained one another in an extended family. Michael and Jerry's first joint political effort called for a decentralized third party presidential platform in 1968 which demanded withdrawal from Southeast Asia, support for Black Power, and a guarantee of jobs or income. Their program attracted no takers, either from SDS leaders or from leaders of the mobilization committees which emphasized big marches while Michael pushed local orientation, realizing that demonstrations alone would not sway masses.

I stayed with Michael and Ann over Thanksgiving and had a grand time telling confrontation stories, being with old friends from camp. There was something joyous about our reunion and the obvious happiness Michael and Ann shared. I got a little depressed about not enjoying a similar relationship, for Elli had left Earlham to spend a year in Kentucky. It is not clear to me whether the affection I had had from both sets of parents or Michael and Ann's relationship stimulated me to think in terms of marriage and a family, but as a nineteen-year-old I entertained such thoughts. I was unhappy to discover that Michael and I were developing new distances between us. I was more of a hippie. Also, politics for him seemed to me to be an intellectual, letter-writing, party-building affair, for me a series of confrontations. He was discouraged by SDS's detour toward student power, and I was part of that shift. Scared by the possible depths of our disagreements, we avoided politics rather than argue, and grew further apart.

Michael "wanted to do something" and was preoccupied with the issues of the Vietnam war and oppression of blacks. Though he judged student power and black power to be good organizing tools, he felt the only successful method for effecting basic change would be achieved by coalitions of groups of oppressed people. In 1968 he and some friends, spurred by the fact that California's Peace and Freedom Party had won a spot on the ballot and agreed to a coalition with the Black Panther Party (whose main spokesman at the time — with Huey Newton in jail — was Eldridge Cleaver), originated the Wisconsin Alliance, which still exists. Within two years they'd elected a member to the City Council and two to the County Board. While Eugene McCarthy supporters worked on his primary campaign, Michael stumped the neighborhood to promote a referendum for total withdrawal from South Vietnam, even shaving his beard in the interest of the cause. Also he became a frequent caller on radio talk shows, offering logical and dispassionate reasons for America's getting out of Vietnam, to illustrate the ways capitalism destroyed people, to support black liberation, centuries overdue.

When I returned to Earlham, Hernán confronted me with the fact that through a mutual friend he'd found out who my parents were. Initially, he'd been dubious; two days of research in the library convinced him. As I had wanted to tell him, I was relieved that he knew.

In the winter term, I completed the transition to student power, associating this reaction against America's system of values with politics and anti-war sentiment. Now our hall didn't merely bend the rules, we ignored them. Women sneaked in "illegally," we even had a co-ed showering incident. I started writing a weekly column, "Out On A Limb," for the college paper, in which I attacked regulations or student passivity. In one column, I advocated Earlham's locating a different base of financial support from the extremely conservative Eli Lilly Corporation. With liberal or left money, the stagnant administration could be replaced. That issue had been published when trustees and fat cats of the college were meeting. The president summoned me to his office. I still regret not declining and inviting him instead to talk to all of us on the hall, but intimidated by power I complied.

Once before I had provoked him over the *View Book,* a public relations project for prospective freshmen. Without faculty or student knowledge, much less their approval, he had added a paragraph in the book to the effect that Earlham did not condone the revolution in sex and drugs; anyone who would not be satisfied with the simple Quaker life should look elsewhere. This was a slap at us and threatened our supply of new recruits. So I added a line at the end of an article, "Whoever wrote those lines in the *View Book* should be congratulated for imposing his small mind on Earlham College." Subsequently I'd learned the president wrote the material, and now, naturally, I accepted his summons with trepidation. We talked aimlessly but amicably for nearly an hour before he came to the point, telling me about a student who couldn't adjust to Earlham and transferred to Williams College, where he was much happier. The parable amused me. Recently I had been accepted at Michigan but I didn't give him the satisfaction of knowing I wouldn't be returning.

Our political activity had been attracting students, increasing our membership to a sizable minority. Nevertheless, I felt remote from society, from those not connected with college life, and Earlham would not alter that situation. Requesting applications from several colleges, Hernán and I had completed the one for the University of Michigan, which didn't require any essays. I also had a sound, academic reason for transferring — now that earning A's for the first time gave me mobility. My fascination with my courses in geology, vertebrate paleontology and human evolution had culminated in a decision to major in physical anthropology. Earlham offered no courses in the field, while Michigan had an entire department. Delighted to get me out of his hair, the dean wrote a strong recommendation. Both Hernán and I were accepted.

We had one last fling before leaving. Our friend Nick had discovered where the *View Books* were stored, approximately fifty boxes of them weighing fifty pounds each, in a locked building.

Eight of us had to find a way to sneak into the building, avoid the security guard and remove the boxes from the campus in the early morning, planning to hide them in the woods and demand a ransom. One of our group regularly used the elevator in that building and gave us the key. We timed the guard's rounds, left a cohort in the building before it was locked and parked three cars in the lot behind the building. At 3:30 A.M. our man inside let us in. In less than an hour we removed all but fourteen boxes which we scattered around the building — the last place they'd look. We drove the remaining thirty-six boxes off campus and went to bed. The next day we drove through the graveyard on the way to our hiding place. Just as on television, our perfect heist had a flaw. It was Memorial Day, and the graveyard was crawling with townspeople paying their respects to the dead. Three cars full of freaks and boxes drew plenty of attention, so the administration easily uncovered our stash a few days later. We posted an anonymous ransom note anyway.

My father arrived to take me home. During the summer I worked as a telephone operator and editorial assistant at the *National Guardian* in New York, living with my friend Mike in Brooklyn. The *Guardian* paid scant attention to student power, and I was uncomfortable discussing politics there, because most of my colleagues — professional, experienced activists — intimidated me, and I was silent for fear of sounding silly. Mike and I were moving in opposite directions. He was in the process of becoming a hippie and ultimately turned to spiritualism; I was a politico with a youth-culture orientation, so we didn't have much to offer each other. New York was hot, dirty, smelly; I wasn't digging the city I'd previously regarded as the coolest in the world. I looked forward to returning to the Midwest in the fall.

At the beginning of August I flew out to Ann Arbor for a three-day orientation session, staying with old friends, one of whom, Karen, promised to find me an apartment. My father and I drove to Ann Arbor in time for my first classes.

11

The New Left and the Commune, 1967–1971

NEITHER KAREN NOR HER HUSBAND, Terry, had any luck in locating a decent apartment for me, so I had to settle for one lousy room without kitchen facilities in the attic of a house. Women and alcohol were not permitted on the premises. Hernán lived on north campus two miles away in an upperclassmen's dorm. As his roommate didn't show up that term, I spent at least half my nights sleeping in his vacant bed.

SDS held a planning meeting, and I was very pleased when 150 students crammed into the room. SDS spearheaded the left movement at Michigan. The local chapter called itself Voice Political Party because of its involvement in student government campaigns. Its slate of candidates usually won. I was awed by its power. Many of the students who ran the *Daily,* the college newspaper, with a circulation of more than 7000, backed the chapter. SDS possessed a lot of clout, was a force to be reckoned with. I was graduating to the big leagues after doing my time in the minors. However, unlike Earlham where activists agreed about almost everything, here people were at each other's throats even though they shared similar views. The meeting bogged down in faction fights. Karen was elected president, and the discussion turned to the fall campaign and joining an upcoming university employee's strike.

Maintenance and service personnel were striking for union recognition. The majority of students opposed the strike — they missed having their meals cooked for them, their sheets laundered. The teamsters honored the picket line and stopped delivering food. If picket lines could be maintained around the clock at all delivery entrances the university would be left in a weak position. The union asked SDS to supply an all-night picket around the services building. Singing old union songs, we camped out on the building steps. With no trucks in sight, the picketers played a midnight football game in the vacant lot across the street. I was euphoric — we were finally reaching out to the real world. Students and workers had joined together in a demonstration, just the sort of experience I'd left Earlham to find. I was somewhat nervous about the outcome should delivery trucks roll in, but none did. At 2:30 in the morning the university acquiesced. Victorious, we whooped it up a little, proud of ourselves.

SDS now directed an attack against secret military research on campus, but meetings were dull, filled with parliamentary wrangling that was often manipulative. In October, Michigan staged a teach-in on third world guerrilla movements. Speaker after speaker openly advocated revolution, no longer afraid to say that word. A militant spirit pervaded the campus, students talking more about resistance than protest. Those mild October nights I sat on the lawn in the center of campus discussing Ché's activities and Debray's book, *Revolution in the Revolution*.

Several weeks after the teach-in I piled into a beat-up car with friends on their way to the now famous Pentagon demonstration in Washington. I was pretty sick of Washington protests, as they didn't accomplish much, but at the last moment I got carried away by the size of the event. On the rear window we pasted a poster of a World War II veteran in uniform wearing a huge red handlebar mustache marching with an anti–Vietnam war sign. Driving along the turnpike we kept up a running horn-and-finger battle with Ohioans jeering at us. The rest stops were crowded with other kids on their way to D.C., and excitement mounted as we approached the capital. The marchers resembled a large herd, thousands of them packed near the reflecting pool. Spirits were high because of the warmth and unity we felt. The atmosphere was almost carnival as Allen Ginsberg and the Yippies began their chant with which they hoped to levitate the Pentagon clear into the sky. I circled the crowd, bumping into old friends from as far back as E.I. Tension built as we marched across the bridge toward the Pentagon. Strategically, the Pentagon was an absurd place to be heading, since it is isolated from the city. We could all be easily surrounded and cut off without an escape route. A confrontation downtown would be more effective; here, we were playing right into the hands of the military.

At the steps of the Pentagon we shouted, "Out now" and "Hey, hey, LBJ, how many kids did you kill today?" Many sat down on the grass, but a bunch of us pushed forward, closer to the front of the crowd. Already we could smell tear gas. One kid on top of a wall taunted a guard then agilely jumped down as the guard's club connected with air and concrete. Toward evening came rumors that national guardsmen were deserting to join our protest. Demonstrators used signs and pickets from fences to fuel bonfires. I pictured myself a soldier in the revolutionary armed camp before the gates of the foe. Our anxiety increased as soldiers began beating and arresting those in front. A friend and I chose to leave; neither of us relished a licking or arrest. Getting caught was one thing, deliberately letting yourself be arrested another.

Back at Michigan, we learned that Admiral Brown, the Director of Navy Research, was coming to the campus to discuss defense projects with the university trustees. This conference received little publicity, so they were shocked when Karen led a small SDS group into their meeting, making fools of them. The student body responded positively, not appreciating the military engaging in semi-secret discussions with the trustees on campus. Embarrassed, the administration pressed charges before the student disciplinary board to have Karen thrown out of college. In its 150 years, Michigan had never taken such an action. The students rallied to her defense. The student disciplinary board promptly dismissed the charges. How different from Earlham, where student committees acted as an administration rubber stamp.

Politics was exciting, but my social life could have stood improvement. Through Karen and possibly because some members knew my background, I had been accepted into the inner circle of SDS. However, I did not feel entirely comfortable with these old-style activists who did not share my concern with the youth culture. The men did a lot of poker playing, drinking beer and watching late-night movies. It was difficult to get close to them, and I spent most of my time with Hernán. Though the campus sponsored movies, sports events and concerts, we seldom had friends to take along. The first few months were pretty lonely; I even returned to Earlham for a visit. My situation gradually improved after I moved into a house with two SDSers and started to have women friends. I did well academically and enjoyed my anthropology courses, preferring cultural anthropology to physical anthropology.

I had little in common with many of my high school friends so I spent most of my Christmas vacation in Washington with Hernán and some Earlhamites. At a party Elli showed up. I hadn't seen her for almost a year. At the end of the evening she invited Hernán and me to her house for New Year's Eve. Elli and I saw each other as frequently as possible in the next two days, after which she decided to drop out of the California college and live with me in Michigan. I was ecstatic, having fantasized just such an event without daring to think it would happen. Hernán and I talked through the night about the substantial change about to take place in my life.

We were not mistaken — during the term my energy was consumed by my relationship with Elli. Working intensely on this alliance initiated the process of integrating my past with my present. Though I had always been apprehensive about revealing my parent's identity, I managed to tell her the night she arrived. She had known for quite a while, which lightened my task. Suddenly there was a new world to explore with her. For the first time I discussed my emotions about the past.

Elli applied to the art school. To lower her tuition she took a secretarial job for six months enabling her to become a state resident. Hernán and I saw less of each other. I attended Voice meetings regularly, but my spare time was for Elli. One night, listening to Joni Mitchell at a coffee house, we agreed to get married.

The Pentagon march had seemed promising, but Ann Arbor remained unchanged. At SDS meetings we complained that while two thousand would travel to Washington not even five hundred attended a rally in the center of campus. I contrasted the Washington trip to the black riots. Black rioters wouldn't drive to D.C. to launch a protest then drop the matter the next day. In

addition, the blacks' oppression sat on their doorstep; they didn't
need to travel long distances to find it. Whites didn't have a sense
of their own oppression. They couldn't connect their demonstrations with their lives; they treated protests as special annual
events. I vowed not to go back to Washington but to devote my
time instead to local organizing.

Many spring SDS meetings were occupied with planning a fall
campaign against classified research, to be focused on a research
referendum. If we won a solid vote we hoped to gain democratic
legitimacy for the next step — possibly a sit-in at the research labs
(these labs were developing heat-sensing devices later used to
pinpoint the whereabouts of guerrilla bands in Thailand) — which
might prove disruptive. The leadership was committed to this
form of democracy, although many members complained that the
student body had no right to vote on whether the Thais would be
bombed by weapons systems designed in Ann Arbor. Searching
for button slogans to highlight the campaign, I made probably my
most significant contribution of the year by suggesting the slogan,
"Go Michigan, Beat Thailand," to be printed in school colors,
capitalizing on the fall football spirit. Much of the spring and
summer we campaigned for the referendum in the dorms and
prepared for the big push in the fall.

I meshed my studies with politics by taking courses on
revolution and American cities (examining the causes of urban
decay and unrest) with radical professors. I read books such as
Ché Guevara's manual, On Guerrilla Warfare, The Autobiography
of Malcolm X, some of which I'd half-seriously started as a
teen-ager. Six hours a week I worked as a student helper for a
professor in the museum, measuring the teeth of American Indian
skeletons over a thousand years old. The professor's thesis was
that by charting the wear patterns on the teeth, he could
determine whether cultivated or wild plants were eaten. In this
manner he'd be able to trace the introduction of agriculture. I
never did find out his results. I'm not sure how I got through the
term and the sixty-seven pages of papers due the final week;
somehow, they were handed in on time. Then we drove east for
our wedding.

Not wanting a fancy ceremony, we had a party at my parents'
house, and three days later an assistant justice of the peace

married us. Elli and I joked throughout the ceremony. That evening we went with friends to a ballet. The ritual wasn't a big deal for us, especially since we'd been living together for four months. Elli's folks threw a party in our honor; almost all those of our age who came were from Earlham. We had few friends at Michigan.

In less than two weeks we returned to Ann Arbor. Elli had to work until July, and I had signed up for two anthropology courses. The wedding gave us two prized possessions — a new stereo and a fairly new Dodge. Over the summer Ann Arbor was calm, not yet a counter-culture haven.

I became intrigued with a course on the development of anthropological theory. The teacher, a Marxist, assigned Marx's *Pre-Capitalist Economic Formations,* a difficult book, but I was enchanted by the beauty of Marx's formulations, beginning to realize that his vocabulary was not used to obfuscate but rather to crystallize meaning. We spent Memorial Day weekend with Michael and Ann in Madison. For hours Michael and I studied the book, page by page. By this time Michael was a Marxist economist very familiar with Marxist method. I was able to submit an excellent midterm paper. My professor, in charge of the senior honors program, began to notice me. At the end of the term I signed up for the honors seminar, choosing for my thesis topic, "Marxism and Cultural Materialism." I intended to go on to graduate school and imagined myself once again a radical academic. Elli, having finished her six months of servitude, was accepted by the art school. She had spent two and a half years at three different colleges, yet managed to win senior status by talking her way into a term's worth of credits.

That summer we visited Earlham friends, attended SDS meetings and watched the storm brewing over the Democratic Convention in Chicago. We did not back Eugene McCarthy, regarding him as a reformer only the naive believed could institute basic changes. Nor had we danced wildly the previous spring when Johnson announced he would not seek re-election. We were happy to have helped drive him from office, but had no illusions his successor would be an improvement. Although large demonstrations attracted us like magnets, we resolved not to travel hundreds of miles to try to appeal to convention delegates. I did not anticipate the battle that erupted, and was horrified by its brutality. It was sobering to realize that even when police lawlessness was televised throughout the nation, most of America still supported the nightsticks against unarmed students. Nevertheless, it perplexed me that an American would figure that a student yelling "pig" at a policeman deserved a cracked skull in return.

Michael despaired over the reaction to the police riot. To admit the impossibility of swaying the American public would be a confession of helplessness, yet neither terrorism nor personal sacrifices had accomplished much. His reaction was colored by his concern for his children; he was worried that involvement in militant activity would endanger their safety, though he tried not to let his fears influence his judgment. He was also debating whether or not to admit his identity publicly. As I'd turned twenty-one, our parents' request that he wait until I reached that age had been honored. By now he and Ann were settled and comfortable with the name of Meeropol. However, the major reason for not changing his name was that he wanted to live his life in his own right — as a radical economist, a good teacher, an activist, a devoted husband and father. Still, despite this decision, in the mid-1960s, he approached William Kuntsler, one of Morton Sobell's lawyers, with an offer to help in any way possible. Shortly thereafter, the Court of Appeals ruled that Morton had served enough of his sentence to be paroled. Overjoyed, Michael sent Morton a telegram, "Congratulations. Part of my parents is alive in you." They eventually met in 1972.

Chicago stimulated us into action, and the fall SDS retreat was very well attended. We explained to disillusioned McCarthy followers why they should be radical, not liberal; many listened. We were all looking for a cause, and opportunity knocked during the first week of the term.

Mothers on Aid to Dependent Children (ADC) allowances protested their $60 per year per child allotment with which to stave off the harsh Michigan winters. SDS joined the outraged mothers, three hundred of us milling around outside the county

THE NEW LEFT AND THE COMMUNE 317

jail housing a few arrested ADC mothers. As time passed, the crowd dwindled; we disbanded without incident. But the next day forty-two protesters were arrested at a support sit-in in a county building. The day after, a few hundred of us marched around the building then sat down in the lobby. We were ordered to leave when the building closed but refused to budge. Although uneasy about the consequences, I felt pressured to stay and show my support. The mass arrest was peaceful and orderly until we were led outside where hundreds of people shouted at the police, who overreacted. Officers were summoned from three counties. Sharpshooters lined the roofs of buildings in a two-block radius, a team of trained riot dogs was brought in. The city expended more money for the cops' overtime than we demanded for the welfare mothers. Proceeding to the lockup, eight of us were jammed into a four-by-six cell for two hours while being processed. Then we were hauled before the judge, a known SDS hater, who charged us with criminal trespassing. When asked to reduce our bail from $50 to $25, he responded, "When you stick your hand in the fire, you are going to get burned." We argued — to no avail — that his retort indicated his belief in our guilt, and could get him disqualified at our trial. By midnight we were free. Several more arrests occurred the next day, but by then we were occupied with legal matters, so the protests petered out. The ADC mothers were awarded a $10 increase the following month.

At the time I thought getting arrested proved my seriousness; however, I soon regretted it. I was wasting my time and putting myself just where they wanted me. At future SDS meetings I contended that we should stay on the scene until the last possible moment, only to return later and harass city officials. If they got an injunction, we should demonstrate on another block; if they banned demonstrations, we should wait until the ban was lifted. I named my strategy after Muhammad Ali's "float like a butterfly, sting like a bee." Of course, my past and possible trial publicity made me anxious about being in police hands.

I had used this strategy on the draft board, as I didn't want to go to jail for refusing to serve. Nor did I want to quietly obey the rules. Since I didn't apply for a 2-S student deferment, my 1-A classification arrived in January 1969. Only then did I apply for the 2-S I was entitled to, causing extra paper work for the draft board. My bad shoulder ultimately earned me a 4-F.

The SDS leadership plotted the format for the session concerning the classified war research referendum. A new group — the Jesse James Gang — objected to the style of attacking classified research. They preferred more radical action and a stronger identification with the youth culture, debating that since revolution was around the corner, we should all take to the streets. The entrenched leaders fought back, the meeting dissolving into rhetoric. At the next meeting tempers were so frayed fights almost broke out. While I partially sympathized with the Gang's sentiments, I considered them outsiders attempting to overrun the organization. It was decided that each faction choose a speaker to present its side, after which the two programs would be voted on. I gave the moderates' speech, outlining why McCarthy-type reforms were unworkable, maintaining that because we were not at a revolutionary stage, we needed to do unglamorous but necessary base-building and dorm organizing. A leader of the James Gang presented the rebuttal, a rap on how we didn't have all the answers, yet this was the time to stop talking and do something about the horrible war, urging us to act. In this cerebral-vs.-gut approach to revolution, he was far more polished and charismatic. The James Gang won by a small margin, and the old leadership stalked out to form the Radical Caucus. I walked out with them but tried to straddle the fence. Along with others I designed a compromise that prodded one member of the Caucus to dub my politics "mushhead SDS." Compromise proved impossible, so I joined the Radical Caucus. The parliamentary manipulation of the Caucus disgusted me, though the style of the James Gang was as bad; in the long run their lack of procedure increased the manipulation from the top down.

The Caucus was soon dominated by International Socialists advocating that true socialist revolution could only occur in advanced industrial democracies and must take a democratic form — invalidating the revolutions in Russia, China, Vietnam and Cuba. Supporting China, Cuba and North Vietnam, I could not stomach this dogma. Their meetings adhered strictly to parliamentary democracy. However, by controlling parliamentary procedure they forced their planks through in a most undemocratic manner. Their strategy was to issue a liberal demand and use a liberal tactic (like a referendum) though they foresaw the tactic would be unsuccessful. Faced with failure, liberals would be cornered into taking more radical steps. As far as I was concerned, tricking liberals never worked. Fooled in this way, they returned to their old positions when a new issue arose.

Because of the heavy turnout of engineering students, the Radical Caucus lost the referendum on classified war research a month later and didn't know where to go. A national boycott of classes to protest the Vietnam war failed miserably at Michigan as neither faction could organize itself. I finally became disgusted and dropped out of organized politics to concentrate on studies and our social life.

Elli and I found a host of new friends through another young married couple, Randy and Rayna, whom we'd met at the SDS retreat. Rayna was a first-year graduate student in anthropology, Randy a teaching fellow in psychology. They came from Old Left backgrounds but didn't usually attend SDS or Caucus meetings because of the elitism they saw in these factions. I still hung out with Hernán and his pals while Elli attended her studio courses eight hours a day and Saturdays.

Five of us in the undergraduate anthropology club set up more radical courses and gathered two hundred signatures on petitions in our drive to initiate the courses. We had to negotiate with faculty who established a procedure by which any five students suggesting a course title and subject could take the course if a professor could be induced to sponsor it. We organized a seminar on Marxist anthropology, persuading a leading professor in the department to sponsor it and conduct evening classes.

Over Thanksgiving we stayed with Michael and Ann in Madison. We enjoyed the visit, although their perspective considerably differed from ours. Their first child had just been born, and they seemed very settled into a family routine. While we were there, Randy and Rayna invited several friends to a Thanksgiving dinner at which they resolved to start a commune the following fall. We had been included in these plans, and our acceptance led us to examine the pending modification in our life-style.

We met regularly to plan the commune and test our compatibility by eating meals together, and to explore our reasons for living communally. Primarily, we hoped to counteract the antagonistic individualism of our society by building a socialistic foundation in our own lives. We intended to live our politics and function as a political support group, our commune relating as a unit to the outside world. Randy and Rayna, and Elli and I were happy in our strong, close marriages, but felt isolated from others. We expected to use our relationships as a base for expanding our friendships. Elli and Rayna were involved in women's liberation; we all agreed that communal living would help break down the sexual division of labor. Learning each other's skills, everyone would contribute to cooking, cleaning the house and maintaining the cars. We thought children would thrive in a communal setting in which they would be provided with more than one model of an adult male and female. Nuclear families seemed too narrow for us. We expected to store our possessions and pool our incomes. In our idealism we contemplated sustaining our commune forever. This deep commitment fed our feelings about each other — we were joyous together.

Good friends of Randy and Rayna worked with People Against Racism (PAR). By March we were all attending PAR meetings as their community orientation appealed to us. The university was an ivory tower: PAR met off-campus and enlisted nonstudent members, enabling us to reach beyond the campus population. We ignored the university, to focus on community problems. PAR's analysis of the political situation was that race stood as the single most important issue in America. Corporations and government exploited racism to split the working class so they would fight among themselves rather than against their common enemy. PAR predicted that a race war was likely to erupt as the nation grew more polarized. The job of radical whites was to neutralize as many white people as possible before the conflict started. One difference between us and other civil rights groups was that we were aware that racism oppressed us as well; we were really fighting for ourselves. Many whites had a hard time internalizing their oppression, but I never had much difficulty with that. The government had taken an active part in destroying a segment of my life — my anger was not theoretical but internal.

Concentrating our efforts on the racism of the county and city police, we supported Crocket, a black judge, who, refusing to bow to police pressure, had released several black prisoners. However, it wasn't easy to find causes in Ann Arbor, so we spent more time talking than actually doing.

The raised political consciousness of women began to influence PAR. After a women's caucus was created within the organization, males became conscious of dominating meetings. The men in response set up a caucus to delve into sexism in themselves and American society, trying to deal with the changes women's liberation underscored in our relationships and stereotypical sex roles which chained us as well. We rapped about getting in touch with our emotions, relating to others in a noncompetitive way. I had never been very physically combative but practiced verbal one-upmanship routinely. The process of explaining our upbringing and ourselves was both invigorating and frightening for me. I had avoided scrutinizing my past for fear I'd recall events better left forgotten. Still, I began to understand that I would not truly know myself until I did.

My course load was relatively light, freeing me to devote my attention to researching and writing my thesis. I also invested a lot of time in the weekly seminar we had originated. We read the classics of Marx, Engels and Marxist anthropologists, discussing them long into the night. The strong contact with the professor was extremely enlightening, as I dug into the formation of hierarchies in society in order to discover what made society tick.

During the summer I enrolled in summer school, and we moved into the commune's house. Randy and Rayna flew to France to do anthropological field work. Another couple, Ed and Rene, helped us fix up the house for their return. The commune had preferred a house in the country but was unable to find anyone who would rent to a group. Realtors couldn't understand why married couples wanted to share a house, a reaction symptomatic of social attitudes. Anthropology taught me that "human nature" is almost totally mutable. American views of people did not reflect reality but the dominant social postures. In our society, nuclear families were separate units that solved their problems in isolation. We aimed to prove that people could trust and share with one another.

After searching for months, we located a big house in a middle-class black neighborhood in Ypsilanti, eight miles from campus. We were pleased to get away from the student ghetto, though Ypsilanti, home of Eastern Michigan University, had a student population of 18,000. These students, at least, were not the elite of the University of Michigan, which helped us to feel less isolated.

Immediately after the move our trial for the ADC mothers sit-in came up. Elli, I and four others were tried together. Sitting in the courtroom before our trial, we watched a parade of black youths, surrounded by white cops, judges, lawyers and recorders, humiliated when they tried to obtain lenient sentences. It was a totally hateful process, enraging me more than our own treatment. I imagined being a black man controlled by a white establishment not only destroying my life but demanding that I lick its feet as well.

The injustices in our trial were amusing. The prosecution had the "arresting officers" testify without taking the trouble to match up each arrestee with the proper arrester. I remembered the face of the cop who'd arrested me, but he was not the one now testifying against me. It didn't matter since the jury was composed of middle-aged whites extremely threatened by those commie hippies at the University of Michigan. During jury selection one potential jurist apologized to the judge for already considering us guilty. Her apology was not for having an opinion but for not being capable of lying. For his part, the judge would not allow any testimony to be introduced about the political nature of our act. The event was ripped from its social context, and on those terms we didn't have a chance. Our position was that county commissioners were guilty for not responsibly helping the ADC mothers, but we received the sentences — seven days of work for the county or seven days in jail. The blacks hadn't been given any choice. I worked fourteen half days chopping brush away from road signs throughout the county.

Our house was quite large, providing privacy when we wanted it. Things went fairly smoothly though we weren't as close to the third couple, Ed and Rene, and did not experience the intense emotions characterizing our relationship with Randy and Rayna the previous four months. Also, we learned some of the disadvantages of a big house — friends' storing their paraphernalia in our basement, the need to accommodate several frightened women seeking group protection from the Ann Arbor sex murderer then on the loose. The commune contributed to the distance Elli and I felt from Ann and Michael who seemed content with the nuclear family unit, and added to the topics Michael and I sidestepped for fear of disagreeing. In reality, they too were concerned about the isolation of nuclear families, considering their friends an extended family.

Elli and I finished up our final courses. I cut my hair and applied for a job at the local Ford plant, but was overeducated for the available jobs. A good portion of that summer was wasted looking for work. Finally I gave up, doing nothing magnificently for a couple of months.

A large revolt at Wisconsin had occurred in May, while I sat in a coffeehouse with politicos of various leftist persuasions bemoaning Ann Arbor's blissful calm. Wisconsin was followed by the People's Park battle in Berkeley — again, the revolution was passing us by. We figured it was impossible to get anything going in the summer, but we were wrong. Ann Arbor had been transformed into a haven for street people, many of whom were high school and college dropouts attracted by the city's counterculture scene or college graduates who hadn't left town. By 1969 a few thousand had congregated in Ann Arbor. After People's Park, the political leadership of this group, the White Panthers, demanded that three blocks of the street we jokingly referred to as "the strip" be closed to traffic during the evenings. Crowds gathered one night to prevent cars from driving through. When one couple started to realize the slogan, "do it in the road," the crowd increased. Police charged with swinging clubs and tear gas.

We were taken by surprise and thought the action silly. They were merely mimicking Berkeley students; besides, who wanted to get beat up for a strip of concrete. The next evening we held a PAR meeting, while the street people staged a repeat performance. Afterward, we drove a member, Jack, to the campus because he wanted to see the blockade. He was standing quietly when a policeman, frustrated at his inability to catch his fleeing quarry, arrested him instead. Jack was released on bail, but now PAR became peripherally involved. When Jack was convicted he threatened to appeal several irregularities in his trial, and the charges against him were dropped. Two more days of riots ensued before the town quieted down for the summer. We mulled over the fact that Ann Arbor's first violent confrontation occurred after the majority of radical students had left the city. But, worse, we had been thwarted in our efforts to force the ruling class to pay a high price for the continuing war in Vietnam and felt with thousands of sympathizers around town that we were surely doing something wrong.

The police had been brutal during the street riots. The sheriff had been heard yelling, "Give it to 'em" and "Eat raw meat," egging his officers on. As a result of this and Jack's illegal arrest, PAR supported a recall petition drive to oust the county sheriff. Elli and I were cold toward electoral politics. We knew we'd never collect enough signatures; even if we did, the rural vote would sweep the sheriff back into office. When PAR's petition drive failed, some blamed it on our lack of enthusiasm. We lost interest in PAR, though long after we'd dropped out we maintained the importance of the race issue in America as well as the need to overcome white-skin privileges.

Ed and Rene had a baby in August. Elli and I accepted our share of responsibility for our new family member. Every other night I took the 2:00 A.M. feeding. This was a good experience for me. At first the squirmy little thing petrified me; I was certain I would break it. By mid-September I was accustomed to caring for an infant. Randy, Rayna and our seventh member, Susan, returned at the end of the summer. Personality conflicts broke out, snagging Elli and me in the middle. In mid-October Ed and Rene moved away. The five of us remaining felt good about each other, but we'd started out on the wrong foot and a mood of gloom hung over the house.

In graduate school I took the required courses, memorizing the anthropological classics and the grammar of the discipline. Elli found a job teaching a class largely composed of black welfare kids in a day-care center. Living with four graduate students in the commune was hard, and she talked about leaving the student town for the real world.

In the fall of 1969, SDS mounted a campaign against ROTC, fanning a confrontation at the ROTC building, where windows were smashed. Away from SDS for almost a year, I looked on as an outsider. The James Gang leaders had left town, and were involved in the leadership of Weatherman, so they no longer dominated the chapter. The SDSers seemed so young; I didn't know any of them and felt much older. I had always considered myself part of the future radical generation, yet this younger group veered farther to the left than I did. This observation troubled me, exacerbating the general gloomy mood of the commune.

Michael was ambivalent about Weatherman; he was intellectually opposed to violence as he believed the patient convincing of an American majority had not really been tried. They took the position that to convince America was impossible; it was necessary to fight. He was moved by the strength of their commitment, respected some of them, and shared their frustration over the war. Michael thought they were hurting the cause through their terrorist activities and, as always, physical violence frightened him.

Another massive Washington march to end the war was scheduled in November. Initially, the commune had nothing to do with it, then changed its mind. I awoke the commune at 4:00 A.M. to start the eight-hour drive by blasting "Here Comes the Sun" on the stereo, and we had a wonderful time singing and waving to the hundreds of people we passed along the way. At first the march was predictably dull. We joined a group chanting "Peace Now" but couldn't relate to their lack of support for the NLF. A friend instructed us in chanting the phrases we disagreed with without being disruptive. When they yelled "Peace," we

yelled "Beef"; when they yelled "Now," we yelled "Cow." Our
"Beef Cow," sounding like the real chant, threw us into hysterics.
We moved on to the revolutionary contingent, quickly spotted by
their sea of NLF flags, among which we found the Ann Arbor
SDS group. Their spirit captivated us. More than 15,000 strong,
the marchers were eager to do something besides march. The
more liberal parade marshals sensed this, and diverted our group
from Pennsylvania Avenue, away from the rest of the parade and
the inviting plate-glass windows. We heard new chants and new
words like "trashing." One chant started very low,
"cooommmmm," got louder, "mmmuuuunnnn," ended with a
scream, "nniiiissssmmmm!" This was where I wanted to be; these
were the people I had been waiting for since 1959. The march
activated us all. It was only a matter of time before we'd be
enmeshed in politics again. We skipped the night demonstration,
as we were not quite ready for the huge street battle between
members of the revolutionary contingent and the police in front of
the South Vietnamese Embassy. On the return trip we chanted,
"Communism" to the toll attendants on the Ohio Turnpike and
remained explosively high. Socially, the trip was a significant
turning point for the commune. We came home feeling so positive
about each other that a fresh spirit of warmth and trust filled the
house.

My principal concern of the new term was not SDS but money.
Elli was bringing it in and I felt a need to contribute to the
household expenses. Every month we pooled our earnings in a
communal account which we lived on. Between Elli's job and the
fellowships, we managed to get by and even save a little money.
Nevertheless, I wanted to help and took a research job offered by
one of my professors. Part of the communal ideology was to
withdraw from the consumer economy. In fact, we often had
more than we needed and spent less than the average nuclear
family.

The commune, mostly on Ford Foundation grants, planned to
spend the summer doing field work in Europe studying the effects
of modernization on the traditional societies of small peasant
villages. This undertaking reinforced our policy of creating a
group life for the commune. I wasn't overjoyed about leaving the

U.S., retreating from American political realities, but determined that I might as well find out what field work was like. Latin America was my area of specialization; since the grants specified European research, I came as close as possible by going to Spain. In preparation, Elli and I audited a Spanish course.

To satisfy our curiosity about SDS, we attended an evening demonstration after a conference on repression. Typically, everyone stood around talking, but with an element of furtiveness. Abruptly, the crowd, led by SDS, marched to the ROTC building, and before the police had a chance to react, broke windows. Some did what damage they could inside the building. When the police arrived, SDS, splitting into roving bands, smashed several windows of local banks. No one was apprehended. Awed by these successful urban guerrilla procedures, we re-enlisted in SDS. Later I learned the event was entirely spontaneous.

An important tactic of SDS, trashing, was constantly discussed but only sporadically resorted to. It referred to destroying property — no violence was designed against people. I then felt that SDS arguments were very persuasive. For years anti-war demonstrators patiently protested as they were beaten and jailed — while Vietnamese continued to die. The war must be stopped; if demonstrators were required to lay their lives on the line to accomplish that result, they would. They hoped to raise the cost of continuing the war effort by causing disruption at home, hitting the ruling class in the pocketbook, damaging selected targets such as banks and ROTC buildings in which people were trained to conduct the war in Vietnam. SDS pledged to lend active support to revolutionary struggles around the world. This strong commitment and common sense of purpose drew the organization together as happened in no other group I'd belonged to.

SDS had a new structure, organizing members into collectives of eight to fifteen who met separately each week, accepted responsibility for the safety of their members during demonstrations and carried out specific assignments. Once a week all collectives met together to make policy decisions. There appeared to be less elitism in the organization than before, and everyone understood why specific steps were taken; they didn't have to follow blindly. Also, SDS had fashioned a new attitude toward demonstrations, or actions as they were now called. Instead of focusing attention on one large confrontation which could make or break the group for the year, SDS devised a series of actions, which confirmed my own ideas about effective protesting. I summarized this philosophy with the phrase, "another day, another action."

The basic goals of SDS were to bar military recruiters and those employed by war-related industries from campus and to get rid of ROTC. As a recruiter was always around, actions occurred almost daily. A hundred or so SDSers blocked the entrances to rooms in which recruiters conducted interviews. The administration screamed that we were violating the freedom of speech, but we didn't agree that companies should be permitted to recruit those who would help destroy the Vietnamese. To avoid arrest we would split before the police showed up. Usually, by the time the police arrived, prospective interviewees had been scared away. In some cases, recruiters were locked out of their offices and forced off campus. The university started proceedings against disrupters in the student disciplinary court, so we took to wearing ski masks and bandannas to avoid identification. The court generally sympathized, especially in cases concerning military recruiters; few protesters received more than a token slap on the wrist.

February 28, 1970, was the "heaviest" day of political activity I've ever experienced. It started normally enough with an attempt to stop the recruiter from General Electric. Our collective was in charge of security — staking a lookout for police, indicating police undercover agents in the crowd (they were easily spotted, some perpetually wore trench coats) and monitoring police whereabouts. When Randy or I spied an agent, we trailed behind, pointing at him. The agent tried to appear inconspicuous, hoping not to blow his cover — with amusing results. A photographer from the student paper snapped his picture to be published the next day.

At 11:00 A.M. a hundred of us headed across campus to the basement of the engineering building. The engineering students' vigilante committee proved no match for us, and after a brief skirmish we burst through their lines to occupy the basement and harass recruiters, who then locked themselves in but the doors' windows were smashed, and they were flushed out. A few campus police and right-wing professors tried to isolate protesters and pick them off one at a time, but the collectives held together, resisting this maneuver. Then word was passed that the police were on the way, so we scattered, escaping just as they arrived, but not before a cameraman began photographing our exit. It had been hot in the basement, so not everyone was wearing a mask or bandanna. One woman, attempting to cover the camera, was tackled, arrested and dragged to a van. We couldn't stand idly by while a dozen cops hustled her to jail; we set upon the van to free her. Twenty more cops joined the fray and a half-hour street battle commenced. We attacked the van only to be driven back by club-wielding police. Collectives singled out officers after they made an arrest, shoving them to the ground and kicking them in an attempt to free their colleagues.

I was stunned and unable to act. My past paralyzed me with fear as I watched my friends actually fighting with these trained, helmeted, armed men — I ran back and forth in the melee, acting like a chicken with his head cut off. I wound up throwing snowballs with friends on the sidelines but didn't participate in the battle. More arrests were made. Some of my friends formed a chain in front of the van which the charging cops broke. Meanwhile, an audience had gathered. Engineering students hung out of windows to cheer the cops on. The entire street was transformed into a battlefield. Suddenly the van disappeared, and with it the police. Eleven had been arrested. The rest of us regrouped, marched across the campus to besiege the president in his office for two hours. I sat outside in the first bright, warm day of the year to collect my thoughts about soliciting support from radical professors and raising bail money.

In the afternoon word came from those students monitoring the wire services of the verdict in the Chicago Seven trial — the defendants were not found completely innocent. SDS had vowed to make the state pay for a guilty verdict, one of the chants to that effect being, "One, two, stop the trial; three, four, stop the trial; five, six, stop the trial; seven, eight, smash the state." Some SDSers felt the upcoming fight might recast the morning's confrontation as a minor skirmish. Cops patrolled the streets six to a car, their shotguns poking from the windows. Everyone was tense, suspecting that at least one of us would be dead by midnight.

So, marshaling our forces, SDS held a pre-demonstration evening meeting as it began to rain. We were afraid the weather would deter supporters. Because the cops were fully mobilized, we planned to put a halt to all trashing at the march. We felt intimidated but, screwing up our courage, we walked across campus — past the cops and shotguns — and moved the meeting indoors. So many activists crammed into the room that a huge crowd had to wait in the rain. Our march circled the campus, passing the dorms to harvest support and, 5000 strong, aimed for City Hall. The rain turned into snow, but the crowd did not diminish. The march was too large and the strategically placed collectives were helpless to control it. The enormous turnout was unlike anything Ann Arbor had seen. As we left the campus, bank windows shattered. People we never dreamed would join us came out of the woodwork to trash. A cop car mistakenly drove through the crowd. By the time it reached us, the windows were broken, the cops inside clearly frightened and amazed at the crowd's size. We never reached City Hall. As the front line approached the building, they were brutally attacked by police. The sheriff, we later learned, had misled them into thinking we intended to burn down City Hall and destroy all the records. In reality, we had no idea what we were going to do at City Hall. The marchers dispersed, roving bands everywhere. This was an ideal time to trash, but we stuck to our resolve to keep cool and returned to the campus. Our commune collapsed at home hardly able to digest the day's events, thankful we were alive.

At the next meeting, we discovered that in retaliation the cops had shaved the heads of eight arrested in the G.E. brawl. I felt a little guilty about my inability to fight; at least I was honestly able to admit that I was scared. Many others had the same reaction.

SDS immediately went to work organizing white support for the demands of the Black Action Movement (BAM). BAM had presented a list of ultimatums to the administration — opening the university to more blacks at the student, administrative and faculty levels — setting March 17 as "do or die" day. Collectives spoke in the dorms and co-ops to drum up advocates for BAM's cause. On the seventeenth, the demonstration in front of the administration building grew raucous when the university refused to accede to the BAM demands. Elli and Randy spotted the president, who was soon surrounded, but he managed to thread his way safely into a building — after a red stripe was spray-painted down his back. One of the police agents heaved a rock through the window which signaled twenty cops to appear and arrest some BAM members who had done nothing. A fight ensued. SDS was unprepared, and a few collectives huddled in the street half a block from the action. It was an absurd situation, fifty SDSers mulling over a course of action while a street fight erupted under their noses. Within a few minutes it was over, and we went home laughing at ourselves. That evening BAM called a student strike, requesting SDS backing. We spent the following morning convincing students they should assist us. Someone in student government produced stink bombs — the obnoxious odor closed down a few classes. Minor harassment continued. Individual departments, including anthropology, began shutting down. Singing and stomping, BAM members invaded the economics building, and within the hour economics classes were suspended.

We were living on raw energy and very little sleep. The commune felt energized. Never in my life had I been so fulfilled, doing all I humanly could to change things. Elli, having quit her job, was women's liberation delegate to the BAM support strike committee, and brought home daily reports of the fervor and worries of strike leadership. We regarded ourselves as full-time revolutionaries, dedicating our lives to this type of activism.

On the fifth day of the strike the university was nearly shut down but didn't give in. The National Guard camped outside the town. SDS figured they had no choice other than to provoke a confrontation. Fortunately, the BAM leaders were more creative, devising a series of actions that were not disruptive enough to justify calling in the troops. Strike supporters conveniently lost contact lenses in the street, causing minor tie-ups. All afternoon we tramped through the halls of buildings singing. It became impossible to conduct classes as 8000 students snaked their way from one building to another, bringing the campus to a standstill without a single arrest. The university decided to wait us out over the weekend in the hope that the strength of the strike would dissipate by Monday. Four days later BAM announced they had won concessions, victory was at hand. SDS was disappointed by the terms of the truce, BAM compromised too much. As for us, we agreed with SDS although we were happy to win something — hamstringing one of the largest universities in the country. We were not surprised to learn about the news blackout on the strike — no one outside of Michigan knew about it.

A lull in political activity succeeded the BAM strike. The energy that politics had generated we now channeled into social interaction and self-exploration. The past three months had revolutionized my attitudes, politics and emotions. I acquired new insights about myself. Still, I rarely talked about my real parents with those who knew. In the midst of all this, traveling in Europe seemed completely anomalous and irrelevant, though we intended to see the summer through.

Elli and I visited my parents, who had recently moved to Florida. Michael and Ann and their two children flew down as well. It was a strange week. Elli and I were hyped up; our schedule had taken its toll. I had lost twenty pounds; we both had a haunted look. Abel and Anne commiserated with us, though they feared for our safety. In the past year Michael had moved somewhat to the left. While we relaxed in Florida Nixon invaded Cambodia and students were killed at Kent State and Jackson State. The world was exploding around us, and we couldn't wait to get back to Ann Arbor. Michael and Ann were on their way to Chile for his Ph.D. research. His swing left reflected his optimism about the political activity supported by large numbers after the Kent and Jackson State murders; he agreed with me that these actions were significant. He hoped this energy would be channeled into sustained drives against the war. Unfortunately, once again the left lacked staying power — the huge demonstrations dwindled — this had been his fear all along.

The Michigan term was over, so the campus did not detonate as others did. We spent our final week packing and rode to the airport uncertain why we were leaving the war zone. Bewildered and sorry to leave our SDS friends, we felt we had little choice.

The commune had booked passage on a charter flight to London. We toured for ten days in London, Paris and Barcelona before splitting up, at which point Elli and I would hunt for a small peasant village in the mountains of Cataluña, south of the Pyrenees. We required some release from the tension of past months, which was making it difficult for us to travel as a group and cater to everyone else's pace and itinerary.

The Spanish I knew left my head the moment we crossed the border, and Elli was deliriously sick with the flu when we landed in Barcelona. We were anxious about being in fascist Spain, though little surface evidence of fascism existed. In preparation for field work we had cleaned ourselves up and our grants allowed us to travel comfortably, so we weren't handled roughly as "hippies" often were in Spain. We rented a car and drove north toward the Pyrenees in search of a suitable village. As my professor believed in the sink-or-swim method of field work, he gave us scant advice other than suggesting we ask hotelkeepers in the regional center of Vich about small mountain villages in which peasants lived as they had for centuries. The waiter at our hotel told us of ten such villages; we spent the next three days touring them. Luckily, our Spanish had returned. We had only a little more than two months for our work, so it was essential to find a place where the villagers would immediately accept us. We settled in the first village we had seen, which was the right size, beautifully situated in the mountains, and the residents smiled at us. As we drove the twisting roads through lush green mountains, the Ann Arbor actions seemed infinitely remote. It was so pleasant and lovely here that I found it difficult to imagine why I'd done all those crazy things. Being in a peaceful area separated from the news and the Ann Arbor political community was having a rapid, profound effect on me.

In fact, living in a village of 300 people really changed our lives. We worked to learn from them whatever they would tell us and to view their lives from their perspective, and, we came to accept many political, social, economic and religious statements we would have rejected back home. For their part, the villagers regarded us as interesting curiosities, and enjoyed talking to us, while we began to judge the world as a conservative backwoods farmer might. Villagers held to certain opinions because they made sense in their lives. We realized that as outsiders our first duty was to learn the needs and philosophies of those we hoped to organize, rather than jumping in with solutions before we perceived the problems. For instance, we had actually secluded ourselves from most Americans by not tolerating racism, sexism or any other "ism" that wasn't "right on." Only now did it dawn on us that a revolution would not succeed without public support. The fusion of my youth-culture orientation with my political activity had resulted in what I called the "millions of groovy kids theory of revolution" — my thesis that a coalition of alienated white hippie youth, students, women, blacks, Indians and the third world would foment revolution — an absurd formula. A society could not be changed without involving those who produced the food and worked in the factories. I knew that once back in America we had to reach Americans with programs responsive to their needs and living situations. In order to do this we had to start living more like average Americans. We were not sure how we would combat racism and sexism, but we realized we had to find a method that made sense to the majority of Americans.

Clearly, Elli and I were duty-bound to terminate our political isolation and move away from Ann Arbor. We were determined to relocate in the next year, sink roots in a community and be politically active.

Once we adjusted to village life, our anxiety level dropped. The inn in which we stayed served the finest food in the region, increasing our bulk by twenty pounds apiece. The days were occupied with conversations, typing of field notes and long walks. After several weeks we were acquainted with the villagers, knew pretty much what to expect from each of them. I sided with those who boasted that their village was the best place on earth. Even so, these people hadn't forgotten the terrible Spanish Civil War which had claimed over a million lives just thirty years earlier. Franco had decimated the left by killing hundreds of thousands of them and fear was still prevalent. Probably I had much in common with the villagers whose families had been executed, but, like them, I felt unable to dwell on the subject.

In midsummer we took a week's break to meet the rest of the commune for a field conference in the Alps. Apparently, we had all undergone a similar process of political transformation, and at the same time, our good feelings toward each other revived.

The villagers welcomed us back, and we grew attached to several of them. Though the field work was satisfying, I was dubious about devoting my life to studying the lives of others. I didn't want to be cast in the role of an observer of people; rather, I hoped to become one with them. Also, I wanted to live life without worrying so much about its worth. At our send-off party the villagers were sad to see us go and predicted our return. We were ready to go home but had mixed feelings about leaving a place that had seriously altered our lives in such a short time.

Slowly we worked our way across northern Spain to Bilbao and caught a ferry to London, arriving two days ahead of the rest of the commune. We were glad to see signs in English and the large city lights. *Woodstock* was showing at the first movie theater we approached, and we spent a few hours watching our youth culture move by us on the screen. The music seemed violent, the characters caught up in their own sense of coolness — we no longer related to that scene. We were not eagerly anticipating our homecoming. After the peace and reason of the summer, the U.S. resembled a vast insane asylum.

The situation in Ann Arbor had changed almost as significantly as we had. SDS had splintered irrevocably, the movement was losing momentum. After the Kent State shootings demonstrators were much less willing to risk anything to alter the system. A new phrase, "burned out," entered the radical vocabulary. Depressed by this turn of events, I focused attention on my studies, looking forward to leaving college. Having spent most of my life in school, I was due for a change. To judge for myself, I did attend an SDS meeting, which was uninspiring. I couldn't stomach people's not listening to one another. Most of the members were new; their tactics lacked direction. For the next several years I stayed away from all political groups.

The commune planned to leave Ann Arbor the following summer. Relations started to deteriorate because we couldn't agree about arriving in the same city at the same time, and we were pulled in different directions. By Christmas we were only going through the motions of living together; our spirit had dissolved. In January we rented separate apartments. After the excitement of 1970, 1971 began in a zombielike manner. Elli and I were sad and lonely in our apartment. We did become good friends with another couple and planned to move with them the day after I passed my preliminary examinations. Since three of the four of us hailed from the Northeast, we decided to settle in a small northeastern city which engendered a sense of community, preferably a city without a substantial, entrenched left-wing organization, which would only embroil us in sectarian squabbles. We selected Springfield, Massachusetts — a suitable size with diversified industries though struggling economically, surrounded by scenic country (very important to me), having no large leftist movement. In addition, Michael was teaching there at Western New England College, and a couple of Ann Arbor friends had recently landed there. I passed the prelims, and we headed east, detouring to Washington for the May Day demonstration. It was the last major protest of the dying New Left.

Before we settled down in Springfield we went back to Ann Arbor once more to visit Randy and Rayna. I roamed the streets looking at the houses my friends or I had lived in. The town was haunted with many memories. I was overcome with sadness remembering the beauty and strength we had shown in the last four years. Most of it seemed to be lost forever.

12

Settling in Springfield, 1971–1974

To start us out in Springfield, we had some savings to fall back on until we got jobs but were uneasy about the high unemployment rate in the area. When my brother informed me that his college was looking for a teacher for its one anthropology course a year I applied for the job, fully intending to eventually find a working-class-oriented job. I didn't even take exception to Spiro Agnew's speech about the country having too many effete intellectual snobs and not enough carpenters. I almost sent him a note stating that I was an effete intellectual snob who desired to become a carpenter. As I was having no luck in getting a carpenter's job perhaps he could help me. Elli took a job teaching in a Headstart program in a nearby town. The college hired me, and I discovered that teaching appealed to me. I was delighted when the college expanded its anthropology program to include a second course. In order to secure my job I'd have to complete my doctorate, so in a trip to Ann Arbor I put together a Ph.D. committee and drew up a project. I planned to do urban anthropology in Springfield and continue to expand my contacts in the city. Later, Nixon's impounding of educational research funds meant I had to shelve full-time Ph.D. research, so progress on my thesis was slow. The attempt of our friends to sink lasting roots into communities all across the country convinced us of the correctness of our decision to be actively involved in Springfield.

However, our community organizing faltered. It was impossible to get a handle on the community. Residents were spread around the county by their professions, and no community groups existed to organize them. Politically, Elli and I were stymied. For a time we remained fairly isolated, though gradually we made friends and became acclimated to our new home. In May, Elli and several friends formed a women's group that helped open a women's center in Springfield. I got together with a few men to form a men's group, and although we had more than a year of good discussions we couldn't get any projects off the ground. It took me more than a year to overcome my depression over the break-up of the commune.

Elli and I came to know Michael and Ann much better. I was glad to find that his political outlook was similar to mine; and fortunately, we were even able to reconcile some of our previous differences. Ann joined a women's group which founded a Women's Health Counseling Service. Later, after their children were in school, she took a teaching job in an adult education center. Later, Michael, Ann and another couple bought property for the two families to share.

When our first child, Jenny, was born, Elli quit her job, but we soon rearranged our schedule so that she could accept another. My part-time schedule enabled me to split child care equally with her.

While I was not actively participating in ongoing political organizing, much of our plan in coming to Springfield was successful. When we first arrived we'd thought in terms of staying for ten or fifteen years. After several years, we knew the city, began to understand its people and problems. My Ph.D. project taught me how decision-making processes were carried out. We were no longer far-out students but members of a community working and sharing problems. We thought of staying indefinitely.

Part III
Going Public

13

Reopening the Rosenberg Case: The Emperor Has No Clothes

BY ROBERT MEEROPOL

IN FEBRUARY 1973, Louis Nizer's *The Implosion Conspiracy* was published and rose on the best-seller lists. For some time, we had been aware of its pending publication but had not read the book, choosing to ignore it, steadfast in our desire to live anonymously with our friends. However, two months after its publication, a friend informed us that Nizer had read from our parents' prison correspondence on television. When we responded that Nizer had not requested our permission to publish these letters in his book, he suggested we contact a lawyer, which we did—and we read the book. Nizer not only used the letters without permission, he distorted their intent. And his characterization of our parents as political fanatics who neglected us for political causes infuriated us. We were further horrified by the book's ending in which he labeled us "normal, decent citizens." Later, in a pre-trial affidavit, Nizer stated he did this to contrast our happy lives with the sorry lives of our parents—the implication being that we were leading normal, happy lives because we rejected everything our parents represented. This was a vicious characterization, and we realized we would not be able to live with ourselves if we kept silent, permitting millions of Americans to draw the same conclusions.

We discussed the matter thoroughly with Elli, Ann and our parents, deciding that however it disrupted our lives we had no alternative but to coerce Nizer into publically retracting his false, fictitious, and distorted writing. We filed suit against Nizer and his publisher, Doubleday, in Federal court that June. Nevertheless, we hoped to maintain some semblance of privacy, which became impossible when we were forced to sign our names and places of residence on the complaint. Within a few hours the local newspaper tagged us, and the next day we appeared on the front page. Our privacy vanished overnight. We resented not only Nizer's book but his taking the decision to reveal our identities publically (we had every intention of doing so some day) out of our hands. Now we had no time to order our lives and were unprepared for the changes that were bound to come.

The year following the publication of *The Implosion Conspiracy* was one of transition. Once the press publicized our current names and addresses, change became inevitable. Those around us reacted in many ways. A few expressed surprise and shock. Some friends were tearfully emotional, and many told us they knew all along but kept silent because we did. In a few instances, Michael and I knew that others knew, but we pretended not to know to make sure our cover was not blown. For all the gut-wrenching trauma the Nizer book forced on us, the public response was not as cataclysmic as we feared. A couple of articles about us were written in the late spring of 1973, but the press quickly lost interest. That summer we gave a few alternative press interviews. We did our first television interview. It was not aired, however, until 1974 as part of "The Unquiet Death of Julius and Ethel Rosenberg." Michael and I had always envisioned an investigative press phoning us at all hours, trying to ferret out the truth. Our vision was wrong.

We discovered that being a plaintiff in a lawsuit is very expensive. We had very little money. The movie *Daniel* implies that the children of the couple executed for conspiracy to commit espionage had a substantial trust fund. Fourteen thousand dollars split between us seemed substantial then but was not enough to finance a major lawsuit. In any event, the trust was distributed in 1968, and by 1973 most of it had been spent. We planned a series of fund-raising parties in the fall and spring. Those parties, more than media attention, accelerated the change in us.

The parties were emotionally charged events held in private homes and attended primarily by those who had fought to save our parents' lives. The program might include a reading of our parents' last letters or a recounting of their struggle. Having to repeatedly relive those experiences in public was very difficult. Being applauded and receiving special attention simply because of who we were was also disturbing. This was especially so because we had put so much effort into being private people for so long. I was often very nervous before each event and didn't know how to respond when people told me how wonderful I was for embarking on this effort. However, Michael and I were teachers, used to speaking before a classroom. Addressing a hundred people in someone's living room wasn't all that different. We were told that we spoke very effectively. Michael quickly came to enjoy speaking, and I eventually became more comfortable as well. We averaged a party a month, so for many days each month our lives remained much as they had been before the Nizer book was published.

Nineteen seventy-four brought dramatic changes. In January, ABC Television broadcast a feature-length dramatization of our parents' trial as part of a series on trials of the twentieth century. The script, as Michael and I read it, was slanted toward our parents' guilt. The actors' portrayal of the characters, however, left the impression that our parents might have been innocent and that the prosecution witnesses were liars. "The Unquiet Death of Julius and Ethel Rosenberg" was aired the following month on PBS. These events sparked the press. The *New York Times* and Associated Press sent reporters to do feature stories about us. The articles appeared simultaneously in dozens of newspapers on my brother's thirty-first birthday, Sunday, March 10. The *New York Times* article was on the front page. Then the phone started ringing constantly. It appeared that, instead of competing to be the first to uncover the story, newspapers had waited for the "big boys" to cover us before they stepped in.

The National Committee to Reopen the Rosenberg Case was formed that spring. A commemorative rally in Carnegie Hall was planned for mid-June. Michael and I entered negotiations that led to our contracting to write *We Are Your Sons*. Our lives were replete with interviews, meetings and legal consultations. By the time we stood on the stage at Carnegie Hall before 2,500 people, the transition was almost complete. We had become public figures, and a national effort to clear our parents' names had begun.

Our work lives were changing as well. I had been teaching half-time at Western New England College. I knew it would be impossible to continue that work and effectively engage in a national campaign. I had decided to resign when I was called to the dean's office and told that my contract would not be renewed. The dean cited an unwritten rule that part-timers were only hired for three consecutive years. I have since discovered that it was one of those conveniently flickering rules that were selectively applied. I'll never know if the college was nervous about having both Rosenberg sons teaching there. The business school might have played a part in the decision. Business majors who were interested in international marketing occasionally enrolled in my course to enhance their communication with those from different cultural backgrounds. I had resisted business school pressure to cater to their needs. I even once flippantly remarked that I would not help my students sell Coca Cola to "natives," because I had taken a firm stand against tooth decay. In any event, I was not planning to teach in the fall of 1974. Michael planned to take a year's leave of absence in 1975.

We spent that summer writing *Sons,* reading and then selecting for inclusion over a hundred of the 500-plus letters our parents wrote while imprisoned. The committee planned speaking engagements for us in the fall. We did not wish to leave our families for long periods of time, and it was not practical for our families to come with us. In response to these needs, arrangements were made for us to take many short trips interspersed with time at home. Thus, we were to be treated like yo-yos. We tried to limit our travel to ten days each month. This may not seem like an arduous schedule, but we often worked eighteen or more hours a day when we were on the road and returned exhausted. Our time at home was supposedly committed to our families but was also occupied with work on our book, committee meetings, legal meetings, interviews and a growing correspondence.

My first speaking engagement was at Hampshire College in September 1974. It was a good place to start because the audience was sympathetic and the location close to home. Trips of several days each to Louisville and St. Louis followed almost immediately. These trips were often structured around a major campus address. The colleges paid for transportation, and the sizeable speaking fees went to the committee. The committee would try either by long distance or through a local group to secure other speaking engagements or to organize fund-raising parties for us in the local area and fill in the gaps with newspaper, television and radio interviews, talk show appearances, press conferences and meetings with interested people. A typical day might include a major address followed by a long question-and-answer period and press conference, three television appearances, a couple of radio interviews, dinner with a newspaper reporter, and an evening at a fund-raising party followed by a late-night talk show. What I said varied with the medium and the time available and was drawn from a fifty-minute presentation that I entitled "The Emperor's New Clothes."

In this speech I first discussed the historical period in which the case occurred because many in the predominantly student audiences hadn't been born until a few years after my parents were executed. I'd then develop the trial's principal characters, explain the major pieces of evidence, what was said about this evidence and then recount what we had learned about the veracity of the witnesses and the authenticity and weight of the evidence in the last twenty years. I'd close with a discussion of the current significance of my parents' case, particularly in light of the then unfolding Watergate scandal. What follows is a typical speech.

The Emperor's New Clothes

I'm going to take you back to a place and time that many of you will have a hard time believing was America only twenty years ago. Many events happened then that seem incredible to people growing up today, after what we've all gone through in the sixties. The late 1940s and early 1950s are known as the McCarthy period, the period of the great red scare after World War II, the period of the "American Inquisition." It was a time of drastic change. Prior to World War II, our economy was—with some exceptions, especially in Latin America—primarily national. After World War II, we became the world's leading economic power. Prior to World War II, most of the federal budget was expended on New Deal social welfare programs. During the war, the military became the number one priority, and it has remained so since. Before the war, our foreign military presence was small and primarily limited to Latin America. Since World War II, we have become "the cops of the world." Why did the public support these changes, even when they led to increased taxes and the loss of thousands of American lives? Selling the necessity of these changes to the public provided the driving force of the McCarthy period and, ultimately, my parents' case.

But before we focus on the McCarthy period, another thread needs to be picked up. World War II ended with a big bang. The atomic bomb was dropped on Japan. Many felt it was also the first shot of the Cold War that started soon afterward between the United States and the Soviet Union. As the Cold War heated up, as the Soviet Union, our World War II ally, was transformed into our arch enemy, the war-weary public had one great consolation. We had the bomb and we could, as some radio commentators suggested then, drop a few A-bombs on Moscow and Leningrad and take care of the Soviets. We had the secret of the atomic bomb and that secret provided security.

This security was illusory. The basic principle behind the atomic bomb—the principle of nuclear fission—was demonstrated in several countries in the late 1930s. The greatest secret was given away when we dropped the bomb on Hiroshima—the secret that it was feasible! Dr. Edward Condon, one of the atomic scientists, warned in 1946: "The laws of nature, some seem to think, are ours exclusively. . . . So, when other countries make atom bombs, these people will cry 'treason' at our scientists, for they will find it inconceivable that another country could make a bomb in any other way except by aid from Americans." In 1946, Robert Hutchins, president of the University of Chicago, who was close to many Manhattan Project scientists, stated that a concensus of those who made the bomb believed that the Soviet Union would successfully test an atom bomb in five years. But General Leslie Groves, the military commander of the atom bomb construction project, scoffed at this idea and concluded it would take the Soviets twenty years.

It took the Soviets a little more than four years. They tested an atomic bomb during August of 1949. President Truman's announcement of this event a month later caused widespread public dismay. As Condon had predicted, many assumed spies must have stolen our secret. In *The FBI Story*, it is reported that J. Edgar Hoover told his lieutenants that the Russians had exploded a bomb, that spies had stolen the secret, and that they should go get them.

However, as September became October and 1949 became 1950, no atomic spies were caught. Tremendous pressure on the bureau to arrest someone developed. Though no atomic spies were captured in the United States, Klaus Fuchs, a German-born nuclear scientist living in Britain who had worked on the Manhattan Project in the 1940s, was arrested by Scotland Yard in February of 1950. He was charged with spying for the Soviet Union while he worked at Los Alamos. He pleaded guilty after a very brief trial at which the sole evidence presented was his confession. Fuchs received a fourteen-year sentence, the maximum permitted for violating the British Official Secrets Act. Klaus Fuchs appears to have been a spy. Since his release, he has lived in East Germany, where he holds an important government position.

The pressure on the FBI to make an arrest in America increased immensely, because Fuchs said he had an American courier who transmitted secret information to the Soviets. The FBI had to find the courier.

They found Harry Gold in May 1950. Gold had previously been questioned with regard to industrial espionage, but when agents questioned him again, he confessed to being Fuchs' courier. Gold was arrested to banner headlines. More arrests were promised. Gold was tried at the end of the year. The only proof presented at Gold's trial was his confession. When the judge asked how he would respond to the prosecution's trial charges, Gold's attorney, who was a former chairman of the Republican National Committee, said, "I would be perfectly willing, on behalf of the defendant, to accept any statement of the crime that he might make, without any supporting evidence." Gold was sentenced to thirty-years imprisonment.

A month after Gold's arrest, David Greenglass, a man who had worked at Los Alamos as a machinist on the atom bomb project when he was an army sergeant, was arrested. He was charged with conspiring to give the secret of the atomic bomb to Harry Gold so that Harry Gold could carry this information to Anatoli Yakovlev, a Soviet diplomat in New York. David Greenglass is my uncle. He and his wife, Ruth, agreed to cooperate with the government in return for lenient treatment.

In July 1950, my father, Julius Rosenberg, was arrested and charged with recruiting David Greenglass into a spy ring to steal the secret of the atomic bomb. My father was an electrical engineer who operated a small machine shop with David Greenglass on New York City's lower east side. A month later, my mother was arrested and charged with being a member of the spy ring. Finally, late in August, Morton Sobell, a college friend of my father's, was also arrested. [I would then turn to a large blackboard on which I had written

FUCHS———GOLD———GREENGLASS———ROSENBERG

and state these were the links the government sought to forge.]

My parents' trial was not long. It lasted from March 6 to March 29. That included time for jury selection and deliberation. Irving R. Kaufman, then the youngest Federal judge, later the chief judge of the Second Circuit Court of Appeals, presided. He has received many honors since and is considered by many to be one of the most prestigious jurists in the nation. Irving Saypol was the chief prosecuting attorney. He is now a New York State Supreme Court judge. Roy Cohn, one of his assistants, later achieved national notoriety when he worked for Senator Joseph McCarthy. The defense team was led by Emanual Bloch, an attorney who had never before tried a major criminal case. His trial experience was in personal injury cases. He was, however, a well-respected civil liberties lawyer. He was assisted by his aged father and by Gloria Agrin, a recent law school graduate.

My parents were not charged with treason or espionage, but with conspiracy to commit espionage. In order to obtain a conspiracy conviction against my parents, the government didn't have to prove they stole atomic secrets. A conspiracy conviction can be obtained if two or more people are shown to have planned a crime and committed one overt act in furtherance of their plan. For instance, in this case, the government had only to prove that my parents agreed with David and Ruth Greenglass that Greenglass would steal atomic secrets and that Greenglass took one specific action such as giving diagrams to Harry Gold. Conspiracy is much easier to prove than espionage or treason. Physical evidence is not required. A conviction can be based entirely on oral testimony. Evidence provided by alleged co-conspirators is admissable while it would not be in a treason trial. A co-conspirator is someone who says, I did it, but they did it too.

Therefore, at a trial like this, the credibility of the witnesses is paramount. Who will the jury believe? Will they believe David and Ruth Greenglass and Harry Gold when they say they helped the Rosenbergs steal atomic secrets, or will they believe Ethel and Julius Rosenberg when they testify they were not involved? The political climate of the country has a profound effect on who the jury will find credible. During the McCarthy period, was the jury going to believe the government, backed by J. Edgar Hoover and government witnesses who said the defendants were spies, or was the jury going to believe "a bunch of commies"? The war in Vietnam had not yet started. The Watergate revelations of government misconduct were decades in the future. Americans did not believe that the FBI might commit illegal acts. J. Edgar Hoover was seen as a white knight riding into town on a white charger cleaning up crime and Communism wherever he went. Furthermore, we were at war with Communism. My parents' arrest, trial and execution were bracketed by the Korean war. They were arrested at the start of that war, and the armistice was signed soon after they were executed. The trial occurred during some of the most intense fighting of the war.

The McCarthy period produced some truly bizarre occurrences. A few stories would probably give you a better feeling for the period than a dry history. During this time, the city manager of Wheeling, West Virginia, appalled that prizes in chewing gum packets that depicted the world's nations included one inscribed with a hammer and sickle that said "USSR popn. 211,000,000, Capital Moscow," said: "That's a terrible thing to expose children in this city to." After the Cincinnati Reds beat the New York Yankees in an exhibition baseball game, people reacted angrily to the headline "Reds beat Yanks." Many Americans did not like the idea of a team called "Reds." Cincinnati soon began calling themselves the "Redlegs." I guess Reds couldn't even beat Yanks on the sports pages! The city council of Moscow, Idaho, passed a resolution that stated: "Whereas the citizens of Moscow, Idaho, believe they have a prior and superior title to the name . . . Moscow, USSR [should] change [its] from Moscow to some name that will not by association embarrass the citizens of Moscow, USA." A governor of a southern state proposed that membership in the Communist party be made a capital offense.

If you had picked up a newspaper during the trial, you might have seen the following headlines on the front page of the *New York Times*. Right-hand column: "Reds Battle Yanks in Korea, Heavy Casualties." Left-hand column: "Brother says Sister was Spy, Stole Bomb Secret." Across the bottom: "Investigation Continues into Reds at Harvard." Mid-page: "Charge Communists Teach in Westchester Schools." This is not an exact reconstruction, but it's the type of thing you could read every day. The jury could have read it every day, because they were not sequestered during the trial. They went home, could have read the paper every night, and watched television coverage of the trial as well. This was the atmosphere in which my parents were on trial for their lives. This was the atmosphere in which their credibility was pitted against the government's.

They were convicted. Even Morton Sobell, about whom the Greenglasses were silent, was found guilty. Only one witness, Max Elitcher, who never admitted to spying himself, claimed that Sobell tried to get him to be a spy. Elitcher, who had committed perjury by denying he had been a Communist and, thus, faced a possible ten-year sentence, also stated that he once saw Sobell entering my father's apartment building with what looked like a film container. On the basis of Elitcher's testimony, Sobell was convicted and sentenced to thirty years in prison. Morton was released after nineteen years, over five of them spent in Alcatraz. My parents were given the death sentence and were executed on June 19, 1953, despite world-wide protests. David Greenglass was given a fifteen-year sentence and paroled after ten. Ruth Greenglass, who swore she was involved in the "conspiracy," was never indicted and never served a day in prison.

The evidence at the trial was primarily oral. Harry Gold took the stand and testified extensively about espionage activity. The key testimony he gave was that on June 3, 1945, he went to Albuquerque, New Mexico, registered at the Hilton, and went to a man's apartment, where he used the code "I come from Julius" to identify himself to the GI who opened the door. Gold said he then gave this man a cut half of a Jello box top as a recognition device. This testimony appeared very incriminating. The government produced a hotel registration card as physical evidence that Gold was in Albuquerque then. The code with my father's first name pointed to my father.

Gold continued that the man he met matched the Jello box top with one he had and gave him some sketches. At that point during the trial, a series of sketches were introduced as evidence. Gold went on, saying he gave the man he identified as Greenglass $500 and returned to New York with the sketches. A bank record of a subsequent $400 deposit by Greenglass was introduced as physical evidence.

David Greenglass testified to the same story from his perspective. He said that my father recruited him into an espionage ring in November 1944. He claimed my father told him the secret Los Alamos project was building an atomic bomb. Greenglass maintained that in January 1945 he sketched some Los Alamos experimental bomb setups in my parents' apartment. A sketch was introduced as evidence. My father, Greenglass said, told him to go back to Los Alamos, find what he could, and that in six months a woman would visit him. That woman would be a courier and would identify herself by having the other half of the Jello box top my father then gave him. In September 1945, Greenglass claimed he prepared a sketch of the cross-section of the atomic bomb. When this sketch was introduced in evidence, the defense requested that it be impounded to impress the judge with our parents' concern for national security. Greenglass also testified that when my father feared they were about to be arrested he directed that the Greenglasses take passport photos so they could flee the country. Passport photos of David and Ruth Greenglass were then introduced as physical evidence. This too was very damaging because the Greenglasses were supposedly poor people who didn't travel. What would they be doing with passport photos?

Greenglass further testified that my parents had a console table in their house—the kind of folding table that could be very convenient in a small apartment. However, this wasn't an ordinary table because it had a hollowed-out section so that it could be used for microfilming. Greenglass said it was a piece of spy equipment that had been given to my parents by the Russians. Ruth next took the stand and corroborated her husband's testimony. She and David further implicated my mother by saying Ethel typed up written and oral reports that David provided for my father.

There was other testimony and physical evidence. This is, however, the key testimony and evidence. Without it, particularly without the link between Gold and Greenglass, the conviction could never have been obtained. The link between Gold and Greenglass was critical because, while Gold testified about contacts with Russians, he never said he met my father. Conversely, the Greenglasses recounted conversations with my parents, but they never told of meeting Russians. The June 3 meeting was the linch pin of the prosecution's case. Without that meeting, no proof was given to link the Gold-Fuchs part of the alleged conspiracy to the Rosenberg-Greenglass part of it.

There was other testimony. A maid, Mrs. Cox, testified that the console table had sometimes been kept in the closet, implying it had been hidden. The government witness lists included over one hundred names, some of them well-known atomic scientists, but no top scientist was called to testify. John Derry, a liaison officer at the base who held a bachelor of science degree in engineering, was called to authenticate Greenglass's cross-section sketch. When asked if the sketch revealed "the principle involved in the operation of the 1945 atomic bomb," Derry responded, "It does."

The defense was simple. My parents denied they were involved. They testified that they had never had passport photos taken and did not encourage David Greenglass to do so. They knew nothing about code words or Jello box tops or Harry Gold. They did not get the table from the Russians but purchased it from Macy's for approximately $21 around 1944. Morton Sobell did not take the stand.

The prosecution asked my parents if they were Communist party members. The defense objected on the ground that the answer was irrelevant and might be unfairly prejudicial to my parents. The judge overruled the objection, reasoning that political views might show the motivation for the crime. My parents then refused to answer, invoking the Fifth Amendment.

Why rehash this today? I do this because it's important for you to know that an honest jury convicted my parents. They saw passport photos, they heard about recognition signals, they saw the sketches, and they heard the government saying valuable information had been stolen. Given the climate of the times, the result was a foregone conclusion.

But it's not 1950 or 1953 now. It's over twenty years later and we've learned a lot about the witnesses, the testimony, the evidence and the government's conduct since then. Let's take a second look. [I would then turn to the blackboard. Under the list of names I mentioned earlier I would write:]

1) I come from Julius	4) Jello Box Top
2) Hotel Card	5) Passport Photos
3) Atom Sketches	6) $400
	7) Console Table

Take a closer look at these seven key pieces of evidence and bits of testimony. Let's start with the console table because that began to unravel first. The console table was not produced at the trial. The defense assumed it had been sold when my parents' apartment was abandoned. An investigative reporter, however, found the table at my grandmother's house in early 1953. I had lived with her for a year and had walked by it on dozens of occasions. People were so scared that none of the relatives attended the trial. Consequently, they didn't know its significance. Once it was found, an affidavit was obtained from a buyer at Macy's who swore the markings on the table proved the table was sold at Macy's for the price my father estimated. The photographs showed no hollowed-out section; it was a perfectly ordinary table. Judge Kaufman said this evidence was unimportant and denied the appeal. Here, however, we finally had a physical object that key prosecution witnesses described in one way, my parents described in another, and, most importantly, third parties could objectively look at to determine who was lying. When they did, they found the Greenglasses lied and my parents told the truth. [I would then cross out the words "Console Table" on the blackboard.] "I come from Julius." Gold and Greenglass swore that was the code phrase. That phrase helped tie my father to the key meeting between Gold and Greenglass. However, when Walter and Miriam Schneir were engaged in research prior to writing *Invitation to an Inquest,* upon which this talk is largely based, they wrote to Gold and asked for his story. Gold sent them tapes of his discussions with his attorneys. These tapes were recently played during a PBS television showing of the documentary "The Unquiet Death of Julius and Ethel Rosenberg." On tape Gold says the code word was "Bob sent me" or "Benny sent me." The name *Julius* was never mentioned. In fact, an FBI agent interviewed in the following scene of the documentary said he suggested the name *Julius* to Gold. This "suggestion" was not reported at the trial. So the original code was not "Julius sent me," and the FBI suggested the name *Julius* to Gold.

What effect would an FBI suggestion have on Gold? Gold was a very suggestible witness. Just months before my parents' trial, he had been cross-examined during the trial of his former boss, Abraham Brothman. Under cross-examination, Gold admitted that he created a fantasy life. He said he invented a brother who had been killed in World War II when he had no such brother. He conjured a wife who was stolen by his best friend when none of this ever happened. The defense counsel asked, "You lied for a period of six years?" Gold answered, "I lied for a period of sixteen years." When asked how he kept from being tangled up in these lies, Gold answered, "It's a wonder steam did not come out of my ears at times." This is the same man who the FBI suggested the code phrase to, and Gold is the only one who corroborates the Greenglass story of the critical Albuquerque meeting. Furthermore, why would Gold, who said he was an experienced spy, use a code name that might incriminate another spy? This appears more like the FBI trying to create evidence than actual spies in action. [I would then cross out "I come from Julius" on the blackboard.]

What about the Jello box top? If you tour the FBI building in Washington, you can see it displayed. Actually, it's not the one from the trial, it's a copy. They call it the Jello box top from the crime of the century. That's what the FBI called this case. In fact, David Greenglass never claimed the Jello box top used at the trial was the same one used in 1945. When Greenglass testified about a Jello box top, the prosecutor handed him a scissors and a Jello box. The prosecutor asked Greenglass to cut the box to demonstrate to the jury how this was done. Greenglass obliged him and then with great solemnity the cut box top was shown to the jury and admitted as evidence of a crime. And a copy was put on display in the FBI building! This isn't proof of a crime; all it proves is that Greenglass knew how to use scissors! [I would then cross off "Jello Box Top."]

What about the atomic sketches? Again, like the Jello box, it was never claimed these were the sketches from 1945. Greenglass said that he drew them from memory shortly before the trial. When the prosecution introduced the cross-section sketch, the defense made an error when they asked the judge to impound it. The sketch was sealed and never made a part of the appellate record.

Morton Sobell, who for years persistently sought a new trial, asked in the 1960s to have the sketch unsealed to help him with his appeals. Government attorneys repeatedly fought disclosure on the grounds that it would hurt our national security. However, in 1965, a judge ordered its release. Sobell's attorney then showed the sketch, along with the sketches that were never impounded, to atomic scientists. Philip Morrison, one of the co-holders of the patent on the atom bomb (yes, those things actually have patents!) looked at the sketches and said they were worthless.

George Kistiakowski, Harvard chemist and atomic scientist, said they were "ridiculous . . . [they don't] tell you anything; a baby drawing. . . ." Victor Weisskopf, former chairman of the physics department at MIT who also worked on the atom project at Los Alamos, called them "uselessly crude." It is now generally conceded that none of the sketches introduced at the trial had much value. The government, however, responded that since the charge was conspiracy, the value of the sketches was irrelevant. The government's attorneys pointed out that they only had to prove our parents **tried** to steal secrets. But it did matter. Can you imagine the headlines during the trial? "Spies Accused of Stealing Baby Drawings," or "Dangerous Red Spy Ring Steals Useless Crudities." It wouldn't have worked. [I would then cross off the phrase "Atom Sketches."]

What about the passport photos? The Schneirs took them to the shop where the photos were taken and asked the owner about them. The owner pointed out that they were not passport photos. The owner said that there could be no mistake; he had a set procedure with passport photos. The photos were the wrong shape, size and pose for passport photos. They were family snapshots. The overwhelmed, understaffed defense was badly fooled. However, the prosecution must have known that the photos were family snapshots. Again the Greenglasses lied about a crucial piece of evidence. The prosecution must have known and still allowed it to happen. [I would then cross out "Passport Photos."]

When the Schneirs checked a copy of the hotel card, they found that the date, 6/3/45, written on the front did not match the date, 6/4/45, stamped on the back. When this discrepancy was explained to the hotel's former manager, the Schneirs were told that the date on the back was controlling. In other words, the card didn't prove Gold was in Albuquerque on the date he said he was. There are other problems with the card. The Schneirs took the card to a handwriting analyst, who studied samples of the hotel clerk's signature and the initials on the card and concluded that the initials on the card were not the clerk's. Unfortunately, the Schneirs only had a photostat of the card, because the prosecution only introduced a copy at the trial. The original was later destroyed.

It was not mentioned at the trial that Harry Gold also registered at the Albuquerque Hilton in mid-September 1945. The September and June cards are dissimilar. Two FBI agents initialed the September card and no such initials appear on the June card. The material used in the June card appeared to differ from that used in the September card. The dates on the back and front of the September card matched and the handwriting expert stated that the handwriting on the September card was authentic. Furthermore, given the Hilton's alphabetical filing system, it seems strange that FBI agents spent days in the hotel's attic going through the files to "find" the June card.

But why not use the September card, you ask? The answer is simple: David Greenglass was on furlough in New York from September 7 to

25, so he could not have met with Gold in mid-September. So why June 3 (or was it 4)? That date fit neatly with a $400 deposit Ruth Greenglass made on June 4.

The date discrepancy renders the card useless as proof. The FBI's actions are more simply explained as an attempt to create a forgery rather than to prove a Gold-Greenglass connection. [I would then cross out the phrase "Hotel Card."]

Finally, the $400. When the Schneirs investigated the Greenglasses' financial affairs in New Mexico, they discovered many deposits made over a number of years; several bank accounts contained more money than David earned. We do not know what Greenglass was doing, but the source of all this money was not Harry Gold. He would have had to be in regular contact with Greenglass and he was not. There is some evidence that David Greenglass stole from the army. Perhaps he was involved in black marketeering. He may have been stealing army equipment and selling it to make extra money. However, we may never discover what the FBI originally had on David Greenglass because in 1969 the record of the initial investigation into David Greenglass' New Mexico activities was destroyed by the FBI. [I would then cross out "$400," leaving no evidence that had gone unrefuted or seriously questioned, turn to the audience and say . . .]

The emperor has no clothes. There was no evidence against my parents. The charade is further exposed once you realize that there was no crime to commit. **There never was a secret of the atom bomb to begin with.** A crime was perpetrated against my parents, not by them. The prosecution witnesses repeatedly perjured themselves. The government attorneys and the FBI fabricated evidence, subborned perjury, and committed Watergate-style dirty tricks.

The government did this so that the people would be convinced that there really was an international Communist conspiracy that was about to destroy us. The government wanted the people to believe that Communism was like a giant octopus out to strangle the world. This octopus had its beak in the Kremlin and tentacles that reached out to places like Korea. Communism would attack us militarily in Korea, where our lines of supply were long, and simultaneously sap our will to resist by infiltrating at home. The American Communist party and left movement, this scenario went, had no domestic basis. American Communists were not really Americans but slaves of Stalin. These Communists aided Stalin's policies by arguing against a strong defense and stealing our military secrets. Thus, another tentacle that directed domestic infiltrators reached into the lower east side of New York City, and that's where my parents came in. This scenario should not be news to you. It provides the justification for Watergate and the war in Vietnam. Obviously, Watergate is not an isolated instance of deception. It is a portrait of governmental abuse of power and manipulation of public opinion that owes much of its foundation to the showcase trials of the late 1940s and early 1950s, including the trial, conviction and execution of our parents.

The conformity of public opinion and the creation of the false issue of national security rising from my parents' conviction opened the way for very significant governmental abuses of power. Foreign policy was mired in secrecy from that time. The publication of the Pentagon Papers in 1971 provided a glimpse of what was festering beneath the surface. The government flagrantly lied to the American public and had no fear that it would be called to account. Extralegal measures against dissenters were instituted in the name of national security. Martin Luther King was harassed by wiretapping; many radical groups were infiltrated by agents provocateurs; local police forces were unleashed to terrorize demonstrators, even beat and kill them. Finally, in national security's name the Nixon administration approved the Huston Plan of using a secret police force to "get" radicals. In a desperate attempt to solidify and manipulate its power, the Nixon administration overstepped its bounds in the Watergate Affair, and the public suddenly woke up.

My brother and I, our parents, the American left are not the sole victims of the Cold War; we have all been victimized. To control public opinion, government agencies fabricated the case against our parents. They convinced American citizens of the dangers of Communism, as well as of the necessity for secrecy, undercover agents, conspiracy trials and surveillance. Next, they sold the public on the arms race, exorbitant military expenditures and, by extension, imperialism. So when American leaders plotted the Vietnam War, few listened to dissenters who warned that we were supporting a dictatorship and killing an entire people. Fifty thousand Americans died in that war; the number of Vietnamese dead vastly exceeded that figure. Our parents died because they adamantly opposed this pattern of deception, but the message of the last twenty years is clear: we will all be destroyed if we do not stand up for the truth.

The American people have paid a heavy price for the "American Inquisition." It is time to explode the myth that the lie of our parents' guilt helped perpetuate. We pledge ourselves to fight in the courts, in the Congress, in the press, on speakers' platforms anywhere until the truth of our parents' innocence is public knowledge.

These are vital political considerations, but I am also personally involved. Part of what I'm doing is trying to pay tribute to my parents. I see all of you as potential jurors. I may never sit on a jury, but some of you will. If my recounting of what happened to my parents can make you a little more critical when you sit in judgment of a defendant who may be someone whose views or appearance are frightening or foreign to you, if I can prevent you from being swayed as the jury in my parents' case was swayed by political prejudice and the climate of the time, if I can save one innocent person from going to prison or worse, then I have paid a very fitting tribute to my parents, and my effort will have been worthwhile. Thank you.

The Question Period

[A question-and-answer period that could last longer than my almost-hour-long talk followed. These are typically asked questions and their answers.]

Q. Why did the government focus on your parents?
A. Because Greenglass supposedly pointed the way to my parents, perhaps I should first answer why Greenglass. This is my theory. Picture yourself as an FBI agent in 1950. There is tremendous pressure to find the atom spies—that there were spies is assumed. What do you do? You refer to your files to see what you have got. I think, at first, the FBI was following several leads. Greenglass was one of them; he was already in the FBI files. The FBI had been investigating Greenglass for something for quite some time. We (myself, my brother, the Schneirs, and others) hypothesize that Greenglass was stealing army equipment and selling it on the black market. We originally asked the United States attorney for the District of New Mexico for these files but coincidentally the FBI has told us that through an "unfortunate accident" those files have been pulped—destroyed.

The console table, an alleged gift from the Russians, which Julius Rosenberg was supposed to have used to microfilm secret information. The bottom shows no hollowed section.

Julius and Ethel Rosenberg in Prospect Park in Brooklyn, New York, in 1945.

Robby (left) and Michael in 1952.

Robby and Michael with Abel and Anne Meeropol. These photographs were taken to show the court the boys' happy adjustment with the Meeropols, who adopted them.

Robert (above) and Michael (below) speaking at a rally in Union Square, New York, June 19, 1978, to commemorate the twenty-fifth anniversary of the Rosenbergs' execution (photo by Lionel Delavigne).

But why would Greenglass name my father? The FBI had proof of his stealing and proof that he lied when he said he had never been a member of a Communist organization. He had been a member of the Young Communist League. The FBI could intimidate him by pointing out that they could get a jury to believe that he was a Communist who lied to get into our secret atom bomb building project and stole army equipment. They could threaten that Harry Gold, a confessed spy, was prepared to testify that Greenglass helped Gold steal the secret of the atom bomb. They could then threaten him with the death penalty, before giving him a way out.

That's where my father came in. He was Greenglass' only Communist relative, and he had a technical background. The FBI wanted to make a political case against Communists in general. While Greenglass had been in the Young Communist League, unlike my parents, he was not politically active. Also, David Greenglass took eight courses beyond high school at Brooklyn Polytechnic Institute and had failed all eight courses. It strained credibility to contend that the same person single-handedly stole the secret of the atom bomb. My father's engineering background made it more plausible.

Proof for this theory comes from a number of sources—from my parents, from Morton Sobell, and from what the FBI agent and prosecutors said on the PBS TV documentary. Morton Sobell stated, "The first thing the government agents, the FBI, told me . . . when they met me was did I know that I faced the death penalty." James Kilsheimer, one of the prosecutors, stated, "If the Rosenbergs had been willing to tell what they knew about Russian espionage, we would have had the most gigantic espionage case in the history of this country." You could almost see the gleam in his eyes as he said that, even twenty years later!

My parents were presented with the same choice Greenglass was: die or confess and name others. They wouldn't lie and were executed.

Q. Why was the government's case so weak? If the government wished to frame people, wouldn't they do a better job?
A. The case was not so weak. In the McCarthy period, failure to deny a government charge of Communism was proof of guilt. The atom bomb was cloaked in mystery; people could easily be convinced that the crime was possible. The jury honestly was convinced. Once my parents were convicted and that conviction affirmed, public faith in the integrity of our judicial process assured that, even if the frame-up were

exposed, the exposers would not be believed. The fact that people were convicted by a fair and honest jury would be enough. Anyone who then claimed frame-up would be facing a presumption of guilt, not a presumption of innocence. Once guilt is assumed, almost anything goes. We shouldn't think that we are so different.

I'm sure many of you are familiar with the TV series "Kojak." In the first scene of the typical show, we see a criminal committing a brutal murder. During the remainder of the show, Kojak zeroes in on the killer. By the time the show is half over, Kojak knows who did it, but either the bureaucracy or the Constitution gets in the way. He knows the criminal won't be convicted. The climax comes when the killer is cornered. Kojak has him against a wall and says: "I'm so mad, I could blow you away. No one would know. Hey, Sapperstein, keep a lookout. If this guy doesn't talk, I'm going to do society a favor." Of course, the killer breaks down and confesses. Kojak is committing a crime. Threatening to kill someone, holding a gun to his head unless he talks, is a felony. Kojak should go to jail, but we approve of what he does. We approve because we know the guy he is threatening is guilty. Would we approve if Kojak's victim was me or you or someone who might be innocent? In the same manner, the FBI and the public presumed all Communists were guilty and, therefore, my parents were also guilty. We become blinded and don't care about the rights of someone we already presume to be guilty. The government only needed to present enough evidence to convince a jury that was already inclined to believe them and inclined not to believe my parents to get a conviction. Once that was accomplished, the presumption of guilt and faith in the judicial process would insure that the frame-up would never unravel.

Q. Are you saying there was a giant conspiracy against your parents?
A. No. Think about Watergate. Nixon didn't need to tell his underlings to commit burglaries and break-ins. He just said that the Democrats had to be stopped. Underlings transmitted this to people who were to do whatever was necessary to insure Nixon's victory. In the same way, J. Edgar Hoover and FBI officials didn't have to say, "Let's frame people." The FBI already "knew" Communists were spies. They told field agents to obtain evidence to convict these dirty Commies. The agents would then develop the evidence. Those who developed evidence were rewarded. They didn't think they were framing inno-

cent people. They thought they were insuring the conviction of guilty people and saving American democracy from Communism. The higher-ups might not even have known that the evidence was fabricated. A climate is created that leads to these excesses, but it's not necessarily a giant, self-conscious conspiracy to frame people.

Q. Why don't you change your name back to Rosenberg?

A. There are a number of reasons why I haven't done this. It was a courageous act for our adoptive parents to take us in. They provided us with a home and love. We are grateful to them for raising us. The name is a tribute to them—a way of saying that we will never forget.

It would also be artificial to change my name to Rosenberg. I was named Rosenberg for the first six years of my life, but I've been a Meeropol for twenty. That's how I think of myself. Meeropol is a very uncommon name. I'm not hiding who I am. If I wanted to hide, I'd be more anonymous once again having the more common name of Rosenberg.

Finally, maybe it's a way of maintaining a little distance. When you become a public figure engaged in a public campaign, who you are can become submerged in that public campaign and that public image. If I were to change my name back, it would be like merging myself with a public image. So maybe keeping this name is a way of maintaining myself, a way of saying I am also a person apart from this reopening effort.

The Ongoing Effort

As our Freedom of Information Act law suit began to force the release of government files, important new information would be incorporated into our talks. The first such incorporation occurred early in the process. By the fall of 1975, after four months of stalling, the government released 735 previously secret pages. We pointed out that at that rate it would take over 200 years for all the files to be released. Also, some of the pages released were so heavily censored that they were of no value at all.

As time went by, many more censored and uncensored files were released. A number clearly showed that the case against my mother had been fabricated only weeks before the trial. Material released by the Atomic Energy Commission related to a February 8, 1951, meeting between members of the AEC, the prosecution and the Joint Congressional Committee on Atomic Energy. At that meeting, Myles Lane, one of Prosecutor Saypol's assistants, said, "The only thing that will break this man Rosenberg is the prospect of a death penalty . . . plus that if we can convict his wife, too, and give her a stiff sentence . . . that combination may serve to make this fellow disgorge and give us the information. . . ." Later, during the meeting, Lane admitted, "The case is not too strong against Mrs. Rosenberg. But . . . I think it is very important that she be convicted, too, given a stiff sentence." At the time of my father's arrest, Assistant Attorney General McInerney had told the FBI, "There is insufficient evidence to issue process against her [my mother] at this time . . . [but he was of the opinion] that it might be possible to utilize her as a lever against her husband." Basically, all that the government "had" was a statement by Ruth Greenglass that my mother had helped Julius convince her [Ruth] to go out to Albuquerque to convince David to be a spy. When questioned in August 1950, David Greenglass denied my mother's presence at the supposed September 1945 meeting where the famous sketch of the cross-section of the atom bomb was drawn. At the time he did this, he was under oath, preparing for his grand jury testimony. Despite his denial, my mother was arrested one week later. Two weeks after Myles Lane made the above statement to the joint congressional committee, Greenglass "recalled" that my mother had been present and had typed up his notes. Thus, there was no evidence against my mother even months after her arrest, and the evidence that led to her conviction and execution was developed after the prosecution decided to use her as a lever against my father.

As I said above, the meeting between Gold and Greenglass on June 3, 1945, was the key to the prosecution's case. That Gold and Greenglass agreed that the code was "I come from Julius" was one of the few points at which Gold and Greenglass corroborated each other's story, and it implicated my father. However, the Schneirs uncovered the fact that Gold, in his original statements to his attorneys, had used the phrase "Bob sent me" or "Benny sent me." Harry Gold's interview with Assistant Prosecutor Myles Lane in early August of 1950 was included in the first set of material released. There, under oath, Gold stated that the code was "I bring greetings from Ben in Brooklyn."

Meanwhile, Greenglass was saying nothing about a recognition signal, only that Gold introduced himself as "Dave from Pittsburgh." We knew the story was changed sometime between Gold's early 1950 arrest and his testimony at the trial in March of 1951. Just as our father maintained to Mr. Bennett (see above p. 210), we knew that Gold and Greenglass must have been brought together to iron out the differences in their story. Documents released in 1979 revealed that we were absolutely correct.

The first major release of documents occurred in November 1975 and included only FBI material from the Washington headquarters. The government responded to our protests that the "raw materials" of historical research were located in the local FBI field offices with the explanation that anything of significance would have been sent to headquarters. This is one of many examples that demonstrate the inaccuracy of that statement. According to a report from the Philadelphia field office, a report never sent to Washington, "Gold and Greenglass were interviewed simultaneously by the writer for their concerted effort in recalling the incident [the visit to Albuquerque]. . . . Concerning the reported salutation 'Greetings from BEN, GREENGLASS says that he had no recollection of such a statement made by GOLD, pointing out further that the name BEN would mean nothing to him. Greenglass proposed that possibly GOLD had said 'greetings from Julius' which would of course make sense to GREENGLASS. Gold's spontaneous comment to this was that possibly GREENGLASS was right that he had mentioned the name of JULIUS rather than BEN. Gold, however, is not at all clear on this point." Later, on March 5, 1951, one day before my parents' trial began, Gold became "convinced" that he had in fact brought "greetings from Julius." The corroboration of Gold by Greenglass and vice versa of that critical meeting was not independently done; it was orchestrated by the FBI and the prosecution!

Another set of documents focused on the debate over whether Fuchs identified Gold as his courier. Was Gold the mysterious "Raymond" Fuchs referred to as his courier? The files reveal that Fuchs initially refused to identify Gold as his courier. However, after Gold confessed, Fuchs changed his story and said Gold was the man. This reversal has a number of interpretations. One explanation is that Fuchs wanted to protect Gold but that once Gold confessed there was no point in carrying on the charade. Another is that Fuchs didn't identify Gold because

Gold was not the courier; Fuchs' subsequent acquiescence in Gold's story was designed to protect the real Raymond. Also, by identifying Gold, Fuchs was doing what his captors wished him to do.

The files revealed that the FBI interviewed Fuchs' sister and brother-in-law, Kristal and Robert Heineman. Both claimed to have met "Raymond," but even after Gold had "confessed," they denied that Gold was Raymond. Later on, Kristal agreed that Gold was Raymond. At the time of this reversal, however, she was in a mental institution undergoing electric-shock treatments. Thus, her statement may not be reliable. Her husband, who was not institutionalized, continued to deny that Gold was Raymond, even after being brought face to face with Gold in a New York restaurant. Thus, the files cast further doubt on Fuchs' identification of Gold as his courier.

Other files provide hints about the original, spring-of-1945 investigation of David Greenglass. Greenglass was one of the potential targets of a general FBI search for what they called the "unknown subject." The existence of this investigation confirmed our earlier hypothesis that Greenglass was already in the FBI files before Gold was arrested. Because of this investigation, the FBI had an easy time manipulating Gold to weave Greenglass into the alleged conspiracy. It was also able to use Gold's cooperation to force Greenglass to "confess" and point his finger at appropriate others.

This new information weakened the government's case. The government's files showed that their witnesses repeatedly lied, that the links in the chain of conspiracy the prosecution relied on were faulty, and that crucial evidence against our mother was manufactured two weeks before the trial.

Not all of the new information came from the newly released FBI files. Some of it came from the Atomic Energy Commission. Many of these files concerned the decision of the AEC and the Joint Congressional Committee on Atomic Energy to have Greenglass testify to stealing very sensitive information about the atomic bomb. The object of this testimony was to impress the jury and judge with the seriousness of the crime in order to obtain a death sentence against my father. When more of the scientific information was released later, my brother and Jerry Markowitz collaborated on an article published in *Science and Society* exposing the fraud behind the claims that our parents had committed the "crime of the century." In 1975, however, we had only a few hints. One of them was from the diary of Gordon Dean, once director of the AEC (the "good friend" of prison director James Bennett [see above, page 209]). On February 7, 1951, he had conferred with James McInerney, the head of the Criminal Division of the Justice Department. Dean asked McInerney if my father had given any indication of "breaking." He reported, "McInerney said there is no indication at this point and he doesn't think there will be unless we get a death sentence. He [McInerney] talked to the judge and he is prepared to impose one if the evidence warrants."

14

"He Talked to the Judge"

BY MICHAEL MEEROPOL

"HE TALKED TO THE JUDGE." These words leaped off the page at me. Others had seen them before I did and had been similarly affected. Kaufman had agreed to give the death sentence before the trial had begun. (I immediately assumed "the judge" was Kaufman.) We had always questioned Kaufman's objectivity. We had always felt that his sentence of death was an extremely cruel and politically motivated punishment, used to attempt to coerce my parents into cooperating with the government, used to strike terror into the hearts of all American radicals. Yet we did not think that he had actually overstepped the boundaries of proper judicial conduct and legality. However, in a letter dated February 12, 1953, my father had intuited that such improper behavior had to have occurred: "The judge's antagonistic conduct, his prejudgment of issues before all facts were in, his anticipatory examination of Government witnesses and his protection of them when in danger because of cross-examination and his ready knowledge of facts not yet adduced from the witness stand proves he had prior knowledge of either statements by witnesses or he had read F.B.I. reports or he had been briefed in the major points the U.S. attorney planned to present. In short collusion on the part of Judge Kaufman."

On the basis of the line "He talked to the judge" in Gordon Dean's diary, I added an affirmation of my parents' intuition to the first edition of this book just before it went to the printer. Members of the National Committee to Reopen the Rosenberg Case tried to interest the media in the Gordon Dean document as well as the February 8 meeting of the Joint Congressional Committee. They were successful. A series of articles was published by *Newsday* under the title "Papers Suggest U.S. Manipulated the Rosenberg Case" and syndicated in many cities.

The series formed the basis of my speech at a small rally on the night of June 18, 1975, at the Ethical Society in New York City. Robby and I and others spoke. There was music, dramatic readings. The only thing I really remember about my speech was informing the audience that I was thirty-two and that my father had been thirty-two at the time of his arrest. I then noted that he was thirty-five at the time of his execution and asked the audience to resolve with me that by the time I was thirty-five we would have succeeded in opening up the files and demonstrating convincingly that my parents were innocent. I also spoke to the audience about the *Newsday* series and noted implications of collusion between judge and prosecutor before the trial. Then I called Kaufman a murderer. At the time I didn't think anything of it. It seemed obvious from the document.

The next day the National Committee to Reopen the Rosenberg Case organized a demonstration in downtown Manhattan at Foley Square, the Federal Courthouse. Every time I go down to that section of Manhattan, I wrack my brains for memories of walks with my father from our home in Knickerbocker Village along East Broadway to Chatham Square. There the Third Avenue El would split, sending one line only one stop along Park Row to City Hall. The other line went all the way to South Ferry, from which we could walk directly onto the Staten Island Ferry without descending to the street. Sometimes, we would just walk all the way down to City Hall. I remember looking down streets off of Park Row which had signs in Chinese calligraphy, but I don't believe I ever walked with my father in Chinatown.

The Third Avenue El was long gone when I got off the subway right at the Foley Square Courthouse. I immediately recognized Park Row and tried to envision where the Third Avenue El ended (I couldn't). Foley Square is right in the same area as City Hall. It is across the street from the New York State Supreme Court, which had been the scene of our family's first legal victory when Justice McNally took Robby and me away from the city welfare department and let us stay with our grandmother.

Not only is Foley Square the building where my parents were convicted, it remains to this day the building where Judge Kaufman has his chambers and conducts business as (now retired) chief judge of the U.S. Court of Appeals for the Second Circuit. I had been to Foley Square only once before, for a hearing at the very inception of our lawsuit against Louis Nizer, but I had not really made much of the Kaufman connection in my mind.

I looked around the City Hall area and noted that in the State Supreme Court building sat Irving H. Saypol, the chief prosecutor in my parents' case. Robby and I have constantly charged him and his assistants with subornation of perjury and conspiracy to deprive my parents of their civil rights by false prosecution. This was a good place to beard the giants in their dens.

Foley Square has a very long and wide set of stone steps that leads up through the inevitable pillars to the front door. The difference between it and most other courthouses is that it is very tall and takes up a whole city block. By comparison, the U.S. Supreme Court building is tiny. In front of this imposing structure at noon on June 19, 1975, we took out our picket signs and the bullhorn and began to demonstrate, not just for the news media and the lunchtime crowds, but for Kaufman and Saypol as well. After overcoming my initial shyness about abruptly shattering the relative silence within which the citizens on the sidewalk were having conversations either with others or themselves, I began to really enjoy talking through the bullhorn. Though the signs and the theme of the demonstration were based on our demand that the FBI open their secret files (the FOIA lawsuit had not yet been filed, not a page had been released four months after our requests had been sent), the magnet of Kaufman's presence up on the twenty-second floor of that building (I don't even know if he was there in fact but his presence was sensed) drew all of us who spoke that day to refer to the phrase from Gordon Dean's diary: "He talked to the judge . . . talked to the judge . . . the judge agreed to impose the death sentence . . . agreed to impose the death sentence." Over and over again we said it. "And what does this mean?" we rhetorically asked the crowd, some of whom actually were listening. "They aren't supposed to behave like this. A judge is supposedly an impartial guardian of the law. How can this be possible when he's consulting with prosecution officials before the trial even begins and agrees on the most severe form of punishment?"

In our speeches, we demanded Judge Kaufman answer the implication of that statement. Was he in fact the judge that Dean referred to? I felt good to be participating. Not only had some new material come out but it felt personally good to be down at Foley Square paying

Kaufman and Saypol back a tiny percentage of the anguish they had caused our family. I had heard that after the television shows of 1974, Kaufman couldn't even go to a party without people starting to argue with him about the Rosenberg case. My grandmother had demanded to look into his eyes when she and my aunts came to beg him to reduce my parents' sentence in late 1952. He had refused and covered his face. I have always believed that that gesture indicated that he was vulnerable—that his facade of judicial rectitude and self-assuredness was very thin. I hoped he could hear Robby's and my voices over the bullhorn in his air-conditioned chambers surrounded by the awards he had received for all his years of "service." I knew he could *feel* our presence, and though it really wasn't advancing the struggle to open the files and vindicate our parents, I enjoyed the thought of his discomfort.

Back at the offices of our lawyer, Marshall Perlin (known as "Mike"), I learned that a number of past presidents of the Bar Association of the City of New York had issued a statement condemning unfounded attacks upon Judge Kaufman and defending the correctness of the judicial proceedings that had been held in my parents' case. A *New York Post* reporter called me and asked to confirm that I had called Kaufman a murderer the night before. The tone of the question and reiteration that "we have it on very good authority" signaled to me that the reporter thought they had caught me doing something I shouldn't have. I sidestepped the question by referring to the Gordon Dean quote in the *Newsday* article and stating that I had until then never dreamed Kaufman had done *illegal* things but merely that he had been biased and unfair. I must have been convincing because the article, when finally written, didn't deal with that issue at all. But when I got off the phone, Mike Perlin chastized me for my statement the night before. "Do you know that 'the judge' was Kaufman?" "He only agreed to give the death sentence *if the evidence warrants it.*" That stopped me. Morton Sobell had once told me, "We always have been very careful to claim only what we know for certain. We can't afford to go off half-cocked because the Establishment will shoot us down." In other words, our side in the dispute cannot jump to conclusions. Every step in our arguments must be clearly demonstrable so that no smart media manipulator can disparage it. Mike Perlin said to me, "I don't want to stifle you, but you've got to be careful to be able to back up everything you

say. This Bar Association thing is just the beginning of their counter-
attack." I realized he was right. When I'd given speeches at colleges
and been on talk shows, I had been extremely careful to keep to the
research work done by the Schneirs and Wexley and the information in
the documentary "The Unquiet Death of Julius and Ethel Rosenberg."
I had bent over backwards to present pro-government counterargu-
ments. Somehow, in the context of the meeting with a friendly crowd,
flushed with the publication of the series of articles in *Newsday,* I had
overstepped the evidence. I resolved from that point forward to use the
same standards in speeches and the media that I would use if submitting an article to a scholarly journal.

The Discovery and Publication of The Kaufman Papers

A year later, I got a chance to do just that. While on tour in May of
1976 publicizing the paperback edition of this book, I discovered that
the first batch of FBI papers that we had obtained in February were
revealing a lot about the activities of Judge Kaufman—here explicitly
mentioned by name. Our lawyers, together with the staff of the National Committee to Reopen the Rosenberg Case, hastily prepared a
statement and arranged a press conference. Robby and I were briefed
over the phone and we pulled out all of our media contacts to see if we
might get full coverage, even on television. On June 10, thirty FBI
documents which we published as *The Kaufman Papers* were released.

Here was vindication not only of my parents' intuition but of my
charges of the previous year that had "jumped the gun." "The judge"
in Gordon Dean's diary became Judge Kaufman or often "Irving" in the
memos of some high FBI officials. The actions ranged from agreeing
to give the death sentence before the trial was over to interfering with
the appeals process. In general the papers show a judge who had
stripped himself of his impartiality and enlisted on the prosecution's
team—who became, in the words of Harvard Law School professor
Vern Countryman, "a judge obsessed with protecting the verdict, judgment and sentence entered in the trial over which he presided, and with
stifling criticism of that trial—and driven by his obsession to conduct
which would *not be acceptable from a prosecuting attorney* much less
a judicial officer."

Before I go further into what *The Kaufman Papers* say and mean, it is essential to clear up something. Many of the FBI documents represent hearsay: some FBI agent says Kaufman said something; sometimes an FBI agent reports what somebody else told him Kaufman said. Thus, these papers are not definitive *proof* of anything. It is important to say that these documents *if true* represent evidence of illegal, or at least improper, behavior and would warrant an impeachment inquiry. Impeachment inquiries themselves *do not presume guilt.*

Some of the papers are not hearsay, but letters written by Judge Kaufman and Prosecutor Saypol. I consider them direct evidence, but even there the signatures would have to be verified on the originals. In fact, that is why our lawyers sent Kaufman a set of the papers and asked him to make his personal records (logs of phone calls, visits, etc.) available so these could be checked. They also invited him to comment or respond. We thought then and still think now that only a Congressional investigation that would compel Judge Kaufman to respond to the implications of these documents would ultimately determine the veracity of our charges. However, one reason why I believe these files reflect the truth is because the FBI did not think there was anything wrong with what Kaufman was doing. These files were not attempts to "get dirt" on someone the FBI considered an enemy. Thus, it is hard to believe the FBI would create files to damage Judge Kaufman. In fact, Kaufman had a friendship with J. Edgar Hoover that went back before his tenure as a judge. Nevertheless, the reader should remember the statement that these documents indicate certain things *if they are true.* I will not repeat this caveat in the following analysis, though the reader should keep it in mind. I should also make it clear that I believe these documents *do* indicate what happened, that the facts as reported *are true.*

Since 1976, the original thirty documents have been supplemented by new discoveries. I think it is valuable for the purposes of analysis to group the Kaufman document into three categories of actions: (1) improper behavior by Judge Kaufman relating to the sentencing; (2) improper and at times apparently illegal activities in the course of the various appeals; and (3) improper activities in relation to public discussion and commentary on the case.

The Sentencing

Before the defense had presented its case, the FBI learned that Raymond Whearty, a high official in the Department of Justice, "knew" Kaufman would sentence my father to death "if he doesn't change his mind." This is excellent confirmation that "the judge" in the Gordon Dean diary was in fact Judge Kaufman, because Whearty had been instrumental in setting up that February 8 meeting that led to McInerney's talk with "the judge" that was recorded in Dean's diary. In an award-winning series of articles about *The Kaufman Papers,* a law school newspaper queried whether this might not be an indication that the judge was biased at the time of the trial and thus should have disqualified himself. This point becomes especially important later on because Judge Kaufman continued to rule on motions for a new trial until 1956.

When the verdicts were in, before imposing sentence, Judge Kaufman stated from the bench, "Because of the seriousness of this case and the lack of precedence I have refrained from asking the government for a recommendation." It would appear that Judge Kaufman did secretly ask Assistant U.S. Attorney Roy M. Cohn, two other judges, and Prosecutor Saypol for recommendations. Asking prosecutors *without the presence of the defense attorney* is a violation of the canons of judicial ethics. The reason this prohibition is in the canons is to guarantee that any evidence that prosecutors might bring to the judge can be rebutted by defense counsel.

The intent of these canons is clear. Judges should not permit themselves to be influenced by one side in a judicial proceeding without letting the other side have equal access and the opportunity to counter whatever is said. In this situation, Kaufman apparently used the secret contacts with the government to keep from the defense a very important fact: the prosecutors were divided as to whether or not my mother should get the death sentence.

According to the FBI, Assistant U.S. Attorney Cohn advised against sentencing my mother to death. If Manny Bloch had been present when that discussion occurred, he could have made the point at the sentencing hearing that some prosecutors did not desire the death penalty for my mother. Another fact Manny might have learned is that, according to his own account, Prosecutor Saypol, at the request of

Judge Kaufman, may have sounded out officials of the Justice Department and J. Edgar Hoover as to what they wished him to recommend, and there was conflict there as well. Hoover agreed with Cohn that my mother should not be executed, but that Mort Sobell should be. With the differing opinions of various prosecutorial officials, Manny could have made an irresistible argument against imposing the death penalty on my mother.

Thus, the apparent violation of the rules of the game by Kaufman is not a mere technical violation signifying nothing. When he told the prosecutor to refrain from making a recommendation and then from the bench asserted that he had not asked for such a recommendation, he was not only speaking falsely, he had acted in such a way as to preclude a proper defense presentation of the reasons why he should not impose the death penalty.

Interfering with the Appeals Process

After the initial trial verdict was affirmed on appeal, my parents and Mort Sobell filed motions for a hearing based on new evidence under section 2255, one in late 1952, the second in June of 1953 (see the chronology above, p. xxxi and pp. 188–93). Mort filed three such motions in 1956, 1959 and 1966. Judge Kaufman heard the 1953 motion from my parents as well as the 1956 motion from Morton.

When any defendant goes before a judge, our legal system guarantees that the judge must act as an impartial arbiter, fairly dispensing the law to all. In fact, the fairness and impartiality of the judiciary is considered one of the keys to the Anglo-Saxon system of justice. Unlike totalitarian societies where the courts are mere instruments of the state, our society is supposed to be a government of laws rather than of individual people. Even the president of the United States is subject to the law, as Richard Nixon discovered to his everlasting regret in 1974. If a judge feels it impossible to impartially pass on the legal merits of a motion because of personal feelings, prejudices, etc., about either of the parties appearing to contest the issue, then the judge is duty bound to disqualify him- or herself from hearing those motions. My parents succeeded in getting Kaufman to disqualify himself on the 1952 motion, but after that the chief judge ruled that Kaufman would hear all future Rosenberg petitions.

With this as background, let us consider the events of January and February 1953. My parents' first motion for a new trial had been denied by both the District Court and the Court of Appeals. After denying the motion to reduce our parents' sentences on January 2, 1953, Kaufman had stayed execution until after the consideration of my parents' clemency petition so long as there were no motions pending anywhere (see above, p. 177). Behind the scenes, he was trying to rush the process along. According to the FBI, at Kaufman's request Assistant U.S. Attorney Kilsheimer

> called Pardon Attorney Dan A. Lyons . . . and asked when Lyons would get the Application for Pardon papers to the President. . . . Lyons indicated it would be at least three weeks. . . . Kilsheimer stated that it was desired that the matter be expedited. Lyons advised Kilsheimer that no one could get this matter expedited unless he was directed to do so by the Attorney General or the President.
>
> Kilshemer furnished this info to Judge Kaufman and thereafter Judge Kaufman called someone in the Department in an effort to get this matter expedited.

On February 11, less than two weeks later, Eisenhower denied clemency, so Judge Kaufman may well have influenced the speed with which this request was processed. He then fixed the execution for the week of March 9, only to be thwarted when the Court of Appeals granted a stay on February 17 (see above, p. 187). On February 19, Kaufman contacted the special agent in charge of the New York FBI field office, Mr. Boardman. What follows is a quote from Boardman's memo to the file:

> Judge Kaufman then went on to say "I would like to see the Department of Justice take a firm stand on this matter and appeal directly to the Supreme Court for an immediate decision." He stated the Department has already taken a very strong stand with the President and that the President had already declined Presidential pardon. Judge Kaufman then commented he can foresee that this case can go over until fall. . . . I asked Judge Kaufman if he desired that I bring his comments to the attention of the officials in Washington. He stated he didn't think it would be desirable for there to be any indication that he was taking an affirmative position in instant matter because of his judicial situation. He then stated

"I think what I will do is go to Assistant U.S. Attorney Kilsheimer and suggest the possibility to him that the U.S. Attorney's Office move aggressively in this matter."

It is clear from this that Judge Kaufman was acting as a member of the prosecution team. It is also clear that he knew what he was doing was improper.

There are two reasons why he opposed delay. On the record, he stated to Boardman that during "the intervening period of time, the propagandists would have an excellent opportunity to completely air the entire matter." In other words, Kaufman was in tune with the political aspects of my parents' case. He knew that delays in the execution would permit further momentum in the clemency campaign to be built up. Perhaps he also believed that when my parents were ultimately confronted with the fact that all hope was gone unless they cooperated they would at that point confess and begin to name names. Second, I believe he was aware of how weak the case was and was afraid that either the Supreme Court or Eisenhower would yield to the mounting pressure. I think he knew how much his handling of the trial had overstepped the bounds of fairness and was afraid of what a full Supreme Court review of the record would bring. * His coaching of the government to help speed the appeal through the Supreme Court before adjournment for the summer recess was, in my opinion, an effort to immunize his own personal conduct and the sentence from the full scrutiny of the higher courts.

Less than four months later, he was to sit in judgment as the motion described above (pp. 192–93) was argued before him. He should have disqualified himself from hearing that motion. Instead he received the papers Friday, heard oral arguments on Monday, and denied the motion in an opinion he had written before hearing the oral arguments. A year after the first release of *The Kaufman Papers,* we discovered a new document that indicated that the FBI had briefed Judge Kaufman about some of this new evidence almost a month before the motion was filed before him. Probably that is one of the reasons he was able to come up with his reasoning denying the motion so quickly!

---

* After the execution, Justice Black reminded everyone of a fact that has been conveniently forgotten by pro-government commentators on the case: "This Court has never reviewed this record and has never affirmed the fairness of the trial below."

From 1953 to 1969, Mort Sobell remained in jail. But he never gave up trying to force a new hearing and a new trial. If our side had had the opportunity to put Greenglass and Gold back on the witness stand anytime after 1951 as the new evidence was uncovered and to confront them with what had been discovered proving they committed perjury at the trial, we would have blown the government's case out of the water. One such possibility arose as a result of Mort's first motion for a new trial after our parents were executed. According to an FBI memo, before he had heard oral argument, "Kaufman . . . indicated that if the motion comes before him, he will deny the motion without a hearing." It did come before him and after putting Mike Perlin (then Mort's attorney) through futile hours of oral arguments he denied the motion, not permitting them to subpeona any witnesses.

In 1957, the Supreme Court ruled that using a defendant's prior assertion of the privilege against self-incrimination provided by the Fifth Amendment to suggest guilt or attack credibility when testifying at the trial was such an extreme error as to require setting aside the conviction. At the trial, my mother was subjected to a long string of such questions by both Judge Kaufman and Prosecutor Saypol. Mort therefore asked the Supreme Court to reconsider their earlier denial of a review. Kaufman expressed concern to the FBI. In 1962, Mort went further. The same legal point had been raised in the District Court and was then on appeal before the Court of Appeals. Kaufman had been promoted to the Court of Appeals, so he was no longer able to sit on the motion. The panel of judges included Thurgood Marshall, later to be named to the Supreme Court.

During the discussion with the attorneys, Judge Marshall asked, "If Ethel Rosenberg were tried, say last spring, and we had her conviction before this court today, wouldn't we have to reverse on the authority of Grunewald [the case described above]?" The U.S. attorney stated, "This court would probably have to rule in favor of the defendant." I remember reading about that exchange in the *National Guardian* in 1962. Somehow the FBI reporter or Judge Kaufman (I'm not sure who is at fault) mis-stated the question as applying to Sobell: "If Sobell had been tried last spring and we had him before us today, wouldn't it be necessary for the Court to reverse the decision, particularly in view of the Grunewald decision?"

According to the FBI document, the U.S. attorney's response was,

"Probably." Judge Kaufman was furious and told C. D. DeLoach, one of Hoover's top lieutenants, that this was a "stupid" response, that this might be the "straw that breaks the camel's back and . . . obtains Sobell's freedom." He suggested the FBI might want to acquaint the Justice Department with this serious turn of events. Finally, according to the FBI, Kaufman stated he "raised Hell with Thurgood Marshall inasmuch as he considered Marshall to be somewhat naive and certainly inexperienced on the bench."

Now this stopped me. Here is an Appeals Court judge browbeating another Appeals Court judge who is in the process of making a determination about the first judge's actions. This interference can be interpreted as obstruction of justice. It also worked. When the decision was handed down, the Court of Appeals panel (Judge Marshall included) claimed that the Grunewald precedent could only have applied to my mother, not to Mort Sobell. Since she was safely dead, there were no grounds for a new hearing.

Kaufman had told the FBI that the Grunewald decision "is not good law and certainly does not apply to this case." * The Appeals Court ruling accepted at least the second part of Kaufman's statement.

Behind the Scenes

In addition to improper (and at times illegal) activities in his judicial capacity, Kaufman was a very active participant in the larger political issues created by this case. Around the same time he was coaching the FBI and Justice Department on how to speed the clemency decision by President Eisenhower and the consideration of the stay by the Supreme Court (January-February 1953), he attempted to browbeat Manny Bloch into controlling the activities of the National Committee to Secure Justice in the Rosenberg Case. On February 14, in open court, "He reminded Bloch that he was an officer of the Court and had a duty to the Court and wanted to know if the half truths and untruths that the Committee was publishing had been approved or considered by Bloch and admonished Bloch that he had the obligation to tell the committee when it was in error."

---

*This prompted Professor Countryman to observe to a Yale Law School audience that this is the first time he had ever heard of an Appeals Court judge overruling the Supreme Court!

He even pressed Manny on the sources of his fees because some of the money had been raised by the committee. This bullying pattern had, of course, begun with the trial. Manny had been decorous, respectful, a dignified "officer of the Court" in a losing battle to develop some sympathy from the jury and/or judge to protect my parents from the death penalty. Unfortunately, with hindsight it is clear that when you are before a biased judge who conducts the trial in an obviously partisan fashion and seeks to intimidate and push around defense counsel, such a tactic is bound to fail. The tactics of radical lawyers in the 1960s and early '70s, particularly in the Chicago Conspiracy Trial of 1969–70, proved more effective in exposing the bias of the judge and in presenting a defense. Nevertheless, given the temper of the early 1950s, it is possible that all Manny would have gotten for his pains would have been a long prison sentence for contempt of court.

But Kaufman was also at work behind the scenes. After my parents' execution and in fact continuing at least until 1975, there was a constant stream of commentary between Kaufman and the FBI about articles and other public actions relating to the Rosenberg-Sobell case. Contrary to the assertions of his defenders and of Kaufman himself that he never comments on cases he has dealt with, in 1956 he prepared a detailed rebuttal of a letter published in the (British) *Manchester Guardian* by Bertrand Russell. He sent this in memorandum form to Herbert B. Swope. Included in the memo was an argument that has since been used repeatedly. At the trial, Manny had followed the tactic described above right up to the end of the trial. He thanked Judge Kaufman for "treating defense counsel with utmost courtesy . . ." and conducting the trial "like an American judge." This has been translated into Manny giving his blessings to the trial as a fair trial. Nothing could be further from the truth. At the time of his death, Manny was facing disbarment proceedings because of the statement about animals he made on the day of executions and other "intemperate" remarks at my parents' funeral.

Kaufman continued his public display of silence in 1957 when he wrote to Attorney General Brownell (a year after preparing the memo to Swope), "I have not uttered a word—as indeed I should not—in answer to these horribly concocted Communist charges concerning my conduct in the trial. . . . I have observed that over the past year or so this propaganda has become intensified and it has been a frustrating experience to feel that no one was making a reply to these accusations. . . ." Note the continuation of the pattern established in the FBI memo of February 19, 1953. He works behind the scenes but he doesn't even want the Justice Department to know. So he fibs a little to Brownell while working diligently with the FBI to (a) help reporters write stories favorable to the government side in my parents' case and (b) make sure pro-Sobell, pro-Rosenberg comments from people like Dr. Harold Urey are answered quickly and decisively. The latter exercise is clearly set out in a memo of February 17, 1955: "Judge Irving Kaufman is very proud of his counteraction of Dr. Harold C. Urey's statement last Saturday night. He talked to General Sarnoff of the Radio Corporation of America (RCA) and last night . . . a total listening audience of some 25,000,000 . . ." had been treated to Kaufman's rebuttal masquerading as news reporting over that network. The memo continued, "Irving is all steamed up to do a lot more to counteract some of the so-called intellectuals." The writer of this memo, L. B. Nichols, seems to have been on a friendly, first-name basis with Kaufman. In the same memo, he noted that he warned the judge that the newly formed Fund for the Republic (later to become known as the Center for the Study of Democratic Institutions) would "probably be probing around on the Rosenberg case. . . . Irving . . . stated something would have to be worked out. He is going to see what he can do with a few of his friends in New York."

Need I remind the reader that in 1956, one year after this memo was written, Judge Kaufman put on his "other hat" as an impartial judge and ruled on Mort Sobell's motion for a new trial? In rendering that decision, he made the following statement from the bench:

> During the course of my deliberations on this matter as any other matters involved in this case from its inception, there have been many attempts to bring extra-judicial utterances and actions to my attention. Many of these have been designed to influence judicial determination in a way that is alien to our judicial process—and in some instances they constituted a subtle attack upon it. Freedom of Speech should and does permit untrammeled discussion and differences of opinion, but judicial impartiality required that the courts be free from extraneous and conflicting pressures—these procedures and safeguards have been the sole guideposts of this court.

In 1955, John Wexley's *The Judgement of Julius and Ethel Rosenberg* was published. The FBI reviewed it as it was coming from the printers, as did Kaufman. Kaufman later (in the above-mentioned letter to the attorney general) commended Brownell for assigning Benjamin Pollock, a Justice Department attorney, to write a definitive rebuttal to Wexley. Later, it appeared that the writer and columnist Jim Bishop had taken up the task of writing a book on the case. Due to FBI–Justice Department rivalry, the FBI was not involved with Bishop because he was using Pollock's work. Kaufman was concerned and tried to hasten the book's completion. Bishop ultimately abandoned the project in 1959. Earlier, Kaufman had tried to enlist J. Edgar Hoover in an effort to dissuade Bishop from meeting with Helen Sobell to hear her side of the story.

And on and on it goes. In 1969, the play *The United States versus Julius and Ethel Rosenberg*, based on the trial record, opened in Cleveland. Kaufman expressed concern that the *New York Times* had reviewed it two weeks in succession. The FBI dug up whatever dirt they could on the writer and forwarded it to Kaufman. This prompted what we called the "Dear Edgar . . . Love, Irving" letter in the original Kaufman papers.

Robby always was very impressed with this point when he spoke: "Kaufman got Hoover to do legwork for him because some writer had the nerve to use the First Amendment rights of free speech to put on a play with a different point of view from Kaufman."

Even as late as 1974 and 1975, when the National Committee to Reopen the Rosenberg Case was formed and when the Public Television documentary had just thrust the case back into the public eye, Judge Kaufman was involved in behind-the-scenes efforts, together with the FBI, to counteract the rising tide of debate. "Judge Kaufman advised that Simon H. Rifkind . . . was preparing an article which would appear in TV Guide and stated 'they' would attempt to get the article in 'The New York Times.'" The FBI arranged for the article to be distributed to all the field offices for use in response to inquiries or complaints they might receive on the case. *TV Guide* gave the FBI reprint rights for free. Ultimately, the article or a variation of it appeared on the Op-Ed page of newspapers all over the country.

In 1975, the committee had been functioning for a year. A full-page ad was set to appear in the *New York Times* demanding the FBI open its

CHAMBERS OF
IRVING R. KAUFMAN
CIRCUIT JUDGE

May 7, 1969

Dear Edgar:

Thank you so much for your letter of May 2, furnishing me with the background information of the gentleman responsible for writing the play, "The United States v. Julius and Ethel Rosenberg."

I believe you will be interested in seeing a copy of a letter sent by former Federal Judge Simon Rifkind to The New York Times concerning their extensive reporting of this play.

With my gratitude and affection, I am

Sincerely yours,

Irving R. Kaufman
United States Circuit Judge

Enclosure

The Honorable John Edgar Hoover
Director, Federal Bureau of Investigation
United States Department of Justice
Washington, D. C. 20535

files. The first edition of this book was coming out. *Esquire* published an article about the jury in my parents' case as well as a short side-bar interview with Robby and me. Kaufman phoned Assistant Director W. LaPrade. He expressed concern about the *Esquire* article, the actions of the committee, and "he emphasized he thought that a counter-move should be taken. He alluded to the fact that during the days of J. Edgar Hoover there were many such actions taken and he understands that the FBI today is not as aggressive. . . . He volunteered that if he could ever do anything with the Department to provide support in these matters he would not hesitate to call Deputy Attorney General Tyler." *

The Kaufman-LaPrade phone call produced the most recently dated Kaufman document we have so far received from the FBI. We later learned that in the summer of 1975, while we were preparing to file our lawsuit which ultimately forced the FBI to release what later became *The Kaufman Papers,* Kaufman had been in touch with Tyler and reportedly cautioned him about releasing documents. This is consistent with Kaufman's knowledge that what he was doing was not right (see above, p. 374). He was clearly worried.

The Establishment Circles the Wagons

Even before the Kaufman papers were released, Kaufman's buddy and former judicial colleague Simon Rifkind set up a three-man subcommittee of the American Bar Association to "review and evaluate current charges being made with respect to the trial of Julius and Ethel Rosenberg. . . . To scrutinize the unfolding publicity . . . to make certain that public support for law and for the judicial process is not subverted by unfounded charges . . . to counteract unwarranted criticism directed to . . . Judge Irving R. Kaufman." The ABA in its press release went on to echo a familiar theme of Rifkind's: Kaufman's "conduct of the trial has been more extensively and more carefully scrutinized by the appellate courts than any other case in American history. It has been found flawless."

---

* Deputy Attorney General Tyler was a former District Court judge under Kaufman. In an interesting coincidence, he was the District Court judge who was first assigned our lawsuit against Louis Nizer. He dismissed half of it without letting us examine Nizer under oath. (See Meeropol *vs.* Nizer 73 CIV 2720.) In his role as Deputy Attorney General, he became one of the defendants in our Freedom of Information Act lawsuit.

This last point is not true. Only one court, the first three-judge panel on the Court of Appeals, scrutinized Kaufman's conduct. In every case that has ever been reviewed by the Supreme Court, the trial judge has had more scrutiny than Kaufman, because in accepting cases for review the Supreme Court actually reviews the record of the original trial. Even at the Appeals Court level, Kaufman's conduct was not considered so flawless by the judge who wrote the opinion. A former student of his once told me the opinion writer, Judge Jerome N. Frank, felt too vulnerable to dissent from the majority who wanted to uphold the conviction, so he instead wrote the opinion putting arrows as it were to certain areas which he felt only the Supreme Court had the prestige and independence to use as a basis for overturning the conviction. Of particular note is his reference to Kaufman's admission of testimony about Communist party membership: "This Court and others have recognized that the Communist label yields marked ill-will for its American wearer. . . . Whether and how much of this kind of evidence should come into a trial like this is a matter for carefully-exercised judicial discretion. We think the trial judge here did not abuse that discretion. Each time party membership was alluded to, and again in his final charge, the judge cautioned the jurors 'not to determine the guilt or innocence of a defendant on whether or not he is a Communist.' It may be that such warnings are no more than an empty ritual without any practical effect on the jurors."

This is the same Judge Frank who cried at his impotence on the day of my parents' death because, though the point before him had legal merit, he felt constrained not to intervene (see above, p. 234). Later, it was his dissent in Grunewald *vs.* U.S. that the Supreme Court upheld, making the cross-examination of my mother the basis for a new trial. Though the Appeals Court held that Grunewald applied only to my mother, not to Sobell, it provides total refutation of the Bar Association point. Frank's dissent in Grunewald (which the Supreme Court upheld) could have been written about Kaufman's questioning of my mother!

Aside from the Bar Association committee's reasoning, the formation of the committee just two months after the first major batch of FBI documents became available to us, but before we had actually paid for our copies, raises an interesting question. Did Rifkind know about *The Kaufman Papers* before we released them? The day of the release, the

New York Post chose not to attend the press conference but was able to headline its article, "Rifkind Rebuts Rosenberg Charges." Later, in an interview with *Juris Doctor* Rifkind defended Kaufman. His tack was either to deny the veracity of the implications of some documents ("triple hearsay," "courtroom gossip") or to claim that there was and is nothing improper about the various activities described in the papers. It is interesting that the Bar Association panel never publicly released their response to *The Kaufman Papers*. The *New York Times* obtained a copy in September of 1983 and wrote a news article about it indicating the committee bought Rifkind's line. Kaufman himself knew better, as evidenced by the request to the FBI that they not let the Justice Department know of his involvement because of his "judicial situation." The ABA committee and Rifkind have never publicly responded to the import of that February 19 Boardman memo.

Meanwhile, for the most part the media has been extremely reluctant to go digging around to either confirm or refute the implications of the documents. From the day we released *The Kaufman Papers*, we knew that the journalistic and legal establishment of New York had decided to close ranks behind Kaufman. No investigation was launched by any of the self-policing agencies of the Bar. After that first day, the story disappeared from the mainstream newspapers. Dorothy Schiff, publisher of the *New York Post*, was actually quoted as saying that Judge Kaufman was a family friend and would never be the subject of a derogatory article in her paper. I was outraged but not surprised. Here was a judicial Watergate in which people actually died and the media was playing deaf, dumb and blind.

Perhaps the most remarkable document involved even more powerful figures than Judge Kaufman. There was evidence in one of the documents that the chief justice of the U.S. Supreme Court, Fred Vinson, had agreed with Attorney General Brownell that if Douglas were to grant the stay on June 17, 1953, he would call the Court back into special session to vacate it. We were amazed. If this actually occurred, one could say "a fix was in" at the Supreme Court, as one of our attorneys put it. Not one newspaper article that dealt with *The Kaufman Papers* mentioned this incredible meeting. Here was the chief justice of the United States agreeing with the chief law enforcement officer of the United States to vacate a stay of execution that had not yet been granted without reading the opinion of his colleague. By now, my capacity for outrage should be exhausted, yet it never fails to amaze me how the news media follow the theme that historian William A. Williams stated in his comments on the first edition of this book: "Reveal as Little of the Truth as Is Necessary to Save the Establishment."

Still Waiting for Justice

A group of law professors headed by Vern Countryman of Harvard Law School wrote to the House and Senate Judiciary committees about the Kaufman documents, and the National Committee to Reopen the Rosenberg Case engaged in lobbying efforts. Ultimately, Congressman John Conyers (D. Michigan) hosted a briefing for Congressional staffers at which Professor Countryman presented the case against Kaufman as evidenced from the documents. Nothing further came of it. Without the groundswell of public opinion that forced Congress to act on Nixon's impeachment, that was as far as we got.

In late 1976, one of Professor Countryman's co-signers attempted to get the American Civil Liberties Union to come out for a Congressional investigation of Judge Kaufman. Simon Rifkind pulled out all of the stops to block the action, and for a time it appeared he had succeeded in convincing a majority of the ACLU board that Judge Kaufman's actions had been "flawless." Our committee responded by sending every member of the board a copy of *The Kaufman Papers* and a rebuttal of Rifkind's arguments. In March 1977, the ACLU adopted a resolution asking Congress to investigate Kaufman's contacts with the prosecutors to see if legislation would be necessary to prevent such actions. It was somewhat wishy-washy but it did imply Kaufman had done something wrong. The *New York Times* weighed in with an editorial that didn't deal with any of the Kaufman documents but instead attacked the ACLU for implying the Rosenberg case was tainted without presenting new evidence. We had to raise over $16,000 to take out a full-page ad reprinting some of the documents to get the facts behind the attack on Kaufman before the *Times'* readers. They had not printed any articles about either Professor Countryman's letter or any of the other issues before the ACLU about Judge Kaufman. Again, my mind continued to boggle at the duplicity of the "free press."

Personal Confrontations

In June of 1977, our committee was again back at Foley Square. That very day, a man named Pedro Archuleta was being hauled before a Grand Jury ostensibly looking into some terrorist bombings carried out by a Puerto Rican nationalist group called the FALN. In fact, the Grand Jury was seeking to tar the radical Hispanic movement with the terrorist brush by interrogating anyone involved in Hispanic struggles. Just the fact of the interrogation makes a connection in the minds of the public—with a little help from the media! It was a typical fishing expedition. None of the people called before grand juries were indicted for participation in the bombings. The purpose of harassing Hispanic independence groups and drying up their support from religious organizations was very clear. Two of the people subpoenaed and later jailed for refusing to answer questions were involved in the Episcopal church's Hispanic section.

Radicals have learned that one must be silent before grand juries. My mother had been a case in point. She took the Fifth Amendment before the Grand Jury and that was used against her at the trial to imply she was hiding something from the Grand Jury. Our committee's demonstration was joined by members of the Grand Jury Project who were seeking to support people who refused to cooperate with these fishing expeditions. Our speakers constantly reminded the lunchtime crowd through the inevitable bullhorn that my mother trusted the grand jury system and look what happened to her. One slogan was, "No more Rosenbergs, stop the Grand Jury." This was an example of what Robby and I had been hoping for since the very first Carnegie Hall event three years earlier: to use the example of my parents' case to support current struggles against repressive government activities.

We also raised the bullhorn until it faced the upper floors of the imposing courthouse and read sections of *The Kaufman Papers* to the lunchtime strollers, news media, and, we hoped, Judge Kaufman. Justice Saypol of the New York State Supreme Court had since died but not before being indicted for influence peddling unrelated to our case. We were sorry he had gotten away before being fully exposed. It had been a year since *The Kaufman Papers* had been released, a year since we had sent Judge Kaufman the material and asked him to respond. It was time to go even further. Accompanied by Mike Perlin and tingling with anticipation (I don't believe it was fear), we took the elevator to the eighteenth floor and asked to see Judge Kaufman. The secretary dialed the number. I got on the phone with one of the judge's law clerks.

My fears at speaking to a Very Important Person evaporated and my anger took over. "My name is Michael Meeropol. I sent Judge Kaufman a number of FBI documents over a year ago and he has not responded to them. I wish to see him to get his response." There was a pause at the end of the line.

"Judge Kaufman is a very busy man."

"That's not good enough. I've waited over a year for some response and I think he at least owes me that."

Now he got indignant. "You can't just walk off the street and see a Federal Appeals Court Judge." (I envisioned him speaking in capital letters as he said this.)

"All right. How about this? I'll give you my phone numbers and address and you tell me when Judge Kaufman *can* see me."

Then I slowly, meticulously, gave my phone numbers and address. To top it off, we sent him a registered letter confirming my request for an interview with him. He never answered. He did tell a writer from the *New York Times* that "the Rosenberg Committee has joined forces with the FALN," at the demonstration outside Foley Square. (Note how the defense of a person's right to remain silent before a Grand Jury is interpreted as support for a terrorist organization.)

This last encounter was made especially significant for me when the next batch of FBI documents was released in February of 1978. A memo from the New York field office of the FBI dated January 18, 1952, stated: "Judge Kaufman informed me that . . . during the time the Rosenberg children were being handled by the Jewish Welfare Board they appeared to be in a very maladjusted state of mind. The older boy particularly seemed to have developed a complex and allegedly stated that he was going to devote his life to avenging his parents. Judge Kaufman was wondering whether he ought to send for the boys and talk with them." *

As I noted above (p. 29), I have always been drawn to themes in

---

*On the basis of my behavior since 1974 Judge Kaufman obviously believes that I have indeed devoted my life to avenging my parents. He once was described by someone who knows him as believing that I wake up every morning, look in the mirror and chant, "Kaufman! Kaufman! Kaufman!" Even now he has extraordinary delusions of grandeur.

literature and drama that relate to people being wronged and exacting revenge as in the song "Just You Wait." This quote is probably a totally correct assessment of my state of mind in 1952. The question is, How much desire for revenge is still left within me.

I have reread *The Count of Monte Christo* as an adult and remarked to myself that by the end of the book Edmund Dantes is not a particularly nice or happy person. He had heroic qualities while he was struggling for survival in prison and ultimately planning and making good his escape. By the time he had crushed all those who did him wrong, he had forfeited claims on humanity, and, not surprisingly, his victory had brought him no peace of mind. Intellectually, I knew that revenge was a stupid reason to do anything.

Yet, beneath all the civilized rationalizations and well-written arguments about why the Rosenberg case needed to be reopened, not as "a personal or historical exercise," but because of the political lessons it can bring us today, I must confess to feeling an animalistic desire for retribution. I do not believe in the retribution theory of punishment. That is in fact why I oppose capital punishment. Yet I sympathize with families of victims who cry out for vengeance. I guess I'll just have to admit a deep conflict between my thoughtful self and the strong feelings that were set at least as far back as 1952. Even then, however, my taste in vengeance is more intellectual than physical. I relish the thought of Kaufman's discomfort and of his possible exposure.

The Kaufman Papers also challenge another of my intellectual beliefs. I have always believed that history moves, by and large, as a result of the operation of structural forces. Historical actors, in Marx's words, "make their own history, but they do not make it just as they please; they do not make it under circumstances chosen by themselves, but under circumstances directly encountered, given and transmitted from the past. The tradition of all the dead generations weighs like a nightmare on the brain of the living."

Thus, I have always thought of my parents' case as an inexorable tragedy rather than a cheap melodrama of coincidences. I recall Jean Anoilh's *Antigone,* in which the chorus digresses on the difference between tragedy, where everything must happen and the audience knows it, and melodrama, where if only the car hadn't broken down at that moment, etc., then the outcome would have been different. *The Kaufman Papers* and all discoveries of new evidence in my parents' case always prompt a flash of longing. If only Kaufman's improper actions had leaked out before my parents' death, they would be alive today. I know these thoughts are stupid. My parents had much more than Judge Kaufman against them. Still and all, sometimes lying awake at night, I envision what a field day Manny Bloch would have had before the Court of Appeals if he had been able to attach *The Kaufman Papers* to his motions for a new trial. Make no mistake about it. The Kaufman documents bear directly on a key issue in my parents' case: did their trial prove them guilty beyond a reasonable doubt? Confronted by Kaufman with his obvious bias, unable in large part because of Kaufman's actions to challenge the prosecution with newly discovered evidence that the case was a fraud, my parents and Mort Sobell were railroaded in a totally tainted proceeding. Had Kaufman not done what he did, certainly there would have been further evidentiary hearings after the initial trial, and my parents might well be alive today.

But What Will Happen as a Result of These Revelations?

Our investigation of the role of Judge Kaufman has revealed a lot more than the utter corruption of the legal process in my parents' case. It also revealed that this case is still very important to some very powerful people—especially in the news media and established legal circles. All the wagons have been drawn up around Judge Kaufman, and I am sure that his death will bring forth near unanimous accolades from both quarters. This is particularly sad, not just because a man I consider a criminal is getting away. It is sad because his immunity is a signal to all judges that, no matter how flagrant their behavior, even if they are found out they will not be forced to account. President Nixon was held accountable, but it appears the judiciary will not be so held. This is the lesson of Judge Kaufman's successful avoidance of a reckoning. Just as he symbolically refused to see me, so he never publicly responds to charges. He probably is continuing to work behind the scenes but is not doing it with the FBI, whose papers are subject to the Freedom of Information Act. Even though I sometimes get discouraged, at least the record is here and available for anyone who wishes to see it. Maybe someday—sooner rather than later—enough people will embarrass Congress with questions that they will be forced to act. I won't hold my breath.

15

The Attempted Reconviction of
Our Parents: Toward a New Cold War

BY MICHAEL MEEROPOL

IN MAY OF 1975, Jerry and Adrienne Markowitz paid us a visit and told of a story that James Weinstein had told Ronald Radosh. Weinstein and Radosh had both distinguished themselves as left-wing historians in the 1960s. Jerry and I were acquainted with their work. I had met Radosh once at a National Committee meeting. The story went as follows: Once in late 1949, Weinstein, at the request of his roommate, Maxwell Finestone, had given my father a lift in his car from Ithaca, New York, to just outside New York City. Some months later, Finestone had moved in with Weinstein in New York. One night, my father came to the house looking for Finestone, who was not at home. When Finestone arrived home, he got very upset with the news and said something like my father should not have come. When Weinstein read of my father's arrest, he decided that "something" had been going on. His surmise was that perhaps there was some industrial espionage going on and that the government had seized upon this to concoct the atomic espionage fraud.

Up to that point, I had accepted the Schneirs' discussion of the alleged "other spy ring" in the first edition of *Invitation to an Inquest*. The involvement of people like Joel Barr and Anne Sidorovich was totally unsupported by any evidence save the Greenglasses' oral testimony. As I saw it, the Schneirs had meticulously pursued every possible piece of evidence about the alleged espionage activities of Barr, Sidorovich, Vivian Glassman, William Perl, Weldon Bruce Dayton and Alfred Sarant. Sarant and Barr had actually left the country, disappearing from contact with friends and relatives. Government apologists asserted or implied they had fled in fear of espionage prosecution. The

Schneirs had concluded that there was no evidence any of the above people were ever involved in espionage.

Some of Greenglass' trial testimony had been about an apartment in Greenwich Village, which the FBI quickly matched up with 65 Morton Street, the residence of Alfred Sarant, the target of an intensive FBI investigation from the early 1940s. Before Finestone had moved in with Weinstein in 1950, he had lived in that building.

Radosh had suggested to Jerry that there might be more to this than the Schneirs had found. I wondered about this and discussed it with Mike Perlin, who said the Weinstein story was evidence of nothing. I did begin to focus my thoughts, however, on the "other spy ring." This included wondering why Joel Barr and Alfred Sarant had left the country. About six months later, I received a call and visit from Alfred Sarant's son, Jeremy. He told me that in fact he and his mother had never heard a word about his father since he had left the country in 1951 in the company of Carol Dayton, the wife of their neighbor, Weldon Bruce Dayton. He wondered if I knew anything about his father's whereabouts. Of course, I didn't and when he met with the Schneirs they could tell him nothing more than what was in their book.

Did my complete faith in my parents' innocence get shaken by the Weinstein story? I believe that because I knew I had an emotional investment in my parents' innocence, I have been too prone to worry about any possible loose end that might suggest that something to support the government's contentions might be true. Thus, my first, rather simple response to the news from Radosh was to check the trial record and see if my father had been asked about and denied going to Ithaca. Though I had by then been speaking about the case for over a year and thought I knew the transcript very well, the "other spy ring" had never been the focus of my concern. I reasoned that denying such a trip would reduce my father's credibility. Asked about supposed trips to Schenectady and Cleveland to make contact with members of the spy ring, he had denied he had ever been to those places. However, on page 1198 of the trial record, I discovered my father not only admitted going to Ithaca but stated that he had gone to borrow money from Alfred Sarant. This convinced me that there was probably an innocent explanation to Weinstein's story, and my initial concern was reduced.

Enter Jerome Eugene Tartakow

That fall (1975), the first files from the FBI were released. The press immediately discovered that there had been a jailhouse informer, one Jerome Eugene Tartakow, supposedly talking to the FBI while housed together with my father before, during and shortly after the trial. Tartakow claimed that my father had confessed to him and revealed details about his far-flung espionage ring. Involved in the ring, according to Tartakow, were not only the people featured in the Schneirs' chapter—Sarant, Barr, Perl and Bruce Dayton—also included were James Weinstein and Maxwell Finestone. We found the Tartakow story incredible on its face. To believe him, you would have to believe that my father, who died rather than confess, who never said a word to his lawyer about his involvement, who never left any kind of message for Robby and me (so as to justify his actions to his sons, who would someday grow up to be adults), would confess to a total stranger while on trial for his life. I immediately recalled that when I interviewed my mother's psychiatrist and Mrs. Phillips while writing the first part of this book they both volunteered that they assumed every conversation they had in the prison was bugged. "Where are the recordings?" we used to ask if anyone brought up Jerome Eugene Tartakow.

However, we wanted to know exactly what Tartakow had allegedly told the FBI. Therefore, we amended our FOIA request to include the names of everyone mentioned by Tartakow as participants or even as possible participants in the Rosenberg spy ring. We were confident when we asked for the files that they would refute Tartakow. In fact, we already had in our possession a document that convinced me that Jerome Tartakow's story was a tissue of lies and half-truths and not the dramatic revelation forever convicting my father in the judgment of history. This document was the Justice Department's exhaustive summary of the evidence they had been able to obtain from all sources about the so-called spy ring. After years of investigation and analysis, the Justice Department concluded, "While certain of the information furnished by Tartakow has been corroborated, the majority has not." The report then went over every story Tartakow told the FBI and demonstrated how it had either been refuted or was impossible to verify. They even rejected calling a Grand Jury, granting some of the individuals immunity, and trying to force them to testify against each other under the threat of a contempt citation. After reading this report, I sincerely believed that no decent, objective researcher would ever take Tartakow seriously.

This is not to suggest that everything Tartakow told the FBI was untrue. It is certainly possible that my father was friendly with and talked to Tartakow in prison, just as he was friendly with and talked to Carl Marzani, Oscar Vago, Abraham Brothman, Eugene Dennis, and no doubt others.

In 1978, we became aware that Radosh and a journalist named Sol Stern had begun researching in the files. This led, in 1979, to the publication in the *New Republic* of "The Hidden Rosenberg Case," and finally, in 1983, to the release of *The Rosenberg File,* for which Radosh was joined by Joyce Milton. Jerry was in personal contact with Radosh and Stern and told me how they were gleefully reading and accepting Tartakow's nonsense. By the time they called Robby and me for an interview, we had decided that anything we would say to them would merely enhance their self-proclaimed status as impartial academic observers and seekers after truth. We declined to be interviewed. I did begin in 1979 and 1980 to research the files of the members in the so-called other spy ring in preparation for the publication of the book.

The "Selective Release" of the Material

Before going to the heart of the reconviction effort, let me first respond to one of the points initially raised in Radosh and Stern's *New Republic* article. They implied that Robby and I and others seeking to vindicate our parents had been "selectively releasing" the FBI documents rather than giving them the comprehensive analysis they deserved. In fact, interviewers have often asked me, "Why have you only selectively released documents?" My anwer to this is in two parts. First, there is a false premise involved. Robby and I were never in a position to "selectively release" anything. It is the FBI that has selectively released material—withholding over 100,000 pages on one premise or another as well as deleting significant passages from many of the documents that they did release. Every page available to us *has already been released.* The press, researchers, any citizen, in fact, can just walk into the FBI reading room in Washington and use the FBI files. Actually, the real meaning of the complaint is that we selectively publicized only those documents that supported our contentions. My answer is that, aside from the Tartakow material, those were the significant documents. Robby and I have responded to that material in print and speech ever since the fall of 1975. All of our written analyses and speeches have taken the government's case very seriously. All users of archives selectively quote from them. The honest historian seriously considers information that tends to cast doubt on the thesis proposed. The most serious challenge to our interpretation of the case was the Tartakow material. Nothing else in the FBI files provides independent corroboration of the oral testimony of David and Ruth Greenglass and Harry Gold. What is new and what we have publicized is evidence that the Greenglasses and Gold committed numerous perjuries at the trial.

The question still remains, Why have we not tried to put together a full-length monograph? The answer is that the files remain woefully incomplete. Thus, in our opinion, they do not deserve a full-length treatment unless one would be content with an ambiguous result. Among the many serious omissions has been the lack of any of the control files. These are the government's own internal administrative discussions of the case they were building. Other omissions have been the result of the FBI's selective destruction of documents and whole files that we suspect had information detrimental to the government's case. Robby's typical speech above already has mentioned the destruction of the Albuquerque file on David Greenglass. Even more important, the original handwritten notes taken by the FBI agents as they interviewed David Greenglass for the very first time about espionage have been destroyed. Thus, the file begins with the signed statement of June 15, 1950, in which he confesses and implicates Ruth Greenglass and my father. The absence of the FBI logs of the Greenglass interview means that we probably will never be able to prove that Greenglass was tricked or coerced into falsely confessing and implicating my father unless he and Ruth decide to tell the truth sometime before they die. (Given the relish with which they spoke to Radosh and Stern, I doubt they have ever considered "coming clean" as did the chief accuser of Captain Dreyfus in France.)

It thus became very apparent, even as we found little tidbits that confirmed our earlier charges about the perjury of the Greenglasses and Gold, that it would be impossible to write a complete history of the case from the government's files alone. In fact, by 1980, I had pretty much given up my initial naive hope that there would be some "smoking gun"—something like J. Edgar Hoover writing to some agents saying, "nice frame-up, guys!" The material we discovered about our mother's typing was pretty dramatic, and I did use that in a number of speeches as well as on "Good Morning America" the morning of June 19, 1978. Jerry and I summarized the argument in our article in *Science and Society.*

Similarly dramatic was the "I come from Julius" document, which made the front page of the *Los Angeles Times* in 1978. From the other side, the Tartakow revelations were considered dramatic. Yet before Radosh came on the scene, neither our side nor the other side felt that there was enough material in the files to make a definitive statement. I had thought historian Allen Weinstein, whose book *Perjury* had been based in part on the FBI's Alger Hiss files, was going to write a book on my parents, but he didn't. When you can't make such a total analysis, it is best not to try. We contented ourselves with pointing to the tidbits we had uncovered and insisting that the government release the tens of thousands of withheld pages. In December of 1982, I joined the Schneirs, Mike Perlin and Aaron Katz (the director of the National Committee to Reopen the Rosenberg Case) at a Congressional hearing asking for an official investigation by Congress into this case. Perhaps the current controversy will spur them to heed our request. At one point, Radosh wrote a letter to the *New York Times* calling for a full inquiry. I wonder if he still feels the same way.

The Rosenberg File: *A Trip through the Looking-Glass*

Then, in June of 1983, I obtained a set of galleys for the Radosh-Milton book. To understand how the book hit me, one has to understand what I expected from it. In the *New Republic* article it appeared that Stern and Radosh had concluded that our mother was framed (and the Greenglasses lied on the witness stand to accomplish this), and that our father was guilty of masterminding a post-World-War-II spy ring that included Sarant, etc. This "split the difference" judgment was supplemented by material Jerry and I had already collected and written up in *Science and Society* (though it was not published till a year later), proving, as Robby described above, that the government knowingly exaggerated the accuracy and significance of Greenglass' scientific information in order to get a death sentence against my father.

Thus, I felt that, while I disagreed with Radosh and Stern's conclusions, even if I were wrong and their charges about the post-World-War-II spy ring were true, that did not change the lack of credibility of the Greenglasses and Gold. In fact, I felt that their exposure of the Greenglasses as liars about my mother made it very difficult for them to maintain that they were telling the truth about my father. At a number of speeches, I bent so far backward that I admitted that it was even conceivable that their postwar spy-ring story might have something to it, though I hadn't seen any convincing evidence of that. Once, when I said this in the presence of a person for whom I have a great deal of respect who is also somewhat agnostic on my parents' case, he told me I was being too generous to Stern and Radosh. I knew. I was merely trying to compensate for my emotional desire for them to be totally wrong by forcing myself to examine as intellectually dispassionately as possible whether there could be anything to their charges. Thus, before I read the book, I was prepared to force myself to be open-minded about the so-called postwar spy ring. I was, however, totally unprepared for just how far Radosh and his new collaborator, Joyce Milton, would go to reconvict my parents.

The Rosenberg File aims to rehabilitate completely all of the government's contentions about my parents. Harry Gold and the Greenglasses were telling the truth. Even Elizabeth Bentley, the so-called "blonde spy queen" who had named scores of people as spies before a grand jury and had parlayed her story into a living by writing an autobiographical account of her years as a "spy," was telling the truth. Even though the typing evidence against my mother was created two weeks before the trial, Radosh and Milton concluded that the Greenglasses were probably telling the truth about her involvement. They even try to argue that the scientific evidence was not as worthless as our side had been saying.

As I read on, I became more and more incredulous. My mind boggled. Was it possible that any of this could be true? Here were unnamed Communists as well as ex-Communists John Gates and Junius Scales saying that in the 1950s they had no doubt my parents were spies. According to Radosh and Milton, Jerome Eugene Tartakow was corroborated when the FBI found a photographer who had taken passport photos of our entire family just weeks before my father's arrest. He was further corroborated in one of his most dramatic tales, a marathon photo-copying session in my family's apartment over some July 4 weekend, when the FBI discovered that one of the alleged participants in that session had checked out lots of classified documents from Columbia University's Pupin Laboratory over that weekend. They also argue that the trip from Ithaca that James Weinstein told Radosh about and the association of Maxwell Finestone with my father that Weinstein had observed corroborates Tartakow's stories to the FBI about my father's travels to Ithaca and his "recruiting" of Finestone.

Having finally and completely disposed of the question of guilt, Radosh and Milton then went on to describe the campaign to save my parents as a grisly dance to death in which the American Communist party and Manny Bloch connived to not permit a re-hearing in court, preferring to see my parents die rather than risk exposing the party and the larger espionage ring in further legal proceedings. As for my parents, according to Radosh and Milton's perverse reading of their prison letters, they engaged in political posturing of the worst sort and willingly died as "soldiers of Stalin." While hiding their guilt as spies, their letters, according to Radosh and Milton, reeked of ideology. *

Introduction to a Refutation

Before I begin an excursion through Radosh and Milton's book, it is important to clear up what I am trying to accomplish in this chapter. As I mentioned above, I do not feel that there is enough in the files to prove my parents were innocent. Even the material on my mother only proves she was framed. You can frame guilty people. Proving innocence is almost impossible, which is why our system of justice starts from a presumption of innocence until guilt is proven. Thus, I am at-

---

*Despite their nastiness about the published *Death House Letters,* Radosh and Milton assert in their bibliographical note that *We Are Your Sons* has an "unexpurgated" version of the letters. We leave it to the readers to decide if these letters reveal a "contempt for their countrymen . . ." displayed by "rigid self-righteous ideologues . . . reveling in the knowledge that they were earning for themselves a place in history." The letters above speak for themselves.

tempting not to prove my parents innocent but to demonstrate that
however "logical" Radosh and Milton's story might appear to some
people, that story is put together one of two ways. If one wishes to be
generous, one can say it is a terribly flawed work that avoids all evidence that would tend to contradict its conclusions. If one wishes to be
harsh, one can say that it is based on deliberate misrepresentation of
the material.

To demonstrate this, I am going to investigate the case that Radosh
and Milton make in their book. Aside from embellishing what Gold
and the Greenglasses said in the trial, their book weaves what many
observers have called a "web of circumstance." Each strand in this web
represents a "tidbit" of information gathered from either interviews or
the FBI files, particularly material from Tartakow. I propose to demonstrate that many of the most crucial new tidbits are based upon
misrepresentation of interviews, misrepresentation of the files, unwarranted conclusions drawn from the files and/or interviews, or assertions with no documentary record to back them up. I also propose to
demonstrate that in many cases Radosh and Milton totally ignored information that would tend to cast doubt on their conclusions. Unfortunately, this process involves what many people have dismissed as "nitpicking." But how else can we demonstrate that Radosh and Milton's
book is flawed? If, after all the "nits" are picked, there is nothing left
of Radosh and Milton's thesis, then we will have succeeded in our task.
People may still think Radosh and Milton are correct, but they cannot
find proof for that belief in *The Rosenberg File.*

Specifically, I will show that Radosh and Milton

1. provide no evidence for their assertion that my parents dropped
out of the Communist party in a manner that indicated they were
spies,

2. fail to rehabilitate the credibility of the Greenglasses, especially
in relation to the console table testimony,

3. are totally unconvincing in their attempts to paint Harry Gold as a
"functional," rather than a pathological, liar,

4. have ignored or distorted all evidence that casts doubt on Tartakow's credibility,

5. have distorted the record in their efforts to rehabilitate the credibility of Elizabeth Bentley and Max Elitcher.

A Significant First Example

Perhaps the most important indication of how Radosh and Milton planned to confront the issue of the Greenglasses' credibility is in the chapter that introduces the Greenglasses and my parents to the readers of *The Rosenberg File*. "Sometime late in [1943] . . . [Julius] and Ethel quietly dropped out of the Party activities that had been so important to them since they were teenagers. . . ." Thus begins a long discussion designed to support the Greenglass assertions at the trial that in 1943 my parents had dropped out of Communist party activities and gotten involved in espionage. What evidence do Radosh and Milton bring to bear on this important issue? The first point is that, though the FBI files clearly indicate my parents' membership in the Communist party in 1943 and though the FBI forwarded information (obtained in a burglary of a Communist party headquarters) as to my mother and father's transfer to a local neighborhood party club in 1944, Radosh and Milton assert with no supporting evidence that they both "failed to take up their new assignment." Instead, they claim that such "separation" from the Communist party "fit the pattern followed by those who were tapped for some form of secret work." They then quote three former Communist party functionaries about this pattern. Max Gordon, former writer and editor for the *Daily Worker,* is quoted as saying, "By and large anyone who became a spy for the Soviet Union was completely separated from the Party." Max Gordon has complained that this is an out-of-context answer to a hypothetical question because he never knew of or heard of anyone spying for the Soviets, but let us for a minute let that pass. Instead, let us recall that this is not evidence to support the assertion that our parents in fact quit the party. That has been assumed into the argument without any evidence, except of course the Greenglass trial testimony.

The next quote is from John Gates, former editor of the *Daily Worker,* and it is much stronger: "Julius Rosenberg was very active in City College . . . and one fine day he disappeared. We knew there was only one explanation . . . in our movement at the time. It could have been for only one reason." Radosh and Milton go on to tell their readers that Gates made clear espionage was the reason. This quote is very curious. John Gates had never heard of my father until he was arrested. He had no direct knowledge as to my father's "disappearance." Even Green-glass' trial testimony didn't say that my father had disappeared. It is unclear where Gates got this erroneous idea, but clearly his opinion about something he had no personal knowledge of does not corrobo-rate the Greenglasses!

Radosh and Milton continue by stating, "Gates recalled that when the Rosenbergs left the Party, their subscription to the *Daily Worker* was cancelled not in the regular manner by the subscription department but by a direct order from the Party's Central Committee. . . . Gates told us, 'one of the surefire things was that their subscription to the [Sunday] *Worker* and the *Daily Worker* were cancelled.'" Queried by the *New York Times,* Gates admitted he was speaking "generally." Since he had not heard of my parents, he had not heard whether they had a subscription or whether or not it ever was cancelled. In the pa-perback edition Radosh and Milton scrambled to fix everything up in view of the obvious contradictions between their writing and the facts. In the new introduction they assert that Gates "vouched for the ac-curacy of the quotes attributed to him in our book." Yet despite that bravado, they omitted from the paperback all references to Gates talk-ing about the alleged *Daily Worker* subscription.

Radosh and Milton then bring in Junius Scales, a former head of the Communist party in North Carolina, who spent time in jail as a result of a Smith Act conviction. He had been quoted about a supposed *Daily Worker* subscription cancellation by Stern and Radosh in the *New Re-public* in 1979. Scales had written to deny that he himself had any di-rect knowledge of that cancellation. Yet in Radosh and Milton's book the same quotes he had repudiated in 1979 were printed again: "Scales recalled hearing from a colleague at the time that the Rosenbergs quit the Party that 'the task [of canceling their subscriptions] was handled at the very highest level at the time.' . . . Because he had been told this, Scales was not surprised when Julius and Ethel Rosenberg were later arrested on spy charges." Back came another letter from Scales to the *New York Times.* He denied that he had heard of my parents before their arrest. He reiterated what he had told the *New Republic* readers in 1979. He heard a story about this alleged cancellation in the 1970s, over twenty years after my parents' arrest. On October 20, 1983, at New York's Town Hall, the Nation Institute and the *New Republic* spon-sored a debate between Radosh, Milton, and Sol Stern, and Walter and

Miriam Schneir entitled, "Were the Rosenbergs Framed?" During his contribution to the debate, Radosh apologized to Scales for his misunderstanding but continued, "In fact, he didn't make it clear until recently that he learned this episode twenty years later." This is not true. Scales had "made it clear" in the *New Republic* in 1979, four years before Radosh made the same "mistake" again! In the paperback, Scales' disclaimer that he learned about this alleged action years later is now (finally) acknowledged in the text. Also, Scales' belief in my parents' guilt is no longer connected to the time of their arrest.

In summary, Gates didn't know or say anything about a *Daily Worker* subscription cancellation. Scales heard about it from somebody else. On these grounds, Radosh and Milton persist in believing the Greenglasses were telling the truth about my parents dropping out.

But wait. What was this truth that the Greenglasses were telling that Scales and Gates supposedly corroborate? Here's the trial testimony of Ruth Greenglass: "Julius said that I might have noticed that for some time he and Ethel had not been actively pursuing any Communist Party activities, that they didn't buy the *Daily Worker* at the usual newsstand." That's it! Nothing about a subscription. In fact, this statement about buying the *Daily Worker* is in one of the early FBI files reporting the Greenglass story from the summer of 1950. There is nothing in the Greenglass testimony either to the FBI or to the trial jury about a subscription. Well, that doesn't mean much, you might respond. They could have made an error in detail. But Radosh and Stern had a chance to clear that up with the Greenglasses when they interviewed them. We may never know if they attempted to do this because Radosh refuses to release his tapes. Radosh and Milton (and Stern before her) first misrepresented the knowledge of their interviewees to corroborate the Greenglasses. Now, having corrected their mistakes, they are left with unnamed, uninvestigated hearsay statements from Junius Scales that directly contradict the Greenglass statements that they were trying to support.

One final point before we leave this discussion. Recall that there was no evidence in the book or in the FBI files released so far that in fact my parents had dropped out of Communist party activities. I made this point at a speech in September of 1983. A month later, I received a letter from a writer named David Evanier that began, "While you and I would probably not agree about the Rosenberg Case, . . ." The letter went on to read in part, "Sarah Plotkin, who died last year at the age of 84 was an honest woman. I have no doubt of her integrity. She told me with absolute certainty that Julius and Ethel Rosenberg were taking part in such [Communist] party activities as selling the *Daily Worker*, attending meetings and gatherings, up to a couple of weeks before your father's arrest. Sarah Plotkin was no longer a party member or supporter when she told me this; in fact she had contempt for the party."

A phone call to the writer of this letter elicited the following transcription of the interview he had with Ms. Plotkin:

I met the Rosenbergs a few times at the home of a friend of mine for dinner. My friend was secretary of the party district. They were very genuine, quite naive. They couldn't agree the capitalist world was as ruthless as it actually was . . . they weren't involved in struggles where bones were broken, where clubs were broken over your bones . . .

He and she were very idealistic, nice to everybody, even the capitalists. Even capitalists, they said, could also be a human being. . . . They were very devoted to the party, to getting subscriptions and contributions for the *Daily Worker*. It was only a month before they were arrested: they were seated with us and said they had gotten two subscriptions and contributions. A month later they were arrested as spies for Russia! . . . I was also at meetings with them. They were still vocal, they were still active in the party. Even I, if I hadn't known that, would harbor a suspicion.

One memory does not make a case. Radosh and Milton try to salvage their failure to include any documentation of their assertion, except that of the Greenglasses, by adding to their treatment of Max Gordon's interview the following statement: Gordon "acknowledged that he and other Communists knew full well at the time of their arrest that 'the Rosenbergs had for some time not been active in the Party.' Gordon stressed that their having dropped out of the Party 'was no secret'; that a 'lot of people knew it' and had talked about it at the time."

I was curious and wrote to Max Gordon. As he has said repeatedly in print, the alleged interview he had with Ronald Radosh was a phone conversation in which Radosh posed a number of hypothetical questions and Gordon responded in a speculative vein. Here is one such exchange that was played at Town Hall:

Ronald Radosh: I've heard this by the way from three or four other people that Julius became unavailable and he dropped out of the Party . . .

Max Gordon: Well that was . . . the discussions at the time were along those lines and a lot of people knew it because we've talked about it. I mean there was no secret that they had dropped out of activity earlier, some years earlier.

Gordon's letter to me read in part, "I cannot recall, or even imagine, my making the statement about everyone knowing they had dropped out of the party except possibly as an indication of common gossip at the time."

Max Gordon's recollection of common gossip is a rather weak reed for Radosh and Milton to lean on. But perhaps the most important point is that in fact the issue of whether or not my parents dropped out of the party is nowhere near as important as what this section of *The Rosenberg File* reveals about Radosh and Milton as researchers. My parents may have withdrawn from political activity in 1943. I said as much on pages 95–96 above. I don't know whether they did or did not despite Sarah Plotkin's recollection. The *fact* is irrelevant to the much more important conclusion that Radosh and Milton assert this as fact with no evidence in their first edition and virtually none in the paperback, and then misuse the interviews with Gates and Scales to demonstrate that this alleged "dropping out" was due to becoming involved in espionage. There thus remains no proof that my parents dropped out of Communist party activities to become spies except the word of the Greenglasses. Therefore, their first major building block in rehabilitating the Greenglasses' credibility has crumbled away.

The Greenglasses' Credibility

The Greenglass passport pictures, discussed in the Emperor's New Clothes speech, are dealt with by Radosh and Milton by ignoring the entire incident. Readers of their book never even learn about the Greenglass trial testimony about the passport photos. Instead, they focus on the supposed Rosenberg passport photos and the testimony of photographer Ben Schneider. The proximity fuse discussion (see above, pp. 190–92) is never confronted, perhaps because if Radosh and Milton had done so they would have found support for what the investigative reporter, Leon Summit, discovered in 1953.

The other major element in the Greenglass trial testimony is the console table. At the trial, in the context of testifying about gifts from the Russians in return for spying, David Greenglass said, "I believe they told me they received a console table from the Russians." On cross-examination, he elaborated that "that console table was used for photography." Ruth Greenglass was more explicit. She stated, "Julius . . . turned the table on its side to show why it was so special. . . . There was a portion of the table that was hollowed out for a lamp to fit underneath it so that the table could be used for photograph purposes." Our parents' testimony that it was an ordinary table bought at Macy's was corroborated when the table was found by Leon Summit. How do Radosh and Milton deal with these contradictions?

They start by asking the question we have asked: "There would seem to be two possibilities. Either another table had been substituted for the original one, or the production of the real table would tend to confirm the Rosenbergs' innocence." Since they had touted their book as a result of exhaustive research into the FBI files, one would have expected them to trace David and Ruth Greenglass' stories about the console table through the files. Also, perhaps they might have asked David and Ruth about it during their interviews.

But no. Instead they turn to an FBI report about Jerome Eugene Tartakow. The first statement from Tartakow to the FBI confirms our parents' version of the console table's purchase. He was "convinced that Rosenberg purchased the table as claimed." The next day, Tartakow is reported to have told the FBI, "Rosenberg stated that the console table which has three holes in it was left at his sister's house and was the one he used for photography work. Claims he photographed a one-thousand page booklet on radar onto a small roll of microfilm, using this table." Radosh and Milton are willing to allow that Tartakow could have made up the espionage act to impress the FBI. Their point is to suggest that the three holes mentioned by Tartakow and confirmed in Malcolm Sharp's book *Was Justice Done?* somehow would have been incriminating to our parents. The reference to the table being "left at his sister's house" suggests that the defense claims that they knew nothing about the location of the table during the trial were untrue. This leaves them to speculate that the reason the defense did not introduce the table was that the three holes would have been difficult to explain without giving credence to the Greenglass story that it had been altered for microfilming.

And that is the end of it. They do not assess the significance of the discovery that Ruth Greenglass perjured herself when she described the table as being hollowed out for microfilming. They do not follow the record of when the Greenglasses first mentioned the table in talking to the FBI and what efforts were made to corroborate their statements. Finally, there is something Radosh and Milton could not have known. My father, not knowing that Tartakow was an FBI informer, had written a physical description of the table for Manny Bloch in a letter dated February 14, 1953. In it, he explains the three holes as follows:

> I remember it was around Christmas time, the end of 1949 or beginning of 1950 that I got the bright idea to fix the console table and steady it. I planned to fix the table top permanently and add a center leg on the long straight side to give the table greater stability. I hunted up some tools that I found. A brace and a couple of steel metal drills. I recall I couldn't find any wood drills. Then I began to drill a couple of holes but I never completed the job as a matter of fact I believe I didn't quite finish enlarging the holes. * Also, I didn't get to go much further. I was afraid I might damage the thin table top by putting more screws in it. The possibility occurred to me it might even weaken the top sufficiently and during constant use as our dining table the top might split. This attempt at repair was done about ½ year before our arrest."

For the first edition of this book, I had interviewed Leon Summit orally and written down his recollections. After seeing what Radosh and Milton had done with the console table issue, he set down his memories in writing. He described the "work" Mrs. Cox remembered on page 189 above in detail: "Mr Rosenberg, who was an engineer and had a lot of tools, was always working with it in the evenings and he was constantly putting toothpicks in the screw holes to tighten the screws up and also drilled holes to tighten the table more." Mr. Summit turned the table over and Mrs. Cox said, "Thems the holes I saw Mr. Rosenberg drill."

Since Mrs. Cox was not working for my parents in 1949, she must have seen my father do other work on the table. What is crucial about

---

*These holes were the ones that held the plug to the top and the table on the frame, the ones referred to above as having to be constantly stuffed with "toothpicks" (p. 188). Now, I discover from my father's letter that these were really wooden matches. These holes shouldn't be confused with the three new holes my father is describing.

her recollection is that if the work were part of the altering of the table for microfilming, if there were anything suspicious about the table that would lead my father to not want to introduce it at the trial to prove the Greenglasses liars, why would he have done that suspicious work in front of Mrs. Cox? Radosh and Milton's concentration on the three holes represent nothing but an elaborate smokescreen for their effort to explain away this proof of the Greenglasses' perjury.

But let us return to their revelation that Jerome Eugene Tartakow told the FBI that the table was in my aunt's house while the trial was going on. Why did the defense not introduce it as evidence? Perhaps the reason was that my father never said this to Tartakow. My first reaction was to wonder if the FBI, rather than my father, had known what happened to the table and that this was one more piece of information they had fed to Tartakow. This is quite logical. Knowing where the table was would have put my parents in the position to prove the Greenglasses perjurers at the trial. Introducing the table in an effort to gain a new trial would be legally dangerous because the hurdle you must jump over is quite high. Thus, this is a possibility. But there is nothing in the files so far released to suggest this.

If we must assume my father knew what had happened to the table, I speculate that without the sales slips from Macy's the physical production of the table would not prove that this was the table the Greenglasses were talking about. By February 1953, with the petition for executive clemency on the way to the president, Manny Bloch was looking for any possible angle to try and get a new hearing under Section 2255 should the president's decision be adverse. My father was asked to send Manny a letter and Manny gave it to Leon Summit. I am suggesting that Manny fudged on the affidavit claiming "no knowledge" of where the table was because if they had known where the table was at the time of the trial, they had no legal right to a hearing based on its discovery. Gloria Agrin strongly denied to me that Manny knew about the table's whereabouts until Leon Summit found it. Thus, this is clearly speculation on my part. The key issue remains that the table does not corroborate the Greenglasses. It does not even corroborate Tartakow, since my father's talk about the table in prison need not have been directly to Tartakow. Any number of people in the jail might have heard my father talking about the table. I reiterate, we do not claim that my father never spoke with Tartakow in prison. We only deny that he confirmed to him the details of his non-existent espionage career!

What do the files say about the Greenglasses' story? Radosh and Milton just hint by noting that the console table was among bits of testimony that "David Greenglass had not considered important enough to mention in any of his early statements to the FBI." In fact, just as with the typing "evidence" against my mother, it was Ruth Greenglass who first mentioned it to the FBI. According to Ruth, "He [Julius] . . . rigged up an attachment for the camera to be fitted on the bottom of a dropleaf table in the apartment." Though from the context of the document, Ruth is referring to one of the other so-called spy apartments, not our home, one wonders why the FBI agents who searched our apartment thoroughly when my father was arrested did not seize the table with its suspicious alterations. Ruth's story is contained in a document dated July 19, two days after my father's arrest but almost a month before my mother's arrest. Again, why did the FBI not come back to the apartment and seize the table? We have always assumed that the FBI knew that the story about the table was bogus and were willing to let the story be told at the trial when it became apparent that the apartment had been given up and the furniture sold for junk. Radosh and Milton, despite all their wriggling, cannot expunge the fact that the discovery of the table proves the Greenglasses lied. Again, one wonders if the transcript of the Greenglass interviews indicates any effort on the part of Radosh to probe on this testimony.

The Rehabilitation of Harry Gold

Instead of a pathological liar, the Harry Gold in Radosh and Milton's book is a "functional liar" whose lies were part of his espionage cover. "Gold had admitted to conscious lies, not delusions." Radosh and Milton assert that the FBI files corroborate Gold, with the one exception of the "I come from Julius" testimony, which they claim Gold resisted until the day before the trial. However, in answering the question whether or not Gold was Klaus Fuchs' courier, they discount the fact that until Gold had confessed Fuchs refused to identify him as the courier. While Radosh and Milton assert that the early Fuchs and Gold statements provide corroboration for each other, the Schneirs have concluded that the statements "cannot be usefully compared for consistency because the FBI . . . relay[ed] information between Fuchs and Gold." Here Radosh and Milton fail to tell their readers that Robert Heineman, Fuchs' brother-in-law who together with his wife, Kristal, met Fuchs' courier, continued to deny that Gold was Fuchs' courier even after a face-to-face meeting, and that the FBI got Kristal to change her story while she was in a mental institution getting shock treatments.

Perhaps even more striking to me is evidence that, even after Gold had started to confess to the FBI, he continued to give false information. Three supposed espionage contacts of his were well under investigation when the interrogating agents had to sheepishly report to FBI headquarters in Washington that they did not even exist. Gold even told the FBI two different reasons for these falsehoods. In one document, Gold states that "he merely furnished the information concerning [the three men] to the Bureau Agents in an effort to preclude his naming his actual espionage associates." In another (and perhaps more revealing) document, Gold "explains further his previous falsehoods as being due to his inability to 'suddenly start telling the truth after having lived a life composed of a web of lies and falsehoods for so many years.'" Needless to say, Radosh and Milton never tell their readers about the three non-existent "espionage contacts" and the two conflicting excuses in the FBI files. At the debate at New York's Town Hall, Walter and Miriam Schneir challenged Radosh and Milton on a number of points. Here was their chance to respond to some of the factual attacks to which their book had been subjected. Joyce Milton responded to charges about Gold by reminding the audience that Gold kept notes to keep track of his various fictitious lives, which were supposedly part of his "functional lying." "As far as I know, pathological liars don't keep notes and schizophrenics don't keep notes. It's spies who keep notes." End of argument.

Jerome Eugene Tartakow: Radosh and Milton's Pièce de Résistance

The main body of new evidence introduced in Radosh and Milton's book is concentrated in their chapter-long treatment of Jerome Eugene Tartakow. It is essential that they convince their readers to believe Tartakow, perhaps not in all specific details but certainly on basic issues, because without Tartakow there is no confirmatory evidence of my father's spy activities—especially in the "other spy ring."

It took me two readings of the Radosh-Milton galleys and one detailed look at their footnotes when the book arrived before I realized that nowhere in the book do they even mention the Justice Department report that formed the basis of my initial dismissal of Tartakow's story. There are many contradictions between the report and what Tartakow allegedly told the FBI, but readers of *The Rosenberg File* never learn of these contradictions.

First they try to assuage one's natural skepticism that my father would be willing to trust his most vital secrets to a man he had just met in a jail he assumed was full of informers and probably bugged. Tartakow told Radosh and Stern in 1978 that their common Jewish working-class background as well as former membership in the YCL drew them together. Radosh and Milton also say that because the U.S. Communist party wanted nothing to do with my parents' case, Tartakow was chosen by Eugene Dennis, the head of the U.S. Communist party and incarcerated in the same prison, to serve as a liaison with my father. According to Tartakow, "Gene Dennis didn't want the three of us [Rosenberg, Dennis and Tartakow] to be seen together at the time." Radosh and Milton then devote two pages of footnotes to disputing Dennis's widow Peggy's claim that Dennis and my father were friendly in prison and had no need for an intermediary. At the Town Hall debate, Mike Perlin got to ask Radosh and Milton some questions as part of the formal program: "Was it true when Tartakow reported to the FBI that the closest friends of Julius Rosenberg were two people, in jail, Eugene Dennis and Oscar Vago?" Yes, there is an FBI document in which Tartakow provides evidence to refute himself. Radosh's response at Town Hall was that he interpreted that comment from Tartakow as reflecting what my father wished to be the case, not what actually was the case. Yet in *The Rosenberg File* this document is neither mentioned nor explained. In fact, Tartakow's liaison story is something he thought up in 1978 to buttress his own credibility. Such a story is not found anywhere in the files.

In the same two pages of footnotes cited above, Radosh and Milton cite "a source close to the Rosenberg defense effort over the years" as "confirming to us that Dennis had been friendly with Tartakow. After Tartakow's release from prison, this source said, Dennis had recommended to Bloch that he hire Tartakow." In the text they write, "Not long after his release from the House of Detention, Tartakow showed up at Manny Bloch's office armed with a letter of reference from Eugene Dennis." The source Radosh and Milton cite is Bonnie Brower, a National Lawyers Guild official who joined the Freedom of Information Act lawsuit in 1975 and who was involved in the National Committee to Reopen the Rosenberg Case and the early years of the Fund for Open Information and Accountability. She is about my age and I have always had a great affection for her both personally and politically. I felt for her the first time we read the statement in Stern and Radosh's *New Republic* article that she had told them of Dennis's friendship with Tartakow and recommendation to Manny Bloch. I can still see her fuming in Mike Perlin's office: "How could they make this up! I had no knowledge." She ultimately demanded a retraction and sued when they persisted. The case was dismissed on a technicality. I personally have watched her and Sol Stern call each other liars. She seemed angry. He seemed to be enjoying himself. But I am not one to judge their credibility. I believe her totally!

But let's ask the crucial question, How would she know? She was eight years old at the time. * At Town Hall, Ronald Radosh said, "We believe [the report about Dennis' letter] to be true because the person who told it to us would have no earthly reason to make up such a thing." But wait. There is an independent test of whether or not Dennis recommended Tartakow to Manny Bloch. One of Mike Perlin's questions at Town Hall was, "You would imagine that if the informer got a letter from Eugene Dennis to Manny Bloch that a copy of it would end up in the files of the FBI. Have you found such a letter?" Milton's response was, "We said he had a reference from Dennis; that's what we said." Now go back and read the quote about Tartakow showing up at Bloch's office in Radosh and Milton's book! * *

Seeking another independent source, I asked Gloria Agrin about Tartakow. She said she'd never met him and never heard about him by name although she did know that someone my father had known in prison drove me, Robby and Manny up to Sing Sing. She said she was

---

*Note how in calling Bonnie "a source close to the Rosenberg defense effort over the years" Radosh and Milton imply that she was involved in the defense efforts at a time when she might have had direct knowledge of this fact!

* *Unfortunately, nobody called her on this at Town Hall.

in the office regularly after November 1951, and if he had come highly recommended, she would have met him.

Another aspect of Radosh and Milton's efforts to elevate Tartakow's credibility is their conclusion that much of the information he provided to the FBI about the activities of the "other spy ring" checked out. The most important part of this chapter is Radosh and Milton's revelation of Tartakow's statement to the FBI that William Perl had used a holiday leave to return to Columbia University, remove some secret files, and engage in a "marathon photography session" with my father and two other men. They play this to the hilt: "As soon as the FBI received Tartakow's information, they moved to check it out. Rather to their amazement, since they still had serious doubts about Tartakow's reliability, the story fit the facts. . . . During his visit to Columbia, the FBI learned, Perl had checked out and signed for a huge amount of classified material." This is the closest that they come in the entire book to a real live incident of espionage. When I read this in galleys, I was concerned. If the FBI had been able to corroborate Tartakow, then Perl certainly would appear to be guilty, and Tartakow's statements about my father gain in credibility.

The first time I discussed this with Walter Schneir, he said, "You know there's something wrong with that story. There was no system for checking out anything at that lab." Thus we had to run down the source. The reference in Radosh and Milton was to a report of Agent O'Donoghue of the FBI from the Perl file of July 2, 1951. There were no direct quotes from the report. We turned to the Justice Department report, which we must recall was nothing more than a summary of the FBI's investigations, and found the following: "Investigations at Columbia University failed to disclose evidence that Perl removed any classified material at Columbia University. There was no system for checking out material and none of the persons interviewed had seen or knew of Perl removing documents from the building."

In the September 29, 1983, issue of the *New York Review of Books*, Walter and Miriam Schneir called readers' attention to the Justice Department report and Radosh and Milton's failure to respond to it. I did the same in *New York Magazine* (October 24, 1983). Radosh and Milton never responded to the above quote until forced to at Town Hall. Instead, they insisted that the O'Donoghue report was crucial. But none of us could find the O'Donoghue report. Why? Because Radosh and Milton's peculiar method of footnoting omitted the FBI serial numbers. Jerry Markowitz spent a couple of days looking. A *Guardian* reporter went to the FBI reading room in Washington and could not find it in the Perl files. Radosh and Milton stonewalled: "The July 2, 1951, report of S. A. O'Donoghue does exist. . . . The report (which we have shown to Sam Roberts of the *New York Times*) . . . summarizes agent John F. Buscher's report of September 21, 1950, which presents the list of exact documents that Perl 'receipted for' on July 3, 1948— probably the material Rosenberg told Tartakow about."

Sam Roberts was reporting for the *New York Times* about the controversy surrounding the case, and especially the controversy surrounding Radosh and Milton's book. He was therefore able to get Radosh to show him the "O'Donoghue report." We learned from him that the report was shown without its cover page, thus he did not see any FBI serial number on it. As with Radosh and Milton's book, his article didn't have any direct quotes from the report. But unlike Radosh and Milton's characterization in their text, Roberts' article made it clear that the report stated that Perl had "receipted for" classified material at this lab. I stated on numerous occasions that one signs a receipt when material comes into the lab, not when checking something out. Radosh and Milton dismissed this as "preposterous" in *New York Magazine*. That same week, the Town Hall debate took place. Miriam Schneir revealed that she and Walter had found the "O'Donoghue report." I enjoyed her presentation so much that I am going to reproduce it verbatim to give the flavor of the evening:

Was it in the Perl file? No. From the Julius Rosenberg headquarters file. Was it dated July 2, 1951? No. February 29, 1952. Was it prepared by Agent O'Donoghue? No. Agent John A. Harrington. (It is serial number 1258, in case anyone is interested.) . . . This document says nothing at all about Perl checking out material from the lab. Let me read you a few significant passages from it. On Page 30: "Perl was Von Karman's technical assistant at Pupin Physics Laboratory, Columbia University, and in Von Karman's absence, Perl handled certain of Von Karman's affairs, which included receiving classified material on behalf of the latter. . . . Such classified material was sent to Von Karman by registered mail." On page 41: "Dr. Von Karman said his office at Columbia maintained no records of the various reports received and did not have a charge-out system. . . . In this connection Dr. Von Karman remarked that all reports received were receipted for in writing."

I felt pleased and vindicated and was quite interested to see how Radosh and Milton would finally respond to the Justice Department report. Joyce Milton responded, "Perl had the key to the files of Dr. Theodore Von Karman, . . . and the combination of Von Karman's safe. . . . So, once Perl signed the receipt accepting these documents into his responsibility, no one had any way of checking whether he put them in the safe, put them in the files, or put them in his briefcase and walked out with them." That was her response! Clearly, the Schneirs had shown conclusively that the Tartakow story to the FBI did not check out. The only way Radosh and Milton could persuade their readers that it did was to totally misrepresent the phantom O'Donoghue report (now Harrington) and ignore the Justice Department report.

The reader may recall that in their statement in *New York Magazine* Radosh and Milton refer to the work of Agent John A. Buscher. In *The Rosenberg File,* readers never learn about Buscher, and for good reason. The FBI was interested in Perl's potential access to classified documents at Columbia University and had been investigating him in relation to Columbia in the summer of 1950, long before Tartakow told the FBI anything. Mentioning this in the book would have provided support for the hypothesis that the FBI used Tartakow as a mouthpiece for their suspicions or frame-up efforts. Despite Radosh and Milton's insistence that Tartakow refused to be a witness in any trial, the bureau considered him a likely witness against Perl. Tartakow stated that he would be willing to testify after his release from prison. Thus, the FBI could have been priming Tartakow to be a witness. In this context, it is interesting that Tartakow "remembered" the conversation with my father about the photocopying only after my father had been transferred from the Men's House of Detention to Sing Sing's Death House. This suggests it was the FBI's interest in Perl that "jogged" Tartakow's "memory."

After their disaster at Town Hall, Radosh and Milton engaged in some "damage control" in their paperback edition. They changed the text reference to Perl from "checked out and signed for" to "receipted for." Even better, they changed the footnote reference to the original

Buscher report as well as Harrington's summary. Thus, the footnote they use to demonstrate that the FBI moved to check out Tartakow's story refers to a report that was prepared over a year before Tartakow told that story!* This supports our alternative interpretation that the FBI had been building a case against Perl since the summer of 1950 and was trying to develop evidence from Tartakow to help them do that. Even in the paperback, however, they still do not acknowledge the existence of the Justice Department report.

Spurred on by the Schneirs' discovery of contradictions between the Radosh and Milton analysis and the Justice Department report, Jerry Markowitz took off about three weeks from his other work and meticulously ran down every footnote in Radosh and Milton's chapter on Tartakow. His efforts uncovered example after example of omissions and misrepresentations. Only some of them found their way into his review of *The Rosenberg File* in *Science and Society*. I'll give just one example.

Radosh and Milton refer to speculation that Perl succeeded in getting information to the Russians that permitted the Soviets to build the MIG 15 planes which at the time of my parents' trial were shooting down American aircraft in Korea. In April of 1951, J. Edgar Hoover had asked if Perl's activities had helped the Russians use American designs in constructing the tail of the MIG. Radosh and Milton quote from Hoover's query and from a newspaper article, but they neglect to inform their readers that the San Francisco field office responded to Hoover's speculation with reports from three government agencies that added up to a loud "No" in answer to Hoover's question.**

Confronted by this and other information at Town Hall, Joyce Milton insisted that they never claimed William Perl was a spy. She referred to their book: "Whether or not William Perl actually did supply data to the Soviets through Julius was never definitively established." They

---

* A page later, Radosh and Milton return to their initial misstatement by noting "Perl had also checked out substantial numbers of reports in May and June." Since they had changed the wording on the previous page, the word "also" must appear curious to the unknowledgeable reader.

** "NACA, by letter dated March 20, 1951, reported that there is no indication to date that the engineering features of the Soviet MIG are based upon research conducted by NACA . . . G-2 advised that the files of the Asst. Chief of Staff, G-2, Intelligence, disclosed nothing to support speculation that data from U.S. research had been incorporated into MIGs.

Department of Air Force . . . has no indication that the MIG-15 contains engineering developments originating from U.S. classified research. The Air Force observed that German, rather than U.S., influence is apparent in the design."

also say, "It is difficult to understand why such a brilliant and dedicated young scientist would have risked his future to become involved with Julius Rosenberg's spy project." This maneuver cannot hide their use of the Perl episodes to demonstrate that Tartakow was telling the truth. If Tartakow was telling the truth, Perl was guilty. Radosh and Milton either believe Tartakow or they don't.

William Perl was pressured by the government to be a witness against my father, and he refused despite being threatened with "frying" by FBI interrogators in the summer of 1950. He was convicted of perjury for initially denying he knew my father and Morton Sobell to a grand jury, though he himself subsequently changed his Grand Jury testimony to admit knowing them. * Not only was he given the maximum five-year sentence, but his scientific career was ruined. When I began giving speeches about the case, someone introduced himself to me and told me Perl was teaching at the New Jersey College of Medicine and was "an extremely nice guy." I now regret never having sought him out, for he died in 1977. His refusal to become another David Greenglass makes him one of many unsung heroes in my parents' case. I'm sorry I never got a chance to thank him personally. He deserves a much better epitaph than to be convicted of espionage by Radosh and Milton in their haste to justify their belief in Tartakow.

But Why Would the FBI Feed All This Stuff to Tartakow Just to Stick It in Their Files Where Nobody Would Ever See It?

Well, say Radosh and Milton and their defenders, there you go nitpicking. Even if Tartakow is wrong on some details, or even if he lies to the FBI, who else would he get his information from? Radosh and Stern said in *The New Republic* that Tartakow knew "details that could have come only from Rosenberg." Our response is that he could have gotten them from the FBI. The FBI was on the trail of every member of the so-called Rosenberg spy ring and many others as well before they ever met Tartakow. Perl, Barr, Sarant, Sidorovich and Bruce Dayton were among the people whose pictures were being exhibited to everyone they interviewed. Maxwell Finestone shows up as an active suspect

---

*Perl continued to deny knowing the people the government tried strenuously to link him with, Ann and Michael Sidorovich (Michael Sidorovich was supposedly one of the four in the photocopying marathon), and the jury believed him!

in September of 1950, when David Greenglass was shown his picture. When Tartakow expressed an interest in telling the FBI what my father was saying in prison, they no doubt saw not only a way to find out what my father was thinking and doing, but also a way to see if their suspicions could be fleshed out. Historian Eric Foner has done research using informer files, and he says they must be used with extreme care: "They always blend accurate and specific minor details with a web of questionable allegations and spurious contentions geared to the conclusions the informer thinks his employers want to reach." There is no question that the FBI gave Tartakow information. The Schneirs discovered one such example: "On January 18, 1951, Tartakow stated to the FBI that Julius Rosenberg did not know agents had contacted Ann Sidorovich and her husband. How then did Tartakow know? Obviously, the FBI had told him."

But, persist Radosh and Milton: "What point would there be to fabricating an entire set of communications from an ersatz source if the FBI never intended to use the documents publicly? And if it did intend to set Tartakow up as a public accuser, why continue to fill the documentary record with negative comments on his reliability?" First of all, the communications may not be fabricated. Tartakow may very well have said those things. He just did not get the information from my father! But a fair question is, What was the FBI's motivation? A hint exists in the fact that whereas the New York field office of the FBI quickly began to accept Tartakow's reliability, the Washington headquarters of the FBI persisted in calling Tartakow "an informant of unknown reliability," the status he enjoyed in the Justice Department summary of 1956. I believe agents in the New York field office were using Tartakow to support the case that they had already made by asking him leading questions about Perl, Sidorovich, etc. Tartakow would then tell the FBI things that my father had allegedly told him which weaved information about Perl, etc. given by the FBI into a tale of espionage from my father's mouth! The reports to Washington would not only enhance the local agents' standings, but would transform unprovable suspicions within the FBI into "facts." These facts would then be the basis of further interrogations by agents who did not know the facts were manufactured to try and find another David Greenglass or Harry Gold. However, Washington remained skeptical about Tartakow because they were not "creating" his stories. The suggestion that he might be used as a witness came from New York. On the TV show "The Unquiet Death of Julius and Ethel Rosenberg," Mike Perlin described the making of a frame-up in classic terms: "Very often when a frame-up is done, it isn't done on a mass scale and involve a whole host of people. Or just the entire matter. Little bits of evidence 'get developed.' And possibly the last person to receive the evidence [FBI headquarters] might believe it's true. Although the donor of that evidence [someone in the New York field office] might know it's false."

Historian Edward Pessen, writing in *New York History*, suggests another motive for the FBI: "In writing a secret memo to the Attorney General two weeks before the Rosenbergs' execution, [J. Edgar] Hoover cited the informer's evidence as extra-judicial proof of the Rosenbergs' guilt and why presidential clemency should be denied them. Hoover's statement is proof not that the FBI necessarily fed Tartakow information but that it would indeed have been in their interest to have done so."

Now, just as it is impossible to *prove* my parents' innocence, it is also impossible for me, or anyone for that matter, to prove that my father did not say such and such a thing to Tartakow. Yet, given the well-known unreliability of informers in general, and also given the number of outrageous statements Tartakow has made, the burden of proof is on Radosh and Milton and the others who wish to use Tartakow as evidence of my father's guilt.

But Radosh and Milton claim they have independent proof that Tartakow told the truth about at least one aspect of my father's espionage activity—his recruiting of Maxwell Finestone and having him drive my father to Ithaca, New York. Remember, James Weinstein's original story to Radosh (see above, p. 390) described a lift he had given to my father from Ithaca to New York City in late 1949. According to Radosh and Milton's construction, here is a story the FBI never heard until Tartakow told them, and it is independently corroborated by James Weinstein. Weinstein's story that Finestone was involved in secret work and frightened by my father's visit supports in their mind Tartakow's statement that my father had recruited Finestone.

But these stories that Tartakow told the FBI are not corroborated by Weinstein. The point about my father recruiting Finestone could have been a leading question from the FBI. Remember, they had been showing Finestone's picture as early as September of 1950. The trip-to-

Ithaca story is even less supportive of Radosh and Milton. The trip Tartakow describes supposedly occurred in June of 1950. It involved Finestone driving my father to Ithaca and back in a car he borrowed from James Weinstein. How could Weinstein's recollection of driving my father from Ithaca to New York in late 1949 have supported Tartakow's story? My father's testimony at the trial can be read as confirming the Weinstein story, or at least as confirming his presence in Ithaca in late 1949 or early 1950. When Saypol pressed him about going to Ithaca in June of 1950, my father said it could not have been that late.

The June trip to Ithaca was mentioned by David Greenglass at the trial and by Tartakow around the same time. Here is another example of how the FBI used Tartakow and how he took advantage of his ability to figure out what the FBI wanted to hear. Tartakow must have heard from either the FBI or my father about Greenglass' trial testimony, and he told the FBI that my father had gone there. Much later, in July of 1951, Tartakow filled in the details of the June trip, placing my father in Finestone's company in Weinstein's car. Weinstein's personal knowledge of my father's presence in Ithaca in late 1949 and the fact that he gave my father a ride back to New York can only confirm Tartakow in Radosh and Milton's world of flim-flam. Again, since Radosh and Milton tout this in their book as "independent confirmation of the existence of a postwar spy network," the fact that their argument has been shown to be specious is not trivial.

Near the end of their treatment of Tartakow, Radosh and Milton return to their effort to bolster Tartakow's credibility. They write, "Jerry Tartakow's secret reports may not have led to any further espionage convictions, but when it came to keeping his promise that he would be able to infiltrate the Rosenberg camp, he proved as good as his word." The fact is, the FBI files of Tartakow's own reports reveal that he had only six visits with Manny Bloch. Manny did not see Tartakow after December 12, 1951. The files also show Tartakow had trouble catching Manny on the phone. The last telephone conversation was January 12, 1952. After that, he seems to have been completely frozen out. On March 12, 1952, he told the FBI he had called Manny a number of times and never reached him.

In their zeal to build up Tartakow's relationship with Manny, Radosh and Milton exaggerate his role as chauffeur. I have a vague recollection of a man driving Manny, Robby and me up to Sing Sing in the fall of

1951, and perhaps his name was Jerry. But see Radosh and Milton: "Beginning in October, 1951, Jerry Tartakow took over the task of chauffeuring Manny Bloch and the children on their trips to Ossining." The FBI files—which, remember, are Tartakow's own reports to the FBI—show that he drove me and Robby to Sing Sing once, Bubbie Sophie once as well. Tartakow doesn't claim as much chauffeuring as do Radosh and Milton!

But, one might protest, doesn't this activity show that the Rosenbergs and Manny Bloch trusted him? To "trust" him to drive Manny, Robby and me to Sing Sing means what? Manny expected he wouldn't crash the car or attempt to kidnap or murder us? Why does that "trust" translate into the kind of confidence Radosh and Milton make the centerpiece of their book, my father's trust which induced a full "confession"? Anyway, the following information is available from one of the FBI reports of the overheard prison conversations (the FBI bugged or listened in on the prison visits in the Death House, both with family members and with counsel!): "Bloch indicated that someone had stolen $1000 which was supposed to be turned over to the defense fund. . . . Mrs. Rosenberg asked Bloch if he suspected 'Jerry.'" Thus, my parents obviously didn't trust Tartakow completely.

Back to the Trial Testimony

Radosh and Milton have attempted to rehabilitate the testimony of Harry Gold and the Greenglasses, not by refuting our charges about the various perjuries committed at the trial, but by convicting my father through the statements of Jerome Eugene Tartakow and thus by implication making my father guilty of what Greenglass charged him with. As a result, in the minds of critics, the case against my father has become a web of circumstantial evidence all pointing toward his guilt. People have even written to me that it does not matter if I or anyone else succeeds in knocking the props out from any of Radosh and Milton's specific points because there are so many other points that remain. Yet, in fact, all points except for the specific incidents, the testimony at the trial, and the reports Tartakow gave the FBI are mere inferences. Tartakow's reports either have not checked out or are only evidence that my father did in fact talk to him in jail. Reports that do not check out do not strengthen a web of circumstance; they obliterate it. The Greenglasses' evidence remains oral, uncorroborated, and false in a number of specifics. Harry Gold, despite Radosh and Milton's efforts, remains a pathological liar.

Their detailed effort to refute the Schneirs' charge that the FBI forged Gold's Hilton Hotel registration card founders on one outstanding piece of new evidence. Until the trial testimony, no document in the FBI files contains an oral or signed statement by Gold that he had registered at the Hilton Hotel for a few hours on the morning of June 3, 1945. Compare that to the way the FBI came upon Gold's September card at the same hotel. On the same day that the FBI log refers to Gold mentioning this stay, a request was sent to Albuquerque and the card was found immediately. As Rob noted above, the September card has FBI agents' initials, the date of acquisition, and even a case code on its back, while the June card has no FBI marking on it whatsoever. The original of the June card was returned to the hotel in August of 1951 while the September original was retained by the FBI until 1960 and then destroyed by them. Radosh and Milton keep this differential treatment from their readers. "Some years after the trial [the cards] had been returned to the Hilton, where they were routinely destroyed in 1957." If this is an honest mistake, it certainly has the advantage of misleading their readers. The June card was returned to the hotel before the first appeal was even argued. Had my parents' conviction been overturned, the original, forged card would have already been destroyed, safe forever from analysis for age of paper. (Age of ink analysis would have been impossible as the FBI made sure it was filled out in pencil.) Meanwhile, as the Schneirs reported in their new edition, the original reference in the FBI documents to Gold's alleged stay at the hotel in June is an FBI teletype that flatly contradicts the FBI logs of Gold's interrogation that day. In my opinion, the Schneirs make a very good case for the conclusion that this teletype was faked.

Two other witnesses gave some peripheral support to the government's case at the trial. One was Elizabeth Bentley. She was used to develop two points for the prosecution. One was the proclivity of Communists to be spies for the Soviet Union; the other was to establish, if only vaguely in the jury's mind, my father's connection with Bentley's alleged espionage superior, Jacob Golos. Since Bentley has often been ridiculed for her sensational and unproven charges against many Americans in her various testimonies before congressional committees and federal grand juries, Radosh and Milton's task was to thoroughly demonstrate her credibility. When I saw how they attempted to do it, my mind boggled again.

Here is Bentley's earliest FBI statement about a "Julius" who was an engineer: "In 1943, Julius and the others in the group proceeded to Norfolk, Virginia, where they secured employment." Bentley said she once saw Julius from a distance and he wore wire-rimmed glasses. I remember reading this material some time after the Bentley file arrived in Mike Perlin's office and saying to myself: Well, there goes another prop in the government's case. My reason? My father had neither lived nor worked in Norfolk and never wore wire-rimmed glasses. So the Julius Bentley testified about at the trial had been adjusted to fit my father between her original statement to the FBI and the trial.

So how can Radosh and Milton conclude "in her testimony at the Rosenberg-Sobell trial . . . Elizabeth Bentley had told the truth"? They give three reasons over three paragraphs as to why "the FBI and the prosecutors had good reason to think that . . . the focus of Rosenberg's espionage activities through 1944 had been an attempt to penetrate the Navy Bureau of Ordinance." They may have accurately reflected the prosecution's viewpoint; I can't tell. There are no footnote references to these three paragraphs. One of the statements in their exposition has since been acknowledged by them as an error. They write that Mort Sobell "had gone to Norfolk and boarded a ship that housed fire-control devices . . . and received a briefing." In September of 1983, they admitted they had made a mistake. It was Max Elitcher who boarded the ship. Now Max Elitcher was the only witness against Mort Sobell, and he also gave some testimony against my father. But the FBI did not believe he was involved in espionage, and Radosh and Milton agree. So what does his presence on the ship prove? Radosh and Milton blithely substitute Elitcher for Sobell in the paperback edition without any explanation as to why that helps their argument.

In *New York Magazine,* in answer to my complaint about their ridiculous effort to make Bentley's Julius into my father, they insist "what is important is that Bentley told the FBI that a spy called Julius was organizing a group of engineers to steal navy secrets, which confirms the testimony of Max Elitcher that Rosenberg had tried to recruit him into such a spy ring." They dismiss the Norfolk connection as immaterial ("Bentley . . . got the information that he worked at Norfolk from a third party.") even though they had titled the chapter "The Norfolk Connection," and they believe the rest of Bentley's information, which of course also came to her from the same alleged third party! Thus, for Radosh and Milton, Max Elitcher's charges that my father attempted to recruit him into a spy ring are confirmed.

What Radosh and Milton never tell their readers is that one Julius Korchien, a naval architect and member of my father's union (the FAECT), was under investigation by the FBI before Bentley made her statement in 1945. He was the person they tried to connect with Golos until the opportunity to adjust the original Julius to fit my father arose.

And what of Max Elitcher's credibility? Facing ten years in prison for perjuring himself on non-Communist affidavits, Elitcher could have been very willing to cooperate with the FBI. He could have been pressured just as William Perl was in the summer of 1950. Elizabeth Bentley's information about a Julius could have been suggested to Elitcher, who himself had been under investigation as early as 1948. To demonstrate Max Elitcher's credibility in the early discussions he had with the FBI, Radosh and Milton use an ingenious device. We have always maintained that the crucial evidence that the case was a frame-up is contained in the contradictions between what the key prosecution witnesses first told the FBI and what they later told the trial jury. Also important, as noted above in the cases of Gold and Fuchs as well as Gold and Greenglass, is the fact that two witnesses told the same story at the trial whereas they told very different stories earlier. The FBI reconciliation, so dramatically revealed in the case of the "I come from Julius" password, is prima facie evidence for a frame-up as well. Radosh and Milton are aware of this argument, and they use it to their advantage in the case of Max Elitcher and his wife, Helene. They claim that Max and Helene Elitcher at their very first interviews with the FBI *independently* confirmed that my father had visited them in Washington, D.C., in June of 1944 and at that first meeting had asked Helene to leave the room. When she was out of the room, my father supposedly asked Max Elitcher to become a spy. Here is how they write it: "She [Helene] had given a statement about her social contacts with Rosenberg that confirmed her husband's version of events—right down to Julius' request during his first visit to her house that she leave the room so he and Max could speak privately."

The references for those pages are to a statement signed by Max

Elitcher, July 20, 1950, an FBI report of a concurrent interview with Helene Elitcher, and a handwritten statement given by Helene Elitcher to her lawyer. It may be hard to believe, but Radosh and Milton have totally misrepresented these documents. First, Max Elitcher's statement makes no reference to Helene being asked to leave the room; in fact, he doesn't even indicate if Helene was there. Second, Helene Elitcher's statement was that she remembered nothing of the conversation and believed she was present the entire visit. In addition, Max Elitcher said the conversation lasted three-quarters of an hour while Helene said the visit went on until midnight.

A month later, in a handwritten note to her attorneys, Helene Elitcher wrote, "Max says I went out of the room for a while—at Julie's request." So that was when the story of the request to leave the room was created. It was *not* in the first independent interviews with the FBI. This time, Radosh and Milton have been caught red-handed. Recall their statement in the text: "She had given a statement . . . that confirmed her husband's version . . . right down to Julius' request. . . ." But her statement did not confirm her husband's version. And her husband's version was not what it later became! There was no such request by my father in *either* of their first *independent* statements! So much for their effort to buttress Max Elitcher's credibility.

What about the Testimony of the Photographer?

Well, say Radosh and Milton, we have one surefire proof that Julius Rosenberg confided damaging information to Tartakow in jail. According to the FBI documents, Tartakow told the FBI that my father was worried that they might find the photographer who had taken passport pictures of him and my mother and Robby and me. Quickly, the FBI fanned out over the lower east side and found Ben Schneider. He had no negatives and no records, but he did remember my parents when showed their pictures by the FBI. His courtroom testimony impressed the jury very much. My parents had categorically denied having passport pictures taken and here was a seemingly disinterested witness proving they had committed perjury. Even more important for Radosh and Milton, according to the FBI files it was Tartakow who led the FBI to Schneider. Thus, this supports their view that my father confided intimate secrets to Tartakow.

Here Radosh and Milton's failure to analyze the Greenglass passport pictures makes their case appear stronger than it is. The FBI had gotten Greenglass to cooperate in passing off family snapshots as passport photos. Unfortunately, though they seized over ninety photographs from my parents' apartment (and years later ended up destroying almost all of them), they never found any that they could label passport photos. Thus, they needed a passport photo story. I believe they got Schneider to help them. Why he may have been willing to do that, I have no idea. But Schneider was not on the witness list. What justification could they have for "finding" Schneider so late? They asked Tartakow a leading question. Tartakow responded. They then had the justification to "find" Schneider. They gave the game away, however, when they brought Schneider into the courtroom a day before his time to testify so he could get a good look at my father so as to accurately identify him. When Manny Bloch strongly cross-examined Schneider and probed when he had last seen my father, Prosecutor Saypol objected, attempting to prevent Manny from stumbling upon Schneider's perjury. Kaufman intervened to help Saypol.

Manny clearly believed Schneider was perjuring himself. At a prison visit with my parents overheard by the FBI, Manny "advised ROSENBERG that he was having the photographer investigated because he believed that he was a 'phony.'" In 1952, Manny found out that Schneider had been in the courtroom the day before and had perjured himself on the stand. The Court of Appeals said he hadn't "meant" to perjure himself! If you think Schneider was perjuring himself, as we have since the first discovery of this "unintentional" perjury, then Tartakow's statements to the FBI only confirm the fact that the FBI was feeding him material! If you believe Schneider, Tartakow still is not necessarily the first source of the FBI's information. They might have been probing photographers' studios ever since the Greenglass passport story was fabricated. Radosh and Milton's failure to confront the discovery of the *Greenglasses'* perjuries re passport photos now emerges as more than a mere omission. Readers of *The Rosenberg File,* deprived of knowledge of the Greenglasses' fabrications, are less likely to smell a rat in Schneider's testimony if they don't know about the dirty little trick the FBI pulled with the other photos. Radosh and Milton also never tell their readers about the overheard prison conversation.

Even if Schneider were telling the truth, that would not prove my parents were spies. It would only prove that they were planning to leave the country and thought it would "look bad" if they admitted it on the witness stand. I don't think that is the case, because on other occasions they admitted things that "looked bad," such as my father's trip to Ithaca to see Sarant in 1949 and his association with Joel Barr at City College. Thus, what Radosh and Milton claim is their final crowning proof turns out to be nothing at all.

Finally, I must admit that this question of Schneider's role in the case is a loose end. One of the reasons that Robby and I never felt comfortable writing a full monographic treatment of the case from the FBI files alone was the presence of too many of these unprovable suspicions. We suspect Schneider perjured himself, but we cannot prove it. The crucial point is that Radosh and Milton cannot use Schneider to prove my parents' guilt or to prove that Tartakow was giving accurate reports to the FBI about what my father was telling him in prison.

What about the Two Engineers Who Went to Russia?

So what is left? Joel Barr and Alfred Sarant did end up in the Soviet Union. Radosh has been quoted as saying that Sarant's move to the Soviet Union and his career there in micro-electronic research is the same thing as espionage. The logic of this escapes me, especially since the micro-electronic industry did not exist when Sarant lived in the United States. It is pure supposition that the reason Barr and Sarant moved to the Soviet Union was because they were spies. At the Town Hall debate Miriam Schneir made short shrift of the Radosh-Milton construction:

> Joel Barr and Alfred Sarant did not leave the United States together. At the time of the arrest of David Greenglass in June 1950, Barr had already been living in Western Europe for two and a half years, studying and traveling. Our opponents say that Barr disappeared from Paris precipitously on the very day of David Greenglass's arrest, inferring that these two events were connected. But the files dispute this inference. They show that two weeks before Greenglass's arrest Barr told a friend that he was planning to leave Paris. To support their false claim that Barr's departure from Paris was a sudden, desperate flight, our opponents offer this dramatic scene: Barr left behind him "his clothes, his books, and a brand new motorcycle that was his pride and joy." . . . In

fact, he abandoned only a few personal items, the value or nature of which the files do not describe. As for the motorcycle, a person Barr knew in Paris told the FBI that he had offered to purchase it but Barr had advised it was in too poor condition to sell to a friend. This information is in the files, as accessible to our opponents as to ourselves. Why did they ignore it?

To turn to Alfred Sarant. Did he leave, disappear, at the time of David Greenglass's arrest? No, he did not. He stayed at home in Ithaca, New York, and continued working as a building contractor. A few days after the arrest of Julius Rosenberg, Sarant was visited by the FBI. He submitted to FBI questioning for a full week and voluntarily permitted agents to search his house. He denied their allegations that he was a spy or a member of a Rosenberg spy ring. Eventually, he slipped away from FBI agents surveilling him and left the United States with his neighbor [Carol Dayton], with whom he was having a love affair. . . .

Our opponents' book hopelessly muddles the chronology of the Sarant investigation. They seem to think the bureau did not begin to investigate Sarant until after Julius Rosenberg's arrest. Did they simply miss the extensive files on an earlier investigation? Or did they choose to suppress the fact that the FBI investigated Sarant months before Julius Rosenberg's arrest? Whatever, nowhere in the Radosh-Milton book can the reader discover that the FBI crept up behind Sarant *in early 1950.* At that time, according to our opponents' thesis, he was still an active espionage agent. He could have been caught, so to speak, red-handed. The FBI investigated Sarant thoroughly. They interviewed his neighbors and his associates, looked into his financial records, checked his telephone records, and watched his mail. The picture of Sarant in their files does not in any respect fit the image of an underground Soviet operative propounded by Radosh and Milton. The FBI files show that Sarant was an open political activist: A CP member during 1944 who canvassed for Congressman Vito Marcantonio; in 1948, active on behalf of Henry Wallace and the Progressive party (his picture appeared in an upstate New York newspaper addressing a Wallace rally); subsequently, he belonged to the American Labor party. . . . The last document we have from this "Soviet agent" hiding his red tinge was a telegram he sent to his U.S. senators, Herbert Lehman and Ives, in April of 1950. It read: "Urge you work for defeat of the Mundt bill, which would destroy freedom while claiming to defend it."

When it came their turn, Radosh and Milton failed to respond to any of Miriam's points. Mark Kuchment, a Soviet emigré who was the source of some details about Sarant's life as a Soviet scientist, supplied the right note of caution with a letter to the *New York Times* in October of 1983 entitled, "A Rosenberg Friend Prematurely Condemned":

> Information [about Sarant] has been used as evidence in the current polemics between those who feel that the Rosenbergs were innocent and those who are trying to prove, by using primarily circumstantial evidence, that they were indeed guilty. . . . I regard such use of my findings as strange indeed. I have absolutely no direct proof which would allow me to conclude that Alfred Sarant was a Soviet spy. . . .
>
> Being from the Soviet Union myself, and having known personally victims of Stalin's purges who spent up to 18 years in concentration camps on the strength of circumstantial evidence, I prefer patience to zealotry, prudence to so-called inner logic, and some measure of human compassion to a ruthless and unscrupulous drive for "objective truth."

Possible Motivations

People are sometimes incredulous when we make our charges about Radosh and Milton's work because they cannot imagine what would cause them to deliberately misrepresent the facts, as we charge they have done. I will not speculate as to their personal motivations. Personal motivation is pretty irrelevant to one's conclusions about this book. One can have bad motivation and still write an analysis that stands the test of time. One can be a most judicious, honest scholar and still write a terribly flawed and incorrect interpretation.

However, when a work of history is terribly flawed, it sometimes means the writer has some kind of political axe to grind. I will try to show how (particularly) Radosh's political predilections may have led him to misuse the FBI documents and cast all the circumstancial evidence in a light that supported his previously-arrived-at conclusions. I then will pose a new question: What has motivated the literary and political establishment to embrace this book so heartily?

Radosh and Milton's political blinders are no better illustrated than in their revealing treatments of the role of Manny Bloch and his defense strategy and the role of the American Communist party in the effort to save my parents' lives. Radosh and Milton assert several times that Manny's strategy of conceding much of the government's case at the trial (accepting the involvement of Gold and Greenglass in espionage, not cross-examining Gold) and resistance to the effort of Daniel Marshall and Fyke Farmer to win my parents a new trial reflected neither

errors nor incompetence, as some have argued, but were the results of
Manny's belief that my parents were guilty. According to Radosh and
Milton's interpretation, Manny was trying to protect other spies, and
particularly the Communist party, from exposure. They even suggest
that when Farmer and Marshall succeeded in getting Justice Douglas
to grant the last-minute stay Manny sabotaged the oral argument before the Supreme Court because he "had to know that the Communist
element which by now dominated the Committee, could only be satisfied by the Rosenbergs' martyrdom." This is total speculation. Much
worse, however, is the fact that their book can be read to suggest that
what Manny did or did not do in the wake of Douglas' stay had a bearing on the outcome before the Supreme Court. In the same section of
their book, Radosh and Milton quote from Justice Felix Frankfurter's
notation on his copy of the written opinion vacating the stay: "The fact
is that all minds were made up . . . I have no doubt . . . before we
met." The famous "fix" document in the FBI files, which stated that
before Douglas had even granted the stay, Chief Justice Vinson had
promised Attorney General Brownell that if Douglas were to grant the
stay "he will call the full court back into session Thursday morning
[June 18] to vacate it," also shows that the final hearing was a hollow
formality.

Manny can be criticized. We all benefit from 20-20 hindsight. Manny
himself realized that he had made a number of serious blunders that
helped the government and made appeals more difficult. Nevertheless,
given the attitude of Judge Kaufman and the way the power of the
United States government was arrayed against my parents, it is doubt-
ful if F. Lee Bailey or Charles Garry or Clarence Darrow would have
achieved an acquittal. The really despicable part of this attack on
Manny is that the only evidence Radosh and Milton present that can
even remotely be connected with their view is Tartakow's statement to
the FBI that Manny admitted my father was involved in some manner
of espionage. Even this does not justify the construction Radosh and
Milton put on Manny's behavior, and I do not believe Tartakow. Gloria
Agrin assured me that Manny never doubted my parents' innocence.
Radosh and Milton quote Justice Douglas' speculation that Manny's
actions were motivated by the desire of the Communists to see my parents dead. This prompted columnist George Will to assert on the TV
show "Nightline" that the "fix" at the Supreme Court, far from oc-

curing when Vinson and Brownell got together to agree to vacate the stay before it was granted, actually occurred when Manny made sure Farmer's point would not be upheld by the Court. Douglas' view is not proof and Frankfurter's statement that the minds of the justices were "made up . . . before we met" proves Will wrong.

Gloria Agrin explained to me that Manny and she felt that the original formulation of Farmer's point was not valid. Douglas' brilliant mind, she said, had ungarbled Farmer's original affidavit and had set it out in a manner that was logically and legally impeccable. Manny and Gloria's desired strategy before the Supreme Court was to "play for time" by asking to properly brief this extremely important and valid legal point. Their dispute with Farmer was based on his desire to argue the merits of the point right there. Whether Gloria or Farmer were right in their approaches, this represents a much more benign interpretation of what went on at the Court that day than does Radosh and Milton's.

Manny Bloch ruined his health trying to save my parents and died while trying to raise money for Robby and me. He made the marvelous decision to place us with Anne and Abel Meeropol just before he died. Harried, overworked, and ultimately defeated in his efforts to save my parents, he still had time to give Robby and me love and affection whenever we were together. I know I'm not objective when it comes to Manny Bloch, but I have to emphasize that Radosh and Milton provide not a shred of evidence to support the interpretation that he threw the case and the appeals and that he knew my parents were guilty. Because this interpretation is not based on any real evidence, the fact that they make it so strongly indicates how they permitted their own prejudicial view (that Communists would prefer to see my parents dead) to take them well beyond the boundaries of responsible historical speculation. Their willingness to ascribe to Manny actions in furtherance of these cynically manipulative motivations is a result of their political attitudes.

The Role of the American Communist Party

In discussing the role of the American Communist party, Radosh and Milton build on the fact that the party did not organize any defense of my parents before and during the trial, and failed to join with the Committee to Secure Justice in the Rosenberg Case until months after it was formed. Their interpretation of this inaction is that the Communist leadership was aware of my parents' guilt and did not want to support them for fear that they might confess and implicate the party. They say that only when it became clear, in November of 1952, that my parents were not going to talk and only when it became necessary to divert public opinion, especially in Europe, from the show trial of Slansky and his associates in Czechoslovakia did the world Communist movement adopt my parents' case. Even then, according to Radosh and Milton, the Communist purpose was not saving my parents but making political capital out of their martyrdom. It takes a lot of rereading, but following this argument through the footnotes of *The Rosenberg File* leads one to discover that this whole structure is built on *one piece of evidence*. Radosh and Milton allege that John Gates remembers that just after my parents were sentenced to death, V. J. Jerome, a member of the central committee of the U.S. Communist party, told him, "They're heroes. They're going to their death and not saying a word." This quote and Gates' interpretation of it is the foundation for their entire analysis.

Now, first of all, my parents could have been innocent heroes in the mind of V. J. Jerome for going to their deaths rather than falsely identifying the Communist party as an espionage recruiting ground. Second, assuming a more sinister interpretation, if this quote accurately reflected the view of the Communist leadership, they would have immediately become involved in a campaign to save my parents because, believing my parents would never talk, they could immediately have begun to make political capital out of that coming "martyrdom." Alternatively, if the Communists were uncertain that my parents would maintain their resolve not to talk and "expose" the party, why would they change their strategy in November of 1952? In fact, the danger of my parents talking would have increased as their appeals became exhausted and they got closer and closer to the electric chair.

The Communist party was not alone in its standoffishness. Nobody—liberals, socialists, Trotskyists, independent leftists—got involved in questioning the justice of the trial and organizing to support my parents until the Reuben series in the *National Guardian*. Radosh and Milton's misrepresentation of the Reuben articles makes me wonder at their contempt for people's intelligence: did they assume no one would read the series to check out their characterization? They attack the series for "the . . . paucity of evidence brought forward" and for "attacking the very premise that some American nationals might have been involved in spying for the Soviets." In fact, Reuben in that series accepted the defense's contention that Greenglass and Gold were spies and suggested that the Greenglasses were buying lenient treatment by helping to frame my parents. He could not have denied that these American nationals were involved in spying for the Soviets. The value of the series was that it boiled down the trial record for the reader. Readers could see that the government's case was dependent on nothing but the oral testimony of confessed accomplices and thus immediately suspect. Therefore, Radosh and Milton's critique of the series is completely invalid.

The National Committee to Secure Justice in the Rosenberg Case was formed as a result of the Reuben series. Radosh and Milton state that until the Communists joined in November 1952, the committee had had virtually no success in attracting support. However, there were many large crowds to hear Bill Reuben speak throughout the winter and spring of 1952—up to 2,000 people came to hear him. Even though the *Daily Worker* was not heavily involved in publicizing the effort, individual public Communists such as William Patterson and Herbert Aptheker made speeches on behalf of my parents well before November 1952. Radosh and Milton deal with this counter-evidence with a method that by now should be anticipated by most readers— they ignore it! At the very least this discussion should show that the role of the American Communist party is a bit more complicated than the centralized cynical manipulations that are the centerpiece of Radosh and Milton's treatment. Again they have let their politics lead them away from responsible scholarship.

Let's Get Out of the Trees and Look at the Forest

BY ROBERT AND MICHAEL MEEROPOL

All of this brings us to the much broader issue of perspective, or paradigm, if you will. We think Radosh and Milton's view of the roles of Manny and the Communist party reveal a fundamentally flawed interpretation of what was going on in the United States in the late 1940s and early 1950s. From reading Radosh and Milton's book, one gets no idea that the late forties and early fifties were one of the most repressive periods in American history. It's ironic that Radosh flaunts his credentials as a "trained historian," because the book is actually a-historical. The events of our parents' case are torn from the context of McCarthyism. The government activities that denied our parents due process were all "excesses." But this is not the only period in our history when government's repressive efforts against the left, the labor movement, and the black liberation movement were accompanied by political frame-ups. Radosh and Milton claim that the Communist party brought the repression down upon itself. We should know too much about the role of secret police agencies to accept Radosh and Milton's "blaming the victim" interpretation.

What is Radosh and Milton's perspective? They claim to be objective. They claim to have risen above the debate that has swirled around this case. They distinguish themselves from centrist or right-wing government apologists who seek to prove that the government did no wrong, and those on the left who in an equally partisan manner seek to prove our parents did no wrong. They immediately establish their credentials by asserting that their left-wing political background and initial belief in our parents' innocence prove this objectivity. There is no reason in the world why these pre-existing attitudes guarantee an objective treatment. What they did in their research indicates whether they approached it and the FBI files objectively.

There are now close to 200,000 released pages relating to this case. How is a researcher to determine what is important in them? How is a researcher to determine which of the files tell the truth and which perpetrate falsehood? The choice of files to publicize provides a key to what the perspective of the researcher is, since that perspective is what will lend coherence to the picture that emerges.

We have made no secret of our perspective. We feel the same forces that created McCarthyism created our parents' frame-up. The government used this case as a graphic demonstration of a number of points: (1) that members of the American Communist party were "un-American"—agents of Stalin and not deserving of the protection of the Bill of Rights and the Constitution; (2) that the equation dissenter = Communist = spy is a valid one; (3) that secrecy is essential to our survival because without it we cannot guarantee our national security against an aggressive world-wide Communist menace. These points served a two-fold purpose: (1) to gather support for our global economic and military expansion and (2) to destroy any domestic opposition to those policies.

Radosh and Milton do not discuss their perspective. To the average American, American leftists may seen the same. Just because Radosh and Milton claim to be on the left does not mean that they view the Communist party with sympathy. Nothing could be further from the truth, especially in the case of Ronald Radosh. A significant part of the Socialist left detest the American Communist party. They feel that the failure of the left in this country to attract more than a tiny minority to left-wing positions is largely because of the bad taste the U.S. Communist party has left in the mouths of average Americans. They particularly point to the party's complete adherence to the positions of the Soviet Union as an obstacle to the growth of the American left. Ronald Radosh is squarely in this camp.

Thus, he brought a perspective to the files. He viewed American Communists as pawns in Stalin's hands. He reasoned that young zealots would volunteer to help the Soviet Union gather information about America's defenses. In fact, that is precisely where he starts his book. The interviews with Scales, Gates, and others attempt to prove this point. As a result, Radosh does not question the original Gold and Greenglass stories too closely. He does not acknowledge that, throughout its history, the FBI has followed a consistent pattern of attempting to harass and discredit the left. He does not see that the FBI's efforts to build the "other spy ring" is part of that pattern. Because he views the spy activities that the FBI was trying to associate with the Communists as plausible, he does not critically analyze the unfolding FBI scenario; in fact, he ignores contrary evidence. In other words, unlike government apologists, he does not presume our parents were guilty, but because they were Communists, he starts off with a strong suspicion that they must have been doing something. Ultimately this not only colors his view of the meaning and trustworthiness of the files, but also provides a convenient justification for reaching his own conclusions even when the files won't support them. The point he is making is a political one, not a scholarly one. His purpose is to expose the manipulative nature of the Communist party and its uncritical acceptance of Soviet espionage by party members.

Because Radosh has a perspective doesn't mean he is wrong. However, most historians inform their readers of their perspective so that those readers can make an informed judgment. Stung by criticism like this, Radosh and Milton petulantly complain in the introduction to the paperback edition: "We never claimed, as the Meeropols suggest, . . . to have come to the . . . Rosenberg case without what they call 'a perspective.' Only infants and fools have no perspective; although in fact, as we have explained elsewhere, our perspective included our original belief in the Rosenbergs' innocence."

The first point to be made about this is that this original belief by Ron Radosh had been "corrected" as a result of his conversation with James Weinstein in 1975. Second, all this statement says is that they had a perspective. It *still* does not tell the reader what that perspective was. Radosh's perspective leads him to accept the FBI files at face value. Radosh and Milton never adequately evaluate the files that they depend on so heavily. Usually, when historians use primary sources such as private letters, private diaries, official communications, etc., they are reasonably certain that the facts revealed by these documents are truthful representations of how the writers (thinking they were writing for each other or themselves, not for some historian a hundred years in the future) viewed their reality. Unfortunately, the FBI files cannot be so confidently used. The FBI is not necessarily telling the truth, even within the government, about what witnesses said or what they said to witnesses.

This is a major shortcoming of Radosh and Milton's book. They never analyze these files in the light of what we know about FBI behavior. They assume that the FBI files chronicle the actions of a police agency that was trying to find out *if* something happened. But during the 1950s (and many other periods) J. Edgar Hoover was a fanatical anti-Communist who believed that anybody with left-of-center views was a threat to America, and, further, that the FBI had a duty to God and Country to investigate these people because they already "knew" something was happening and they knew these people were doing it. The FBI's tactics in interrogation demonstrate this preconception and modus operandi. The FBI doesn't ask witnesses if they know something. They instead tell them what they want them to say.

The records of the original question session with David Greenglass, our parents, Morton Sobell, etc., were all destroyed by the FBI at some point over the last thirty years. However, we are fortunate to have one very revealing document. This is Ruth Greenglass' account written for her lawyer of her first encounter with the FBI. Ruth was in the hospital at the time, recovering from a severe burn. The FBI entered her room and told her that David had been arrested. "They said that Gold claimed that . . . he came to the house and my husband gave something to him, and that he returned and gave something to my husband. . . . I said this was not so, I did not know the man and such a thing never happened. They said my husband had admitted all this to be true. I said this could not be possible. . . . They asked was I calling them liars? Or didn't I believe my husband? I said I was not calling them liars, that I did not believe my husband had made such statements, that I would have to hear it from his mouth and then I would not believe it because it was not true."

There are a lot of interesting things we can glean from the existence of this statement. First of all, it demonstrates that the FBI told Ruth what they wanted her to corroborate rather than asking information questions. Second, it completely contradicts the FBI's own internal report of the interview. In the FBI's report, there is no description of the FBI putting words into Ruth's mouth, no description of their "persuasive" efforts to win her cooperation. Ruth is merely quoted as saying she would not believe the story until she heard it from her husband. The crucial words, "and even then I would not believe it because it was not true" were omitted from the FBI's internal report. We believe Ruth Greenglass' statement to her lawyer, because telling him this version casts doubts upon her and David's credibility at the trial, where they stated they told the truth to the FBI from the beginning. Thus, she would have no reason to fabricate this story. The FBI reports, of course, are consistent with the story the agents wanted accepted.

This example should sound a warning to everyone that the FBI files, when they describe what people allegedly told the FBI, present a sanitized and partial record of the actual exchange. Radosh and Milton do not inform their readers about Ruth Greenglass' version. Instead, they quote the FBI's version of the interview, either accepting it at face value or purposely keeping Ruth's version from their readers.

We think most of the files reflect what the FBI wanted witnesses to tell them. The files reflect the FBI's biases and even obsessions. Because they also reflect the biases of Ronald Radosh in this case, they have told Radosh what he wanted to hear. From any rational perspective, not just ours, such material in the files should be expected. After all, the FBI was under tremendous political pressure to find spies. In line with their belief that Communists were spies, they had been investing a lot of resources and personnel to keep tabs on Communists. They would especially focus on Communist party members with technical and scientific backgrounds. One should expect files on people like our parents and those in their social circle of friends. Gatherings and trips were suspect. Under these circumstances, one would expect there to be a mass of circumstantial evidence in the files, all cast in the most suspicious light. In fact, when all of the "nits" are "picked," that is what remains—lots of circumstantial evidence in lots of files focused on our parents, their friends, and people with similar political as well as technical and scientific backgrounds. When one places this mass of circumstance in this proper historical setting and integrates it with the FBI's attitude towards Communists, the files provide a great deal more insight into how the FBI sought to destroy the lives of political dissidents than they provide about espionage! And of course when files contradict trial testimony they are extremely significant, because they provide direct evidence from the FBI and its witnesses that the trial testimony was being fabricated.

Toward a New Cold War

Finally, let us turn to the question of why the literary and intellectual establishment has embraced this book so completely. First, the book's conclusions support the argument that the Communist party contained a group of traitors who actually succeeded in damaging our nation's security.* In the 1950s, such a view justified a repressive apparatus of secret police agencies, witch-hunts, etc. Today, in the 1980s, when McCarthyism has supposedly been discredited, along comes this "dispassionate search for the historical truth" that concludes that the FBI, whatever its excesses, was chasing real spies and actually succeeded in catching them. This conclusion dovetails with the perceived need of at least some in the political establishment to reconstitute the secret po-

---

*Radosh and Milton never say this explicitly, but since they do not argue against this interpretation, it is a fair one that can be gleaned from their book, particularly from the material about Perl and the tail of the MIG.

lice apparatus so damaged by the 1960s and 1970s in time for possible future periods of repression. The equation of the left with treason helped erect a monolithic, uncritical, public opinion in the 1950s that would never even take left-wing opposition views seriously. The message of this book, whatever the intentions of its authors, can be used by those who wish to smear the left wing of the current opposition to an interventionist and militarist foreign policy. No better example could exist than the following excerpt from the *New Republic* editorial which accompanied Radosh and Stern's article. The editorial warned against those who would ally themselves with "the old fellow-travelling left. Let us recall that left: its soft spot for dictators, its contempt for scruples, its abuse of language and people, its dogmatism and intolerance, its instrumental notion of ethics. These people could not be trusted; their word was their dishonor. Those who see them as heroes can't be trusted either."

Thus, Radosh has told the neo-liberal and conservative establishments what they want to hear. They accept the fact that evidence may have been fabricated, that there was no need for the death sentence, but they are comforted to know that they are justified in supporting a strong defense and rejecting the legitimacy of left politics because American Communists really did try to steal the secret of the atom bomb.

But it's not true. The truth does not always lie somewhere in the middle. The government did frame two innocent people. The McCarthy period was a disgusting witch-hunt, not merely an overreaction to a real menace. The liberals were not justified when they refused to get involved in the efforts to save our parents and nothing will excuse their behavior.

We can do no better than to close with what Michael said, spontaneously speaking for both of us before the Congressional subcommittee, trying to persuade them to request a full-scale inquiry into the case:

I am not asking this for myself or my family. Norman Thomas once was asked about raucous demonstrations in the United States, people burning the flag, and he said, "I wouldn't want to burn the flag. I might want to wash it sometime, but I wouldn't want to burn it." I feel that way. I feel the people who framed my parents trampled the American flag in the mud. I think it is up to us to wash it. This case poisoned the functioning of our democracy. It made reasoned debate, particularly about foreign policy, very difficult. Smearing dissenters with the brush of treason became too easy. Our nation suffered.

I am not only asking for this so that my children, who are now older than I was when my parents were killed, will know that their nation agrees with me that their grandparents were innocent.

I am also asking so that our country does not have to go through the same kind of situation again. The French reopened the Dreyfus case. The governor of Massachusetts proclaimed the exoneration of Sacco and Vanzetti. Governor Altgeld rehabilitated and pardoned the people in the Haymarket affair.

I am asking you to start the long overdue process of review over my parents' case while the still living participants can be made to testify. If we can learn from the past, we will escape having to repeat it, but first we must learn the whole truth about the past. Please help us learn that truth.

Notes

1. THE ARRESTS AND THE DISSOLUTION OF THE FAMILY

page

10. The exchange in prison between our father and a fellow prisoner is reported in Virginia Gardner, *The Rosenberg Story* (New York: Masses and Mainstream, 1954), p. 90.

10–11. The encounter between our mother and her mother was described by our Aunt Ethel in an interview in 1974.

20. Information about seeing the social worker at the Jewish Board of Guardians was obtained in an interview with Mrs. Elizabeth Phillips, M.S.W., who was my social worker in 1950.

22. Information on my lack of eating obtained from the Mrs. Phillips interview.

22. The understanding of our parents' lawyers was published in John Wexley's *The Judgement of Julius and Ethel Rosenberg* (New York: Cameron and Kahn, 1955), pp. 141f. The same information was obtained from a recording of a speech given by Emanuel Bloch on September 22, 1953, in Detroit.

22–23. Letter from Sam Greenglass to our mother in possession of the authors.

24. The October 25, 1950, letter is in the possession of the authors.

24. Tessie's threat to dump us at a police station was reported in Wexley. The same conversation was reported in the Bloch speech.

25. Conversations between Sophie Rosenberg and Julius Rosenberg and our grandmother's exhortation to her other children reported in the Aunt Ethel interview.

31. Fear of taking us into their homes affirmed in the Aunt Ethel interview.

34. Judge Irving Kaufman's sentencing speech is quoted in Walter and Miriam Schneir, *Invitation to an Inquest* (New York: Pantheon Press, 1983), pp. 169–71.

35. The trial transcript is on file at the Federal Records Center in Bayonne, N.J.: "U.S. *vs.* Rosenbergs, Sobell, Yakovlev and Greenglass" (Cr. No. 134–245). It has been reprinted from the submission of the transcript to the United States Supreme Court which was filed along with the first petition for a writ of *certiorari* on June 7, 1952. The page references are to the printed copy which the National Committee to Secure Justice in the Rosenberg Case duplicated and sold in an effort to acquaint the public with the flimsiness of the prosecution's case. This

printed transcript is available in many libraries in the United States, particularly in law school libraries. Henceforth, the transcript will be referred to as "Record." David Greenglass' testimony about the console table is in Record, pp. 521, 630f. Ruth Greenglass' references are on pp. 706f. Our parents' counter-testimony is on pp. 1054, 1136f., 1205–11 and 1297f. The reference to the alleged curtailment of Communist activities is in David Greenglass' testimony on pp. 423f. and Ruth Greenglass' on p. 679. Our parents' counter-testimony is on pp. 1054, 1136f., 1205–11 and 1297f.

35. The Court of Appeals opinion upholding the conviction was also reprinted by the Committee and is included in Record, pp. 1640–82. The quoted passage is from p. 1648.

35–36. Testimony about the sketch was impounded at the trial and finally unsealed in 1966. The testimony and sketch are reprinted in Schneir, p. 465.

36. Affidavits by Morrison and another scientist are discussed in Schneir, p. 464.

36. For Wexley's discussion of the hotel registration card, see pp. 384–91, 411. For the Schneirs', see Ch. 29 and pp. 445–50. Photos of the hotel registration card are in Schneir.

36. The discovery of the perjury about the passport photos is in Schneir, pp. 350–55.

39. Interview with our mother's psychiatrist in 1974.

40. Our mother's affidavit is on file at the Federal Records Center in Bayonne, N.J. (Cr. No. 134–245).

59. Dr. Wertham's letter written in 1974 is in the possession of the authors.

2. PULLING TOGETHER

68. Quote from an interview with Rabbi Irving Koslowe in 1974.

69. Information from the Aunt Ethel interview.

70. Quote from the Rabbi Koslowe interview.

71. Information and quotes from the psychiatrist interview.

81. Most of Mr. Reuben's work was later expanded and published in book form: *The Atom Spy Hoax* (New York: Action Books, 1954).

3. CLINGING TO MEMORIES

91. Quote is from Julius' letter to Ethel, July 24, 1950 (see above, p. 9).

91–92. Information from social worker in the Mrs. Phillips interview.

94. Information on having to remove me from my mother so she could rest in the Aunt Ethel interview.

94. Psychiatrist interview.

94–95. The quote and the description of my mother's feeding technique from the Mrs. Phillips interview, as is also the information about my mother's idealism.

95–96. For the Greenglass testimony, see Record, pp. 423f., 679.

4. LIFE WITH GRANDMA SOPHIE, 1951–1952

98. Interview with Gloria Algrin in 1974.
108. In the course of the interview, Gloria Algrin severely criticized S———. From this I learned that Manny shared my parents' views as to the source of the problem in Grandma's home.
111. Information about how I came to spend time with the Minors from an interview with Dr. Frances Minor in 1974.
116. Information on my traveling to the music teacher's and leafleting from Dr. Minor interview.
116–17. Information about P——— from a phone conversation with Michael Minor in 1974.
117. Incident with the neighbors and the quotes from the Dr. Minor interview.
117. Social worker corroboration and quote contained in an interview with the woman who was my social worker at this period. The interview was conducted in 1974.

5. A NEW HOME

136. Information about the decision to move us from the Gloria Algrin interview and the Bloch speech.
145. Information on our clinging to Manny Bloch from the Gloria Algrin interview.
146. We have had numerous talks with Emily and David Alman throughout the years and have learned many things from them that have been incorporated into our own memories. Thus, it is hard to pin down specific factual debts to them.
147. One of the observers of our state while watching television was Gloria Algrin.
147. Cedric Belfrage's recollections were obtained in an interview with him in 1974.
148. Information on our mother's worries from the psychiatrist interview.
148. Quote from the Bloch speech.
149. Quote from the psychiatrist interview.

6. WAITING FOR JUSTICE

151. Quote from Justice Frankfurter's memorandum on Rosenberg *vs.* U.S. 344 U.S. 889–890.
173. See Wexley, pp. 490–94, especially the last two pages, for a description of the court's harsh language and a discussion of its reasoning. For the opinion of the Court of Appeals, see 200 Fed Second 666.
187. Learned Hand is quoted in Wexley, p. 494.
189. For Saypol's question, see Record, p. 1211.
189* For the Macy's employee's affidavit, see Wexley, p. 644.
192–93. Manny's motion was filed June 5, 1953, and is available at Bayonne, N.J. (Cr. No. 134–245). Some of the affidavits are reprinted in Wexley, pp. 637–48.
193. Quote from Dr. Urey in the *National Guardian*, July 6, 1953, p. 6.
229. All subsequent references to activity in New Haven obtained from discussions

with Marshall Perlin and Samuel Gruber. See also Arthur Kinoy, *Rights on Trial* (Cambridge: Harvard University Press, 1983), pp. 115–27.

231. Quote from James Kilsheimer in the book that is a transcript of the television documentary by the same name: Alvin H. Goldstein, *The Unquiet Death of Julius and Ethel Rosenberg* (New York: Lawrence Hill & Co., 1975), n.p.

232. Quote from Justice Jackson's opinion in the *New York Times*, June 20, 1953, p. 8.

236. Manny's statement before the television cameras is in Goldstein.

237** Manny's recollection of my mother's statement in the Bloch speech.

7. ORPHANS OF THE COLD WAR

239. My plans with Shelley obtained from Michelle Alman.

242. Quote from the Bloch speech.

244–45. All tape-recording information is from my personal memory.

246. Fineberg's statement is in the possession of Dr. Emily Alman.

246. The Neglect Petition was filed in the Domestic Relations Court of the City of New York—Children's Court Division of the County of New York—in the matter of Abel Meeropol, Anne Meeropol, the custodians of children under sixteen years of age alleged to be neglected. Present: the Honorable Jacob Panken. Date: February 1954.

247. Memories of the events described were reinforced by discussions with Anne Meeropol in 1973 and Abel Meeropol in 1973 and 1974.

248. Interview with my social worker in 1974.

248. Information on how the Jewish Board of Guardians saw its responsibility to protect us is in the social worker interview.

248–49. Material from the transcript of the hearing before Justice McNally, Supreme Court, New York County Special Term, Part II: "In the matter of the application of SOPHIE ROSENBERG, ABEL MEEROPOL, and ANNE MEEROPOL for a writ of *Habeas Corpus* to bring up the bodies of Michael Rosenberg and Robert Rosenberg infants, for the purpose of awarding custody of these said infants!" (pp. 19f).

251. Gloria Algrin's remarks in Justice McNally hearing, pp. 46f.

252. Justice McNally's remarks in hearing, p. 52.

252–53. The court maneuverings leading up to the Surrogate's decisions can be followed in the *National Guardian*, March 8, 1954, p. 3; March 15, 1954, p. 6; April 5, 1954, p. 6; April 12, 1954, p. 5.

253. Quote and information from Dr. Wertham's letter to the authors.

13. REOPENING THE ROSENBERG CASE: THE EMPEROR HAS NO CLOTHES

References to FBI documents related to our parents' case are by file name, file location, and document number. JR is Julius Rosenberg, DG is David Greenglass, MS is Morton Sobell, ME is Max Elitcher, EB is Elizabeth Bentley, HG is Harry Gold, KF is Klaus Fuchs. HQ is FBI headquarters, NY is the New York field office of the FBI,

Phila. is the Philadelphia field office of the FBI. Thus, a reference to JR NY 1255 means the Julius Rosenberg file from the New York field office, number 1255. Documents from the Department of Justice and the Atomic Energy Commission are referred to by date and name and, only in some cases, by number. One can go to the FBI reading room in Washington, D.C., and request any one of these documents by file and document number. Our own personal collection is still in the office of our attorney, Marshall Perlin, and may under some circumstances be available for copying at cost.

342. Our interviews were published in *University Review,* October 10, 1973, pp. 12–17, and *Ramparts* (November, 1973): 37–41, 49–52.

345. This typical speech contains material that will repeat facts and arguments from earlier sections of this book. For the purposes of giving the flavor of the speech and arguments as well as the extent of our knowledge then, we have chosen to include these duplications. To refresh the reader's memory: pp. 187–89, 192–97 above discuss the console table; pp. 32–36 discuss the trial, the conspiracy, the console table, the implosion sketch, the hotel card, the passport photographs and Harry Gold.

345. With regard to military expenditures: between 1972 and 1980, the percentage of the federal budget devoted to the military began to decline as social security spending rose rapidly. This was not true in the 1950s and is no longer true.

346. For the full statement of Edward Condon, see E. Condon, "Appeal to Reason," *Bulletin of the Atomic Scientists of Chicago,* March 14, 1946, pp. 6–7.

346. For the full statement of Robert Hutchins, see "Peace with Russia," *Bulletin of the Atomic Scientists of Chicago,* March 1, 1946, p. 1.

346. For General Groves' quote, see Schneir, p. 38.

346. Among those who assumed spies had stolen atomic secrets was then Congressman Richard Nixon. He is quoted in Schneir, p. 53. His speech was reported in the *New York Journal-American,* September 24, 1949, p. 1.

346. For Hoover's reaction, see Don Whitehead, *The FBI Story* (New York: Random House, 1956), p. 305.

346. Reports of Fuchs' trial appeared in the *London Times,* March 2, 1950, p. 2.

347. The statement of Gold's attorney is contained in the transcript of his trial, United States District Court of the Eastern District of Pennsylvania (Cr. No. 15769).

348. Irving Saypol has since died.

349. The quote from the city manager is documented in Cedric Belfrage, *The American Inquisition 1945–60* (New York: Bobbs-Merrill Company Inc., 1973), p. 172.

349. The resolution from Moscow, Idaho, is quoted in Ibid., p. 175.

350. Elitcher's statement about Sobell and the film can is in Record, p. 207. More generally the examination of Elitcher is found on the following pages: Direct, p. 197; Cross, p. 264; Redirect, p. 379; Recross, p. 388.

350. Gold's statements about the code appear in Record, pp. 822 and 825, and about the $500, p. 826. Gold's testimony appears in Record, p. 798.

350–51. David Greenglass' statement about the Jello box appears in Record, p. 448; "Julius sent me," p. 457; $500, p. 460; atom bomb sketch, pp. 490–91; Ethel did the typing, p. 510; console table, p. 521; and passport photos, p. 524. David Greenglass' examination appears in Record, pp. 394–406, 438–66, 489–500, 510–76.

351. Ruth Greenglass' statement that my mother did the typing appears in Record, p. 704. Her examination appears in Record, pp. 677–715.

351. Mrs. Cox's testimony appears in Record, pp. 1406–12.

351. John Derry's quote appears in Record, p. 910. His testimony appears on pp. 903–12.

352. My father's cross examination about the console table appears in Record, p. 1211; Direct examination, pp. 1056–1159; Cross, pp. 1159–99; Redirect, pp. 1282–86; Recross, pp. 1308–30.

352. My mother's cross examination about the console table appears in Record, p. 1136; Direct examination, pp. 1311–43; Cross, pp. 1343–98; Redirect, pp. 1398–1400; Recross, pp. 1400–1401; Redirect, p. 1401; Recross, p. 1401.

352. Examination that focused on the Fifth Amendment is found in Record, pp. 1159–81.

352–53. A more complete discussion of the console table appears above at pp. 187–89, 192–97, and 404–6.

353. The suggestion of the password to Gold by the FBI is dramatically demonstrated in Goldstein. Also see the note on p. 353 of this chapter for what we discovered in 1978.

353. The exchange between Gold and his cross examiner is reported in Schneir, pp. 363–65.

354. The prosecutor's request that David Greenglass cut the Jello box top appears in Record, p. 448.

354. The exhibition was removed in 1977 because, said the FBI, of waning interest in the case. However, this removal came after several demonstrations deriding it staged by the Washington Committee to Reopen the Rosenberg Case outside the FBI building.

354. Greenglass' statement that he recently drew the sketch from memory appears in Record, p. 460.

354. The impounding of the sketch appears in Record, p. 500.

354. The hearing to release the sketches is described in Walter and Miriam Schneir, *Invitation to an Inquest* (Baltimore: Penguin Books, 1973), pp. 432–36. This description does not appear in the Pantheon, 1983, edition.

354. Victor Weisskopf and George Kistiakowski are both quoted by Daniel H. Yergin in "Victims of a Desperate Age," *New Times Magazine,* May 1975.

354. Why the value of the sketches was irrelevant was discussed by government attorneys at the hearing described in Schneir (Penguin Books, 1973), pp. 432–36.

355. The passport photo story was developed in Schneir (Pantheon, 1983), pp. 350–55.

355–56. The hotel card is discussed in detail in ibid., pp. 378–90, 445–50.

356. The Greenglass accounts are discussed in ibid., p. 393.

356. When we filed our Freedom of Information Act law suit, we learned that the FBI

and the U.S. attorney for the District of New Mexico had destroyed the original records of the New Mexico investigation of David Greenglass.

358. The phrase "American Inquisition" is taken from the title of an excellent book by Cedric Belfrage referred to above in the notes for page 349.

359. David Greenglass' college failures appear in Record, p. 611.

359. Morton Sobell's recounting of FBI death penalty threats appears in Goldstein, *The Unquiet Death*. The Kilsheimer quote is also from that documentary.

362. The deal "talk or die" is discussed in detail in the text, pp. 209–17.

362. The use of my mother as a lever against my father is discussed in the transcript of a meeting of U.S. Joint Congressional Committee on Atomic Energy, February 8, 1951, p. 6, AEC Documents, and in A. M. Belmont to Ladd, July 17, 1950, JR HQ 188.

362. David Greenglass' denial of my mother's presence when the atom bomb sketch was drawn appears in an interview of David Greenglass by Myles Lane, August 4, 1950, DG HQ 332. He later "recalled" my mother's presence and typing activity in a telegram, NY to Washington, February 26, 1951, JR HQ 813.

362–63. Harry Gold said he brought greetings from Ben in Brooklyn in HG HQ, August 3, 1950, while David Greenglass said Gold introduced himself as Dave from Pittsburgh in DG HQ 332.

363. Gold and Greenglass' meeting is reported in HG Phila. 3–599, December 28, 1950. The report that Gold was later convinced the name *Julius* appeared in the code is reported in HG HQ 799, March 5, 1951.

364. The report of Robert Heineman's face-to-face meeting with Gold is in NY Report, June 8, 1950, HG HQ 491, Boston Teletype, May 25, 1950, KF HQ 1238.

364. The original investigation of Greenglass as the "unknown subject" is discussed in Schneir, pp. 436–38.

364. Bennett's visit to my parents is discussed in the text, pp. 209–17.

365. Quote re the discussion with Assistant Attorney General McInerney is from Gordon Dean's diary, February 7, 1951, AEC documents.

14. HE TALKED TO THE JUDGE

366. Quote from letter in *We Are Your Sons*, 1st ed. (Boston: Houghton Mifflin, 1975), p. 390.

366. For my affirmation of my parents' intuition, see ibid., p. 392.

366. David Gelman, "Papers Suggest U.S. Manipulated Rosenberg Case," *Newsday*, May 25, 1975.

367. For our first victory in a court, see above pp. 246–55.

370. *The Kaufman Papers* were and are available from the National Committee to Reopen the Rosenberg Case. They were published in booklet form in 1976 and consisted of only thirty FBI documents. Since that time we have discovered many more documents pertaining to this issue. In all of the references to Kaufman documents in this chapter, the note will cite them by FBI file, serial, and document number except in those cases where the document number is undeci-

pherable. Those released with the initial Kaufman Papers will be designated with the addendum [K]. The complete text of *The Kaufman Papers* as well as some additional documents were read into the Congressional Record at a hearing in 1982. See U.S. Congress, *Hearings before the Sub-Committee on Criminal Justice of the Committee on the Judiciary, House of Representatives 97th Congress, First and Second Sessions on Federal Criminal Law Revision*, Serial No. 132, Pt. 3, App. 2, "The Death Penalty (Rosenberg Case)," December 16, 1982, pp. 2255–486 (hereinafter cited as *Hearings*). *The Kaufman Papers* appear on pp. 2337–403.

370. Vern Countryman, professor of law, Harvard Law School, to the Honorable James O. Eastland, chairman, Senate Judiciary Committee, September 17, 1976, p. 5. This letter is in the possession of the authors and is also available in *Hearings*, pp. 2404–11. A version of Professor Countryman's conclusions was published in the *New Republic* under the title, "Out, Damned Spot," October 8, 1977, pp. 15–17.

371. For evidence of the Kaufman-Hoover friendship see Yergin.

372. Quote from Whearty in Belmont to Ladd, JR HQ 894, March 16, 1951 [K]. Also in *Hearings*, p. 2348.

372. Law School newspaper articles in *Lex Brevis* (Western New England College School of Law), Vol. 5, No. 2 (September, 1976), pp. 2–3. The suggestion that this indicated prejudice on the part of Kaufman was contained in "Comment: What It Might Mean," by Bill Whitman, Gerry Hecht and John Hargrove, p. 2.

372. Quote from Kaufman in Record, p. 1612.

372–73. For Kaufman's secret contacts with Cohn, Saypol, et al, see memo, Ladd to Hoover, JR HQ (number undecipherable), April 3, 1951 [K], also in *Hearings*, p. 2349. See also memo, Roy J. Barloga to file, JR NY 1579, April 3, 1951. See also Saypol to Kelley, JR HQ 2498, March 13, 1975 [K], also in *Hearings*, p. 2391f.

372–73. Re the canons of judicial ethics, Professor Countryman's letter asserts: "Canon 3 of the Code of Judicial Conduct, adopted by the American Bar Association in 1972, expressed no new concept of judicial propriety in this respect by providing that, 'except as authorized by law,' a judge should 'neither initiate nor consider *ex parte* or other communications concerning a pending or impending proceeding.'" (Countryman to Eastland, p. 5, *Hearings*, p. 2309).

372–73. For Cohn's recommendation see memo, Barloga to file.

373. For evidence about the divisions among FBI and Justice Department people re sentencing recommendations, see J. Edgar Hoover, memo for the Attorney General, JR HQ 944, April 2, 1951, also in *Hearings*, p. 2335f. This memo expressed Hoover's reasons for recommending my mother not be sentenced to death. In addition, Hoover added his recommendation that Mort Sobell be sentenced to death because he "had undoubtedly furnished high classified information to the Russians, although we cannot prove it."

374. See decision of the Court of Appeals, December 31, 1952, 200 Fed 2nd 666 (1952). See also 109 F Supp 108 (1953) for Kaufman's denial of a reduction in sentence.

374. Quote re Kilsheimer-Lyons contacts in Cleveland to Belmont, JR HQ 1466, January 27, 1953, also in *Hearings,* p. 2399.

374. As a result of the stay of February 17, we are able to discover that not only the Court of Appeals (see above, p. 173) but at least three Supreme Court Justices were outraged by Saypol's conduct at the trial (Michael Parrish, "Cold War Justice, The Supreme Court and the Rosenbergs," *American Historical Review,* Vol. 82, No. 4 [October 1977] pp. 805–42.) When this stay got to the Supreme Court, a majority quickly agreed to deny *certiorari,* but Justices Frankfurter and Jackson thought about filing a dissent to attack Prosecutor Saypol's conduct. In Jackson's private words to Frankfurter, "I don't think you can be too hard on Saypol" (ibid., p. 822). On May 22, Justice William Douglas circulated a memo stating that he had changed his original position and now believed that Saypol's conduct had prejudiced my parents' chances for a fair trial. This led Frankfurter, according to his own accounts of the event, to believe that he, Douglas, Black (who had always voted for *certiorari*) and Jackson could force a Supreme Court review of the case. Yet, at the May 25 conference, Jackson switched his vote, leaving only three judges in favor of a review. The intricacies about how and why this occurred are discussed in detail in Parrish's article (pp. 823–25), and Douglas appears to be the villain in this account. We must remember, however, that Parrish used mostly Frankfurter's diary and correspondence as a source, and Frankfurter was a notorious enemy of Douglas'. For an alternative interpretation of Douglas' behavior, see William Cohen, "Justice Douglas and the *Rosenberg* Case: Setting the Record Straight," *Cornell Law Review,* Vol. 70, No. 3 (January 1985), pp. 211–52. See also Michael Parrish, "Justice Douglas and the *Rosenberg* Case: A Rejoinder," *Cornell Law Review,* Vol. 70, No. 6 (August 1985), pp. 1048–57.

374–75. Quote from SAC [special agent in charge] Boardman to file, JR NY 2188, February 19, 1953, pp. 1–2.

375. From the opinion of Justice Hugo Black, *New York Times,* June 20, 1953, p. 7.

375. The document indicating the briefing of Kaufman says "ASAC [assistant special agent in charge] Whelan of the New York Office advised . . . that Judge Kaufman was contacted on Monday, May 11, 1953, and briefed concerning the new statements which have recently been published and the facts surrounding the theft of copies of these statements from the office of defense attorney, O. John Rogge. Judge Kaufman expressed his appreciation to the Bureau for keeping him advised regarding this matter." Memo, Hennrich to Belmont, JR HQ 1641, May 13, 1953, also in *Hearings,* p. 2353.

376. Quote from Hennrich to Belmont, MS HQ 1264, May 16, 1956 [K], also in *Hearings,* p. 2356.

376. For the 1957 case see Grunewald *vs.* U.S. 353 US 391.

376. For my mother's cross-examination see Record, pp. 1373–98. See also Morton Sobell, *On Doing Time* (New York: Charles Scribner's Sons, 1974), pp. 221–39.

376. Kaufman expressed concern to the FBI: Nichols to Tolson, MS HQ 1402, September 16, 1957 [K], also in *Hearings,* p. 2361.

448 # NOTES

376. Exchange between Judge Marshall and the U.S. Attorney reported in the *National Guardian*, December 13, 1962, p. 12.

376–77. Quotes from memo, DeLoach to Mohr, MS HQ 1506, December 21, 1962, p. 1 [K], also in *Hearings*, p. 2364f.

377. For the Appeals Court decision restricting the Grunewald precedent to my mother only, see U.S. *vs.* Sobell, 314 Fed 2nd 314 (1963), pp. 318–25.

377. Quote from Kaufman in DeLoach to Mohr.

377–78. February 14 quote from teletype, Boardman to Hoover, JR HQ 1529, February 14, 1953, pp. 1–2.

378. See *The Conspiracy Trial*, ed. J. Clavir and J. Spitzer (New York: Bobbs-Merrill, 1970).

378. For evidence that Manny might have gotten prison for contempt, consider the trial of the first group of U.S. Communist party leaders who were convicted under the Smith Act for "conspiring to teach the advocacy of overthrowing the government by force and violence." During that trial, their lawyers engaged in spirited exchanges with Judge Medina and received stiff prison sentences for contempt. See the comments of one of those lawyers, now Congressman George Crockett, (D. Michigan) in *Hearings*, p. 2272f. See also Parrish, "Cold War Justice," p. 822, for what Justice Frankfurter thought of Judge Medina.

378. For the stream of commentary, see a not-exhaustive list: teletype, Boardman to Hoover, JR HQ 2227X, October 14, 1953; memo, Nichols to Tolson, UREY HQ 157, February 17,1955; memo, Hoover to SAC, NY, JR HQ 2201, May 11, 1955; memo, Nichols to Tolson, JR HQ 2227, October 8, 1955; letter, Kaufman to Nichols, JR HQ 2248, April 9, 1956; memo, Nichols to Tolson, MS HQ 1309, July 3, 1956 [K], also in *Hearings*, p. 2357; letter, Kaufman to Nichols, MS HQ (file number indecipherable), July 5, 1956 [K], also in *Hearings*, p. 2358; letter, Kaufman to Brownell, MS HQ (file number indecipherable), October 15, 1957 [K], also in *Hearings*, p. 2362; memo, Hoover to Tolson and Nease, JR HQ 2338, November 12, 1957 [K], also in *Hearings*, p. 2363; memo, SAC to file, Rosenberg-Sobell Committee, NY 2985A, May 14, 1958; memo, Branigan to Sullivan, JR HQ 2417, May 2, 1969 [K], also in *Hearings*, p. 2376f; memo, Branigan to Wannall, JR HQ 2470, March 12, 1974 [K], also in *Hearings*, pp. 2385–87; memo, Heim to Franck, JR HQ 2471, April 10, 1974 [K], also in *Hearings*, pp. 2388–90; memo, SAC, NY to Director, JR HQ 2505, May 4, 1975 [K], also in *Hearings*, p. 2393f.

378. For the memo to Herbert B. Swope, see JR HQ 2245. The FBI has a cover letter, Kaufman to Nichols, JR HQ 2248, April 9, 1956, which reads, "I enclose a copy of a Memorandum which I sent to Mr. Swope today in connection with Bertrand Russell's letter to The Manchester Guardian attacking the F.B.I. and his irresponsible assertion that the Rosenbergs and Sobell were innocent."

378. Quotes from Manny, Record, pp. 1452–53, 1603. Manny went out of his way to tell the jury that these "thank yous" were "certain social amenities, certain preliminaries, certain graces that one goes through before one gets into the facts of the case" (p. 1452).

378. For Kaufman's translation of Manny's statements, see memo to Herbert B.

Swope. Nowhere in the Record is there a statement from any defense attorney pronouncing the trial as a "fair" one.

378–79. Kaufman to Brownell.

379. Memo, Nichols to Tolson, UREY HQ 157, February 17, 1955, p. 1.

379. Ibid., pp. 1–2.

379. Sobell vs. U.S. 142 F. Supp. 515 (D.C. SDNY, 1956).

380. Re Kaufman's aid to Bishop, see memo, SAC to file, R/S Committee, NY 2985A, May 14, 1958. Re the prevention of Helen Sobell's meeting with Bishop, see memo, Hoover to Tolson and Nease.

380. Quote from memo, Branigan to Wannall; see also memo, LePrade to Dens, JR NY 3090, May 2, 1975.

381. Kaufman to Hoover, JR HQ unrecorded before 2420, May 7, 1969 [K].

382. Quote from memo, Branigan to Wannall; see also memo, LaPrade to Dens, JR NY 3090, May 2, 1975.

382. "Kaufman had been in touch with Tyler. . . ." See Hon. Bella S. Abzug (D. New York) to Deputy Attorney General Harold R. Tyler, Jr., July 29, 1976. The letter from the chair of the subcommittee of the House Committee on Government Operations, which has oversight responsibilities for the Justice Department's handling of the FOIA, read in part:

> It has come to my attention, through both public and private reports, that there were *ex parte* communications between yourself and Judge Irving R. Kaufman during the pendency of Freedom of Information Act requests for documents relating to the prosecution of Julius and Ethel Rosenberg. According to these reports, your conversations with Judge Kaufman pertained to aspects of the Rosenberg trial, at which Judge Kaufman presided, and events regarding subsequent government actions. As the Justice Department official in charge of FOIA matters, I am certain that you are sensitive to the questions which these *ex parte* communications raise. I would ask that you supply me with the following information at your earliest convenience:
>
> (1) The dates, time and duration of all communications between yourself and Judge Kaufman while you have been at the Justice Department which touched on any and all matters relating to the Rosenberg case and/or Freedom of Information Act requests for any or all documents relating to that case; and
>
> (2) The substance of those conversations, memoranda based on those conversations, or copies of written communications.

Tyler never responded. The letter was attached to a motion filed by Mike Perlin in an effort to demonstrate to the Court of Appeals which was about to hear our appeal of the dismissal of the Nizer suit that Kaufman was so obsessed with the case that he was always interfering, making their effort to hear our appeal with "judicial detachment" impossible. (See Meeropol vs. Nizer, Civ. 2720, United States Court of Appeals for the Second Circuit, Docket No. 76–7434, Affidavit of Marshall Perlin, September 30, 1976. The Abzug letter is attached to the Perlin affidavit as Exhibit 3. See also my reply affidavit, October 14, 1976.) Needless to say, the Court of Appeals didn't accept our request (See Meeropol vs.

Nizer, 429 US 1337) but that doesn't mean Kaufman has not continued to work behind the scenes as the Abzug letter suggests.

382. Quotes from press release, American Bar Association Task Force on Courts and the Public, January 8, 1976.

383. For Frank's opinion on the appeal, see Record, pp. 1649–58.

383. Quote from appeal decision, Record, pp. 1655–56.

383. My discussion of the events in New Haven concerning Judge Frank was originally based on some conversations with Mike Perlin and Samuel Gruber. Since then, the third lawyer, Arthur Kinoy, has set down his recollections in a chapter in his book *Rights on Trial,* pp. 115–27. Kinoy revealed something that Perlin and Gruber had not told me—namely, that Judge Swan had already indicated that not only would he sit on a three-judge panel, but that he *would have voted for the stay!* Thus, Frank's failure to act cost my parents their lives!

384. *New York Post,* June 11, 1976.

384. For Rifkind's defenses of Kaufman, see Rod Townley, "A Spectre Is Haunting Irving Kaufman," in *Juris Doctor,* November 1977, p. 24. When Townley started reading from the Canons of Judicial Ethics about *ex parte* communications (relating to the issue of Kaufman's private consultations prior to imposing the sentences), Rifkind responded: "I don't care what the rule says! I don't care what the rule says! It doesn't apply to this. . . . It has never been treated as applicable to this situation [sentencing] . . . Because otherwise then every judge I've known has behaved badly" (ibid.).

384. For the *Times* article about the Bar Association committee report, see p. B4, September 23, 1983.

384. For the promise by Vinson, see memo, Belmont to Ladd, JR HQ 1823, June 17, 1953 [K], also in *Hearings,* p. 2353. The report reads: "Judge Kaufman . . . very confidentially advised that at the meeting between the Attorney General and Chief Justice Vinson last night [June 16], Justice Vinson said that if a stay is granted he will call the full Court into session Thursday morning [June 18] to vacate it."

384. Though no newspaper article mentioned the "fix" at the Supreme Court, historian Michael Parrish took note of this extraordinary fact. See Parrish, "Cold War Justice," p. 835.

385. Quote from William Appleman Williams on the back cover of the dust jacket of the first (hardback) edition of *We Are Your Sons.*

385. The *New York Times* editorial, March 20, 1977, Sec. 4, p. 16.

385. Our ad was on the back of the "News of the Week in Review" section of the *New York Times,* June 19, 1977.

386. For the Grand Jury harassment of Mr. Archuleta in 1977, see the *Guardian,* May 11, 1977, p. 9, and June 8, 1977, p. 9. For background on the investigation of alleged links between the FALN and the Hispanic section of the Episcopal Church, see *Guardian,* March 9, 1977, p. 5, March 16, 1977, p. 4, and April 6, 1977, p. 9. See also the *New York Times,* April 5, 1977, p. 37, April 17, 1977, pp. 1, 49, and July 1, 1977, p. A21.

386. For my mother at the Grand Jury, see above, note to p. 376.

386. For the drawing of parallels between the Grand Jury activities against Mr. Archuleta and the others and my parents' case, see the *Guardian,* June 29, 1977, p. 9

387. Quote from memo, Scheidt to file, JR NY 1890, January 28, 1952.

388. Quote from Karl Marx, *The Eighteenth Brumaire of Louis Bonaparte* (New York: International Publishers, 1963), p. 5.

15. THE ATTEMPTED RECONVICTION OF OUR PARENTS: TOWARD A NEW COLD WAR

390. The Schneirs' discussion of the alleged spy ring is in *Invitation to an Inquest,* Ch. 23.

391. For the FBI's investigation of 65 Morton Street, see JR NY 89 July 13, 1950, JR HQ 120 (outgoing), July 25, 1950. See also William Perl HQ 38, August 16, 1950.

391. For my father's testimony about Schenectady and Cleveland, see Record, p. 1107.

392. One of our earliest responses to the Tartakow story was published on the Op-Ed page of the *New York Times,* January 8, 1976, p. 31.

392–93. The Justice Department report mentioned is Thomas K. Hall, Securities Activities Section, to William F. Tompkins, assistant attorney general, Internal Security Division, Justice Department, 146–41–15–133, November 5, 1956. The quote is on p. 2.

393. For discussion of the friendships my father had in prison with Marzani and Vago, see Ann-Mari Butraigo, "The Fraud of the Century," in *Our Right to Know, Special Issue: The Rosenberg Controversy Thirty Years Later* (New York: Fund for Open Information and Accountability, 1983), p. 15.

393. Radosh and Stern's "The Hidden Rosenberg Case" was in the *New Republic,* June 23, 1979, pp. 13–25; Ronald Radosh and Joyce Milton, *The Rosenberg File* (New York: Holt, Rinehart and Winston, 1983), hereinafter referred to as RM.

393–94. In further pursuing the "selective release" charge, in the introduction to the paperback edition of their book, Radosh and his collaborator, Joyce Milton, accuse us of ignoring information that does not support our case (Ronald Radosh and Joyce Milton, *The Rosenberg File* [New York: Vintage Books, 1984], hereinafter cited as RM [pb], pp. xiv–xv) by quoting out of context from an interview we did with *Socialist Review* ("New Light on the Rosenberg Case: An Interview with Michael and Robert Meeropol," Vol. 13, No. 6 [November–December 1983], pp. 71–96). For details of the treatment they give us, see Michael Meeropol and Robert Meeropol, "New Chapter in the Rosenberg Controversy," *Socialist Review,* Vol. 15, Nos. 4 and 5 (October–July 1985), pp. 1, 202–3.

394. For the first signed statement of David Greenglass, see report of Agent Leo H. Frutkin, DG HQ 65–15336–149, June 23, 1950, pp. 32–34, 37.

394. For Gold's logs, see for example HG Phila 1–B–16 (logs). For discussion of their implications, see Schneir, pp. 442–45.

395. The *Los Angeles Times* article is Robert Sheer and Narda Zacchino, "Documents

Tell of Meeting by 2 Rosenberg Witnesses," *Los Angeles Times,* March 10, 1979, p. 1.

395. For the Congressional hearing, see U.S. Congress, *Hearings,* December 16, 1982, pp. 2255–486. For my testimony, see pp. 2412–20.

395. Radosh's letter to the *New York Times* is in the July 26, 1979, issue on p. 18.

396. For Elizabeth Bentley's version of her story, see *Out of Bondage* (New York: Devin-Adair Co., 1951).

396. For a devastating expose of Elizabeth Bentley, see the Taylor brief quoted extensively in Schneir, pp. 318ff.

396. For Radosh and Milton's analysis and conclusion about my mother, see RM, pp. 98, 102, 162–69, 450. Stern and Radosh had said they were "unconvinced that the typing incident ever took place" (Stern and Radosh, p. 21). Interviewed on television in June of 1983, Radosh said Greenglass lied about that incident. This statement was made eight months after the book's galleys were reproduced! Will the real Ron Radosh stand up?

396. For their discussion of the scientific evidence, see RM, Ch. 30.

396. For the un-named Communists and Gates and Scales, see RM, pp. 56–57, xiii.

397. For the corroboration of Tartakow, see RM, Ch. 20.

397. For the role of Manny Bloch and the American Communist party, see RM, Chs. 21–27 passim, especially pp. 328 and 409.

397. For RM's characterization of our parents and specifically the letters, see Ch. 22, especially p. 452, and the long endnote on pp. 547–50.

398. For an example of RM actually falsifying trial testimony, compare their quote from Ruth Greenglass' testimony, p. 67, with the actual trial record, p. 679.

399. Quote on dropping out, RM, p. 54.

399. For the Greenglasses' testimony on the alleged "dropping out," see Record, p. 679; RM, pp. 54–57; above, pp. 95–96.

399. Quote about failure to take up new assignment, RM, p. 54.

399. Quote about those tapped for secret work, ibid., p. 56.

399. Max Gordon quote, ibid, p. 56.

399. Max Gordon has expressed his complaints in letters to the editor of *In These Times* (November 16–22, 1983) and the *New York Review of Books* (November 10, 1983).

399. Quote from John Gates, RM, p. 57.

400. Second quote from Gates, ibid.

400. Gates' admission to the *New York Times,* referred to on September 23, 1983, p. B4.

400. RM (pb), p. xvii.

400. To see the difference between the paperback and the original treatments of Gates and the subscriptions, compare p. 57 (second full paragraph) in the two editions.

400. Scales' letter to the *New Republic* was published in a section headed, "The Rosenberg Letters," August 4–11, 1979, p. 27.

400. Scales' recollections according to Radosh and Milton in RM, p. 57.

400. Scales' reiteration is contained in a letter from Junius Scales to the *New York Times Book Review,* September 18, 1983, p. 16.

401. Radosh's comment about Scales is in the unofficial transcript of Walter and Miriam Schneir *vs.* Ronald Radosh, Joyce Milton and Sol Stern, "Were the Rosenbergs Framed?" Town Hall debate, New York City, October 20, 1983 (hereinafter referred to as THD), p. 44. The transcript is available from the Nation Institute.

401. For the changes in the treatment of Scales in the paperback, compare p. 57 (second full paragraph) in the two editions of RM.

401. Quote from Ruth Greenglass' testimony in Record, p. 679.

401. For the FBI file on the Greenglass story about purchasing the *Daily Worker*, see JR HQ 130, outgoing Hoover to Attorney General, July 17, 1950, p. 4.

401–2. Quote from David Evanier to Michael Meeropol, October 4, 1983, in possession of the authors.

402. Second quote from David Evanier to Michael Meeropol, October 20, 1983, in possession of the authors.

402. Quote from Max Gordon from RM (pb), p. 56.

403. Quote from THD, p. 57.

403. Quote from Max Gordon to Michael Meeropol, December 5, 1984, in possession of the authors.

403. For RM on Schneider, see RM, pp. 264–66, 295.

403. For FBI files on the proximity fuse investigation, see memo to file, JR NY 596, August 17, 1950, which describes an interview with one of the men mentioned in my father's letter. The man told the FBI that my father would not have been able to piece together a fuse: This man "had never seen the specifications of the complete fuse. . . . if such plans were not available to him, they would not be available to Rosenberg" (p. 2). Furthermore, the chief engineer of special production, my father's supervisor, stated that "Rosenberg had absolutely nothing to do with the proximity fuse during his private employment with Emerson in 1945" (ibid., p. 2).

404. Quote from David Greenglass' testimony in Record, p. 521.

404. Quote from David Greenglass' cross-examination, ibid., p. 631.

404. Quote from Ruth Greenglass' testimony, ibid., p. 707.

404. Quote from RM, p. 364.

404. Quote from FBI report on Tartakow, JR HQ 914, March 26, 1951, teletype, Scheidt to Director.

404. Quote from next day FBI report on Tartakow, JR HQ 969, March 27, 1951, teletype, Scheidt to Director.

404. The reference in Malcolm Sharp's *Was Justice Done?* (New York: Monthly Review Press, 1956) is on pp. 12–13.

405. Julius Rosenberg to Emmanuel Bloch, February 14, 1953, in possession of the authors.

405. Quoted (typed) recollections of Leon Summit, in the possession of the authors.

406. The document from March 27, 1951, has been challenged as a fabrication by Jack Gold. He bases this view on the fact that the date on the document does not correspond to the events described by Tartakow in the document. I would not dismiss this idea out of hand, but I have no direct evidence to support it. Mr.

Gold has done some ingenious detective work and in fact has entitled his study "The Historian Detective." I refer to the unpublished manuscript by this title that Mr. Gold has kindly sent to me.

406. Gloria Agrin's denial occurred during a discussion we had on September 15, 1983.

407. Quote about David Greenglass, RM, p. 261.

407. Quote from Ruth Greenglass' statement to the FBI in JR HQ 131, N.Y. to Director.

407. Quote about Harry Gold, RM, p. 465.

407–8. Quote about Fuchs and Gold in Schneir, p. 440.

408. For Robert Heineman's denial, see above, p. 364.

408. For the three imaginary contacts of Gold, see HG HQ 403, June 6, 1950. See also HG Phila 614, June 23, 1950. The first quoted explanation is from HG HQ 403, the second for HG HQ unrecorded after 576X.

408. Quote from Joyce Milton at Town Hall, THD, p. 30.

409. Quote from Tartakow, RM, p. 293.

409. For RM's two pages of footnotes, see ibid., pp. 535–36.

409. Quote from Mike Perlin at Town Hall, THD, p. 72.

409. The FBI file where Tartakow refutes himself is JR HQ 639, p. 4.

409. Radosh's response at Town Hall, THD, p. 73.

409–10. Quote about the Dennis recommendation for Tartakow, RM, p. 535.

410. Quote re Tartakow at Manny Bloch's office, RM, p. 314.

410. For Bonnie's demand for a retraction and Radosh and Stern's refusal, see the *New Republic,* August 4-11, 1979, p. 27.

410. Quote from Radosh at Town Hall, THD, p. 73.

410. Quote from Mike Perlin at Town Hall, ibid., p. 73.

410. Quote from Joyce Milton at Town Hall, ibid., p. 73.

411. Quote re FBI checking Tartakow's information, RM, p. 299.

411. The report of Agent O'Donoghue is referred to in ibid., p. 537.

411. Quote from Justice Department report, Hall to Tompkins, p. 5.

411. For the Schneirs' and my citing of the Justice Department report, see the *New York Review of Books,* September 29, 1983, p. 56, and *New York Magazine,* October 24, 1983, pp. 9–10.

412. On RM's peculiar method of footnoting and why this is so crucial, see Gerald E. Markowitz, "How Not to Write History: A Critique of Radosh and Milton's *The Rosenberg File,*" *Science and Society* (Spring 1984), p. 77n.

412. RM quote about the July 2, 1951, report from *New York Magazine,* October 24, 1983, p. 10. At Town Hall Joyce Milton tried to suggest that the FBI didn't really investigate Perl's activities at Pupin Lab until after Tartakow talked to them (THD, pp. 36–37), yet Radosh and Milton's response in *New York Magazine* indicates that all the "O'Donoghue" Report did was summarize Buscher's work— work which had occurred in the summer of 1950, months before Tartakow started talking to the FBI. See above, pp. 413–14, for what Radosh and Milton do to try to recover from this fiasco in their paperback.

412. Sam Roberts' article is in the *New York Times,* September 23, 1983, p. B4.

412. RM dismissed my point as preposterous in *New York Magazine,* October 24, 1983, p. 10.

412–13. Quote from Miriam Schneir at Town Hall, THD, p. 26.

413. Quote from Joyce Milton at Town Hall, THD, p. 36.

413. For the FBI investigation of Perl at Columbia in the summer of 1950, see Perl 129, Multiple Referral 53, WFO to HQ, September 21, 1950.

413. For the FBI consideration of Tartakow as a likely witness against Perl, see JR HQ 1041, April 3, 1951.

413. For Tartakow's willingness to be a witness, see JR NY 995.

413. For RM's change to "receipted for," see RM (pb), p. 299.

414. For RM's change of footnote reference, see ibid., p. 544.

414. For RM's reference to Hoover's query, see RM, pp. 538, 303–4.

414. Quote that Perl's espionage was never proved, RM, p. 303.

414.* Quote in footnote, ibid., p. 300.

414.** Quote in footnote, SAC, SF to Director, FBI, May 8, 1951, JR Multiple referral No. 89 Perl HQ 390.

415. Second quote about Perl, RM, p. 304.

415. The FBI files do not admit such pressure on Perl in the summer of 1950. Perl's own description of this is in Schneir, p. 289, from his trial testimony.

415. For Perl's trial, see Schneir, pp. 288–92.

415. Quote about Tartakow knowing details from Stern and Radosh, pp. 17–18.

415–16. For FBI files on the attempt to link all members of "Tartakow's spy ring" and others to espionage as early as the summer of 1950, see memo, SA to file, JR NY 757; memo, O'Connor to file, JR NY 770; memo, Harrington to file, JR NY 762, September 12, 1950.

415.* For the jury's decision in Perl's trial, see Schneir, p. 291.

416. Quote from Eric Foner's letter to the *New Republic,* August 4–11, 1979, p. 27.

416. Quote from Schneir, p. 476. See JR HQ 656, January 19, 1951.

416. Quote in support of Tartakow's credibility, RM, p. 310.

416. For the Justice Department characterization of Tartakow, see Hall to Tompkins, p. 2.

416. For an example of how the FBI pursued the Sidoroviches in an attempt to make them into another pair of Greenglasses, see Schneir, pp. 300–302.

416–17. For the suggestion that Tartakow might be a witness against Perl, see above, p. 413.

417. Quote from Mike Perlin, in *Goldstein,* n.p.

417. For quote about Tartakow and the FBI's possible motivation, see Edward Pessen, "The Rosenberg Case Revisited: A Critical Essay on a Recent Scholarly Examination," *New York History* (January 1984): 91.

417. For an outrageous statement by Tartakow, see JR HQ 639, p. 4, where Tartakow said my father expected there to be a Soviet America in five years! Radosh admitted at Town Hall that my father probably did not say that to Tartakow (THD, p. 72).

417. For RM's version of how the alleged recruitment of Maxwell Finestone is corroborated, see RM, pp. 304–5.

418. For trial testimony about Ithaca, see Record, p. 1198.

418. Quote about "independent corroboration," RM, p. 312.

418. Quote re Tartakow, RM, p. 314.

418. For FBI files about Tartakow's alleged "infiltration," see Scheidt teletype, July 24, 1951, JR NY 1791; SAC NY to Director, JR NY 1891, January 28, 1952; SAC NY to Director, JR NY 1945, March 12, 1952; SA W. F. Norton, Jr., to SAC, JR NY 2152A, January 26, 1953.

419. Quote re chauffering, RM, p. 316.

419. On Tartakow's reports of chauffering, see JR NY 1841, October 25, 1951; JR NY 1891.

419. Quote from FBI file of overheard prison conversation, JR HQ 1258, February 29, 1952.

420. For the Hilton Hotel card discussions, see RM, pp. 455–70; Schneir, pp. 443– 50, especially 447–48. See also Radosh and Milton in the *New York Review of Books*, July 21, 1983, pp. 17–21, and the Schneirs' response, September 29, 1983, pp. 55–59.

420. Quote re destruction of the cards, RM, pp. 461–62.

420. For Bentley's testimony, see Record, pp. 973–80, 986–96.

421. For RM on Bentley, see RM, Ch. 14.

421. Quote from Bentley's statement, EB NY 264, December 5, 1945, p. 106.

421. For a full discussion of the Bentley issues, see Walter and Miriam Schneir, "The Story of 'Red Spy Queen' Didn't Tell," *The Nation*, June 25, 1983, pp. 790–94.

421. Quote with RM's conclusion, RM, p. 234.

421. Quote supporting Bentley's veracity, RM, p. 230.

421. To observe the lack of footnote references, see RM, pp. 230–31, 527.

421. Quote about Morton Sobell, RM, p. 231.

421. For RM's admission that it was Elitcher on the ship, see "Reply to Schneirs," *New York Review of Books*, September 29, 1983, p. 60.

421. Max Elitcher's testimony was so innocuous the Court of Appeals said that only the Greenglass testimony was the key to my parents' conviction. See Record, p. 1648.

421. For the substitution of Elitcher for Sobell, compare RM, p. 231, with RM (pb), p. 231.

421. Quote from RM in *New York Magazine*, October 24, 1983, p. 12.

421–22. Parenthetical quote re Bentley, ibid, p. 12.

422. For information that the FBI was interested in pursuing Julius Korchien before Bentley spoke to them, see memo, March 24, 1947, EB NY See Reference Batch No. 11, (Julius Rosenberg et al). They note an ongoing investigation of Korchien, "since sometime in June 1941" (p. 5). Though Radosh and Milton mention the FBI's interest in Korchien, they neglect to tell their readers that this interest *predated* Bentley's original 1945 statement.

422. For Max Elitcher's testimony, see Record, pp. 197–263.

422. For the early investigation of Elitcher, see ME HQ 7X, June 15, 1948.

422–23. For the RM effort to develop Elitcher's credibility, see RM, pp. 132, 133. Their footnote references are on pp. 513–14.

423. For the actual statements of Max and Helene Elitcher, see ME HQ 75, pp. 3, 36.

423. This example of Radosh and Milton's dishonesty was discovered by Walter and

Miriam Schneir and presented by them to a debate sponsored by the City University of New York Academy of Sciences on November 17, 1983. The debate was supposed to include Radosh and Milton, but after their disaster at Town Hall, they dropped out of it, so Walter and Miriam presented their material to the audience without Radosh and Milton having to explain it. The quote is from page 2 of a six-page, handwritten statement to her attorney prepared by Helene Elitcher subsequent to engaging the law firm of O. John Rogge (who also represented the Greenglasses) on July 26, 1950. The actual date of this memorandum, which describes my father's visit to the Elitchers' Washington apartment in 1944, is uncertain, but it was at least six days after the interview with the FBI reported in ME HQ 75. This document is in the possession of the authors, courtesy of Walter and Miriam Schneir. Researchers may obtain their own copies by writing to the Schneirs in care of Pantheon Books.

423. For RM's analysis of Tartakow and the photographer, see pp. 264–66, 295.

423. For my parents' denials and the photographer's testimony, see Record, pp. 1277–80, 1362–66, 1424–40.

424. For Manny's cross-examination, Saypol's objection and Kaufman's intervention, see Record, p. 1437.

424. Quote from FBI report JR HQ 1185, November 19, 1951.

424. For how the Court of Appeals handled the Schneider perjury, see Schneir, pp. 180–83.

425. For information about Barr and Sarant, see, for example, the Schneirs' response to Radosh and Milton, New York Review of Books, September 29, 1983, p. 56.

425. For Radosh's quote, see the New York Times, September 21, 1983, p. B4.

425–26. Long quote from Miriam Schneir, THD, pp. 20–21; quote by Miriam Schneir from RM, p. 104. On p. 117 they admit the two-week advance notice given by Barr without acknowledging that it reduces the credibility of their precipitous departure scenario.

427. Quote from letter to the editor of the New York Times from Mark Kuchment, October 20, 1983, p. A26. Kuchment has recently suggested that Sarant and Barr may have been spies. See "Beyond the Rosenbergs: A New View from Russia," Boston Review, Vol. 10, No. 4 (September 1985), pp. 5–6, 23–24. His evidence is based, ironically, on the different fortunes of Sarant and Carol Dayton when they tried (successfully) to get from Mexico to Europe and of Morton Sobell, who was unsuccessful (see ibid., p. 24). The introduction to the article queries "Is it possible that Sarant and Barr were the important spies, part of a much more significant espionage apparatus with which the Rosenbergs were unconnected?" Kuchment himself draws no such firm conclusion. His measured presentation of the evidence with questions but no rush to judgment is in marked contrast to Radosh and Milton's behavior. My view on Sarant and Barr is the same view all people interested in justice should have: they are innocent until proved guilty.

427–28. For an outright suggestion about Manny's strategy and motivations, see RM's views on Manny's decision to impound the sketch of the so-called "secret of the Atom Bomb" (see above, pp. 351, 354). Instead of seeing it as a grandstand play to impress the judge with my parents' patriotism (which of course failed), they suggest that "he was privately convinced of his clients' guilt and wanted to spare the Communist Party the embarrassment of having the details exposed in the press" (p. 192).

428. For Farmer and Marshall and the last-minute stay, see above, p. 228.

428. Quote about Manny at the Supreme Court, RM, p. 409.

428. Quote from Frankfurter, RM, p. 411. All of their discussion of the Supreme Court appears to be restating the work of Parrish: "Cold War Justice," pp. 805–42.

428. Quote from Belmont to Ladd, JR NY 1823, June 17, 1953. See above, p. 384.

428. For Tartakow's report to the FBI that Manny admitted my parents' guilt, see RM, p. 314f.

428. Quote from Justice Douglas, RM, p. 407.

428–29. For George Will's assertion, see the transcript of ABC News, "The Rosenbergs: A Thirty Year Debate," on "Nightline," October 20, 1983, Show #639, p. 9.

430. For their assertions about the motivations and actions of the world Communist movement, see RM, pp. 347ff.

430. For an assertion that the Communists were only interested in making political capital out of my parents' martyrdom, see, for example, RM, p. 409.

430. Alleged quote from V. J. Jerome, RM, p. 328. For Gates' long quote to Radosh and Stern, see THD, pp. 57–58.

430. For the Reuben series, see above, p. 81.

431. Quote re Reuben series, RM, pp. 324, 325.

431. For evidence of large crowds hearing Reuben in early 1952, see JR NY 1955, which included a committee press release dated March 12, 1952, about a meeting in New York which drew over 2000.

431. For a William Patterson speech about my parents, see above, pp. 201–3.

432. For RM's claim that the Communist party brought repression on itself, see RM, p. 453.

433. For Radosh's anti-Communist credo, see THD, pp. 39–49.

433. On volunteering to help the Soviets, note that this is not the same point made by James Weinstein, who participated in the Town Hall debate as a "first questioner" from Radosh's side. Weinstein said, "I know that we would have willingly done the same thing [engage in espionage] if we had been asked" (THD, p. 69). "We" here refers to members of the American Communist party. But Radosh accepts the Greenglass testimony, and the Greenglasses said our father "sought out" the Soviets and made himself available to engage in espionage. This is a far cry from James Weinstein's hypothetical willingness to engage in secret activity.

434. Quote from RM (pb), p. xv.

435. Quote from typed copy of handwritten statement prepared by Ruth Greenglass for her attorneys in June of 1950. This statement is in NY to Washington, JR NY 1636 In., May 1, 1953. Note when this got into the FBI's files. The FBI acquired this because of the new evidence that had been publicized in the spring of 1953 about David and Ruth Greenglass' original interviews with their attorneys,

which contradicted the trial testimony somewhat (see Schneirs, pp. 203–10). The FBI wanted to know what other material the defense might throw at them in the next motion for a new trial so they could brief Judge Kaufman fully (see above, p. 375). Had the original statements not been published in France, the files would only have the FBI's version of the Ruth Greenglass interview.

435. For the FBI's omission of Ruth's crucial words, see, for example, report of Agent John W. Lewis, DG HQ 193, p. 38: "She said she would not believe any such admissions by her husband unless he himself told her so."

435. For RM's ignoring of Ruth Greenglass' version of that conversation, see RM, p. 85. At the Town Hall debate, I asked them why they had omitted those crucial last words of Ruth. On a TV show a month earlier, Walter and Miriam had called Radosh and Milton on that omission, yet at Town Hall, in response to my question, Radosh said, "We don't have documents in front of us, I don't know what lines he's referring to. . . ." (THD, p. 82). For my question see THD, pp. 81–82.

437. Quote from an editorial in the *New Republic*, July 28, 1979.

437–38. Quote from U.S. Congress, *Hearings*, p. 2416f.

Index

Bach, Sonia (*continued*)
  mentioned in letters, 142, 145, 146,
  147, 198, 203, 206; and Rosenberg
  executions, 238; and Rosenberg rally,
  203–4
Barnett, Zade, 19
Barr, Joel, 390, 392, 415, 425
Bass, Charlotta, 144
Belfrage, Cedric, 147, 236
Bennett, John V., "talk or die" offer
  of, to Rosenbergs, 207–18, 363
Bentley, Elizabeth, 209, 396, 398,
  420–21
Bishop, Jim, 380
Black, Hugo, 181, 223, 285
Black Action Movement (BAM),
  330–32
Bloch, Alexander, 45, 248, 348
Bloch, Emanuel (Manny): and assessment of trial's fairness, 378; on chances
  of conviction, 10; and copies of Rosenberg correspondence, 48; and David
  Greenglass, 81–82; death of, 246;
  decision not to cross-examine Harry
  Gold, 270, 427; and denial of motion
  for new trial, 173, 373; efforts on behalf of Rosenberg children, 109, 110,
  114, 136, 145, 147; on Eisenhower,
  245–46; Ethel's letters to, 37, 41, 51,
  100, 101, 176, 181, 182, 183, 184,
  205, 213, 219, 227, 230, 235, 237;
  on Ethel's removal to Sing Sing, 40;
  and Ethel's therapist, 71; excluded
  from conferences with Kaufman, 372;
  experience of, 348; and introduction
  of new evidence, 192; Julius on, 120;
  Julius' letters to, 92, 99, 131, 134,
  157, 161, 167, 172, 174, 175, 177,
  179, 190, 207, 213, 220, 229; Kaufman's attempt to reprimand, 377–78;
  last-minute efforts of, 224, 228, 229,
  231–32, 233–34, 236, 238; meetings
  with Tartakow, 410, 418–19; mentioned in letters, 8, 9, 12, 16, 18, 43,
45, 48, 49, 55, 60, 61, 67, 72, 73,
88, 90, 106–7, 118, 119, 125, 126,
137, 153, 154, 160, 161, 166, 180,
202; mistakes of, 428–29; and motion
for evidentiary hearing, 218; and
prison visits of Rosenberg children to
their parents, 85–86, 87, 106, 224;
recollections of Michael on, 27; as
representative of Rosenbergs to their
children, 81, 144; responsibilities toward children after executions, 241,
242, 243, 247, 253, 429; and Supreme Court's refusal of execution
stay, 222; and visits between Rosenbergs at Sing Sing, 61, 62–63, 70, 86
Boardman, Mr., 374, 384
Brothman, Abraham, 353, 393
Brower, Bonnie, xvii, 410
Brown, Admiral (Director of Navy Research), 312
Brownell, Herbert, Jr.: Bloch's comments on, 233, 245; and Douglas'
  stay of execution, 228, 384, 428;
  Kaufman's comments to, 378–79, 380;
  and "talk or die" offer, 207, 208, 212
Buscher, John F., 412, 413
Butraigo, Ann Mari, xvii

Carnegie Hall, commemorative rally
  at, 343
Carroll (U.S. Marshal), 207
Castro, Fidel, 277
Center for the Study of Democratic In-
  stitutions. *See* Fund for the Republic
Chicago Conspiracy trial, conduct of
  lawyers during, 378
Chicago Seven, 329
"Chutcha" (sister of Tessie Greenglass),
  19, 22–23, 25, 26, 31, 111
Citron, Alice, 242–43
Clark, Tom, 234, 236, 285
Cleaver, Eldridge, 307
Cohn, Roy M., 348, 372, 373
Cold War: impact of on American so-

ciety, vii; impact of on Rosenberg case, 183; politics of, 345; victims of, 357

Collins (of Surrogate's Court, N.Y.), 255

Communism: American attitude toward, 143–44, 302; FBI conspiracy against, 356–57, 359, 360–61, 432–33; Julius on, 131–32, 159, 165; Michael accused of, 112; and SDS, 290, 291–92

Communist party: American attitude toward, 143, 349, 356–57; European attitude toward, 302; revisionist analysis of, viii; Robert's dismissal of, 291; role of in Rosenberg case, 429–31; Rosenberg's membership in, 399

Conard, Joseph W., 285

Condon, Dr. Edward, 346

Console table, as evidence against Rosenbergs, 35, 188–90, 193, 194, 204, 351, 352–53, 404, 405–7

Conyers, John, 385

Countryman, Vern, 370, 385

Court of Appeals, U.S. Circuit: affirmed denial of motion for new trial, 173, 176; appeal on denial to stay execution, 229; convictions of Rosenbergs upheld by, 128–29, 151; failure to overturn Ethel's conviction, 377; and Kaufman's trial conduct, 383; opinion on Rosenberg case, 192; parole of Morton Sobell by, 316; stay of executions by, 187

Cox, Evelyn, 188–89, 351, 405–6

Crocket (judge), 321

Daily News, 265

Daily Worker, Rosenberg subscription to, 399, 400, 401

Daniel (movie), 342

Danzis, M., 164

Davis, Angela, 266

Dayton, Carol, 391

Dayton, Weldon Bruce, 390, 391, 392, 415

Dean, Gordon, 209, 216, 365, 366, 368, 370

DeLoach, C. D., 377

Democratic Convention (Chicago), brutality at, 315–16

Dennis, Eugene, 393, 409

Dennis, Peggy, 409

Denno (warden at Sing Sing), 233

Derry, John, 351

Diem, Ngo Dinh. *See* Ngo Dinh Diem

Doubleday, lawsuit against, 341

Douglas, William O., and stay of execution, 223, 224, 228–29, 231, 285

Du Bois, W. E. B., 243, 267, 277–78

Du Bois, Shirley Graham (Mrs. W. E. B.), 243

Einstein, Albert, 212

Eisenhower, Dwight D.: Bloch on, 245–46; and clemency, 31, 144, 223, 224, 229, 236; decision on clemency of, 230–31, 232; denial of clemency by, 186–87, 233, 237, 374; Ethel's letter to, 224–26, 237; and Kenneth Johnson, 253; Michael's letter to, 222

Eisenhower, Mamie (Mrs. Dwight D.), 226

Eliot, George, 178, 237, 238

Elitcher, Helene, 422–23

Elitcher, Max, 349–50, 398, 421–23

Emerson Radio Corporation, 190–91, 192

Engels, Friedrich, 321

Espionage Act, 158

Esquire, article on trial jury in, 382

Evanier, David, 401

FALN, investigation of bombings by, 386

Farina, Richard, 304

Farmer, Fyke, 229, 427

Federal Bureau of Investigation (FBI): arrest of Julius by, 5–6, 188; con-

Note on the Authors

Robert Meeropol holds degrees in anthropology from the University of Michigan and a degree in law from Western New England College. He was admitted to the Massachusetts state bar in 1985. He lives with his wife, Ellen, and their daughters, Jennifer and Rachel, in Springfield, Massachusetts.

Michael Meeropol studied economics at Swarthmore College and at Kings College, Cambridge University, and received his Ph.D. from the University of Wisconsin. He now teaches economics at Western New England College in Springfield, Massachusetts, and lives near Springfield with his wife, Ann, and their children, Ivy and Gregory.